Lecture Notes in Computer S‹

Commenced Publication in 1973
Founding and Former Series Editors:
Gerhard Goos, Juris Hartmanis, and Jan van Leeuwen

Yvo Desmedt (Ed.)

Information Theoretic Security

Second International Conference, ICITS 2007
Madrid, Spain, May 25-29, 2007
Revised Selected Papers

 Springer

Volume Editor

Yvo Desmedt
Department of Computer Science
University College London
Gower Street, London WC1E 6BT, UK
E-mail: y.desmedt@cs.ucl.ac.uk

Library of Congress Control Number: 2009938103

CR Subject Classification (1998): E.3, D.4.6, F.2.1, C.2, K.4.4, K.6.5

LNCS Sublibrary: SL 4 – Security and Cryptology

ISSN	0302-9743
ISBN-10	3-642-10229-8 Springer Berlin Heidelberg New York
ISBN-13	978-3-642-10229-5 Springer Berlin Heidelberg New York

springer.com

© Springer-Verlag Berlin Heidelberg 2009
Printed in Germany

Typesetting: Camera-ready by author, data conversion by Scientific Publishing Services, Chennai, India
Printed on acid-free paper   SPIN: 12787302   06/3180   5 4 3 2 1 0

Preface

ICITS 2007, the Second International Conference on Information Theoretic Security, was held in Madrid, Spain, May 25-29, 2007. The first one was held on Awaji Island, Japan, October 16-19, 2005, as the 2005 IEEE Information Theory Workshop on Theory and Practice in Information-Theoretic Security (ITW 2005, Japan). The General Chair of ICITS 2007, Javier Lopez, and the Organizing Committee were responsible for local organization, registration, etc.

Modern unclassified research on cryptography started with Shannon's work on cryptography using information theory. Since then we have seen several research topics studied, requiring information theoretical security, also called unconditional security. Examples are anonymity, authenticity, reliable and private networks, secure multi-party computation, traitor tracing, etc. Moreover, we have also seen that coding as well as other aspects of information theory have been used in the design of cryptographic schemes.

In the last few years there have been plenty of conferences and workshops on specialized topics in cryptography. Examples are CHES, FSE, PKC and TCC. In view of the multitude of topics in cryptography requiring information theoretical security or using information theory, it is time to have a regular conference on this topic. This was first realized by Prof. Imai (then at University of Tokyo, Japan), who organized the first event in October 2005. The goal is to continue this event on a regular basis.

There were 26 papers submitted to ICITS 2007, of which one was withdrawn. Of the remaining ones, 13 were accepted. Ueli Maurer was the invited keynote speaker on "Random Systems: Theory and Applications." The other invited speakers were Amos Beimel, on "On Linear, Non-linear and Weakly-Private Secret Sharing Scheme," Iordanis Kerenidis on "An Introduction to Quantum Information Theory," Eyal Kushilevitz on "Zero-Knowledge from Secure Multiparty Computation," Renato Renner on "Can We Justify the i.i.d. Assumption?," Junji Shikata on "Construction Methodology of Unconditionally Secure Signature Schemes," Alain Tapp on "Anonymous Quantum Message Transmission," and Raymond Yeung on "Network Coding and Information Security."

The proceedings contain the slightly revised versions of the accepted papers and summaries of the keynote address and some invited papers. Each submitted paper was sent to at least three members of the Program Committee for comments. Revisions were not checked for correctness on their scientific aspects and the authors bear full responsibility for the contents of their papers. The invited talks were not refereed.

I am very grateful to the members of the Program Committee for their hard work and the difficult task of selecting roughly 1 out of 2 of the submitted papers. Submissions to ICITS 2007 were required to be anonymous. Papers submitted by members of the Program Committee were sent to at least five referees (and, of course, no Program Committee member reviewed his or her own paper).

The following external referees helped the Program Committee in reaching their decisions: Masucci Barbara, Anne Broadbent, Ingemar Cox, José Manuel Fernandez, Robbert de Haan, Goichiro Hanaoka, Tetsu Iwata, Kazukuni Kobara, Hiroki Koga, Thomas Martin, David Mireles-Morales, Maura Paterson, Krzysztof Pietrzak, Dominik Raub, Junji Shikata, Kazuhiro Suzuki, Alain Tapp, Yongge Wang, Takashi Satoh, Alain Tapp, Juerg Wullschleger, Frédéric Dupuis. (I apologize for any possible omission.) The Program Committee appreciates their effort.

Thanks to the Organizing Committee, for maintaining the website of the conference, the registration, and the services corresponding to a conference. Neil Marjoram is thanked for setting up iChair and the e-mail address for submission-related issues for ICITS. Several people helped the General Chair with sending out the call for papers, registration, etc. I would also like to thank the General Chair for all his advice. Also, special thanks to Gilles Brassard for helping to format the preproceedings.

Finally, I would like to thank everyone who submitted to ICITS 2007.

September 2009   Yvo Desmedt

ICITS 2007

Second International Conference on Information Theoretic Security

Universidad Carlos III de Madrid, Spain
May 25-29, 2007

General Chair

Javier Lopez   University of Malaga, Spain

Conference Chair

Arturo Ribagorda Garnacho   Universidad Carlos III de Madrid, Spain

Local Co-chairs

Julio César Hernández Castro   Universidad Carlos III de Madrid, Spain
Maria Isabel González Vasco   Universidad Rey Juan Carlos, Spain

Program Chair

Yvo Desmedt   University College London, UK

Program Committee

Carlo Blundo	University of Salerno, Italy
Gilles Brassard	University of Montreal, Canada
Ronald Cramer	CWI, The Netherlands
Matthias Fitzi	Århus University, Denmark
Hideki Imai	National Institute of Advanced Industrial Science and Technology, Japan
Kaoru Kurosawa	Ibaraki University, Japan
Keith Martin	Royal Holloway, UK
Rei Safavi-Naini	University of Calgary, Canada
Doug Stinson	University of Waterloo, Canada
Stefan Wolf	ETH, Switzerland
Moti Yung	RSA & Columbia University, USA
Yuliang Zheng	University of North Carolina, USA

Steering Committee

Carlo Blundo	University of Salerno, Italy
Gilles Brassard	University of Montreal, Canada
Ronald Cramer	CWI, The Netherlands
Yvo Desmedt, Chair	University College London, UK
Hideki Imai	National Institute of Advanced Industrial Science and Technology, Japan
Kaoru Kurosawa	Ibaraki University, Japan
Ueli Maurer	ETH, Switzerland
Rei Safavi-Naini	University of Calgary, Canada
Doug Stinson	University of Waterloo, Canada
Moti Yung	RSA & Columbia University, USA
Yuliang Zheng	University of North Carolina, USA

Organizing Committee

Julio César Hernández Castro	Universidad Carlos III de Madrid, Spain
Maria Isabel González Vasco	Universidad Rey Juan Carlos, Spain
Ana Isabel González-Tablas	Universidad Carlos III de Madrid, Spain
Javier Lopez	University of Malaga, Spain
Arturo Ribagorda Garnacho	Universidad Carlos III de Madrid Spain

Table of Contents

Authentication II

Invited Talk

Secret Sharing

Invited Talk

Applications of Information Theory

Commitment and Authentication Systems

Alexandre Pinto, André Souto, Armando Matos, and Luís Antunes

DCC-FC & LIACC
University of Porto, Portugal
R. Campo Alegre 1021/1055
4169-007 Porto*

Abstract. In the present paper, we answer a question raised in the paper *Constructions and Bounds for Unconditionally Secure Non-Interactive Commitment Schemes*, by Blundo et al, 2002, showing that there is a close relation between unconditionally secure commitment schemes and unconditionally secure authentication schemes, and that an unconditionally secure commitment scheme can be built from such an authentication scheme and an unconditionally secure cipher system.

To investigate the opposite direction, we define optimal commitment systems and show that these must be resolvable design commitment schemes. Then, a proof is given that the resolvable design commitment schemes are a composition of an authentication system and a cipher system and the conclusion follows that this is the case for all optimal commitment systems.

We also show how to build optimal schemes from transversal designs that are easy to build and can be more efficiently implemented than the proposal in the previously cited paper.

Keywords: Commitment, Authentication, Unconditional Security, Galois Field.

1   Introduction

Commitment schemes were introduced by Blum ([2]). It is not possible to build unconditionally secure commitment schemes with only two parties, but Rivest ([9]) proposed the first unconditionally secure non interactive commitment scheme with a trusted initializer.

In [3], the authors begin a mathematical formalization of such commitment schemes. They also prove some lower bounds on the binding probabilities and propose and analyse implementations of optimally secure systems. They give a general description of a commitment scheme in Rivest's model that uses encoding and authentication keys and also a simplified scheme where the authentication key is not necessary. Then they offer a construction of commitment schemes based on resolvable designs and analyse its binding probabilities.

---

* Partially supported by KCrypt (POSC/EIA/60819/2004), the grant SFRH/BD/13124/2003 from FCT and funds granted to LIACC through the Programa de Financiamento Plurianual, FCT and Programa POSI.

Y. Desmedt (Ed.): ICITS 2007, LNCS 4883, pp. 1–22, 2009.

They list two open problems: finding a lower bound on the amount of information that has to be pre-distributed to the users and sent by the sender to the receiver; and the existence of some relation between these schemes and authentication codes.

The first of these questions was answered in [8], while the present paper proposes to answer the second one. We show that an unconditionally secure commitment scheme with trusted initializer can be built from

- a composition of an unconditionally secure authentication code without secrecy, without splitting and with no arbitration
- and an unconditionally secure cipher system.

This relation suggests an attack already referred in [8] that is the counterpart of the impersonation attack of an authentication system. We give a combinatorial and an information-theoretic lower bound for its probability of success. The second of these bounds is already present in [8] but while their proof used techniques from hypothesis testing, ours uses only the definition of mutual information and the log sum inequality.

We begin by giving some definitions and notation in Section 2, as well as formal definitions of unconditionally secure cipher, authentication and commitment systems. We then analyse the possible attacks against commitment schemes in Section 3, and show how these can be built from a cipher system and an authentication code.

In Section 4, we define the notion of optimal commitment scheme and show that such a scheme is a resolvable design commitment scheme as proposed in [3]. We follow with the main results of this paper, showing that optimal systems must be resolvable design commitment schemes and that all of these can be decomposed into a cipher system and an authentication code.

We then propose a generalization of the affine plane commitment scheme in [3] that is efficiently implementable in both hardware and software by allowing an alphabet of source states with size $|S| = 2^n$ rather than having $|S| = p$ for prime p. In the former case, the needed arithmetic operations reduce to bit shifts and bitwise logical operations, which have very fast hardware and machine-code implementations.

We show that this is possible for every n, by building an appropriate Transversal Design and using a result due to Stinson ([14]) to turn it into an unconditionally secure authentication system. Our commitment scheme follows from composition with the One-Time Pad cipher system. By the previous results, this scheme is optimal.

Finally, Section 6 contains some concluding remarks and possible directions for future work.

2   Preliminaries

We denote alphabets by calligraphic type, e.g. $\mathcal{P}, \mathcal{C}$. Depending on context, these alphabets can be seen as subsets of $\mathbb{N}$ or of $\{0,1\}^*$. Elements of these alphabets are usually represented by lowercase letters. The size of a set is denoted by $|\cdot|$. Random variables over these sets are represented by uppercase versions of the name of the set, like P, C and so on. Greek letters are reserved for some probabilities and real parameters not greater than 1. Probability expressions of the type $\Pr[X = x]$ and $\Pr[X = x|Y = y]$ are sometimes simplified to $p(x)$ and $p(x|y)$ respectively. The function $E(\cdot)$ denotes the expected value of some distribution.

Sometimes, functions of two arguments are written as parameterized functions of one argument. For example, $f(k,s)$ is the same as $f_k(s)$. The function $H(\cdot)$ and its variants denote Shannon's entropy function.

The users of the protocols bear the standard names of the literature: Alice and Bob are the legitimate participants, Eve is a passive eavesdropper, Oscar is a malicious opponent with complete power over the channel between Alice and Bob, and Ted is a trusted initializer. Alice is always the sender and Bob the receiver. In the commitment scheme, both Alice and Bob can be malicious and try to break the protocol.

We now give formal definitions of the cryptographic constructions used in this paper.

2.1   Cryptographic Systems

Cipher Systems

Definition 1. *A cipher system is a tuple denoted $CP(\mathcal{P}, \mathcal{C}, \mathcal{K}, f(k,p))$ where $\mathcal{P}$ is the alphabet of plaintext messages, $\mathcal{C}$ is the alphabet of ciphertext messages and $\mathcal{K}$ is the alphabet of secret keys. For each $k \in \mathcal{K}$, there is a function $f_k : \mathcal{P} \mapsto \mathcal{C}$ with $f_k(p) = f(k,p)$ that is injective and defined for all $p \in \mathcal{P}$.*   ⋄

A cipher system is unconditionally secure if the random variables $P, K, C = f(K, P)$ satisfy:

$$H(P) = H(P|C).$$

Authentication Systems. We give only the details needed for authentication codes and refer the reader to [10], [11] and [12] for more information.

Authentication codes without secrecy allow a party to send a message composed of a source value s and an authenticator a such that an attacker has at most a probability α of forging a new message or a probability β of altering a known valid message such that the receiver will accept these forgeries as valid.

If the attacker sees i valid messages before sending his forgery, this is called a deception attack of level i. The most basic attacks are the impersonation attack ($i = 0$) and the substitution attack ($i = 1$) and are the only ones considered in this paper. The probability of success for an attack of level i is denoted P_{d_i}.

The participants of the scheme share a secret key that allows the sending party to compute the right authenticator for a source value, by computing $a = f(k,s)$, and the receiving party to decide if a message is a forgery or not, by evaluating $g(k, \langle s, a \rangle)$.

There is always some positive probability of success for any attack. We list some bounds from the literature: $\log P_{d0} \geq H(K|M) - H(K)$ ([10]), $\log P_{d1} \geq -H(K|M)$ ([6]), $P_{d_0} \geq \frac{|S|}{|M|}$ and $P_{d_1} \geq \frac{|S|-1}{|M|-1}$ ([13], [14]). An authentication code is unconditionally secure if the maximum probabilities of success meet these bounds. We only consider systems where any pair (s, a) is valid for at least one key.

Authentication Attacks. In an impersonation attack, the attacker sends a forgery $(s, a) \in \mathcal{S} \times \mathcal{A}$ without seeing any valid message. The probability of the receiver accepting this message as valid is

$$\text{payoff}(s, a) = \sum_{k \in \mathcal{K}, \, g_k(s,a)=1} \Pr[K = k]$$

In a substitution attack, the attacker knows that (s_1, a_1) is a valid message before sending a forgery $(s, a) \in \mathcal{S} \times \mathcal{A}$. The probability of the receiver accepting this message as valid is

$$\text{payoff}(s, a, s_1, a_1) = \frac{\sum_{k \in \mathcal{K}, \, g_k(s,a)=1, \, g_k(s_1,a_1)=1} \Pr[K = k]}{\sum_{k \in \mathcal{K}, \, g_k(s_1,a_1)=1} \Pr[K = k]}$$

Definition 2. *An authentication code without arbitration, without splitting and without secrecy is a tuple denoted $AC(\mathcal{S}, \mathcal{A}, \mathcal{K}, f(k, s), g(k, \langle s, a \rangle), \alpha, \beta)$ where $\mathcal{S}$ is the set of source states, $\mathcal{A}$ is the set of authenticators and $\mathcal{K}$ is the set of the secret keys. For each $k \in \mathcal{K}$, there is an injective encoding rule $f_k : \mathcal{S} \mapsto \mathcal{A}$ with $f_k(s) = f(k, s)$ that computes the message authentication code (mac) for each source value $s \in \mathcal{S}$. For each $k \in \mathcal{K}$, a verification function $g_k : \mathcal{S} \times \mathcal{A} \mapsto \{0, 1\}$ with $g_k(s, a) = g(k, \langle s, a \rangle)$ can be defined as $g_k(s, a) = 1$ iff $f(k, s) = a$.*

The value α is the maximum chance of success for an impersonation attack and β is the maximum chance of success for a substitution attack. Formally, for any fixed $k \in \mathcal{K}$,

$$\max_{(s,a) \in \mathcal{S} \times \mathcal{A}} \text{payoff}(s, a) \leq \alpha$$

and

$$\max_{(s,a),(s_1,a_1) \in \mathcal{S} \times \mathcal{A}} \text{payoff}(s, a, s_1, a_1) \leq \beta$$

◇

Commitment Systems. Commitment schemes with a trusted initializer allow a sender to commit to a value and send that commitment to a receiver such that the value she committed to remains hidden from this. In a second step, the sender reveals her commitment and the receiver may verify that the sender is not fooling him. The third participant is required only to give the other two some information that enables them to carry out the protocol. This third participant is completely honest and trusted by the other two.

A commitment scheme must satisfy a Concealing Property, i.e., the receiver can guess the value committed to only with a probability equal to a uniform random guess. On the other hand, the sender's commitment must effectively bind her, which means she can not open to the receiver a value different from her commitment. As shown in [3], a commitment system can not be completely binding, and so we say a system is $(1-\epsilon)$-binding if the probability of the sender deceiving the receiver is at most ϵ.

Definition 3. *A commitment scheme is a tuple denoted $CM(\mathcal{X}, \mathcal{Y}, \mathcal{K}, \mathcal{V}, f(k,x),$ $g(v,k), \alpha, \beta)$ where $\mathcal{X}$ is the source states alphabet, $\mathcal{Y}$ is the coded states alphabet, $\mathcal{K}$ is the alphabet of the committer's keys, $\mathcal{V}$ is the alphabet of the verifier's tags. For each $k \in \mathcal{K}$, there is an injective encoding rule $f_k : \mathcal{X} \mapsto \mathcal{Y}$ with $f_k(x) = f(k,x)$ that computes the encoding of each possible commitment $x \in \mathcal{X}$. For each $v \in \mathcal{V}$, there is a verification function $g_v : \mathcal{K} \mapsto \{0,1\}$ with $g_v(k) = g(v,k)$.*

The values α and β are the maximum chances of success for the two kinds of attack described in Section 3.1. Formally,

$$\max_{k \in \mathcal{K}} \sum_{v \in \mathcal{V}_k} \Pr[V = v] \le \alpha$$

and

$$\max_{k,k' \in \mathcal{K}} \frac{\sum_{v \in \mathcal{V}_{k'} \cap \mathcal{V}_k} \Pr[V = v]}{\sum_{v \in V_{k'}} \Pr[V = v]} \le \beta$$

⬦

2.2   Combinatorial Designs

Design theory is a large body of research dedicated to statistical constructions known as designs. We give only the results and definitions we need in this paper and refer the reader to some textbook in design theory.

Definition 4. *A $t-(v, k, \lambda, b, r)$ design is a pair $(\mathcal{D}, \mathcal{S})$ where $b = |\mathcal{D}|$, $t \le k < v$, $\lambda > 0$, $\mathcal{S}$ is a set of v distinct elements, called points, and $\mathcal{D}$ is a collection of subsets of $\mathcal{S}$ each with exactly k elements, called blocks. Besides, every point occurs in exactly r blocks and every subset of $\mathcal{S}$ with exactly t points occurs in exactly λ blocks.*

These constructions are called t-designs. When $t = 2$, they are usually called Balanced Incomplete Block Designs (BIBD).   ⬦

Definition 5. *A design is said to be resolvable if its blocks can be partitioned into sets $\mathcal{P}_i$ called parallel classes, each with exactly v/k elements, such that the blocks in each parallel class form a partition of $\mathcal{S}$.*

A resolvable $1-(v, k, \lambda, b, r)$ design is called affine if for any two blocks B_1, B_2 belonging to different parallel classes, it happens that $|B_1 \cap B_2|$ is equal to k^2/v.   ⬦

Theorem 1. *If* $(\mathcal{D}, \mathcal{S})$ *is a* $t - (v, k, \lambda, b, r)$ *design, then* $b = \dfrac{\lambda\binom{v}{t}}{\binom{k}{t}}$. *Furthermore,*

each point occurs in exactly $r = \dfrac{\lambda\binom{v-1}{t-1}}{\binom{k-1}{t-1}}$.

Definition 6. *A transversal design* $TD(k, n, \lambda)$ *is a pair* $(\mathcal{D}, \mathcal{S})$ *such that* $|\mathcal{S}| = k \cdot n$, *the points in* $\mathcal{S}$ *can be divided into exactly* k *groups of* n *elements each, there are* $\lambda \cdot n^2$ *blocks, each of them containing at most one point from each group, and any pair of points from distinct groups occurs in exactly* λ *blocks.* ◇

It is easy to see from the definitions that a transversal design is not a 2-design because two points from the same group are never contained in any block.

3   Analysis of Commitment Schemes

This section presents an analysis of the possible attacks against a commitment scheme and shows how to build such schemes from a cipher and an authentication scheme.

3.1   Security

In a commitment scheme, both participants can launch attacks.

Bob Attacks. The security of a commitment scheme can be measured by the probability that Alice has of cheating Bob while Bob can not cheat Alice with more than a priori probability. Bob's chances at guessing each x should not be altered by his knowledge of v and y, i.e., for all triples (x, y, v), $p(x|y, v) = p(x)$. This can be summarized using Shannon's entropy with $H(X) = H(X|Y, V)$.

Alice Attacks. Let Alice commit to a value x and send $y = f(k, x)$ to Bob where k is her secret key. Alice cheats Bob if she can reveal a $k' \neq k$ such that $f_{k'}^{-1}(y) = x'$ with $x' \neq x$, and Bob accepts k' as valid, i.e., $g_v(k') = 1$.

It is proved in [3] that a Commitment Scheme can not be invulnerable against all of Alice's attacks: Alice can compute the set $\mathcal{V}_k = \{v \in \mathcal{V} : p(v|k) > 0\}$ of all the tags that Bob may have. She then picks the tag $v_0 \in \mathcal{V}_k$ that maximizes $p(v|k)$. Let $\alpha = p(v_0|k)$. By an averaging argument, $\alpha \geq 1/|\mathcal{V}_k|$. Now, Alice picks two values $x \neq x'$ and computes $y = f(k, x)$. But by the concealing property, there is a key k' such that $f(k', x') = y$ and $g(v_0, k') = 1$ which allows Alice to cheat successfully if Bob's tag is v_0. The success probability of this attack is the probability that Bob is holding the tag chosen by Alice, α. It is shown in the same paper that the average probability of this attack is at least $2^{-H(V|K)}$ and therefore there's at least one instance with at least this probability of success.

There is yet another attack that Alice can perform, which has been pointed in [8]. The attack described above is the counterpart to a substitution attack in an authentication system. The following is the counterpart of an impersonation attack. These relations are a consequence of the construction of commitment schemes from authentication codes.

In the previous attack, Alice makes the best possible use of her private information, but she can also launch an attack ignoring it altogether. To do this, Alice simply computes for each key the probability that Bob accepts it, i.e., for a fixed key k she finds

$$\gamma(k) = \sum_{v \in \mathcal{V}_k} p(v) \tag{1}$$

She then picks the key that maximizes the above sum and reveals it to Bob in the revealing step.

We give two combinatorial lower bounds for this attack when the distribution of the keys and tags is uniform.

Theorem 2. *There is some $k \in \mathcal{K}$ with probability of success $\gamma(k) \geq \frac{E(|K_v|)}{|\mathcal{K}|}$, where $E(|K_v|)$ signifies the average number of keys that each tag validates.*

Proof. Consider $\gamma(k)$ as defined above. Its average value is

$$1/|\mathcal{K}| \sum_{k \in \mathcal{K}} \sum_{v \in \mathcal{V}_k} p(v) =$$

$$1/|\mathcal{K}| \sum_{v \in \mathcal{V}} |K_v| p(v) =$$

$$\frac{E(|K_v|)}{|\mathcal{K}|}$$

Then, by an averaging argument, there is some k which has

$$\gamma(k) \geq \frac{E(|K_v|)}{|\mathcal{K}|}$$

Corollary 1. *There is some $k \in \mathcal{K}$ with probability of success $\gamma(k) \geq \frac{E(|\mathcal{V}_k|)}{|\mathcal{V}|}$, where $E(|\mathcal{V}_k|)$ signifies the average number of tags that validate each key.*

Proof. It suffices to note that $\sum_{k \in \mathcal{K}} |\mathcal{V}_k| = \sum_{v \in \mathcal{V}} |K_v|$.

We can show an analog result with Shannon's entropy

Theorem 3. *There is some $k \in \mathcal{K}$ with probability of success*

$$\gamma(k) \geq 2^{-I(K;V)}$$

Proof. By definition of mutual information (see [4])

$$-I(K;V) = \sum_{k \in \mathcal{K}, v \in \mathcal{V}} p(k,v) \log \frac{p(k)p(v)}{p(k,v)}.$$

For each $k \in \mathcal{K}$, $p(k,v) = 0$ for every $v \notin \mathcal{V}_k$. Thus, the above can be written

$$\sum_{k \in \mathcal{K}} \sum_{v \in \mathcal{V}_k} p(k,v) \log \frac{p(k)p(v)}{p(k,v)} \tag{2}$$

The log sum inequality (see [4]) states that

$$\sum_{i=1}^{n} a_i \log \frac{b_i}{a_i} \leq \left(\sum_{i=1}^{n} a_i \right) \log \frac{\sum_{i=1}^{n} b_i}{\sum_{i=1}^{n} a_i}. \tag{3}$$

Applying (3) to (2),

$$-I(V;K) = \sum_{k \in \mathcal{K}} \sum_{v \in \mathcal{V}_k} p(k,v) \log \frac{p(k)p(v)}{p(k,v)}$$

$$\leq \left(\sum_{k \in \mathcal{K}} \sum_{v \in \mathcal{V}_k} p(k,v) \right) \log \frac{\sum_{k \in \mathcal{K}} \sum_{v \in \mathcal{V}_k} p(k)p(v)}{\sum_{k \in \mathcal{K}} \sum_{v \in \mathcal{V}_k} p(k,v)}$$

$$= 1 \cdot \log \sum_{k \in \mathcal{K}} \sum_{v \in \mathcal{V}_k} p(k)p(v)$$

$$= \log \sum_{k \in \mathcal{K}} p(k)\gamma(k)$$

$$= \log E(\gamma(K))$$

where $E(\gamma(K))$ is the average value of the success probability for each k. By an averaging argument, there is at least one k that has probability greater or equal to the average value. For this k:

$$\gamma(k) \geq E(\gamma(K)) \geq 2^{-I(K;V)}$$

A Commitment Scheme is said to be unconditionally secure if it is perfectly concealing and the maximum probabilities of success for these two attacks are equal and meet the lower bounds. This implies $H(K) = H(V|K) + H(K|V)$.

3.2   Construction of Commitment Schemes

This section presents a proof that an unconditionally secure commitment scheme can be built using an unconditionally secure cipher system and an unconditionally secure authentication system without secrecy as building blocks.

Each user in these systems has a function to play. We call that function a "role". In composing a commitment scheme with two different systems, the users of the former will have to play the different roles of the latter at different steps, so we refer to these roles by writing the abbreviation of the system followed by the role played, all within square brackets.

In the remainder of the paper, CP stands for "Cipher System", 'AC stands for "Authentication System" and CM stands for "Commitment system". The cipher system is composed by three roles: [CP.Alice], [CP.Bob] and [CP.Eve]; the Authentication system has roles [CP.Alice], [CP.Bob] and [CP.Oscar].

In a commitment scheme there are two kinds of attacks. The first is against secrecy: Bob must not learn the secret value Alice committed to before the right time, so Alice sends it enciphered. The second attack is against authentication: Alice must not send a fake opening key, so she must send it through an authentication scheme. In the first step, Alice uses a cipher system without receiver. She merely sends Bob an encrypted message, but he must not be able to open it. Essentially, Bob takes the role of [CP.Eve]. After Bob receives a key in the revealing step, he takes the role of [CP.Bob] and opens the ciphertext learning Alice's commitment.

In the second step, Alice sends Bob the key to open the encrypted message he has, but Bob needs to be sure it is the right distributed to her in the initial phase. Essentially, Alice acts as a relay between Ted and Bob. Since she reads what the initializer sends and has a choice of relaying that message or changing it for another one altogether, she has complete control over the channel. In this phase, Ted plays the role [AC.Alice], Alice plays the role [AC.Oscar] and Bob plays the role [AC.Bob]. We summarize the above in Table 1.

Table 1. Roles Played

User	Committing Step	Revealing Step
Alice	[CP.Alice]	[AC.Oscar]
Bob	[CP.Eve]	[CP.Bob] / [AC.Bob]
Ted	. . .	[AC.Alice]

Theorem 4. *Given an unconditionally secure cipher system $CP(\mathcal{P}, \mathcal{C}, \mathcal{K}, f(k, p))$ and an authentication system without secrecy $AC(\mathcal{S}, \mathcal{A}, \mathcal{E}, h(e, s), g(e, \langle s, a \rangle), \alpha, \beta)$ with $\mathcal{S} = \mathcal{K}$, there is a commitment scheme with initializer (per Rivest's model) $CM(\mathcal{P}, \mathcal{C}, \mathcal{S} \times A, \mathcal{E}, f(s, p), g(e, \langle s, a \rangle), \alpha, \beta)$.*

Proof. The several components of the commitment scheme are obtained from the cipher and the authentication system as shown in Table 2.

Table 2. Equivalences between systems

Cipher	Commitment	Authentication
$\mathcal{P}$	$\mathcal{X}$	. . .
$\mathcal{C}$	$\mathcal{Y}$	. . .
$\mathcal{K}$	. . .	$\mathcal{S}$
. . .	$\mathcal{K}$	$\mathcal{S} \times \mathcal{A}$
. . .	$\mathcal{V}$	$\mathcal{E}$
$f(k, p)$	$f(k, x)$	. . .
. . .	$g(k, v)$	$g(k, \langle s, a \rangle)$

Because we have used letters given in the initial definitions, there are two different alphabets labelled $\mathcal{K}$. They are not to be confused. For each $k \in CP.\mathcal{K}$, there are $|\mathcal{A}|$ different $k' \in CM.\mathcal{K}$, all with the same behaviour in the cipher system. Considering the analysis in [3], these $|\mathcal{A}|$ keys form a parallel class of keys in the combinatorial design used as basis for the resolvable design commitment scheme.

The protocol is as follows:

1. **Initialization:** Ted chooses uniformly at random an encryption key $s \in \mathcal{S}$ and an authentication key $e \in \mathcal{E}$, computes the mac $a = h(e, s)$ and sends $\langle s, a \rangle$ to Alice and e to Bob.
2. **Committing Step:** Alice commits to x by sending Bob the encryption $y = f(k, x)$.
3. **Revealing Step:** Alice sends Bob a possibly false key $\langle s', a' \rangle$. Bob checks if $g_e(\langle s', a' \rangle) = 1$ and if so, he decrypts $x' = f_{s'}^{-1}(y)$.

This construction yields a commitment scheme that follows Rivest's model, as is shown next. The crucial point of this construction is that the source value that Ted wants to send Bob in the revelation step is the actual key that the latter must use to open Alice's commitment. The figures in Appendix B can help to understand this.

It is easy to verify that the families of functions $f(k, p)$ and $g(k, \langle s, a \rangle)$ satisfy the formal requirements of the commitment scheme. Now we check the concealing and binding properties.

Concealing. Let x_0 be the value Alice committed to, k_0 the key she holds and $y_0 = f(k_0, x_0)$ the value Bob received. Let e_0 be Bob's tag.

Let $X_{y_0} = \{x \in \mathcal{X} : \exists k \in \mathcal{K} \text{ s.t. } f(k, x) = y_0\}$ be the set of possible plaintexts for the ciphertext Bob holds, $\mathcal{K}_{e_0} = \{k \in \mathcal{K} : \exists a \in \mathcal{A} \text{ s.t. } h(e_0, k) = a\}$ be the set of possible Alice's keys and let $X_{y_0, e_0} = \{x \in \mathcal{X} : \exists k \in \mathcal{K}_{e_0} \text{ s.t. } f(k, x) = y_0\}$ be the set of possible values for Alice's commitment given the information Bob knows.

Because the authentication system does not have splitting, for each possible $k \in \mathcal{K}$ and $v \in \mathcal{V}$, there is exactly one $a \in A$ such that $h(e, k) = a$. Therefore, a is a function of k and so $\mathcal{K} = \mathcal{K}_{e_0}$, implying that $X_{y_0} = X_{y_0, e_0}$.

Bob's probability of guessing Alice's commitment without or with knowledge of e_0 is, respectively, $p(x_0|y_0) = \sum_{k \in \mathcal{K}, f(k, x_0) = y_0} p(k)$ and $p(x_0|y_0, e_0) = \sum_{k \in \mathcal{K}_{e_0}, f(k, x_0) = y_0} p(k)$ and by the above reasoning they're equal. Then

$$H(X|Y, E) = E_{y,v}(H(X|Y = y, E = e))$$
$$= E_{y,e}\left(\sum_{x \in \mathcal{X}} p(x|y, e) \log 1/p(x|y, e)\right)$$
$$= E_y\left(\sum_{x \in \mathcal{X}} p(x|y) \log 1/p(x|y)\right)$$
$$= E_y(H(X|Y = y))$$
$$= H(X|Y)$$

If follows, by assumption, that $H(X|Y, E) = H(X)$ and this commitment scheme satisfies the concealing property.

Binding. Let x_0 be the value Alice committed to and (k_0, a_0) be the key/ authenticator pair that she holds. In order to reveal a value $x' \neq x_0$, Alice needs to make Bob accept a key $k' \neq k_0$.

Alice can make two kinds of attack, as described in Section 3.1. Her chances of success are, for the first attack:

$$\max_{(k',a') \in \mathcal{K} \times \mathcal{A}} \sum_{e \in \mathcal{E},\, g(e,(k',a'))=1} p(e)$$

This corresponds to the impersonation attack against the authentication system and so this probability is at most α.

Likewise, for the second attack:

$$\max_{(k',a'),(k_0,a_0) \in \mathcal{K} \times \mathcal{A}, k' \neq k_0} \frac{\sum_{e \in \mathcal{E},\, g(e,(k',a'))=1,\, g(e,(k_0,a_0))=1} p(e)}{\sum_{e \in \mathcal{E},\, g(e,(k',a'))=1} p(e)}$$

which corresponds to a substitution attack and is at most β. Thus, this commitment is $(1 - \max(\alpha, \beta))$-binding.

Corollary 2. *Given an unconditionally secure cipher system and an unconditionally secure authentication system without secrecy there is an unconditionally secure commitment scheme with initializer (per Rivest's model).*

In the appendix, we show how the different flows of information in the three systems are related.

4 Optimal Commitment Schemes

In [3], the authors propose a general commitment scheme which they call Resolvable Design Commitment Scheme. In this section, we define optimal commitment schemes and show that they are resolvable design affine commitment schemes. Then, we close the circle showing that all resolvable design commitment schemes can be viewed as the composition of a cipher system and an authentication system. For simplification, in what follows, consider that the source values, keys and verification tags are distributed uniformly, since this maximizes uncertainty and therefore security.

The proof that optimal commitment schemes are affine resolvable is long and includes several lemmas, so we list only the results and leave the proofs for the appendix.

Definition 7. *A commitment scheme $CM(\mathcal{X}, \mathcal{Y}, \mathcal{K}, \mathcal{V}, f(k, x), g(v, k), \alpha, \beta)$ is optimal if it is unconditionally secure, $|\mathcal{X}| = |\mathcal{Y}|$ and has the minimum number of keys for a fixed number of source states and the desired security level. Besides, the probability of Alice's cheating should be equal to the probability of Bob's cheating.* ◇

The Lemmas 1 to 2 give some properties that an optimal commitment system must have. Lemma 3 excludes BIBDs as the possible minimal system, and this is necessary because such systems are not resolvable. This means that there can be pairs of blocks with empty intersection and these are counted in Lemma 4.

After these lemmas, we're ready to give the two main theorems: that an optimal commitment system must be affine resolvable and that a resolvable commitment scheme can be decomposed into a cipher system and an authentication system.

Lemma 1. *If a commitment scheme* $CM(\mathcal{X}, \mathcal{Y}, \mathcal{K}, \mathcal{V}, f(k, x), g(v, k), \alpha, \beta)$ *is optimal, then* $\alpha = \beta$ *and* $|\mathcal{V}| = (1/\alpha)^2$.

Lemma 2. *If a commitment scheme* $CM(\mathcal{X}, \mathcal{Y}, \mathcal{K}, \mathcal{V}, f(k, x), g(v, k), \alpha, \beta)$ *is optimal, then* $|\mathcal{X}|^2 = |\mathcal{K}| = |\mathcal{V}|$.

Lemma 3. *If a commitment scheme* $CM(\mathcal{X}, \mathcal{Y}, \mathcal{K}, \mathcal{V}, f(k, x), g(v, k), \alpha, \beta)$ *is optimal, then its incidence matrix can not be a BIBD.*

Lemma 4. *Let* $p = |\mathcal{X}|$. *If a commitment scheme* $CM(\mathcal{X}, \mathcal{Y}, \mathcal{K}, \mathcal{V}, f(k, x), g(v, k), \alpha, \beta)$ *is optimal, then the sum of distinct pairs of keys that don't have any tag in common is* $p^2 \cdot (p-1)/2$.

Theorem 5. *If a commitment scheme* $CM(\mathcal{X}, \mathcal{Y}, \mathcal{K}, \mathcal{V}, f(k, x), g(v, k), \alpha, \beta)$ *is optimal, then it is an affine resolvable commitment scheme, and all keys in each parallel class encrypt each value* $x \in \mathcal{X}$ *to the same value* $y \in \mathcal{Y}$. *That is, the function* $y = f(k, x)$ *depends only on the index of the parallel class containing* k, *and not on* k *itself.*

Theorem 6. *A resolvable design commitment scheme obtained from a resolvable* $1 - (v, k, \lambda, b, r)$ *design* $(\mathcal{D}, \mathcal{S})$ *is a composition of a perfectly secure cipher system and an authentication code with* $P_{d0} = k/v$ *and* $P_{d1} = \frac{\max |B_1 \cap B_2|}{k}$ *for all* $B_1, B_2 \in \mathcal{D}, B_1 \neq B_2$.

5 Generalization to Galois Fields

As noted in [3], affine resolvable 2-designs are optimal among the resolvable designs in terms of binding probabilities, however not many classes of such designs are known to exist. Notwithstanding this, there are other kinds of designs that can achieve the same goals, namely Transversal Designs.

This section addresses this question by showing how to construct a resolvable Transversal Design $TD(2^n, 1, 2^n)$, for any n, that is also a $1 - (2^{2n}, 2^n, 1)$ affine resolvable design. From such a design, we then build an unconditionally secure authentication code and an unconditionally secure commitment scheme.

Theorem 7. *For any positive integer* n, *it is possible to construct a Transversal Design* $TD(2^n, 1, 2^n)$.

Proof. The order of any finite field can be written p^k, where p is a prime and $k \geq 1$ is an integer (see [5]). Let $GF(p^n)$ represent one such field. For any finite field $GF(p^n)$, there is a primitive polynomial of degree n and coefficients modulo p ([5]).

For composite orders p^n, the elements of the field are considered to be polynomials and the operations of the field are addition and multiplication of polynomials modulo the prime p. Addition is denoted by $\oplus$ and multiplication by $\odot$.

Fix some n and some primitive polynomial for $GF(2^n)$. We build a table with 2^{2n} rows and 2^n columns. The rows are divided in 2^n groups of 2^n elements each, and uniquely identified by a pair (a, b) where $a, b \in \mathbb{Z}_{2^n}$. Each column is labelled by a number $x \in \mathbb{Z}_{2^n}$. Cell $((a, b), x)$ holds the value $a \odot x \oplus b$, which is a number in $\mathbb{Z}_{2^n}$.

We show this table represents a $TD(2^n, 1, 2^n)$ transversal design. Consider the set of points $\mathcal{V} = \{0, 1, \ldots, 2^{2n} - 1\}$ and divide them in 2^n groups of 2^n points. Each row represents a block with 2^n points, one from each group. For row j, the ith value represents the index of the point in the ith group that belongs to the jth block. By construction, each block has one point in each group. Finally, each two points from distinct groups can occur in only one block. To see this, let (x_0, y_0) and (x_1, y_1) be two points from distinct groups, where $x_0 \neq x_1$. For both points to be in the same block, there must be a pair (a, b) such that $a \odot x_0 \oplus b = y_0$ and $a \odot x_1 \oplus b = y_1$. Then,

$$a \odot x_0 - y_0 = a \odot x_1 - y_1 \Leftrightarrow$$
$$a \odot (x_0 - x_1) = y_0 - y_1$$

Since $(x_0 - x_1)$ and $(y_0 - y_1)$ are defined and $(x_0 - x_1) \neq 0$, then a is completely determined, and so is b. That means there is only one pair satisfying both equations, which means both points can belong to only one block. This concludes the proof.

This design originates an authentication code $AC(2^n, 2^n, 2^{2n}, 1/2^n, 1/2^n)$, as proved in [14].

With such an unconditionally secure authentication scheme, and using the One-Time Pad as a perfect cipher system, we can build an unconditionally secure Commitment Scheme as outlined in section 3.2.

Let $\mathcal{S} = \{0, 1\}^n$. The protocol is as follows:

1. **Initialization:** Ted chooses randomly a pair $(a, b) \in \mathcal{S} \times \mathcal{S}$ and a number $x_1 \in \mathcal{S}$, computes $y_1 = a \odot x_1 \oplus b$ and sends the pair (x_1, y_1) to Bob and the pair (a, b) to Alice.
2. **Committing Step:** Alice commits to $x_0 \in \mathcal{S}$ by enciphering $y_0 = x_0 \oplus a$ and sending y_0 to Bob.
3. **Revealing Step:** Alice sends (a', b') to Bob, who checks that $a' \odot x_1 \oplus b' = y_1$. If so, he computes $x_0' = y_0 \oplus a'$ and accepts x_0' as Alice's commitment.

The resulting commitment scheme is a generalization of the affine plane commitment scheme. It uses the One-Time Pad as cipher system, which is very fast to implement both in software and hardware. Besides, it allows the use of a complete alphabet of strings of size n, whereas in the affine plane with order p, the alphabet of allowed values does not coincide with any alphabet of all strings of a given size. In general, the latter systems will be less efficiently implemented in hardware and software because the basic instructions are more oriented to a fixed size of bits than the corresponding arithmetic value.

Finally, we address the matter of calculating addition and multiplication in a Galois Field. Each element of $GF(2^n)$ is a binary string of size n, where bit i corresponds to the coefficient of term x^i in a polynomial of degree strictly less than n. Addition is performed by adding the polynomial coefficients degree by degree, which corresponds easily to an exclusive-or between both strings. Thus, this operation can be performed extremely fast both in hardware and software, especially if n corresponds to the size of the word of the microprocessor used.

Multiplication can be computed by shifting one of the strings to the left an appropriate number of positions for each bit 1 in the other string, XORing the several displaced versions together and computing the remainder of the division by the primitive polynomial. This sounds complicated, but can all be implemented with shift and XOR instructions, and both kinds are quickly implemented in hardware and machine-code. A whole analysis of a possible implementation is given in [7].

6   Conclusion and Further Work

This paper continues the work began in [3] and [8] in the analysis of unconditionally secure commitment schemes. It gives formal characterizations of cipher schemes, authentication schemes without secrecy, splitting or arbitration and perfectly concealing commitment schemes with a trusted initializer, as proposed by Rivest. Then, we showed how to build an unconditionally secure commitment scheme using an unconditionally secure cipher system and an unconditionally secure authentication code. Based on this construction, we showed a new proof for an attack against commitment schemes analog to the impersonation attack of authentication codes that had been referred in [8] and gave a similar combinatorial lower bound. Then we showed that the resolvable design schemes proposed in [3] can be built according to our composition and that any optimal commitment system must be a system of this kind. We then considered whether it would be possible to build commitment schemes using the One-Time Pad as the cipher system. This requires the source alphabet to have 2^n elements. A positive answer was given to this question by showing how to build an adequate transversal design and then an authentication code with a source alphabet of size 2^n that is unconditionally secure against impersonation and substitution attacks. With the composition given before, this implies the existence of such commitment schemes that are in fact generalizations of the resolvable design commitment scheme to Galois Fields of composite order. The construction used can be applied to any field of order $GF(p^n)$ for any prime p, and not just $p = 2$.

This answers affirmatively the question raised in [3] about the relation of commitment schemes and authentication schemes, although with a solution different from the one suggested in that paper. Also this shows that a cipher system is needed too. Accordingly, the theory of authentication codes without secrecy can be used in the analysis of commitment schemes. Further work can be done to understand if other kinds of authentication codes can also be used to develop different kinds of commitment schemes and if there are viable alternatives to the cipher system.

References

1. Anderson, I., Honkala, I.: A Short Course in Combinatorial Designs (Spring 1997), http://www.utu.fi/~honkala/designs.ps
2. Blum, M.: Coin flipping by telephone: a protocol for solving impossible problems. In: 24th IEEE Spring Computer Conference, pp. 133–137. IEEE Press, Los Alamitos (1982)
3. Blundo, C., Masucci, B., Stinson, D.R., Wei, R.: Constructions and Bounds for Unconditionally Secure Non-Interactive Commitment Schemes. Designs, Codes and Cryptography 26 (2002)
4. Cover, T.M., Thomas, J.A.: Elements of Information Theory. John Wiley & Sons, Chichester (1991)
5. Lidl, R., Niederreiter, H.: Finite Fields, pp. 50–51, 89–91. Cambridge University Press, Cambridge (1983)
6. Maurer, U.: Authentication theory and hypothesis testing. IEEE Transactions on Information Theory 46(4), 1350–1356 (2000)
7. McGrew, D., Viega, J.: The Galois/Counter Mode of Operation (GCM). Submission to NIST Modes of Operation Process (January 2004)
8. Nascimento, A.C.A., Otsuka, A., Imai, H., Müller-Quade, J.: Unconditionally Secure Homomorphic Pre-distributed Commitments. In: Fossorier, M.P.C., Høholdt, T., Poli, A. (eds.) AAECC 2003. LNCS, vol. 2643, pp. 87–97. Springer, Heidelberg (2003)
9. Rivest, R.L. (ed.): Unconditionally Secure Commitment and Oblivious Transfer Schemes Using Private Channels and a Trusted Initializer (unpublished manuscript) (November 1999), http://citeseer.ifi.unizh.ch/rivest99unconditionally.html
10. Simmons, G.J.: Authentication Theory / Coding Theory. In: Blakely, G.R., Chaum, D. (eds.) CRYPTO 1984. LNCS, vol. 196, pp. 411–431. Springer, Heidelberg (1985)
11. Simmons, G.J.: Message authentication: a game on hypergraphs. Congressus Numerantium 45, 161–192 (1984)
12. Simmons, G.J.: A Natural Taxonomy for Digital Information Authentication Schemes. In: Pomerance, C. (ed.) CRYPTO 1987. LNCS, vol. 293, pp. 269–288. Springer, Heidelberg (1988)
13. Stinson, D.R.: Combinatorial Characterization of Authentication Codes. In: Feigenbaum, J. (ed.) CRYPTO 1991. LNCS, vol. 576, pp. 62–73. Springer, Heidelberg (1992)
14. Stinson, D.R.: Some Constructions and Bounds for Authentication Codes. In: Odlyzko, A.M. (ed.) CRYPTO 1986. LNCS, vol. 263, pp. 418–425. Springer, Heidelberg (1987)

Appendices

A   Proof of Theorems 5 and 6

This section presents the proofs omitted earlier in Section 4.

Lemma 1. If a commitment scheme $CM(\mathcal{X}, \mathcal{Y}, \mathcal{K}, \mathcal{V}, f(k, x), g(v, k), \alpha, \beta)$ is optimal, then $\alpha = \beta$ and $|\mathcal{V}| = (1/\alpha)^2$.

Proof. By definition,

$$\alpha = \max_{k \in \mathcal{K}} |\mathcal{V}_k|/|\mathcal{V}| \geq E(|\mathcal{V}_k|)/|\mathcal{V}|.$$

and by optimality of the system the above holds with equality. Then, $|\mathcal{V}_k|$ is constant for all k. Likewise, and by Theorem 2, $|\mathcal{K}_v|$ must be constant.

By definition,

$$\beta = \max_{k \neq k' \in \mathcal{K}} \frac{\Pr[g(v, k) = 1, g(v, k') = 1]}{\Pr[g(v, k') = 1]}$$

$$= \max_{k \neq k' \in \mathcal{K}} \frac{|\{v \in \mathcal{V} : g(v, k) = g(v, k') = 1\}|}{|\{v \in \mathcal{V} : g(v, k) = 1\}|}$$

$$= \max_{k \neq k' \in \mathcal{K}} \frac{|\mathcal{V}_k \cap \mathcal{V}_{k'}|}{|\mathcal{V}_k|}$$

Let $\mu = \max_{k \neq k' \in \mathcal{K}} |\mathcal{V}_k \cap \mathcal{V}_{k'}|$. Then

$$\beta = \frac{\mu}{|\mathcal{V}_k|}.$$

The value μ can not be 0 because if so each tag would verify exactly one key and Bob would be able to cheat Alice with absolute certainty. Then β is minimum when $\mu = 1$ and

$$\alpha = |\mathcal{V}_k|/|\mathcal{V}|$$
$$\beta = 1/|\mathcal{V}_k|$$

We show that γ is minimum when $\alpha = \beta$. Let $|\mathcal{V}_k|$ and $|\mathcal{V}|$ be such that $\alpha = \beta = \gamma$. Then $|\mathcal{V}_k|^2 = |\mathcal{V}|$. Denote by α_0 and γ_0 the values of α and γ respectively in this case.

Assume for contradiction that there is some combination of values $|\mathcal{V}_k|$ and $|\mathcal{V}|$ such that $\gamma = \max(\alpha, \beta) < \gamma_0$. Assume w.l.o.g that $\alpha > \beta$. Then

$$\alpha = \gamma < \gamma_0 = \alpha_0 \Rightarrow$$
$$|\mathcal{V}_k|/|\mathcal{V}| < |\mathcal{V}|^{1/2}/|\mathcal{V}| \Leftrightarrow 1/|\mathcal{V}_k| > 1/|\mathcal{V}|^{1/2} \Rightarrow$$
$$\beta > \alpha_0 > \alpha$$

Thus we have a contradiction, and so the minimum γ is achieved when $\alpha = \beta$. This implies that $1/|\mathcal{V}_k| = |\mathcal{V}_k|/|\mathcal{V}|$ and $|\mathcal{V}| = |\mathcal{V}_k|^2 = (1/\alpha)^2$.

Lemma 2. *If a commitment scheme $CM(\mathcal{X}, \mathcal{Y}, \mathcal{K}, \mathcal{V}, f(k, x), g(v, k), \alpha, \beta)$ is optimal, then $|\mathcal{X}|^2 = |\mathcal{K}| = |\mathcal{V}|$.*

Proof. Let v be Bob's tag and y the coding of Alice's commitment. Define $\mathcal{X}_{y,v} = \{x : \exists k \in \mathcal{K}_v \text{ s.t. } f_k^{-1}(y)\}$ to be the set of possible commitments for Alice given the information Bob holds. Then, $|\mathcal{X}_{y,v}| \leq |\mathcal{K}_v|$. Because $|\mathcal{K}_v|$ is constant, by Lemma 1,

$$
\begin{aligned}
H(X|Y, V) &= \sum_{y \in \mathcal{Y}, v \in \mathcal{V}} \Pr(y, v) H(X|Y = y, V = v) \\
&\leq \sum_{y \in \mathcal{Y}, v \in \mathcal{V}} \Pr(y, v) \log |\mathcal{X}_{y,v}| \\
&\leq \sum_{y \in \mathcal{Y}, v \in \mathcal{V}} \Pr(y, v) \log |\mathcal{K}_v| \\
&= \log |\mathcal{K}_v|
\end{aligned}
$$

and by optimality of the system $\log |\mathcal{K}_v| \geq H(X) = \log |\mathcal{X}|$.

By the proof of Corollary 1, $|\mathcal{K}| \cdot |\mathcal{V}_k| = |\mathcal{K}_v| \cdot |\mathcal{V}|$ and using Lemma 1, this brings $|\mathcal{K}| = |\mathcal{K}_v| \cdot |\mathcal{V}_k| \geq |\mathcal{X}| \cdot |\mathcal{V}_k|$. But since the system is optimal and the number of keys is minimal, then it must be that $|\mathcal{K}_v| = |\mathcal{X}|$. Bob's chance of guessing Alice's commitment is $1/|\mathcal{X}|$, by definition of security. From Lemma 1, Alice's chance is $1/|\mathcal{V}_k|$. Because in an optimal system Alice's chance of success is equal to Bob's, $1/|\mathcal{X}| = 1/|\mathcal{V}_k| \Leftrightarrow |\mathcal{X}| = |\mathcal{V}_k|$ which implies $|\mathcal{K}| = |\mathcal{X}|^2 = |\mathcal{V}|$.

Lemma 3. *If a commitment scheme $CM(\mathcal{X}, \mathcal{Y}, \mathcal{K}, \mathcal{V}, f(k, x), g(v, k), \alpha, \beta)$ is optimal, then its incidence matrix can not be a BIBD.*

Proof. By Lemma 2, $|\mathcal{V}| = |\mathcal{K}|$. Suppose the incidence matrix of the commitment scheme is a $2 - (v, k, \lambda, b, r)$ Balanced Incomplete Block Design. Then the design is symmetric and by Theorem 2.14 in [1], any two keys have exactly λ tags validating them. By the proof of Lemma 1, the maximum intersection between any two lines should be 1, so $\lambda = 1$. Then, by Theorem 1, each tag validates exactly $r = (v - 1)/(k - 1)$ keys and by Theorem 2.14 in [1], $r = k$. This brings $b = v = k^2 - k + 1$ where $b = |\mathcal{K}|$ and $v = |\mathcal{V}|$. By definition, $r = |\mathcal{K}_v|$.

By Lemma 2, $|\mathcal{K}|/|\mathcal{X}| = |\mathcal{K}_v|$. Then, b/k must be an integer, but

$$
\begin{aligned}
\frac{b}{k} &= \frac{k^2 - k + 1}{k} \\
&= k - 1 + 1/k
\end{aligned}
$$

and this can not be an integer for $k > 1$.

Lemma 4. *Let $p = |\mathcal{X}|$. For a commitment scheme $CM(\mathcal{X}, \mathcal{Y}, \mathcal{K}, \mathcal{V}, f(k, x), g(v, k), \alpha, \beta)$ that is optimal, the sum of distinct pairs of keys that don't have any tag in common is $p^2 \cdot (p - 1)/2$.*

Proof. Consider a square matrix where cell (i, j) contains the value $|\mathcal{V}_{k_i} \cap \mathcal{V}_{k_j}|$ where $k_i \neq k_j \in \mathcal{K}$.

There are $p^2 \cdot (p^2 - 1)$ filled cells. We count the pairs that have a non-empty intersection. Each key has tag v_1 in common with $p - 1$ different keys and since it is validated by p tags, each key contributes with $p(p - 1)$ to the total of the sum

$$\sigma' = \sum_{k_i \in \mathcal{K}} \sum_{k_j \neq k_i \in \mathcal{K}} |\mathcal{V}_{k_i} \cap \mathcal{V}_{k_j}|$$

Therefore, $\sigma' = p^3(p - 1)$. But this sum counts each pair twice, so the total number of distinct intersections is $\sigma = p^3(p - 1)/2$.

We can find the total number of distinct key pairs that don't intersect, recalling that in this particular case all filled cells are either 0 or 1, which means that σ is the sum of all 1s in the table. As before, only a half of the matrix needs to be considered.

Then, the number of distinct key pairs without tags in common is

$$(p^4 - p^2)/2 - p^3(p - 1)/2 = p^2 \cdot (p - 1)/2$$

Theorem 5. If a commitment scheme $CM(\mathcal{X}, \mathcal{Y}, \mathcal{K}, \mathcal{V}, f(k, x), g(v, k), \alpha, \beta)$ is optimal, then it is an affine resolvable commitment scheme, and all keys in each parallel class encrypt each value $x \in \mathcal{X}$ to the same value $y \in \mathcal{Y}$. That is, the function $y = f(k, x)$ depends only on the index of the parallel class containing k, and not on k itself.

Proof. Let $p = |\mathcal{X}|$. From the previous results, there are p^2 keys. Fix some $x_0 \in \mathcal{X}$. The concealing property implies that there must be exactly p keys transforming x_0 into each possible value $y \in \mathcal{Y}$. Then, the keys can be grouped in p groups such that all keys $k_{i,j}$ in group i satisfy $f(k_{i,j}, x_0) = y_i$.

There are exactly p keys validated by each verifier tag. For each two keys k_i and k_j validated by the same tag, it must happen that $f(k_i, x_0) \neq f(k_j, x_0)$ or else there won't be enough keys to hit all the values in $\mathcal{Y}$.

But by Lemma 4 and a counting argument, this implies that all pairs of keys in different groups must have exactly one common tag.

Since there are p disjoint keys in each group, each validated by p tags, each group forms a partition of $|\mathcal{V}|$ and is therefore a parallel class. The design is therefore resolvable and since the maximum intersection between two keys is $1 = k^2/v$ it is also affine.

Now consider a value $x_1 \in \mathcal{X}$ different from x_0. Suppose there are two keys k_i, k_j in different groups that code x_1 in the same way. That is:

$$f(k_i, x_0) \neq f(k_j, x_0)$$
$$f(k_i, x_1) = f(k_j, x_1)$$
$$|\mathcal{V}_{k_i} \cap \mathcal{V}_{k_j}| = 1$$

Following the same reasoning as above, if $f(k_i, x_1) = f(k_j, x_1)$ then they can not have any tag in common, contradicting the previous division in groups.

Therefore, keys in different groups code x in different ways and by a counting argument all keys in the same group transform x into the same y.

Repeating the argument for any $x_l \in \mathcal{X}$ and for all groups, it must happen that all keys k_i, k_j in the same group satisfy

$$f(k_i, x_l) = f(k_j, x_l)$$

and so the theorem is proved.

Theorem 6. A resolvable design commitment scheme obtained from a resolvable $1 - (v, k, \lambda, b, r)$ design $(\mathcal{D}, \mathcal{S})$ is a composition of a perfectly secure cipher system and an authentication code with $P_{d0} = k/v$ and $P_{d1} = \frac{\max |B_1 \cap B_2|}{k}$ for all $B_1, B_2 \in \mathcal{D}, B_1 \neq B_2$.

Proof. Let B be Alice's block and w be Bob's tag in the above system. Then $w \in B$. By Theorem 1, $b = r \cdot v/k$. Then, w can be seen as a number between 0 and $v - 1$.

By definition of resolvable design, B belongs to some parallel class. Then, B can be written (i, j), where i is the index of the parallel class and j is the index of the block within the parallel class. The pair (i, j) can be interpreted as a pair source value / authenticator.

When Alice commits to $x_0 \in \mathbb{Z}_r$, she sends Bob $y_0 = (x_0 + i) \mod r$. Then, x_0 can be seen as a symbol in alphabet $\Sigma = \mathbb{Z}_r$ and y_0 as a displacement of i positions over that alphabet. This corresponds to applying a Ceasar's cipher to the secret message x_0. In general, Ceasar's cipher is not secure, but here the message is composed of only one symbol, which means its size is equal to the size of the key. In this situation, it is equivalent to the One-Time Pad and is unconditionally secure. Since all blocks in the same parallel class encipher x_0 in exactly the same way, the index of the parallel class represents the cipher key used by Alice.

Now we show that the design used to check the validity of the value revealed after the commitment can also be used to make an authentication scheme with r source states, v/k possible authenticators for each source state and v encoding rules.

Any block from the design can be identified by a pair (i, j), where i is the index of the parallel class it belongs to and j its index within that class. Let B be the set represented by a block with indices (i, j).

Then, B can be interpreted as belonging to an authentication code: i represents the source code and j the respective authenticator. Each element $w \in B$ contributes for the definition of an encoding rule in the following way: $f(w, i) = j$. Since each w belongs to exactly one block in each parallel class, there is a unique value associated to each pair (w, i). Since there are k elements in each block, there are exactly k encoding rules associating i to j.

The probability of an impersonation attack is the maximum probability of finding the right authenticator for a specific pair key / source state. There are a total of v encoding rules. The number of rules that associate some source state i to a given authenticator j is by construction k. Thus, for all such pairs (i, j),

$$\text{payoff}(i, j) = \sum_{w \in \mathcal{S}: f(w,i)=j} 1/v = k/v \tag{4}$$

and because this is constant for all pairs, it is the probability of an impersonation attack.

For the substitution attack, suppose the attacker knows that the secret encoding rule associates i_1 to j_1. By construction, there are k such keys. For any pair (i, j), the probability of success is

$$\text{payoff}(i, j, i_1, j_1) = \frac{\sum_{w \in \mathcal{S}: f(w,i)=j, f(w,i_1)=j_1} p(w)}{\sum_{w \in \mathcal{S}: f(w,i_1)=j_1} p(w)} \tag{5}$$

$$= \frac{|B_{i,j} \cap B_{i_1,j_1}|}{k} \tag{6}$$

where $B_{i,j}$ is the block of the design indexed by (i, j). Then, the probability of the substitution attack is $\frac{\max |B_1 \cap B_2|}{k}$ over all $B_1, B_2 \in \mathcal{D}, B_1 \neq B_2$.

B   Flow Analysis

In the conclusion to the paper [3], the authors suggest a possible relation between commitment schemes and authentication schemes with arbitration, but point that the information flows between these systems are different.

Here, we analyse the different flows of information in a commitment scheme, and how these are realized through the flows present in the cipher and in the authentication systems. We understand by information flows the data that is sent from one user to another user. The following pictures help visualize the flows in the different systems.

In these figures, there are blocks representing each participant in the system and arrows representing the messages sent by them, this is, the flows of information between users. Within some blocks is another name within square brackets. This represents the name of the user of the commitment scheme that will be playing the role indicated by the block. For instance, when Alice sends her commitment to Bob, he is playing the role of Eve in the cipher scheme: he receives a ciphertext but can not read it.

Next is shown how each flow is used to implement the flows of the final Commitment Scheme. When necessary, we describe roles with the same notation of Section 3.2. In the following list, we describe the flows in each system and identify them with a name between brackets that indicates the system the flow belongs to and the step when it takes place.

Cipher Scheme

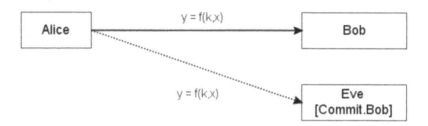

Fig. 1. A Cipher Scheme

Authentication Scheme

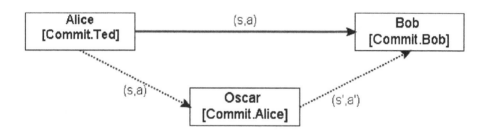

Fig. 2. An Authentication Scheme

Commitment Scheme

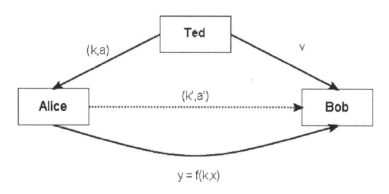

Fig. 3. A Commitment Scheme

When some steps have two similar flows, these are further distinguished with letters 'a' and 'b'.

(CP1)   Alice (a) and Bob (b) receive a secret key[1] by some secure channel.
(CP2)   A message is sent from Alice to Bob (a) and possibly also read by Eve (b).

In an authentication system as described above, there are the following flows:

(AC1)   Alice (a) and Bob (b) receive a secret key by some secure channel.
(AC2)   A message is sent from Alice to Oscar (a), who may change it before relaying it to Bob (b)[2].

In a commitment scheme, there are the following information flows:

(CM1)   Ted gives a key to Alice (a) and a verification tag to Bob (b).
(CM2)   Alice sends her commitment to Bob.
(CM3)   Alice sends her key to Bob to open her commitment.

The information flows of the commitment scheme are carried out by the information flows of the other systems like this:

– Flow (CM1.b) is achieved by flow (AC1.b). Flow (AC1.a) is ignored because Ted does not need to remember the key after he creates a valid message to send Alice. Flow (CM1.a) is achieved by flow (AC2.a), that is, Ted takes the role [AC.Alice] and sends a message to Alice ([AC.Oscar]). Due to the nature of the construction, flow (AC2.a) includes flow (CP1.a), because Alice now has a key for the cipher system.
– Flow (CM2) is achieved by flow (CP2.b).
– Flow (CM3) is achieved by flow (AC2.b). From this message, Bob deduces a key, completing flow (CP1.b), and opens the commitment by flow (CP2.a).

Table 3. Information Flows

Cipher	Commitment	Authentication
(CP1.a)	(CM1.a)	(AC2.a)
. . .	(CM1.b)	(AC1.b) [(AC1.a)]
(CP2.b)	(CM2)	. . .
(CP1.b) (CP2.a)	(CM3)	(AC2.b)

---

[1] This includes the case where they create a key themselves and exchange it.
[2] This is just a simplified model. In reality, Alice sends the message to Bob, but Oscar may intercept and alter it or not.

Unconditionally Secure Blind Signatures

Yuki Hara, Takenobu Seito, Junji Shikata, and Tsutomu Matsumoto

Graduate School of Environment and Information Sciences,
Yokohama National University, Japan
{seito,tsutomu}@mlab.jks.ynu.ac.jp, shikata@ynu.ac.jp

Abstract. The blind signature scheme introduced by Chaum allows a user to obtain a valid signature for a message from a signer such that the message is kept secret for the signer. Blind signature schemes have mainly been studied from a viewpoint of computational security so far. In this paper, we study blind signatures in unconditional setting. Specifically, we newly introduce a model of unconditionally secure blind signature schemes (USBS, for short). Also, we propose security notions and their formalization in our model. Finally, we propose a construction method for USBS that is provably secure in our security notions.

1 Introduction

1.1 Background

The security of most of present cryptographic techniques is based on the assumption of difficulty of computationally hard problems such as the integer factoring problem or the discrete logarithm problem in finite fields or elliptic curves. However, taking into account recent rapid development of algorithms and computer technologies, such a scheme based on the assumption of difficulty of computationally hard problems might not maintain sufficient long-term security. In fact, it has been known that quantum computers can solve factoring and discrete logarithm problems easily. From these discussions, it is necessary and interesting to consider cryptographic techniques whose security does not depend on any computationally hard problems.

The blind signature scheme introduced by Chaum [6] allows a user to obtain a valid signature for a message from a signer such that the message is kept secret for the signer. This blindness property plays a central role in applications such as electronic voting and electronic cash schemes where anonymity is of great concern [7]. Blind signature schemes have mainly been studied from a viewpoint of computational security so far. However, in some applications including blind signature schemes, it may be required to guarantee them in a stronger fashion such as in terms of long-term security. In such a case, blind signature schemes proposed so far cannot provide a solution, since the underlying security of the schemes essentially relies on computationally hard problems. Also, as mentioned above, if the quantum computer would be built in the future, such schemes based on computationally hard problems cannot guarantee their security. Therefore, it is important and interesting to establish blind signature schemes in unconditional security setting.

Y. Desmedt (Ed.): ICITS 2007, LNCS 4883, pp. 23–43, 2009.

1.2   Related Works

Blind signature schemes are first introduced and studied by Chaum [6]. After that, blind signature schemes have been intensively studied and developed [1][2][3][4][5][9][11][12][13][14]. In [12], Pointcheval and Stern proposed the first provably secure blind signature schemes in the random oracle model. In [9], Juels, Luby and Ostrovsky showed provably secure blind signature schemes assuming the one-way trapdoor permutation family, and they also gave a formal definition of blind signatures and formalized two kinds of security notions called *unforgeability* and *blindness* building on previous works [6][12][14]. The notion of blindness was originally considered in the paper of Chaum [6], and the notion of unforgeability was first defined by Pointeval and Stern in [12], and it was called "one-more" forgery. Based on these works, the formal security definition of blind signatures were defined in [9]. The schemes proposed in [9] are the first provably secure blind schemes in the standard model based on general results about multi-party computation, and thus it is inefficient in contrast with efficient schemes in the random oracle model. Recently, Camenisch, Koprowski and Warinschi proposed efficient blind signature schemes, provably secure in the standard model [5]. Also in [3][4], Bellare, Namprempre, Pointcheval and Semanko proved Chaum's blind signature scheme to be secure against the one-more forgery in the random oracle model based on a new hardness assumption of RSA called known-target inversion problem. In addition, very recently, Abdalla, Namprempre and Neven study Blind MAC schemes which are the symmetric analog of blind signature schemes in computational security, and have shown Blind MAC schemes do not exist since unforgeability and blindness cannot be simultaneously satisfied in the symmetric key setting [2].

The definition of blind signatures shown in [9] is briefly described as follows. There are two entities, a user and a signer in blind signature schemes, and the user can obtain signatures for the messages, such that the signer learns nothing about the message that is being signed. More formally, a signer S has public key pk and secret key sk, and he interacts with a user U who has a message m as private input. At the end of the interaction, the user obtains a signature σ on m, while the signer gets no information about σ and m. And security notions of blind signatures, called unforgeability and blindness shown in [9] are as follows. Unforgeability means that it is difficult for any malicious user who engages in s runs of the protocol with the signer, to obtain strictly more than s valid message-signature pairs. And, blindness means that after interacting with various users, it is difficult for the signer to link a valid message-signature pair obtained by some user, with the protocol session during which the signature was created.

1.3   Our Contribution

From a theoretical viewpoint, it is important to study and establish security notions of cryptographic protocols in a formal way, and to show construction which meets the security notions in a provable way. Our contribution is to study unconditionally secure blind signature schemes from this point of view. As mentioned above, blind signature schemes have mainly been studied from a viewpoint of computational security so far. In [2], it is shown that blind signature schemes in the symmetric-key setting (called Blind MAC schemes) do not exist in computational security. The main reason lies in the point that in blind MAC schemes the same secret key is used both to generate a tag and to check the validity of the tag. In fact, the user cannot verify the validity of the tag if he does not know the key with which a tag is generated by a signer. On the other hand, in the scenario that the user holds the same key with a signer, it is always possible for the user to forge a tag. Therefore, in the Blind MAC it is impossible to guarantee both unforgeability and blindness. We also note that the same argument of the impossibility applies to the symmetric-key setting even in unconditional security scenario. In this paper, we propose blind signature schemes in the asymmetric key setting in unconditional security. More precisely, we newly introduce a model and consider security notions of unconditionally secure blind signatures (USBS, for short) based on both blind signature schemes in computational setting in [9] and signature schemes in unconditional setting in [8][16][18]. As a result, we establish three notions, *Unconditional unforgeability*, *Unconditional undeniability* and *Unconditional blindness*, as security notions of unconditionally secure blind signatures, and then formulate the three notions in unconditional setting. We finally provide a construction method of USBS that is provably secure in our security definitions.

2 Blind Signatures with Computational Security

We describe the definition and the standard security notion of blind signature schemes shown in [9]. A blind signature scheme Π consists of (Gen, Signer, User, Vf). Gen is the probabilistic key generation algorithm which on input a security parameter 1^k, outputs a public-secret key pair (pk, sk). Signer and User are two interactive probabilistic Turing machines that run in polynomial time. The Signer machine is given (pk, sk) produced by Gen on his input, and the Signer machine is given pk and a message m to be signed, on his input. Then, the two machines interact to produce a signature on m. At the end of the interaction, the Signer machine outputs either *completed* or *not-completed* and the User machine outputs either *fail* or a signature σ on m. Vf is the deterministic verification algorithm which on input pk, m and σ, outputs *valid* or *invalid*. The security notions of blind signatures, called unforgeability and blindness defined in [9] are as follows:

Unforgeability and Strong Unforgeability: Unforgeability is defined via an experiment parameterized by a security parameter k as follows. In this experiment, there is an adversarial User and he tries to get "one-more" signature. First, a public-secret key pair (pk, sk) for the Signer is generated by the key generation algorithm Gen on the security parameter. Then, the User engages in polynomially many runs of the protocol with the Signer, where the User decides in an adaptive fashion when to stop. Finally, the User outputs l message-signature pairs $((m_1, \sigma_1), (m_2, \sigma_2), ..., (m_l, \sigma_l))$ with $m_i \neq m_j$ if $i \neq j$.

Let s the number that the Signer output *completed*. The advantage of the User is defined by $Adv_{\Pi,U}^{uf}(k) = Pr\left[1 \leq \forall i \leq l,\ \mathsf{Vf}(pk, (m_i, \sigma_i)) = valid) \wedge (s < l)\right]$ and unforgeability means that for any polynomial time adversarial User, the function $Adv_{\Pi,U}^{uf}(k)$ is negligible in the security parameter k. If $(m_i, \sigma_i) \neq (m_j, \sigma_j)$ instead of $m_i \neq m_j$ holds for message-signature pairs output by the adversarial User, the blind signature scheme is called strongly unforgeable.

Blindness: Blindness is defined via an experiment parameterized by a security parameter k as follows. In this experiment, there is an adversarial Signer and tries to guess b which is a random bit kept secret from the Signer. First, a public-secret key pair (pk, sk) for the Signer is generated by the key generation algorithm Gen on the security parameter. Then, the Signer outputs a pair of messages (m_0, m_1) lexicographically ordered. Next, the Signer engages in two runs with two honest Users, they have m_b and m_{1-b} as input, respectively. If the Users get valid signatures on their message, they give them to the Signer, otherwise the Signer has no additional input. Finally, the Signer guesses a bit d and outputs it. The advantage of the Signer is defined by $Adv_{\Pi,S}^{blind}(k) = 2 \cdot Pr\left[b = d\right] - 1$ and blindness means that for any polynomial time adversarial Signer, the function $Adv_{\Pi,S}^{blind}(k)$ is negligible in the security parameter k.

3   The Model and Security Definitions

In this section, we newly propose a model and security notions of unconditionally secure blind signatures, based on those of computationally secure blind signature schemes [9] and those of unconditionally secure signature schemes [8][16][18].

3.1   The Model

We now consider the model of USBS. In a signature scheme based on public-key cryptography, a verification-key for a verifier can be public and shared among all verifiers. However such a signature scheme cannot be secure against an adversary with unlimited computing power (e.g. see [18]). A consequence of this fact is that with a signature scheme that allows an adversary to have unlimited computing power, its key generation algorithm must generate verification-keys for all verifiers, and it is necessary to distribute the verification key to verifiers individually in a secure way. For simplicity, in the model of signature schemes in unconditional setting as well as other schemes [15][16] , it is often the case to assume that there is a trusted authority whose role is to generate and distribute participants' secret keys. In defining the model of blind signature schemes from an information-theoretic viewpoint, we also adopt the model of the *TA model* as follows.

We assume that there is a trusted authority, denoted by TA. In USBS, there are $n + 2$ participants, a signer S, n users $U_1, U_2, \ldots, U_n$ and a trusted authority TA, where n is a positive integer. For convenience, we also use S(resp. U_j) as S's(resp. U_j's) identity. The TA produces a secret key on behalf of each participant. After distributing these secret keys via a secure channel, TA deletes them from his memory. Once being given a secret key from TA, a user generates a blinded message for a message not to reveal the message that is being signed to the signer by using his key. Then, the user sends the blinded message to the signer. On receiving a blinded message from the user, the signer generates a signature for the blinded message by his key, and sends it back to the user. On receiving a signature for a blinded message from the signer, the user can then produce a signature for the original message by using his key from the received signature created by the signer, and then the user verifies the validity of the signature by using his key. The signer can also verify the validity of signature by using his key. In the case of dispute between the signer and a user, an arbiter (an honest user) can resolve the dispute by using his key. A formal definition is given as follows:

Definition 1. (USBS) : USBS Π consists of $n + 2$ participants $(TA, S, U_1, U_2, \cdots, U_n)$, six spaces $(M, M^*, \Sigma, \Sigma^*, E_s, E_u)$ and six algorithms $(Gen, Blind, Sign, Unblind, UVer, SVer)$.

1. **Notation:**
   - TA is a trusted authority.
   - S is a signer.
   - $U_1, U_2, \cdots, U_n$ are users. Let $U = \{U_1, U_2, \cdots, U_n\}$
   - M is a finite set of possible messages.
   - M^* is a finite set of possible blinded messages.
   - Σ is a finite set of possible signatures for the messages.
   - Σ^* is a finite set of possible signatures for the blinded messages.
   - E_s is a finite set of possible signer's secret keys.
   - E_u is a finite set of possible user's secret keys.
   - $GGen$ is a key generation algorithm which on input a security parameter, outputs a signer's secret key and users' secret keys.
   - $Blind : M \times E_u \longrightarrow M^*$ is a blinding algorithm.
   - $Sign : M^* \times E_s \longrightarrow \Sigma^*$ is a signing algorithm.
   - $Unblind : \Sigma^* \times M \times E_u \longrightarrow \Sigma$ is an unblinding algorithm.
   - $UVer : M \times \Sigma \times E_u \longrightarrow \{valid, invalid\}$ is a verification algorithm by the user.
   - $SVer : M \times \Sigma \times E_s \longrightarrow \{valid, invalid\}$ is a verification algorithm by the signer.
2. **Key Generation and Distribution by TA:** The TA generates secret keys $e_s \in E_s$ and $e_{u_i} \in E_u (1 \leq i \leq n)$ for the signer S and users $U_i (1 \leq i \leq n)$, respectively using the key generation algorithm $GGen$. After distributing these secret keys via a secure channel, TA deletes them from his memory. And S and $U_i (1 \leq i \leq n)$ keep their secret keys secret, respectively.
3. **Blinding:** For a message $m \in M$, a user U_i generates a blinded message $m^* = Blind(m, e_{u_i}) \in M^*$ by using his key e_{u_i} not to reveal the message m that is being signed, to the signer S. Then, U_i sends m^* to S.
4. **Signature Generation:** On receiving m^* from U_i, the signer S generates a signature $\sigma^* = Sign(m^*, e_s) \in \Sigma^*$ for the blinded message m^* by using his key e_s. Then, S sends (m^*, σ^*) to U_i.

5. **Unblinding:** On receiving (m^*, σ^*) from S, the user U_i creates a signature $\sigma = Unblind(\sigma^*, m, e_{u_i}) \in \Sigma$ for the original message m from the received signature σ^* for a blinded message m^* by using his key e_{u_i}. The pair (m, σ) is regarded as a message-signature pair of S.

6. **Signature Verification by User:** On generating (m, σ) from (m^*, σ^*), the user U_i verifies the validity of σ for m by using his secret key e_{u_i}. More precisely, if $UVer(m, \sigma, e_{u_i}) = valid$ then U_i accepts (m, σ) as a valid , and rejects it otherwise.

7. **Signature Verification by Signer:** The signer can also verify the validity of σ for m by using his secret key e_s. More precisely, if $SVer(m, \sigma, e_s) = valid$ then S accepts (m, σ) as a valid, and rejects it otherwise.

8. **Resolution for Dispute by a Third Party:** Let $U_A \in \{U_1, \cdots, U_n\}$ be an arbiter(third party) and $e_{u_A} \in E_u$ his key. If dispute occurs between the signer S and a user U_i about whether (m, σ) is legally generated by S or not, U_A judges the validity of (m, σ) following the resolution-rule as follows. If $UVer(m, \sigma, e_{u_A}) = valid$, U_A judges that the signature is valid. Otherwise, he judges that it is invalid. Here, we assume that the arbiter honestly follows the resolution-rule and honestly outputs its result when a dispute occurs.

Note that we call a message-signature pair (m, σ) *valid* if the signature can be generated by using signer's secret key e_s. Otherwise, we call (m, σ) *invalid*. We also note that in unconditionally secure signature schemes an invalid message-signature pair which is accepted as valid by a user may exist.

In the sequel, let t_u, t_s, t_v be a number up to which each user is allowed to request signatures, a number up to which the signer is allowed to generate signatures and a number up to which each participant is allowed to verify signatures, respectively.

3.2   Approaches to Unconditional Security

Here, we consider security notions and their formalization of blind signature schemes from an information-theoretic viewpoint. As mentioned above, Juels, Luby and Ostrovsky defined and formalized two kinds of security notions of blind signatures in computational setting, called unforgeability and blindness, building on previous works [6][12][14]. We interpret those security notions anew from a viewpoint of unconditional security setting, and newly define the three kinds of security notions of USBS, *unconditional unforgeability*, *unconditional undeniability* and *unconditional blindness* as follows.

Unconditional unforgeability: In [9], unforgeability is defined and formalized as the notion that it is difficult for any malicious user that after engaging in s runs of the protocol with the signer, to obtain strictly more than s valid message-signature pairs. When interrupting this notion in information-theoretic viewpoints, we focus on the security notions of signature schemes in unconditional setting [8][16][18]. These notions mean that it is difficult for the adversary who can collude with any users to create a signature that has not been legally created by the signer but will be accepted as valid by a verifier. We modify these notions based on the idea of unforgeability in [9] and call this notion unconditional unforgeability. We note that the notion of unconditional unforgeability covers the notion of strong unforgeability in computational security.

Unconditional undeniability: As mentioned above, in signature schemes in unconditional setting, verification-keys differ by each verifier, and are kept secretly. In such a scheme, in general, a signature which is accepted by a verifier but rejected by other verifiers may exist. Therefore, it is necessary to carefully take into account the attack in which a signer generates a signature, and then denies it. In [16] and [18], security notions against such an attack are defined. Especially, in [16], this kind of attack was called *denial attack*. We note that the same argument applies to USBS. Therefore, we modify the notion of the denial attack in [16] and [18]. Into a form suitable for USBS, and call this notion unconditional undeniability.

Unconditional blindness: In [9], blindness is defined and formalized as the notion that after interacting with many users, it is difficult for the signer to link a valid message-signature pair obtained by some user, with the protocol session during which the signature was created. When interrupting this notion in information-theoretic viewpoints, we focus on the security notions of encryption schemes in unconditional setting as shown in [10][19]. Especially, we focus on the security notions of encryption schemes in unconditional setting, called APS(almost perfect secrecy) [19] or ϵ-perfect secrecy [10] against CPA(chosen plaintext attacks) and CCA(chosen ciphertext attacks), which is the straightforward expansion of the notion called perfect secrecy introduced by Shannon [17]. This notion means that it is difficult for the adversary to obtain any information about plaintext from a target ciphertext in unconditional setting. We modify the notion of APS against CPA and CCA based on the notion of blindness in [9], and call this notion unconditional blindness.

3.3 Security Notions

Based on the above argument, we define security notions of USBS and give their formalizations in this subsection. As mentioned above, let t_u, t_s, t_v be a number up to which each user is allowed to request signatures, a number up to which the signer is allowed to generate signatures and a number up to which each participant is allowed to verify signatures, respectively, and let ω be the number of possible colluders among participants. Let $\mathcal{W} := \{W \subset \{S, U_1, \ldots, U_n\} \,|\, \#W \leq \omega\}$. Here, each element of $\mathcal{W}$ presents a group of possibly collusive participants $\{S, U_1, \ldots, U_n\}$. For a set $\mathcal{T}$ and a non-negative integer t, let $P(\mathcal{T}, t) := \{T \subset \mathcal{T} \,|\, \#T \leq t\}$ be the family of all subsets of $\mathcal{T}$ whose cardinalities are less than or equal to t. With these notations, we define security notions of USBS, called unconditional unforgeability, unconditional undeniability and unconditional blindness, and formalize them as follows.

Definition 2. (Security of USBS) : Let Π be an USBS. The scheme Π is said to be $(n, \omega, t_u, t_s, t_v, \epsilon)$-*secure* if $\max\{P_F, P_D, P_B\} \leq \epsilon$, where P_F, P_D, P_B are defined as follows:

1. **Unconditional unforgeability:** The notion of unconditional unforgeability means that it is difficult for malicious colluders not including the signer S to create a signature that has not been legally generated by S but will be accepted as valid by a user U_j or the signer S. We define this notion exactly as follows.

(1) For $W \in \mathcal{W}$ such that $S \notin W$ and $U_j \notin W$, we define $P_{F_1}(U_j, W)$ as

$$P_{F_1}(U_j, W) := \max_{e_W} \max_{M_\sigma} \max_{M_{\sigma^*}} \max_{M_{U_j}} \max_{M_{U_1}, \ldots, M_{U_i}, \ldots, M_{U_n} (i \neq j)} \max_{M_S} \max_{(m,\sigma)}$$

$$Pr(U_j \ accepts \ (m,\sigma)|e_W, M_\sigma, M_{\sigma^*}, M_{U_j}, \{M_{U_i}(1 \leq i \leq n, i \neq j)\}, M_S)$$

where e_W is taken over all possible combination of keys of W; M_σ is taken over $P(M \times \Sigma, t_s)$ such that any element of M_σ is a valid message-signature pair; M_{σ^*} is taken over $P(M^* \times \Sigma^*, t_s)$ such that any element of M_{σ^*} is a pair of valid blinded-message and its signature; $M_{U_j} = \{(m_j, \sigma_j, UVer(m_j, \sigma_j, e_{u_j}))\}$ is taken over $P(M \times \Sigma \times \{valid, invalid\}, t_v - 1)$ such that $UVer(m_j, \sigma_j, e_{u_j}) = invalid$ for any invalid message-signature pair (m_j, σ_j); M_{U_i} is taken over $P(M \times \Sigma \times \{valid, invalid\}, t_v)$ for $1 \leq i \leq n, i \neq j$; M_S is taken over $P(M \times \Sigma \times \{valid, invalid\}, t_v)$; and (m, σ) is taken over $M \times \Sigma$ such that $(m, \sigma) \notin M_\sigma$. Then, the probability P_{F_1} given as $P_{F_1} := \max_{U_j, W} P_{F_1}(U_j, W)$.

(2) For $W \in \mathcal{W}$ such that $S \notin W$, we define $P_{F_2}(W)$ as

$$P_{F_2}(W) := \max_{e_W} \max_{M_\sigma} \max_{M_{\sigma^*}} \max_{M_S} \max_{M_{U_1}, \ldots, M_{U_n}} \max_{(m,\sigma)}$$

$$Pr(S \ accepts \ (m,\sigma)|e_W, M_\sigma, M_{\sigma^*}, M_S, \{M_{U_i}(1 \leq i \leq n)\})$$

where e_W is taken over all possible combination of keys of W; M_σ is taken over $P(M \times \Sigma, t_s)$ such that any element of M_S is a valid message-signature pair; M_{σ^*} is taken over $P(M^* \times \Sigma^*, t_s)$ such that any element of M_{S^*} is a pair of valid blinded-message and its signature; $M_S = \{(m_s, \sigma_s, SVer(m_s, \sigma_s, e_{u_s}))\}$ is taken over $P(M \times \Sigma \times \{valid, invalid\}, t_v - 1)$ such that $SVer(m_s, \sigma_s, e_{u_s}) = invalid$ for any invalid message-signature pair (m_s, σ_s); M_{U_i} is taken over $P(M \times \Sigma \times \{valid, invalid\}, t_v)$ for $1 \leq i \leq n$; and (m, σ) is taken over $M \times \Sigma$ such that $(m, \sigma) \notin M_{1 \leq i \leq n}$. Then, the probability P_{F_2} given as $P_{F_2} := \max_W P_{F_2}(W)$. And, we define P_F as $P_F := \max\{P_{F_1}, P_{F_2}\}$.

2. **Unconditional undeniability:** The notion of unconditional undeniability means that it is difficult for malicious colluders including the signer S to generate an invalid signed message (m, σ) that will be accepted as valid by the target user U_j. Note that the purpose of the colluders is to deny having sent (m, σ). We define this notion exactly as follows.

For $W \in \mathcal{W}$ such that $S \in W$ and $U_j \notin W$, we define $P_D(U_j, W)$ as

$$P_D(U_j, W) := \max_{e_W} \max_{M_{U_j}} \max_{M_{U_1}, \ldots, M_{U_i}, \ldots, M_{U_n} (i \neq j)} \max_{M_S} \max_{(m,\sigma)}$$

$$Pr(U_j \ accepts \ (m,\sigma)|e_W, M_{U_j}, \{M_{U_i}(1 \leq i \leq n, i \neq j)\}, M_S)$$

where e_W is taken over all possible combination of keys of W; $M_{U_j} = \{(m_j, \sigma_j, UVer(m_j, \sigma_j, e_{u_j}))\}$ is taken over $P(M \times \Sigma \times \{valid, invalid\}, t_v - 1)$ such that $UVer(m_j, \sigma_j, e_{u_j}) = invalid$ for any invalid message-signature pair (m_j, σ_j); M_{U_i} is taken over $P(M \times \Sigma \times \{valid, invalid\}, t_v)$ for $1 \leq i \leq n, i \neq j$; M_S is taken over $P(M \times \Sigma \times \{valid, invalid\}, t_v)$; and $(m, \sigma) \in M \times \Sigma$ runs over invalid message-signature pairs. And, we define P_D as $P_D := \max_{U_j, W} P_D(U_j, W)$

3. **Unconditional blindness:** The notion of unconditional blindness means that it is difficult for malicious colluders to succeed in the following attack. They observe (m, σ), and then try to guess the user who requested it. We define this notion exactly as follows.

For $W \in \mathcal{W}$, we define $P_B(W)$ as

$$P_B(W) := \max_{e_W} \max_{(m_1^*, \sigma_1^*),\ldots,(m_n^*, \sigma_n^*)} \max_{(m, \sigma)}$$

$$\left\{ \sum_{U_j \in U \backslash W} \left| Pr(U_j | e_W, \{(m_i^*, \sigma_i^*)(1 \leq i \leq n)\}, (m, \sigma)) - Pr(U_j) \right| \right\}$$

where e_W is taken over all possible combination of keys of W; $(m_i^*, \sigma_i^*) \in M^* \times \Sigma^*$ is a pair of blinded-message and its signature requested by U_i for $1 \leq i \leq n$; and $(m, \sigma) \in M \times \Sigma$ is a message-signature pair corresponding to (m_j^*, σ_j^*) requested by $U_j \notin W$. And, we define P_B as $P_B := \max_W P_B(W)$.

4   Construction

In this section, we show a construction method of USBS. In [8][16][18], constructions of unconditionally secure signature schemes are proposed by using polynomials over finite fields. Therefore, we use polynomials over finite fields to construct a USBS that is provably secure in our security notions.

The main idea of this construction is to combine USBS in one-time model. In the model of one-time USBS, there are four kinds of secret-keys, a blinding-key, an unblinding-key, a signing-key and verification-keys. And, the user who has the pair of blind-key and unblinding-key can request the signer to generate a signature only once, and other users who have only the verification-key can check the validity of the message-signature pair.

In our construction method, we first provide a set of blinding-key, unblinding-key, signing-key and verification-key for one-time model of USBS, and we independently generate $t_u n$ sets of these keys. And, we give t_u pairs of blind-key and unblinding-key to each users, and $t_u n$ signing-keys to the signer, respectively. And, the user requests the signer to generate a signature by using one of the pair of blinding-key and unblinding-key only once, and, the signer generates the signature by using the signing-key corresponding to user's blinding-key and unblinding-key pair only once. And also, we give $t_u n$ verification-keys to each participants. Here, we note that verification-keys differ by each participant (see section 3). In this construction, we need to keep the relation among the

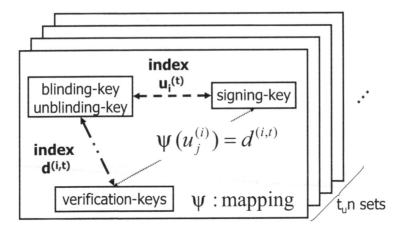

Fig. 1. The basic idea of our construction

keys, because the signer cannot generate a valid signature unless he uses the signing-key corresponding to the blinding-key of the user who request to generate a signature. Thus, each key should be indexed. However, if we trivially index these keys, that is, the relation between indexes of verification-key and signing-key is publicly known, the construction cannot achieve the notion of unconditional blindness. This is because when the signer receives a signature, he can determine the user who requested it by the relation between verification-key and signing-key. Therefore, we make it secret to relate the indexes of verification-key with those of the other keys by meaning of mapping which is secretly given to each user. The details of the construction are as follows.

1. **Key Generation Algorithm:** For a security parameter 1^k, the algorithm *Gen* outputs matching key for each participant as follows. It picks k bit prime power q, and constructs the finite field $\mathbf{F}_q$ with q elements such that $q \geq n + 1$. We assume that a message m is an element of $\mathbf{F}_q$ in this construction. It also picks uniformly at random $t_u n(n+1)$ elements $v_j^{(i,t)} := \left(v_{1,j}^{(i,t)}, \ldots, v_{\omega,j}^{(i,t)} \right) (1 \leq i \leq n, 1 \leq t \leq t_u)(j = s, 1, \ldots n)$ in $\mathbf{F}_q^\omega$. And it generates $t_u n$ mappings $C_j^{(t)}(z) := z + \alpha_j^{(t)}(1 \leq i \leq n, 1 \leq t \leq t_u)$ by picking $\alpha_j^{(t)} \in F_q$ uniformly at random. Also, it chooses uniformly at random $4t_u n$ polynomials $G_0^{(i,t)}(y_1, \ldots, y_\omega)$, $G_1^{(i,t)}(y_1, \ldots, y_\omega)$, $G_2^{(i,t)}(y_1, \ldots, y_\omega)$ and $G_3^{(i,t)}(y_1, \ldots, y_\omega)(1 \leq i \leq n, 1 \leq t \leq t_u)$ over $\mathbf{F}_q$ with ω variables $y_1, \ldots, y_\omega$, in which the degree of every y_i is at most 1, and computes $t_u n$ polynomials $F_j^{(t)}(x, y_1, \ldots, y_\omega)(1 \leq j \leq n)$ by $F_j^{(t)}(x, y_1, \ldots, y_\omega) := G_3^{(j,t)}(y_1, \ldots, y_\omega) - \alpha_j^{(t)} G_1^{(j,t)}(y_1, \ldots, y_\omega) + x G_2^{(j,t)}(y_1, \ldots, y_\omega)$ $(1 \leq j \leq n, 1 \leq t \leq t_u)$. It also computes $H_j^{(i,t)}(z) := G_0^{(i,t)}(v_j^{(i,t)}) + G_3^{(i,t)}(v_j^{(i,t)}) + z(G_1^{(i,t)}(v_j^{(i,t)}) + G_2^{(i,t)}(v_j^{(i,t)}))(1 \leq i \leq n, 1 \leq t \leq t_u)(j = s, 1, \ldots n)$. It also chooses

distinct numbers $u_i^{(t)} (1 \leq i \leq n,\ 1 \leq t \leq t_u)$ uniformly at random from $\mathbf{F}_{q^2}$, and makes n sets $U^{(i)} := \{u_i^{(1)}, ..., u_i^{(t_u)}\} (1 \leq i \leq n)$. Also, it chooses distinct numbers $d^{(i,t)} (1 \leq i \leq n,\ 1 \leq t \leq t_u)$ uniformly at random from $\mathbf{F}_{q^2}$, and makes n sets $D^{(i)} := \{d^{(i,1)}, ..., d^{(i,t_u)}\} (1 \leq i \leq n)$. Next it generates distinct n bijective mappings $\Psi_i : U^{(i)} \rightarrow D^{(i)} (1 \leq i \leq n)$ such that $\Psi_i(u_i^{(j)}) = d^{(i,j)}$. Finally, the algorithm Gen outputs the keys

$$e_s := ((u_1^{(1)}, G_0^{(1,1)}(y_1, \ldots, y_\omega),\ G_1^{(1,1)}(y_1, \ldots, y_\omega), d^{(1,1)}, H_s^{(1,1)}(z), v_s^{(1,1)}),$$
$$\ldots,\ (u_i^{(t)},\ G_0^{(i,t)}(y_1, \ldots, y_\omega),\ G_1^{(i,t)}(y_1, \ldots, y_\omega),\ d^{(i,t)},\ H_s^{(i,t)}(z), v_s^{(i,t)}),\ \ldots,$$
$$(u_n^{(n)},\ G_0^{(n,t_u)}(y_1, \ldots, y_\omega),\ G_1^{(n,t_u)}(y_1, \ldots, y_\omega), d^{(n,t_u)}, H_s^{(n,t_u)}(z), v_s^{(n,t_u)})),$$

where $1 \leq i \leq n$ and $1 \leq t \leq t_s$, and $e_{u_j} :=$
$$((C_j^{(1)}(z), F_j^{(1)}(x, y_1, ..., y_\omega)),\ \ldots ,(C_j^{(t)}(z), F_j^{(t)}(x, y_1, ..., y_\omega)),\ \cdots,\ (C_j^{(t_s)}(z),$$
$$F_j^{(t_s)}(x, y_1, ..., y_\omega)),\ U^{(j)},\ \Psi_j,\ (d^{(1,1)},\ H_j^{(1,1)}(z),\ v_j^{(1,1)}),\ \ldots\ ,\ (d^{(i,t)}, H_j^{(i,t)}$$
$$(z), v_j^{(i,t)}),\ \ldots,\ (d^{(n,t_s)}, H_j^{(n,t_s)}(z), v_j^{(n,t_s)}))),\ \text{where } 1 \leq i \leq n \text{ and } 1 \leq t \leq t_s.$$

2. **Blinding Algorithm:** In the t-th request, for a message $m \in F_q$ and $e_{u_j} \in E_u$, the algorithm $Blind$ computes $c := C_j^{(t)}(m)(= m + \alpha_j^{(t)})$ and outputs $m^* = (u_j^{(t)}, c)$ which is the blinded message for m.

3. **Signing Algorithm:** For a blinded message $m^* = (u_j^{(t)}, c)$, and $e_s \in E_s$, the algorithm $Sign$ picks up $G_0^{(j,t)}(y_1, \ldots, y_\omega)$ and $G_1^{(j,t)}(y_1, \ldots, y_\omega)$ corresponding $u_j^{(t)}$ from e_s , and computes $\sigma^* := \beta^*(y) = G_0^{(j,t)}(y_1, \ldots, y_\omega)$ $+cG_1^{(j,t)}(y_1, \ldots, y_\omega)$. Then it outputs σ^* as the signature for the blinded message $m^* = (u_j^{(t)}, c)$.

4. **Unblinding Algorithm:** For a signature σ^* for $m^* = (u_j^{(t)}, c)$, the original message m and $e_{u_j} \in E_u$, the algorithm $Unblind$ picks up $F_j^{(t)}(m, y_1, \ldots, y_\omega)$ corresponding $u_j^{(t)}$ from e_{u_j}, and computes $r := \beta(y) = \beta^*(y) + F_j^{(t)}(m, y_1, \ldots,$
$$y_\omega) = G_0^{(j,t)}(y_1, \ldots, y_\omega) + G_3^{(j,t)}(y_1, \ldots, y_\omega) + m(G_1^{(j,t)}(y_1, \ldots, y_\omega)$$
$+G_2^{(j,t)}(y_1, \ldots, y_\omega))$. Next, it computes $\Psi_j(u_j^{(t)}) = d^{(j,t)}$, and outputs $\sigma = (d^{(j,t)}, r)$, which is a signature for the original message m.

5. **Verification Algorithm by User:** For a message-signature pair (m, σ), where $\sigma = (d^{(j,t)}, r)$ and $e_{u_k} \in E_u$, the algorithm $UVer$ picks up $H_k^{(j,t)}(z)$ and $v_k^{(j,t)}$ corresponding $d^{(j,t)}$ from e_{u_k}, and outputs $valid$ if $\beta(y)|_{y=v_k^{(j,t)}} = H_k^{(j,t)}(z)|_{z=m}$ holds and otherwise outputs $invalid$.

6. **Verification Algorithm by Signer:** For a message-signature pair (m, σ), where $\sigma = (d^{(j,t)}, r)$ and $e_s \in E_s$, the algorithm $SVer$ picks up $H_s^{(j,t)}(z)$ and $v_s^{(j,t)}$ corresponding $d^{(j,t)}$ from e_s, and outputs $valid$ if $\beta(y)|_{y=v_s^{(j,t)}} = H_s^{(j,t)}(z)|_{z=m}$ holds and otherwise outputs $invalid$.

The security of the above construction method follows from Theorem 1.

Theorem 1. *The above construction results in* $(n, \omega, t_u, t_s, t_v, \epsilon)$-*USBS, where* n, ω, t_u, t_s, t_v *and* ϵ *are taken in such a way that*

$$0 \leq \omega \leq n, \ 1 \leq t_s \leq nt_u \ and \ \epsilon = \frac{2}{q - 2t_v + 2}.$$

Proof. The proof is given in Appendix A.

Also, the efficiency of the above construction is easily shown as follows.

Theorem 2. *The efficiency of the above construction in terms of time complexity of algorithms and memory sizes are estimated as follows: The algorithm Blind requires one addition in the finite field* $\mathbf{F}_q$; *the algorithm Sign requires almost* $\omega + 1$ *multiplication in* $\mathbf{F}_q$; *the algorithm Unblind requires almost* $\omega + 1$ *multiplication in* $\mathbf{F}_q$; *and each of the algorithms UVer and SVer requires almost* $\omega + 1$ *multiplication in* $\mathbf{F}_q$. *The memory sizes required in the above construction are:* $l_\Sigma = (\omega + 3) \log q$ $l_{\Sigma^*} = (\omega + 1) \log q$, $l_{E_u} = (t_u(n\omega + 2\omega + 4n + 5) + t_u!) \log q$ *and* $l_{E_s} = nt_u(3\omega + 8) \log q$, *where* $l_\Sigma, l_{\Sigma^*}, l_{E_u}$ *and* l_{E_s} *are bit length of signatures for messages, signatures for blinded messages, users' secret keys and the signer's secret keys, respectively.*

5 Concluding Remarks

In this paper, we studied blind signature schemes from the viewpoint of unconditional security setting. Specifically, we newly introduced a model of unconditionally secure blind signatures. Also, we proposed security notions and their formalizations in our model. In addition, we provided a construction method that was provably secure in our strong security notions. As far as we know, this is the first achievement of blind signatures in unconditional security. However, the proposed construction may be inefficient. As further works, it would be interesting to investigate more efficient construction methods.

Acknowledgement

The authors would like to thank anonymous referees for their helpful comments.

References

1. Abe, M.: A secure three-move blind signature scheme for polynomially many signatures. In: Pfitzmann, B. (ed.) EUROCRYPT 2001. LNCS, vol. 2045, pp. 136–151. Springer, Heidelberg (2001)
2. Abdalla, M., Namprempre, C., Neven, G.: On the (im)possibility of blind message authentication codes. In: Pointcheval, D. (ed.) CT-RSA 2006. LNCS, vol. 3860, pp. 262–279. Springer, Heidelberg (2006)
3. Bellare, M., Namprempre, C., Pointcheval, D., Semanko, M.: The power of RSA inversion oracles and the security of Chaum's RSA-based blind signature scheme. In: Syverson, P.F. (ed.) FC 2001. LNCS, vol. 2339, pp. 309–338. Springer, Heidelberg (2002)

4. Bellare, M., Namprempre, C., Pointcheval, D., Semanko, M.: The One-More-RSA-Inversion problems and security of Chaum's blind signature scheme. J. Cryptology 16(3), 185–215 (2003)
5. Camenisch, J., Koprowski, M., Warinschi, B.: Efficient blind signatures without random oracles. In: Blundo, C., Cimato, S. (eds.) SCN 2004. LNCS, vol. 3352, pp. 134–148. Springer, Heidelberg (2005)
6. Chaum, D.: Blind signatures for untraceable payments. In: Proc. of CRYPTO 1982, pp. 199–204. Prenum Publishing Corporation (1982)
7. Chaum, D., Fiat, A., Naor, M.: Untraceable electronic cash. In: Goldwasser, S. (ed.) CRYPTO 1988. LNCS, vol. 403, pp. 319–327. Springer, Heidelberg (1990)
8. Hanaoka, G., Shikata, J., Zheng, Y., Imai, H.: Unconditionally secure digital signature schemes admitting transferability. In: Okamoto, T. (ed.) ASIACRYPT 2000. LNCS, vol. 1976, pp. 130–142. Springer, Heidelberg (2000)
9. Juels, A., Luby, M., Ostrovsky, R.: Security of blind digital signatures. In: Kaliski Jr., B.S. (ed.) CRYPTO 1997. LNCS, vol. 1294, pp. 150–164. Springer, Heidelberg (1997)
10. McAven, L., Safavi-Naini, R., Yung, M.: Unconditionally secure encryption under strong attacks. In: Wang, H., Pieprzyk, J., Varadharajan, V. (eds.) ACISP 2004. LNCS, vol. 3108, pp. 427–439. Springer, Heidelberg (2004)
11. Pointcheval, D.: Strenghened security for blind signatures. In: Nyberg, K. (ed.) EUROCRYPT 1998. LNCS, vol. 1403, pp. 391–405. Springer, Heidelberg (1998)
12. Pointcheval, D., Stern, J.: Provably secure blind signature schemes. In: Kim, K.-c., Matsumoto, T. (eds.) ASIACRYPT 1996. LNCS, vol. 1163, pp. 252–265. Springer, Heidelberg (1996)
13. Pointcheval, D., Stern, J.: New blind signatures equivalent to factorization. In: ACM CCS, pp. 92–99. ACM Press, New York (1997)
14. Pointcheval, D., Stern, J.: Security arguments for digital signatures and blind signatures. Journal of Cryptology 13(3), 361–396 (2000)
15. Rivest, R.: Unconditionally secure commitment and oblivious transfer schemes using private channels and a trusted initializer (manuscript), http://theory.lcs.mit.edu/~rivest/Rivest-commitment.pdf
16. Safavi-Naini, R., McAven, L., Yung, M.: General group authentication codes and their relation to "unconditionally-secure signatures". In: Bao, F., Deng, R., Zhou, J. (eds.) PKC 2004. LNCS, vol. 2947, pp. 231–247. Springer, Heidelberg (2004)
17. Shannon, C.E.: Communication theory of secret systems. Bell Syst. Tech. J. 28, 656–715 (1949)
18. Shikata, J., Hanaoka, G., Zheng, Y., Imai, H.: Security notions for unconditionally secure signature schemes. In: Knudsen, L.R. (ed.) EUROCRYPT 2002. LNCS, vol. 2332, pp. 434–449. Springer, Heidelberg (2002)
19. Shikata, J., Hanaoka, G., Zheng, Y., Matsumoto, T., Imai, H.: Unconditionally secure authenticated encryption. IEICE Trans. on Fundamentals (May 2004)

Appendix A: Proof of Theorem 1

The outline of the proof of Theorem 1 is as follow. In Lemma 1, we evaluate the probability of unforgeability: First, in Claim 1 of Lemma 1, we evaluate the probability that the malicious colluder who does not use verification-oracle, forges a valid signature; In Claim 2 of Lemma 1, we show the Relation of probability when verification-oracle exists and when it doesn't exist; Then from Claims 1 and 2, we show the probability P_F that the malicious colluder which uses verification-oracle, forges a valid signature. Next, in Lemma 2, we evaluate the probability of undeniability P_D: First, in Claim 3 of Lemma 2, we evaluate the probability that the malicious colluder who does not use verification-oracle to forge a signature; From Claim 3 and Lemma 1, we evaluate the probability P_D. In Lemma 3, we evaluate the probability of blindness P_B: We show that the malicious colluder cannot guess the user who requests the signature after observing it with probability more than random guessing. Finally, from Lemmas 1, 2, 3, we complete the proof of Theorem 1. The detail of the proof of Theorem 1 is as below.

The detail of the proof of Theorem 1 is as below. To complete the proof of the theorem, we show the following three lemmas.

Lemma 1. P_F *is at most* $\frac{2}{q-2t_v+2}$.

Proof. Without loss of generality it is sufficient to prove P_{F_1} is at most $\frac{2}{q-2t_v+2}$. Let $W := \{U_1, ..., U_w\}$ be a set of colluders. We consider that W tries to produce a fraudulent message-signature pair (m', σ') which is accepted by $U_n \notin W$, and W can obtain most information which are their secret keys, t_s valid message-signature pairs, t_s valid pairs of blinded-message and its signature, $t_v - 1$ verification results on message-signature pairs from $U_n \notin W$, and t_v verification results on message-signature pairs from $U_j (j = 1, ..., n - 1)$. We note that the proposed construction consists of $t_u n$ independent signing-keys, blinding-keys, unblinding-keys and verification-keys, hence when W tries to produce a fraudulent message-signature pair (m', σ') with $\sigma' = (d^{(i,t)}, r')$, obtained message-signature pairs and pairs of blinded message and its signature are not valuable except for them corresponding to $d^{(i,t)}$. We also note that the obtained verification results on message-signature pairs are not valuable except for them from the target user $U_n \notin W$. Thus, the following equation holds in this construction.

$$Pr(U_n \text{ accepts } (m', \sigma') | e_W, M_\sigma, M_{\sigma^*}, M_{U_n}, \{M_{U_j}(j = 1, ..., n - 1)\}, M_S)$$
$$= Pr(U_n \text{ accepts } (m', \sigma') | e_W, (m, \sigma), (m^*, \sigma^*), M_{U_n})$$

where (m, σ) is a valid message-signature pair such that $\sigma = (d^{(i,t)}, r)$, (m', σ') is an invalid message-signature pair such that $\sigma' = (d^{(i,t)}, r')$ and $(m, r) \neq (m', r')$, and (m^*, σ^*) is a pair of blinded-message and its signature corresponding to (m, σ). We first consider the case where the colluders are not allowed to obtain any verification results from the target user $U_n \notin W$, and we show the following.

$$P_{F_1'} := Pr(U_n \text{ accepts } (m', \sigma') | e_W, (m, \sigma), (m^*, \sigma^*)) \leq \frac{2}{q} - \frac{1}{q^2}. \tag{1}$$

We prove (1) as follows. W has the following information corresponding to $d^{(i,t)}$. $\sigma^* = \beta^*(y) = G_0^{(i,t)}(y_1, ..., y_w) + cG_1^{(i,t)}(y_1, ..., y_w)$, $r := \beta(y) = G_0^{(i,t)}(y_1, ..., y_w) + G_3^{(i,t)}(y_1, ..., y_w) + m(G_1^{(i,t)}(y_1, ..., y_w) + G_2^{(i,t)}(y_1, ..., y_w))$, $C_i^{(t)}(z) = z + \alpha_i^{(t)}$, $F_i^{(t)}(x, y_1, ..., y_w) = G_3^{(i,t)}(y_1, ..., y_w) - \alpha_{i,t}G_1^{(i)}(y_1, ..., y_w) + xG_2^{(i,t)}(y_1, ..., y_w)$, $H_j^{(i,t)}(z) = G_0^{(i,t)}(v_j^{(i,t)}) + G_3^{(i,t)}(v_j^{(i,t)}) + z(G_1^{(i,t)}(v_j^{(i,t)}) +$

$G_2^{(i,t)}(v_j^{(i,t)}))(1 \leq j \leq \omega)$ and $v_j^{(i,t)} = \left(v_{j,1}^{(i,t)}, \ldots, v_{j,\omega}^{(i,t)}\right)(1 \leq j \leq \omega)$. We note that $\beta^*(y)$ and $F_i^{(t)}(x, y_1, \ldots, y_\omega)$ are not valuable for them having $\beta(y)$, since the equation $\beta(y) = \beta^*(y) + F_i^{(t)}(m, y_1, \ldots, y_\omega)$ holds. Let $v_j := v_j^{(i,t)} \mathrm{C}(v_{j,1}, \ldots, v_{j,\omega}) := (v_{j,1}^{(i,t)}, \ldots, v_{j,\omega}^{(i,t)})$ and $E(y_1, \ldots, y_\omega, z) := G_0^{(i,t)}(y_1, \ldots, y_\omega) + G_3^{(i,t)}(y_1, \ldots, y_\omega) + z(G_1^{(i,t)}(y_1, \ldots, y_\omega) + G_2^{(i,t)}(y_1, \ldots, y_\omega))$. Then, $\beta^*(y)$ and $H_j^{(i,t)}(z)$ $(1 \leq j \leq \omega)$ can be written with $E(y_1, \ldots, y_\omega, z)$ as $\beta(y) = E(y_1, \ldots, y_\omega, m)$ and $H_j^{(i,t)}(z) = E(v_i, z)(1 \leq j \leq \omega)$. Therefore, the information W has are $E(y_1, \ldots, y_\omega, m)$, $E(v_j, z)(1 \leq j \leq \omega)$ and $v_j(1 \leq j \leq \omega)$. We can write $E(y_1, \ldots, y_\omega, z)$ in the form

$$E(y_1, \ldots, y_\omega, z) := \sum_{k=0}^{1} (a_{0k}, \ldots, a_{\omega k}) \begin{pmatrix} 1 \\ y_1 \\ \vdots \\ y_\omega \end{pmatrix} z^k,$$

where $(a_{0k}, \ldots, a_{\omega k})$ are chosen uniformly at random in $\mathbf{F}_q$. Then, $E(v_j, z)$ and $E(y_1, \ldots, y_\omega, m)$ are written as

$$E(v_j, z) = \sum_{k=0}^{1} (a_{0k}, \ldots, a_{\omega k}) \begin{pmatrix} 1 \\ v_{1,j} \\ \vdots \\ v_{\omega,j} \end{pmatrix} z^k \ (1 \leq j \leq \omega)$$

and

$$E(y_1, \ldots, y_\omega, m) = \sum_{k=0}^{1} (a_{0k}, \ldots, a_{\omega k}) \begin{pmatrix} 1 \\ y_1 \\ \vdots \\ y_\omega \end{pmatrix} m^k.$$

Therefore, the information W has are as follows.

$$C_k := (a_{0k}, \ldots, a_{\omega k}) \begin{pmatrix} 1 & 1 & \cdots & 1 \\ v_{1,1} & v_{1,2} & \cdots & v_{1,\omega} \\ & & \vdots & \\ v_{\omega,1} & v_{\omega,2} & \cdots & v_{\omega,\omega} \end{pmatrix} \ (k = 0, 1) \tag{2}$$

$$D = \sum_{k=0}^{1} (a_{0k}, \ldots, a_{\omega k}) m^k \tag{3}$$

Set $r_j := \begin{pmatrix} 1 \\ v_{1,j} \\ \vdots \\ v_{\omega,j} \end{pmatrix}$ and $t := rank(r_1, \ldots, r_\omega)$ $(1 \leq t \leq \omega)$. Let R be the vector space over $\mathbf{F}_q$ generated by $r_1, \ldots, r_\omega$, i.e. $R = \langle r_1, \ldots, r_\omega \rangle$. Now, we show the following claim.

Claim 1. Let (m', σ') be an arbitrary message-signature pair, where $\sigma' = \beta'(y)$ If $r_n \notin R$, we have

$$\frac{|\{E(v_v, z)|E(v_v, z) \; satisfies \; (2)(3) \; and \; E(v_v, m') = \beta'(v_v)\}|}{|\{E(v_v, z)|E(v_v, z) \; satisfies \; (2)(3)\}|} = \frac{1}{q}$$

Proof. First, we consider the following special case of (2).

$$O = C_k = (a_{0k}, ..., a_{\omega k}) \begin{pmatrix} 1 & 1 & \cdots & 1 \\ v_{1,1} & v_{1,2} & \cdots & v_{1,\omega} \\ & & \vdots & \\ v_{\omega,1} & v_{\omega,2} & \cdots & v_{\omega,\omega} \end{pmatrix} \quad (k = 0, 1) \qquad (4)$$

Then, the followng equations holds.

$$(a_{0k}, ..., a_{\omega k})r_1 = 0$$

$$\vdots$$

$$(a_{0k}, ..., a_{\omega k})r_\omega = 0$$

Next, we choose non-zero vectors $r'_1, ..., r'_{\omega-t+1} \in F_q^{\omega+1}$ such that $\{r'_1, ..., r'_{\omega-t+1}\}$ is a basis of $R^\perp$, where $R^\perp$ is the orthogonal complement of R. Then, we can write $(a_{0k}, ..., a_{\omega k}) = \sum_{i=1}^{\omega-t+1} \mu_{i,k}{}^t r'_i$. Let Γ_0 be the set of $A^{(0)} = ((a_{00}, ..., a_{\omega 0})^{(0)}$, $(a_{01}, ..., a_{\omega 1})^{(0)})$ satisfying (4). Then, Γ_0 is a vector space over $\mathbf{F}_q$ and the dimension is equal to $2(\omega - t + 1)$. Let $A^{(1)} = ((a_{00}, ..., a_{\omega 0})^{(1)}, (a_{01}, ..., a_{\omega 1})^{(1)})$ be some solutions of (2). Then, $\Gamma := \{A^{(1)} + A^{(0)}|A^{(0)} \in \Gamma_0\}$ is the set of solutions of (2).
From (3), we have

$$D = \sum_{k=0}^{1} (a_{0k}, ..., a_{\omega k})m^k$$

$$= \sum_{k=0}^{1} ((a_{0k}, ..., a_{\omega k})^{(0)} + (a_{0k}, ..., a_{\omega k})^{(1)})m^k$$

$$= \sum_{k=0}^{1} \sum_{i=1}^{\omega-t+1} m^k \mu_{i,k}{}^t r'_i + \sum_{k=0}^{1} (a_{0k}, ..., a_{\omega k})^{(1)} m^k$$

Therefore, we have at most $\omega - t + 1$ linearly independent equations. Thus, the set of A satisfying (2) and (3) makes a subset $\tilde{\Gamma}$ of Γ having at least q elements. Next, we define a mapping Φ_{v_n} as follows. For any $v_n \in F_q$, we define

$$\Phi_{v_n} : \tilde{\Gamma} \to \{E(v_n, z)|E(v_n, z) \; satisfies \; (2), (3)\}$$

$$\Phi_{v_n}((a_{00}, ..., a_{\omega 0}), (a_{01}, ..., a_{\omega 1})) = ((a_{00}, ..., a_{\omega 0}) \begin{pmatrix} 1 \\ {}^t v_n \end{pmatrix}, (a_{01}, ..., a_{\omega 1}) \begin{pmatrix} 1 \\ {}^t v_n \end{pmatrix})$$

where we identify $\Phi_{v_n}(a_{00}, ..., a_{\omega 0})$ with its associated function $E(v_n, z)$. Also, we define a mapping $\Phi_{v_n, m}$ as follows. For any $v_n \in F_q$ and any $m \in F_q$, we define

$$\Phi_{v_n, m} : \tilde{\Gamma} \to F_q$$

$$\Phi_{v_n, m}((a_{00}, ..., a_{\omega 0}), (a_{01}, ..., a_{\omega 1})) = \sum_{k=0}^{1} (a_{0k}, ..., a_{\omega k}) m^k \binom{1}{{}^t v_n}$$

Then, we can show that for any v_n such that $r_n \notin R$, Φ_{v_n} is bijective as follows. By the definition of $\tilde{\Gamma}$, it is seen that Φ_{v_n} is surjective. Let $A, A' \in \tilde{\Gamma}$ and suppose that $\Phi_{v_n}(A) = \Phi_{v_n}(A')$, namely, $A_k r_n = A'_k r_n (k = 0, 1)$, where $A = (A_0, A_1)$ and $A' = (A'_0, A'_1)$D Then, by the equation (1) we have $A_k(r_1, ..., r_\omega, r_n) = A'_k(r_1, ..., r_\omega, r_n)(k = 0, 1)$. Since the matrix $(r_1, ..., r_\omega, r_n)$ is invertible, we have $A = A'$, which means that Φ_{v_n} is injective. Therefore, $A = A'$ is bijective. Also, we know that for any v_n such that $r_n \notin R$ and any m' such that $m' \neq m$, $\Phi_{v_n, m'}$ is surjective. It is shown as follows. For any element $A = A^{(0)} + A^{(1)} \in \tilde{\Gamma}$, we have

$$\Phi_{v_n, m'}(A) = \left(\sum_{k=0}^{1} A_k m^k \right) r_n$$

$$= \left(\sum_{k=0}^{1} A_k^{(0)} m^k \right) r_n + \left(\sum_{k=0}^{1} A_k^{(1)} m^k \right) r_n$$

$$= \left(\sum_{k=0}^{1} \sum_{i=1}^{\omega - t + 1} \mu_{i,k} {}^t r'_i m^k \right) r_n + \left(\sum_{k=0}^{1} A_k^{(1)} m^k \right) r_n$$

For simplicity, we assume $t = \omega$. Then, ${}^t r'_1 \cdot r_n \neq 0$ since $r_n \notin R$. Thus $\Phi_{v_n, m'}(A)$ can be written in the form

$$\Phi_{v_n, m'}(A) = k_1 \mu_{1,1} + k_0$$

where $k_1, k_0 \in F_q$ are some constants with $k_1 \neq 0$ and $\mu_{1,1}$ is chosen from $\mathbf{F}_q$ uniformly at random if A is chosen uniformly at random. Therefore, the map $\Phi_{v_n, m'}$ is surjective. Thus, we also know that uniform distribution on $\tilde{\Gamma}$ induces uniform distribution on $\mathbf{F}_q$ through $\Phi_{v_n, m'}$. Also, for the case of $t < \omega$ we can show that $\Phi_{v_n, m'}$ is surjective and uniform distribution on $\tilde{\Gamma}$ induces uniform distribution on $\mathbf{F}_q$ through $\Phi_{v_n, m'}$ by similar ways.

From the above arguments, for arbitrary message-signature pair (m', σ'), where $\sigma' = \beta'(y)$, we have

$$\frac{|\{E(v_v, z) | E(v_v, z) \ satisfies \ (2)(3) \ and \ E(v_v, m') = \beta'(v_v)\}|}{|\{E(v_v, z) | E(v_v, z) \ satisfies \ (2)(3)\}|}$$

$$= \frac{|\{\tilde{A} \in \tilde{\Gamma} | \Phi_{v_n, m'}(\tilde{A}) = \beta'(v_v)\}|}{|\tilde{\Gamma}|} = \frac{1}{q}$$

Therefore, the proof of Claim 1 is completed.

Now, we return to the proof of (1). For arbitrary message-signature pair (m', σ'), with $\sigma' = \beta(y)$, we have

$$Pr(U_n \; accepts \; (m', \sigma')|e_W, (m, \sigma), (m^*, \sigma^*))$$

$$= \frac{|\{(v_n, E(v_n, z)|E(v_n, z) \; satisfies \; (2)(3) \; and \; E(v_n, m') = \beta'(v_n)\}|}{|\{(v_n, E(v_n, z))|E(v_n, z) \; satisfies \; (2)(3)\}|}$$

$$= \frac{\sum_{v_n} |\{E(v_n, z)|E(v_n, z) \; satisfies \; (2)(3) \; and \; E(v_n, m') = \beta'(v_n)\}|}{\sum_{v_n} |\{E(v_n, z)|E(v_n, z) \; satisfies \; (2)(3)\}|}$$

$$\leq \frac{\sum_{v_n \; s.t. \; r_n \in R} |\{E(v_n, z)|E(v_n, z) \; satisfies \; (2)(3)\}|}{\sum_{v_n} |\{E(v_n, z)|E(v_n, z) \; satisfies \; (2)(3)\}|}$$

$$+ \frac{1}{q} \cdot \frac{\sum_{v_n \; s.t. \; r_n \notin R} |\{E(v_n, z)|E(v_n, z) \; satisfies \; (2)(3)\}|}{\sum_{v_n} |\{E(v_n, z)|E(v_n, z) \; satisfies \; (2)(3)\}|}$$

$$= \frac{1}{q} + (1 - \frac{1}{q}) \cdot \frac{\sum_{v_n \; s.t. \; r_n \in R} |\{E(v_n, z)|E(v_n, z) \; satisfies \; (2)(3)\}|}{\sum_{v_n} |\{E(v_n, z)|E(v_n, z) \; satisfies \; (2)(3)\}|}$$

If $r_n \in R$, we have

$$\{E(v_n, z)|E(v_n, z) \; satisfies \; (2)(3)\} = 1 \tag{5}$$

In fact, this is shown as follows. If $r_n \in R$, r_n is expressed as a linear combination of $r_1, ..., r_\omega$ over $\mathbf{F}_q$. Thus, for all matrices $(a_{0k}, ..., a_{\omega k})(k = 0, 1)$ which satisfy (2) and (3), it follows that $(a_{0k}, ..., a_{\omega k})r_n(k = 0, 1)$ are constant vectors from equation (2). Therefore, the associated $E(v_n, z)$ is uniquely determined, which implies equality (5).

Therefore, by the equality (5) we have

$$\sum_{v_n \; s.t. \; r_n \in R} |\{E(v_n, z)|E(v_n, z) \; satisfies \; (2)(3)\} = q^{t-1} \leq q^{\omega-1}, \tag{6}$$

$$\sum_{v_n} |\{E(v_n, z)|E(v_n, z) \; satisfies \; (2)(3)\} \geq q^\omega. \tag{7}$$

Thus, from (5)(6)(7) it follows that, for any (m, σ),

$$P_{F_1'} \leq \frac{1}{q} + (1 - \frac{1}{q}) \cdot \frac{1}{q} = \frac{2}{q} - \frac{1}{q^2}$$

Therefore, the proof of (1) is completed. Next, we show the following claim.

Claim 2. Suppose that for (m, σ), (m', σ') and (m^*, σ^*), where $\sigma = (d^{(i)}, r)$, $\sigma' = (d^{(i)}, r')$ such that $(m, r) \neq (m', r')$ and (m^*, σ^*) is a pair of blinded message and its signature corresponding to (m, σ),

$$Pr(U_n \; accepts \; (m', \sigma')|e_W, (m, \sigma), (m^*, \sigma^*)\}) \leq \epsilon$$

for non-negative ϵ. then, we have

$$Pr(U_n \; accepts \; (m',\sigma')|e_W,(m,\sigma),(m^*,\sigma^*),\beta_i(v_n) \neq E(v_n,m_i)(1 \leq i \leq t-1)\})$$
$$\leq \frac{\epsilon}{1-(t-1)\epsilon}$$

Proof. We first show the following. Suppose that, for $m_1,...,m_s \in M$ and $m'_1,...,m'_t \in M$,

$$\frac{|\{(v_n,E(v_n,z)|\beta_i(v_n) = E(v_n,m_i)(1 \leq \forall i \leq s), \beta'_j(v_n) \neq E(v_n,m'_j)(1 \leq \forall j \leq t)\}|}{|\{(v_n,E(v_n,z)|\beta_i(v_n) = E(v_n,m_i)(1 \leq \forall i \leq s-1), \beta'_j(v_n) \neq E(v_n,m'_j)(1 \leq \forall j \leq t)\}|}$$
$$\leq \epsilon_{s,t} \tag{8}$$

for some non-negative real number $\epsilon_{s,t}$. Then, for arbitrary $m_{s+1} \in M$, we have

$$\frac{|\{(v_n,E(v_n,z)|\beta_i(v_n) = E(v_n,m_i)(1 \leq \forall i \leq s), \beta'_j(v_n) \neq E(v_n,m'_j)(1 \leq \forall j \leq t+1)\}|}{|\{(v_n,E(v_n,z)|\beta_i(v_n) = E(v_n,m_i)(1 \leq \forall i \leq s-1), \beta'_j(v_n) \neq E(v_n,m'_j)(1 \leq \forall j \leq t+1)\}|}$$
$$\leq \frac{\epsilon_{s,t}}{1-\epsilon_{s,t}} \tag{9}$$

This is shown as follows. From the equation

$$|\{(v_n,E(v_n,z)|\beta_i(v_n) = E(v_n,m_i)(1 \leq \forall i \leq s-1), \beta'_j(v_n) \neq E(v_n,m'_j)(1 \leq \forall j \leq t)\}|$$
$$=|\{(v_n,E(v_n,z)|\beta_i(v_n) = E(v_n,m_i)(1 \leq \forall i \leq s-1), \beta'_j(v_n) \neq E(v_n,m'_j)(1 \leq \forall j \leq t+1)\}|$$
$$+ |\{(v_n,E(v_n,z)|\beta_i(v_n) = E(v_n,m_i)(1 \leq \forall i \leq s-1), \beta'_j(v_n) \neq E(v_n,m'_j)(1 \leq \forall j \leq t),$$
$$\beta'_{t+1}(v_n) = E(v_n,m'_{t+1})\}|,$$

we have

$$1 = \frac{|\{(v_n,E(v_n,z)|\beta_i(v_n) = E(v_n,m_i)(1 \leq \forall i \leq s-1), \beta'_j(v_n) \neq E(v_n,m'_j)(1 \leq \forall j \leq t+1)\}|}{|\{(v_n,E(v_n,z)|\beta_i(v_n) = E(v_n,m_i)(1 \leq \forall i \leq s-1), \beta'_j(v_n) \neq E(v_n,m'_j)(1 \leq \forall j \leq t)\}|}$$
$$+ \frac{|\{(v_n,E(v_n,z)|\beta_i(v_n) = E(v_n,m_i)(1 \leq \forall i \leq s-1), \beta'_j(v_n) \neq E(v_n,m'_j)(1 \leq \forall j \leq t), \beta'_{t+1}(v_n) = E(v_n,m'_{t+1})\}|}{|\{(v_n,E(v_n,z)|\beta_i(v_n) = E(v_n,m_i)(1 \leq \forall i \leq s-1), \beta'_j(v_n) \neq E(v_n,m'_j)(1 \leq \forall j \leq t)\}|}$$

Thus, by the assumption we have

$$\frac{|\{(v_n,E(v_n,z)|\beta_i(v_n) = E(v_n,m_i)(1 \leq \forall i \leq s-1), \beta'_j(v_n) \neq E(v_n,m'_j)(1 \leq \forall j \leq t+1)\}|}{|\{(v_n,E(v_n,z)|\beta_i(v_n) = E(v_n,m_i)(1 \leq \forall i \leq s-1), \beta'_j(v_n) \neq E(v_n,m'_j)(1 \leq \forall j \leq t)\}|}$$
$$\geq 1-\epsilon_{s,t}$$

Therefore, it follows that

$$\frac{|\{(v_n,E(v_n,z)|\beta_i(v_n) = E(v_n,m_i)(1 \leq \forall i \leq s), \beta'_j(v_n) \neq E(v_n,m'_j)(1 \leq \forall j \leq t+1)\}|}{|\{(v_n,E(v_n,z)|\beta_i(v_n) = E(v_n,m_i)(1 \leq \forall i \leq s-1), \beta'_j(v_n) \neq E(v_n,m'_j)(1 \leq \forall j \leq t+1)\}|}$$
$$\leq \frac{|\{(v_n,E(v_n,z)|\beta_i(v_n) = E(v_n,m_i)(1 \leq \forall i \leq s), \beta'_j(v_n) \neq E(v_n,m'_j)(1 \leq \forall j \leq t)\}|}{|\{(v_n,E(v_n,z)|\beta_i(v_n) = E(v_n,m_i)(1 \leq \forall i \leq s-1), \beta'_j(v_n) \neq E(v_n,m'_j)(1 \leq \forall j \leq t)\}|(1-\epsilon_{s,t})}$$
$$\leq \frac{\epsilon_{s,t}}{1-\epsilon_{s,t}}$$

Note that (8) and (9) holds for $t = 0$. Thus, by applying (8) and (9) for $t = 0, ..., t - 2$, we obtain the claim.

Now, we return to the proof of lemma 1. From (1), we have

$$P_{F'_1} \leq \frac{2}{q} - \frac{1}{q^2} \leq \frac{2}{q}$$

and from Claim 2, we obtain

$$P_{F_1} \leq \frac{\frac{2}{q}}{1 - (t_v - 1)\frac{2}{q}} = \frac{2}{q - 2t_v + 2}$$

We can also show $P_{F_2} \leq \frac{2}{q - 2t_v + 2}$ in a way similar to the proof of P_{F_1} by the construction. Therefore, we have $P_F = \max\{P_{F_1}, P_{F_2}\} \leq \frac{2}{q - 2t_v + 2}$, and the proof of Lemma 1 is completed.

Lemma 2. P_D is at most $\frac{1}{q - t_v + 1}$.

Proof. Let $W = \{S, U_1, ..., U_{\omega-1}\}$ be a set of colluders. We consider that W tries to produce an invalid message-signature pair which is accepted as valid by $U_n \notin W$, and W can obtain most information which are their secret keys and verification results on message-signature pairs from $U_n \notin W$. We first consider the case where the colluders are not allowed to obtain verification results on any message-signature pair from any participants. Let (m, σ) with $\sigma = (d^{(i,t)}, r)$ be a valid message-signature pair and (m, σ') with $\sigma = (d^{(i,t)}, r')$ be an invalid message-signature pair such that $r \neq r'$. We show the following claim.

Claim 3. For (m, σ) with $\sigma = (d^{(i,t)}, r)$ and (m, σ') with $\sigma' = (d^{(i,t)}, r')$ such that $r \neq r'$,

$$P_{D'} := Pr(U_n \text{ accepts } (m, \sigma') | e_W, (m, \sigma)) \leq \frac{1}{q}$$

Proof. We write r and r' in the form

$$r = b_0 + \sum_{i=1}^{\omega} b_i y_i, \quad r' = b'_0 + \sum_{i=1}^{\omega} b'_i y_i$$

$$(b_0, b_1, ..., b_\omega) \neq (b'_0, b'_1, ..., b'_\omega) \quad (b_i, b'_i \in F_q)$$

Set $r_n := \begin{pmatrix} 1 \\ v_{1,n} \\ \vdots \\ v_{\omega,n} \end{pmatrix}$, then it is seen that (m, σ') with $\sigma' = (d^{(i)}, r')$ is accepted by

U_n as valid if and only if

$$(b_0, b_1, ..., b_\omega) \cdot r_n = (b'_0, b'_1, ..., b'_\omega) \cdot r_n \tag{9}$$

Set $\gamma = (b_0 - b'_0, b_1 - b'_1, ..., b_\omega - b'_\omega)$, then (10) is equivalent to

$$\gamma \cdot r_n = 0 \quad (\gamma \in F_q^{\omega+1}, \gamma \neq 0) \tag{10}$$

Thus, the best strategy that the colluders take is to find $\gamma \in F_q^{\omega+1}$ which satisfies (11). Since v_n is chosen uniformly at random from $\mathbf{F}_q^{\omega}$, we have

$$P_{D'} = \max_{\gamma} Pr(v_n \in \langle\gamma\rangle^{\perp})$$

$$= \max_{\gamma} \frac{|\{v_n \in F_q^{\omega} | \gamma \cdot r_n = 0\}|}{|F_q^{\omega}|}$$

$$= \frac{q^{\omega-1}}{q^{\omega}} = \frac{1}{q}$$

Thus, the proof of Claim is completed. We return to the proof of lemma 2. We can show the following in a way similar to the proof for Lemma 1.

$$P_D \leq \frac{\frac{1}{q}}{1 - (t_v - 1)\frac{1}{q}} \leq \frac{1}{q - t_v + 1}$$

Lemma 3. $P_B = 0$.

Proof. We consider the case where the colluders include the signer. Let $W := \{S, U_1, ..., U_{\omega-1}\}$ be a set of colluders, and W observes (m, σ) where $\sigma = (d^{(k,t)}, r)$, and try to guess the user $U_k \notin W$ who requested it. Here, the message-signature pair (m, σ) with $\sigma = (d^{(k,t)}, r)$ is in the form, $r = \beta(y) = G_0^{(k,t)}(y_1, \ldots, y_\omega) + G_3^{(k,t)}(y_1, \ldots, y_\omega) + m(G_1^{(k,t)}(y_1, \ldots, y_\omega) + G_2^{(k,t)}(y_1, \ldots, y_\omega))$, and the pair of blinded-message and its signature (m^*, σ^*) with $m^* = (u_k^{(t)}, c)$ corresponding to (m, σ) is in the form, $\sigma^* = \beta^*(y) = G_0^{(k,t)}(y_1, \ldots, y_\omega) + cG_1^{(k,t)}(y_1, \ldots, y_\omega)$. If the colluders can link (m, σ) with (m^*, σ^*), then they succeed in guessing the user $U_k \notin W$ who requested it. But, the colluders cannot link (m, σ) with (m^*, σ^*) by the relation between $u_k^{(t)}$ and $d^{(k,t)}$, since they don't have U_k's secret information Ψ_k such that $\Psi_k(u_k^{(t)}) = d^{(k,t)}$. They also cannot link (m, σ) with (m^*, σ^*) by the relation between m and c, since they don't have $C_k^{(t)}(z)$ such that $c = C_k^{(t)}(m) = m + \alpha_k^{(t)}$. Also W don't have the polynomials $G_2^{(k,t)}(y_1, \ldots, y_\omega)$ and $G_3^{(k,t)}(y_1, \ldots, y_\omega)$, hence they cannot link (m, σ) with (m^*, σ^*) from the relation between $\beta(y)$ and $\beta^*(y)$. Therefore, we have $Pr(U_j | e_W, \{(m_i^*, \sigma_i^*)(1 \leq i \leq n)\}, (m, \sigma)) = Pr(U_j)$ for $U_j \notin W$. We can also show $P_B = 0$ in the case where the signer is not included the colluders in a similar way.

Proof of Theorem 1. From Lemmas 1,2 and 3, for $0 \leq \omega \leq n$ and $1 \leq t_s \leq nt_u$, we have

$$\epsilon = \max\{P_F, P_D, P_B\} = \frac{2}{q - 2t_v + 2}$$

Therefore, the proof of Theorem 1 is completed.

Random Systems: Theory and Applications

Ueli Maurer

Department of Computer Science, ETH Zurich
maurer@inf.ethz.ch

Abstract. This short note accompanies the author's keynote lecture delivered at ICITS' 07. The concept of a random system is explained and a few results in the theory of random systems are mentioned.

1 Random Systems

Many cryptographic systems (e.g. a block cipher, the CBC-MAC construction, or more complex games) can be modeled as discrete systems. A discrete system interacts with its environment by taking a (generally unbounded) sequence of inputs $X_1, X_2, \ldots$ (from some alphabet $\mathcal{X}$) and generating, for each new input X_i, an output Y_i (from some alphabet $\mathcal{Y}$). The abstraction of the input-output behavior of such a discrete system, say $\mathbf{F}$, is captured by the following definition of [Mau02]. We also refer to [MPR07] for an introduction to random systems.

Definition 1. An $(\mathcal{X}, \mathcal{Y})$-*random system* $\mathbf{F}$ is a (generally infinite) sequence of conditional probability distributions $\mathsf{p}^{\mathbf{F}}_{Y_i|X^i Y^{i-1}}$ for $i \geq 1$.[1]

This description of a system is exact and minimal in the sense that two systems, say $\mathbf{F}$ and $\mathbf{G}$, with different input-output behavior correspond to two different random systems, and two different random systems have different input-output behavior. Two systems $\mathbf{F}$ and $\mathbf{G}$ are *equivalent*, denoted $\mathbf{F} \equiv \mathbf{G}$, if they correspond to the same random system.

2 Indistinguishability and Game-Winning

Two major paradigms for cryptographic security definitions are:

- **Indistinguishability:** An ideal-world system is indistinguishable from a real-world system. For example, a secure encryption scheme can be seen as realizing a secure channel (ideal world) from an authenticated channel (real world).
- **Game-winning:** Breaking a system means that the adversary must achieve a certain goal, i.e., win a certain game. For example, a MAC is secure if the adversary cannot generate a fresh message together with the correct MAC, even if he can query the system arbitrarily.

---

[1] For arguments x^{i-1} and y^{i-1} such that $\mathsf{p}^{\mathbf{F}}_{Y^{i-1}|X^{i-1}}(y^{i-1}, x^{i-1}) = 0$, $\mathsf{p}^{\mathbf{F}}_{Y_i|X^i Y^{i-1}}$ need not be defined.

Y. Desmedt (Ed.): ICITS 2007, LNCS 4883, pp. 44–45, 2009.

A game can be modeled as a random system with a special monotone binary output (MBO) which indicates whether or not the game has been won. Indeed, an important paradigm in indistinguishability proofs, made formal in [Mau02], is the definition of such an internal monotone condition in a system such that for any distinguisher $\mathbf{D}$ the distinguishing advantage can be shown to be upper bounded by the probability that $\mathbf{D}$ provokes this condition.

In [MPR07], the converse was proved, which we state informally: For two systems $\mathbf{F}$ and $\mathbf{G}$ one can always define new systems $\hat{\mathbf{F}}$ and $\hat{\mathbf{G}}$, which are equivalent to $\mathbf{F}$ and $\mathbf{G}$, respectively, but have an additional MBO, such that

(i) for any distinguisher $\mathbf{D}$ the distinguishing advantage for $\mathbf{F}$ and $\mathbf{G}$ is equal to the probability that $\mathbf{D}$ sets the MBO to 1 in $\hat{\mathbf{F}}$ (or $\hat{\mathbf{G}}$), and

(ii) the systems $\hat{\mathbf{F}}$ and $\hat{\mathbf{G}}$ are equivalent as long as the respective MBOs are 0.

3   An Application: Indistinguishability Amplification

Since analyzing game-winning for a combined game consisting of sub-games appears to be considerably simpler than analyzing the indistinguishability of combined systems, the above mentioned correspondence is very useful for proving amplification results of the following types (see [MPR07]).

Let $\mathbf{F}$ and $\mathbf{G}$ be systems for which the best distinguisher's advantage in distinguishing it from a uniform random function $\mathbf{R}$ within k queries is bounded by ϵ and ϵ', respectively. Then $\mathbf{F} \star \mathbf{G}$, the system consisting of $\mathbf{F}$ and $\mathbf{G}$ in parallel with their outputs combined by the group operation $\star$, can be distinguished with advantage at most $2\epsilon\epsilon'$ from $\mathbf{R}$ (for k queries). This bound is optimal. Another amplification result states that the optimal (adaptive) distinguishing advantage for $\mathbf{F} \star \mathbf{G}$ and $\mathbf{R}$ is bounded by the sum of the *non-adaptive* distinguishing advantages for $\mathbf{F}$ and $\mathbf{G}$.

The combination operation $\mathbf{F} \star \mathbf{G}$ can be generalized as follows, and the above results, appropriately generalized, hold for the general setting. Let $\mathbf{F}$ and $\mathbf{I}$ (and similarly $\mathbf{G}$ and $\mathbf{J}$) be systems for which the distinguishing advantage (of some type) is known to be bounded. A construction $\mathbf{C}(\cdot, \cdot)$ invoking two subsystems is called *neutralizing* for the pairs $(\mathbf{F}, \mathbf{I})$ and $(\mathbf{G}, \mathbf{J})$ of systems if

$$\mathbf{C}(\mathbf{F}, \mathbf{J}) \equiv \mathbf{C}(\mathbf{I}, \mathbf{G}) \equiv \mathbf{C}(\mathbf{I}, \mathbf{J}) \equiv \mathbf{Q}$$

(for some $\mathbf{Q}$). To obtain the above results one sets $\mathbf{C}(\mathbf{F}, \mathbf{G}) := \mathbf{F} \star \mathbf{G}$, $\mathbf{I} := \mathbf{R}$, $\mathbf{J} := \mathbf{R}$, and $\mathbf{Q} := \mathbf{R}$.

References

[Mau02]   Maurer, U.: Indistinguishability of random systems. In: Knudsen, L.R. (ed.) EUROCRYPT 2002. LNCS, vol. 2332, pp. 110–132. Springer, Heidelberg (2002)

[MPR07]   Maurer, U., Pietrzak, K., Renner, R.: Indistinguishability amplification. In: Menezes, A. (ed.) CRYPTO 2007. LNCS, vol. 4622, pp. 130–149. Springer, Heidelberg (2007)

Optimising SD and LSD in Presence of Non-uniform Probabilities of Revocation

Paolo D'Arco and Alfredo De Santis

Dipartimento di Informatica ed Applicazioni
Università degli Studi di Salerno, 84084, Fisciano (SA), Italy
{paodar,ads}@dia.unisa.it

Abstract. Some years ago two efficient broadcast encryption schemes for stateless receivers, referred to as SD (Subset Difference Method) [NNL01] and LSD (Layered Subset Difference Method) [HS02], were proposed. They represent one of the most suitable solution to broadcast encryption. In this paper we focus on the following issue: both schemes assume *uniform* probabilities of revocation of the receivers. However, in some applications, such an assumption might not hold: receivers in a certain area, due to historical and legal reasons, can be considered trustworthy, while receivers from others might exhibit more adversarial behaviours. Can we modify SD and LSD to better fit settings in which the probabilities of revocation are *non-uniform*?

More precisely, we study how to *optimise user key storage* in the SD and LSD schemes in presence of non-uniform probabilities of revocation for the receivers. Indeed, we would like to give less keys to users with higher probability of revocation compared to trustworthy users. We point out that this leads to the construction of binary trees satisfying some optimality criteria.

We start our analysis revisiting a similar study, which aims at minimising user key storage in LKH schemes. It was shown that such a problem is related to the well-known optimal codeword length selection problem in information theory. We discuss the approach therein pursued, pointing out that a characterisation of the properties a key assignment for LKH schemes has to satisfy, does not hold. We provide a new characterisation and give a proof of it. Then, we show that also user key storage problems of SD and LSD are related to an interesting coding theory problem, referred to as *source coding with Campbell's penalties*. Hence, we discuss existing solutions to the coding problem.

1   Introduction

Broadcast Encryption with Stateless Receivers. Broadcast Encryption schemes enable a center to deliver encrypted data to a large set of users, in such a way that only a privileged subset of them can decrypt the data. Applications for these schemes range from pay-tv to systems for delivering sensitive information stored on media like a CD/DVD.

Broadcast encryption works as follows: during a set-up phase, every user receives a set of predefined keys. Then, at the beginning of each data transmission,

Y. Desmedt (Ed.): ICITS 2007, LNCS 4883, pp. 46–64, 2009.

the center sends a broadcast message enabling privileged users to compute a session key, by means of which, the encrypted data, that will be delivered later on, can be decrypted. In broadcast encryption with *stateless receivers*, two main issues are considered: *a)* from time to time, the subset of privileged users *changes* by means of join and revoke operations, but *b)* the sets of predefined keys held by the users *stay the same* for the lifetime of the scheme. Moreover, the scheme has to be collusion resistant, in the sense that even if all the revoked users collude, they cannot compute a session key they are not entitled to.

Previous Work. Berkovits, in [Ber91], addressed the issue of how to broadcast a secret to privileged users. Later on, Fiat and Naor, in [FN94], formalized the broadcast encryption paradigm. Since then, several variants have been considered. *Multicast* [CGI+99] is one of the most interesting and studied ones. It achieves a similar goal but in presence of a dynamically changing set of privileged users which is a proper subset (and often much smaller than) of the universe. Moreover, the emphasis is on many-to-many communication (i.e. group communication) instead of one-to-many, as in broadcast encryption. Due to lack of space, we refer the readers to the full version of [NNL01] and to references therein quoted.

Related work. Many tree-based broadcast/multicast schemes, where users update their predefined keys after join/revoke operations, have been described in the last years. Such "statefull" tree-based schemes are also referred to as Logical Key Hierarchy schemes (LKH, for short) in the literature [WHA99, WGL98]. In LKH schemes the users are associated to the leaves of the tree. To every node of the tree is assigned a key. Each user receives the keys assigned to nodes *along the path from the root to his leaf node*. The session key is (or derived from) the key assigned to the root node. When a user is revoked, all keys along the path from the root to the leaf have to be changed. Hence, all users have to *update* the predefined keys they hold which belong to this set of keys [WHA99, WGL98].

User Key Storage. A few papers [CMN99, SM03, CEK+99, PB01] have studied the problem of how to minimise user key storage in LKH schemes. Lower bounds have been given in [CMN99, SSV01, PB01, MP04]. In particular, the authors of [PB01] studied LKH schemes from an information theoretic point of view. They provided a *characterization* the key assignment to the tree has to satisfy in order to guarantee the security of the scheme. Then, they showed that the problem of constructing LKH schemes minimizing user key storage can be posed as an *optimisation problem* that is abstractly identical to the optimal codeword length selection problem in coding theory. Hence, they showed that the *entropy* of the probability distribution of user revocation quantifies the *average number of keys* to be assigned to a user.

Beyond SD and LSD. A different design approach to broadcast encryption can be found in [JHC+05], where constructions achieving a fine-grained trade-off between user key storage and transmission overhead have been proposed. In [HLL05] a compiler for transforming trasmissions-efficient schemes with high computational overhead and user key storage requirements into schemes with a slightly increasing trasmission overhead but reduced computational and/or key storage overhead has been proposed. Finally, the authors of [GST04, HL06] have instead considered a scenario in which the storage of the devices is bounded i.e., it can contain at most a logarithmic number of keys w.r.t. the total number of users.

Non Uniform Probabilities. It might be of practical interest to optimise SD and LSD for settings in which the probabilities of revocation for the receivers are not all the same. A broadcaster could *estimate* the adversarial behaviors of receivers in different areas and might try to sell different devices, i.e., storing a different number of predefined keys, to more or less trustworthy receivers. However, in this paper we do not attempt to develop methods for computing the probabilities. We assume that they are computable through statistical methods or known a priori.

Our Contribution. The results we show are the following:

- We revisit the analysis done in [PB01] (see IEEE Transactions on Information Theory, Nov. 2001, and Crypto'99), and we show that the characterization of the properties a key assignment for LKH schemes has to satisfy *does not* hold.
- Then, we derive a necessary and sufficient condition the key assignment for a LKH scheme has to satisfy, and we give a proof of it. Moreover, we show that the key assignment given in [CWSP98, CEK+99] is *optimal* w.r.t. center storage for schemes secure against a single revocation.
- Finally, we show that the problem of finding implementations of SD and LSD, minimising user key storage, can be posed as optimisation problems which correspond to optimal codeword length selection problems in coding theory. However, while the optimisation problem of LKH coincides with finding codeword lengths minimising the average codeword length in a prefix-free code, which is a well known and efficiently solvable problem, the optimisation problems we have found consist in finding codeword lengths for prefix-free codes minimising some *non-standard measures*, belonging to the framework of the so called *Campbell's penalties* [Cam66].

2   LKH Schemes: Key Assignment

We briefly review the approach developed in [PB01], in order to cast the problem of how to minimize user key storage in LKH schemes as a coding problem.

LKH Schemes [WHA99, WGL98]. A LKH scheme enables a group center (GC, for short) to establish a *session key* with a group of users. The session key has to be updated when its lifetime expires, or when new users join (or are revoked from) the group. To achieve this goal, every user holds some secret keys, which can be used to recover from a broadcast message, sent by GC when one of the above events occurs, the new session key. In a LKH scheme a logical tree, hereafter referred to as *key-tree*, is used in order to define *a strategy* for giving secret keys to users and for performing revoke and join operations.

Revoke and Join. Let T be a finite full binary tree, i.e., a tree in which every non-leaf node has two children. To each node is assigned a key. Each user is associated to a leaf, and he/she gets the keys assigned to the nodes along the path from the root to his own leaf. The session key is (or can be derived from, by means of a private computation) the root key.

- *Revoke*: once a user is revoked, the leaf associated to the user is removed, and all the keys along the path from the removed leaf to the root are deleted and substituted with other ones. Then, starting from the bottom of the tree, these keys are distributed to the other users. More precisely, the new key assigned to the parent of the removed leaf, is encrypted with the key assigned to the child node and sent along the broadcast channel. Then, going one level up, the new key assigned to the parent node, is encrypted with the keys of the children, and these encryptions are sent along the broadcast channel. The process is repeated until the root node is reached. For example, in Fig. 1 user U_1 gets K, K_0, K_{00}, and K_{000}. When he is revokes, keys K, K_0, and K_{00} are updated with K', K_0', and K_{00}'. Then, GC sends the following encryptions: $E_{K_{001}}(K_{00}'), E_{K_{00}'}(K_0'), E_{K_{01}}(K_0'), E_{K_0'}(K')$, and $E_{K_1}(K')$.

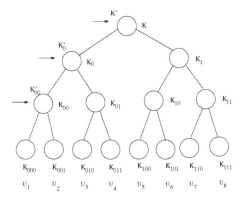

Fig. 1. Key Assignment and Revocation for U_1

- *Join*: when a new user joins the group, if the tree is not full, a leaf is added to an internal node with one leaf. Otherwise, a leaf becomes an internal node with two new leaves, corresponding to the previous user and to the new one. Then, two keys are associated to the new leaves and are securely sent to the two users, respectively. Finally, the keys associated to the nodes along the path from the root to the parent of the new leaf (leaves, resp.) are deleted and substituted with other ones and, starting from the bottom up to the root, encrypted with the keys associated to children and broadcasted.

Hence, if the tree is balanced[1] revoking (resp. joining) a user among (resp. to) a set of n, requires only $O(\log n)$ messages, by means of which non-revoked (resp. old) users can update their secret keys and compute the new session key.

Notice that a key-tree could be constructed *from scratch* through a sequence of join operations. However, usually, when a service starts, a set of initial users is available. Hence, a key-tree is constructed at the beginning with this initial set. Then, the structure is modified according to the join and revoke events taking place during the lifetime of the scheme.

From the above description, no specification about *the properties* the keys assigned to the nodes of the key-tree have to satisfy to get a secure scheme is given. In [PB01] the authors studied this problem, providing a characterization for key assignments. Let us briefly review their findings.

Key Assignment. In assigning keys to users the GC needs to ensure that every valid user can be securely reached when some users are revoked. The GC also needs to make sure that illegal collaboration among two or more revoked users does not enable them to cover all the keys assigned to another user. This "cover-free" property among the sets of keys can be defined as follows:

Definition 1. *[EFF85] Let $\mathcal{K} = \{k_1, \ldots, k_n\}$ be a ground set, and let ω, m be positive integers such that $\omega < m$. A family $\mathcal{A} = \{A_1, \ldots, A_m\}$ of subsets of $\mathcal{K}$ is a ω-cover-free family if, for all distinct $A, A_{i_1}, \ldots, A_{i_\omega} \in \mathcal{A}$, it holds that*

$$\mid A \setminus \cup_{j=1}^{\omega} A_{i_j} \mid \geq 1.$$

The definition guarantees that the union of ω subsets does not completely cover any other subset. Hence, if the sets of keys held by the users are ω-cover-free, the center can always reach safely w.r.t. any ω revoked users, non-revoked users. If the set of keys are $n - 1$-cover-free, then we will simply say that the assignment is cover free.

Users and Key indices. To characterize the properties a key assignment for a LKH scheme has to satisfy, the following definition was given:

Definition 2. *[PB01] Key index (KID, for short) of a member M_i is a string generated by the concatenation of the keys assigned to the member M_i, taken in any order. If the number of keys assigned to member M_i is denoted by ℓ_i, then there are $\ell_i!$ possible different KID strings that can be generated using these ℓ_i keys. Given a KID, all the KIDs that are generated by permuting and concatenating its keys are equivalent with respect to the cover-free property. If the set of keys generating KID_1 is denoted by S_1, and the set of keys generating KID_2 is denoted by S_2, we denote $KID_1 \equiv KID_2$ if $S_1 = S_2$.*

---

[1] Techniques for keeping balanced the tree have been proposed in several papers. We do not address this issue here since our focus in on key assignment and simply assume that the number of new users is approximatively equal to the number of revoked users, and that new users replace revoked users by keeping the tree structure almost balanced.

In [PB01] it was pointed out that, for any key assignment on the trees, cover freeness requires that the KID of a member *should not* be a *prefix* of the KID of any other member, where a prefix of a string is a substring which can be obtained as truncation of the string[2]. Hence, if a KID assignment is cover-free, it has to be prefix-free. However, by means of an example (see Section IV, paragraph C, of [PB01]), it was shown that the prefix-free property is necessary *but not sufficient* to guarantee cover freeness.

Hence, the problem was how to construct a prefix-free KID assignment on the tree that is also cover free.

The answer given in [PB01] was the following: *if we choose all the leaf node keys to be distinct, the prefix-free KID assignment will be necessary and sufficient a) to prevent user collusion from completely disabling the secure communication, and also b) to reach a valid member under deletion of arbitrary number of members.*

Unfortunately, the above characterization[3] does not hold (see Fig. 2).

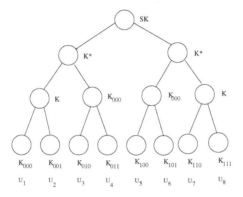

Fig. 2. The keys of U_1 are covered by the keys of U_5 and U_7

The KIDs assigned to the above key-tree define a set of prefix-free strings, and all leaf keys are distinct. However, KID_1 is completely covered by KID_5 and KID_7. Hence:

> The cover-free property of KIDs *is not* equivalent to requiring prefix-free KIDs obtained from a key assignment where all keys assigned to the leaves are distinct.

---

[2] However, notice that, due to the definition of KID and the equivalence w.r.t. permutations of keys, a KID is not a prefix of another KID *if and only* if the set of keys associated to the first KID *is not contained* in the set associated to the second one.

[3] Notice that "choose all the leaf node keys to be distinct" cannot be interpreted as "choose all the leaf node keys to be unique in the tree". In such a case, KIDs are necessarily prefix-free and the proposed characterization does not make sense.

We can say more about LKH schemes. Notice that, in studying the properties that need to be satisfied by a key assignment for a key-tree, cover-freeness is necessary to have a correct scheme, but it is *not enough* to characterize LKH schemes. In *any* key distribution scheme, resistant to attacks performed by coalitions of any size, the key assignment has to be cover-free. But in a LKH scheme user revocation has to be also *efficient*, i.e., it has to take place according to the rule defined by the tree which, as we have seen before, requires $O(\log n)$ messages in presence of n users associated to a balanced key-tree. For example, if the sets of keys are cover-free, then each user shares a safe key with GC. Using such safe keys for encrypting the new session key and sending it to the users is possible but requires the transmission of $n - 1$ messages. In other words, the applicability of the key revocation strategy defined by the tree, has to be *explicitely* considered in the analysis of the conditions that the key assignment has to satisfy.

Building on the above observations, we state the following definition.

Definition 3. *Let T_0 be an initial key-tree, let $< T_1, \ldots, T_\ell >$ be a sequence of key-trees generated from T_0 by GC due to join/revoke events, and let $< B_1, \ldots, B_\ell >$ be a sequence of broadcast messages sent by GC to the users to communicate the updates of the key-tree. A LKH scheme is secure w.r.t. revoked users if, for any $\ell \in N$, for any coalition of users R revoked in session ℓ, and for any admissible history $H_\ell^R = [T_0, T_1, \ldots, T_\ell, B_1, \ldots, B_\ell]$ of key-tree changes up to session ℓ, the coalition R does not get any information about the session key K_ℓ.*

Notice that, in the following analysis we assume *perfect encryption* and, when we talk about distinct keys, we mean *independent*. Indeed, our goal is to focus on the key-assignment and to point out the weaknesses of a key-assignment which associates the same keys to several nodes of the key-tree, in order to reduce GC and user key storage. Therefore, we do not consider attacks again the encryption scheme or attacks made possible by choices of related keys.

The revocation strategy which characterizes LKH schemes implies some constraints on the key assignment to the nodes of the key-tree, in order to construct secure schemes. To identify such constraints, we consider a key-tree with n leaves, and we analyse a scenario in which *users are only revoked*. Moreover, we consider *simultaneous revocations*, i.e., a few users are revoked at the same time. The key-tree update procedure is a trivial extension of the key-tree update procedure for a single revocation: all the keys along the paths from the removed leaves to the root are deleted and substituted with other ones. Then, starting from the bottom, these keys are distributed to non-revoked users. Such a revocation strategy is sometimes referred to as *Clumped re-keying method* [NNL01].

Definition 4. *A key-tree is t-secure if it enables revoking t users simultaneously, in such a way that they do not get any information about the new session key, i.e., the session key after the revocations.*

For each user u, let $KPATH^{(u)}$ be the multi-set of keys associated to the nodes along the path from the root to the leaf associated to user u, and let $HPATH^{(u)}$

be the multi-set of keys associated to nodes hanging off the path, i.e., the nodes at distance one from the nodes of the path. We can show the following:

Theorem 1. *A key-tree is 1-secure if and only if, for each user u, the following conditions hold:*

1. *The keys of the multi-set $KPATH^{(u)}$ are all distinct.*
2. *The keys of the multi-set $HPATH^{(u)}$ are all distinct.*
3. $KPATH^{(u)} \cap HPATH^{(u)} = \emptyset.$

Proof. (Sketch) Conditions 1., 2. and 3. are necessary. Indeed, let us denote by K_i the key assigned to node v_i and let us look at Fig. 3. Point 1. follows because, in Fig. 3.a), if $K_i = K_j$, the users associated to the leaves of the subtree rooted in v_q, the sibling of v_j, cannot be revoked. Similarly, Point 2. follows by noticing that, in Fig. 3.b), if $K_i = K_j$, there is no way to revoke any user associated to one of the leaves of the subtree rooted in v_j. Finally, Point 3. follows because, in Fig. 3.c), if $KPATH^{(u)} \cap HPATH^{(u)} \neq \emptyset$ and, say $K_j = K_i$, then user u cannot be revoked.

On the other hand, Conditions 1., 2. and 3. are sufficient because, if the two multi-sets contain distinct keys and are disjoint, a revoked user u has no way to decrypt the messages sent by GC for communicating to non revoked users the update of the keys along the path from the root to the leaf node associated to u.

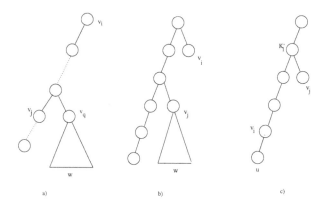

Fig. 3. Conditions for a 1-secure key-tree

□

Notice that, the key-tree used in the scheme proposed in [CWSP98, CEK+99] (see Fig. 4) and analysed in Section VI of [PB01], fulfills the above requirement. Indeed, therein, at any given depth from the root, two new keys are used and are duplicated across the same level of the tree. Hence, it is 1-secure.

Moreover, we state the following result:

Corollary 1. *In any 1-secure key-tree with n leaves, the number of distinct keys is greater than or equal to $2 \log n + 1$.*

Proof. For any root-to-leaf path of length d_u, due to Theorem 1, we have that, $|KPATH^{(u)}| = d_u + 1$, $|HPATH^{(u)}| = d_u$, and $|KPATH^{(u)} \cup HPATH^{(u)}| = 2d_u + 1$. Let d be the lenght of the longest root-to-leaf path. It follows that d is minimal when the key-tree is balanced, i.e., $d = \log n$. Therefore, the number of distinct keys is greater than or equal to $2 \log n + 1$. □

Hence, the key assignment of [CWSP98, CEK⁺99] is optimal w.r.t the total number of keys GC has to generate for 1-secure key-trees.

Theorem 2. *A key-tree is 2-secure if and only if the keys assigned to the nodes of the key-tree are all distinct.*

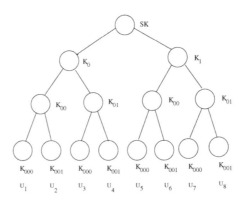

Fig. 4. Optimal Key Assignment for 1-secure key-trees

Proof. (Sketch) Assume, by contradiction, that the tree is 2-secure but two nodes, say v_i and v_j, have equal keys, i.e., $K_i = K_j$. Due to Theorem 1 these two nodes cannot be one a descendant of the other and cannot be siblings. Let T_i be the subtree rooted at v_i and T_j be the subtree rooted at v_j. Then, let v_p be the parent of v_j, let v_q be the sibling of v_j, and let T_q be the subtree rooted at v_q (see Fig. 5).

If user u, associated to one of the leaves of T_i, is revoked, the revocation strategy deletes key K_i and associates to v_i a new key. Then, if user w, associated to one of the leaves of T_q is revoked, key K_p is deleted and a new key is associated to v_p. Such a new key is communicated securely to non revoked users. In particular, this new key is communicated to all leaves belonging to T_j through a message encrypted with K_j. But since $K_j = K_i$, then user u can decrypt such a message, recovering the new key associated to v_p and, subsequently, all other keys the revocation strategy associates to nodes from v_p to the root. Hence, u can compute the new session key. Therefore, the key-tree is not 2-secure. On the other hand, if keys are all distinct, then it is easy to see that the key-tree is 2-secure. Indeed, the GC can revoke both users simultaneously. Moreover, both (revoked) users do not get any information about the new session key. □

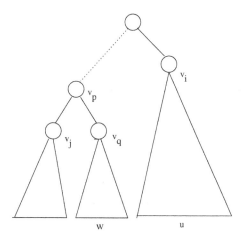

Fig. 5. Node v_j is not a descendant of v_i

A key-tree enabling revoking all users but one is said to be *totally secure*. It is easy to check the following:

Corollary 2. *A key-tree with n leaves, for any $n \geq 4$, is totally secure if and only if it is 2-secure.*

Proof. (Sketch) The "only if" part of the above corollary follows by noticing that an $(n-1)$-secure key-tree must be at least 2-secure. On the other hand, the "if" part follows because distinct keys yield the possibility of revoking securely up to $n-1$ users. □

In the above analysis, we have considered a key-tree with n leaves, and we have focused on revocations. The aim was to find the conditions the key assignment to the nodes of the key-tree has to satisfy for providing secure revocations. If we consider a LKH scheme where join and revoke operations take place, from our analysis it comes up that if the new keys assigned to new leaves and the keys assigned to the nodes of the key-tree during a revoke/join operation are *distinct among them, from all the others, and from previously used and deleted ones*, then the invariant that all keys assigned to the nodes of the key-tree are distinct is maintained. Hence, the key-trees generated due to join/revoke events are totally secure, and the LKH scheme is secure w.r.t. Definition 3. More precisely, we summarise our analysis by stating the following:

Theorem 3. *A LKH scheme is secure w.r.t. revoked users if and only if in the initial key-tree T_0 the keys associated to nodes are all distinct, and the join and revoke operations maintain such an invariant, i.e., at session j, for any $j = 0, 1, \ldots$, all keys of the key-tree T_j are distinct among them and from all the previously used and deleted ones.*

Notice that Definition 3 can be extended to deal with coalitions of joining and revoked users. As well, it is possible to show that the above characterization for the key-assignment holds also for such a more general adversarial settings.

3   The Subset-Cover Framework: CS, SD, and LSD

In a seminal paper [NNL01] a framework for BE algorithms enabling efficient user revocation[4], referred to as *Subset-Cover*, was proposed. We briefly recall it here and refer the reader to [NNL01] for details.

Let $\mathcal{N}$ be the set of all users. Every user $u \in \mathcal{N}$ gets, at the beginning, some secret information I_u. Let $\mathcal{R} \subset \mathcal{N}$ be a subset of r users which should be revoked. The center sends a message M containing a new session key K such that all users $u \in \mathcal{N} \setminus \mathcal{R}$ can decrypt the message correctly, while even a coalition consisting of all members of $\mathcal{R}$ cannot decrypt it.

An algorithm defines a collection of subsets $S_1, \ldots, S_\omega \subseteq \mathcal{N}$. Each subset S_j is assigned (perhaps implicitly) a key L_j; each member $u \in S_j$ can compute L_j from its secret information I_u. Given a set of revoked users, the remaining users $\mathcal{N} \setminus \mathcal{R}$ are partitioned into disjoint subsets $S_{i_1}, \ldots, S_{i_m}$ so that

$$\mathcal{N} \setminus \mathcal{R} = \bigcup_{j=1}^{m} S_{i_j}$$

and the session key K is encrypted m times with $L_{i_1}, \ldots, L_{i_m}$.

A particular implementation of such a scheme is specified by *a)* the collection of subsets $S_1, \ldots, S_\omega$, *b)* the key assignment to each subset in the collection, *c)* a method to cover the non-revoked users $\mathcal{N} \setminus \mathcal{R}$ by disjoint subsets from this collection, and *d)* a method that allows each user u to find its cover-set S and compute its key L_S from I_u.

The schemes we consider in the following are all based on trees, i.e., receivers are associated to the leaves of a full binary tree.

Complete Subtree Method (CS, for short). The collection of subsets $\{S_1, \ldots, S_\omega\}$ in the CS scheme corresponds to all subtrees in the full binary tree with n leaves. For any node v_i in the full binary tree (either an internal node or a leaf, $2n - 1$ altogether) let the subset S_i be the collection of receivers u that correspond to the leaves of the subtree rooted at node v_i. In other words, $u \in S_i$ iff v_i is an ancestor of u. The key assignment method is simple: assign an independent and random key L_i to every node v_i in the complete tree. Provide every receiver u with the $\log n + 1$ keys associated with nodes along the path from the root to leaf u.

For a given set $\mathcal{R}$ of revoked receivers, let $\{u_1, \ldots, u_r\}$ be the leaves corresponding to the elements in $\mathcal{R}$. The method to partition $\mathcal{N} \setminus \mathcal{R}$ into disjoint subsets is as follows. Consider the Steiner tree $ST(\mathcal{R})$ defined by the set $\mathcal{R}$ of

---

[4] The join operation is trivially performed by constructing at the beginning an oversized tree structure, capable of accommodating new users. Hence, the focus is only posed on efficient ways to revoke users.

vertices and the root, i.e., the minimal subtree of the full binary tree that connects all the leaves in $\mathcal{R}$. $ST(\mathcal{R})$ is unique. Then, $S_{i_1}, \ldots, S_{i_m}$ correspond to all subtrees whose roots $v_1, \ldots, v_m$ are adjacent to nodes of outdegree 1 in $ST(\mathcal{R})$, but they are not in $ST(\mathcal{R})$.

Subset Difference Method (SD, for short). The collection of subsets in the SD scheme corresponds to subsets of the form "a group of receivers G_1 minus another group G_2." More precisely, a valid subset $S_{i,j}$ is represented by two vertices (v_i, v_j) such that v_i is an ancestor of v_j. A leaf u is in $S_{i,j}$ iff it is in the subtree rooted at v_i but not in the subtree rooted at v_j

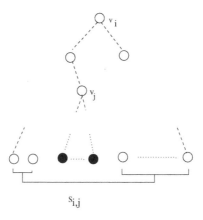

Fig. 6. $S_{i,j}$ contains all leaves descending from v_i but not from v_j

The key assignment method associates to each *internal node* v_i of the full binary tree a random and independent value $LABEL_i$. This value induces the keys for all legitimate subsets of the form $S_{i,j}$. More precisely, let G be a cryptographic pseudorandom generator that triples the input, and denote by $G_L(S), G_R(S)$, and $G_M(S)$ the left, right and middle parts, respectively. Consider a subtree T_i rooted at v_i. The root node is assigned $LABEL_i$. From this label are computed recursively labels for all subtrees associated to subsets $S_{i,j}$: given that a parent node was labeled S, its two children are labeled $G_L(S)$ and $G_R(S)$. Let $LABEL_{i,j}$ be the label of node v_j derived in the subtree T_i from $LABEL_i$. Following such a labeling, the key $L_{i,j}$ assigned to $S_{i,j}$ is $G_M(LABEL_{i,j})$. The information I_u that each receiver u gets consists in a set of values $LABEL_{i,j}$ defined as follows: *for each* subtree T_i such that u is a leaf of T_i, consider the path from v_i to u and let $v_1, \ldots, v_k$ be the nodes adjacent to the path but not ancestor of u (see Fig. 7).

Then, u receives the labels $LABEL_{i,1}, \ldots, LABEL_{i,k}$. Notice that each node v_j that is not an ancestor of u is a descendant of one of the nodes $v_1, \ldots, v_k$. Therefore, u can compute the labels $LABEL_{i,j}$ for any j such that v_j is not an ancestor of u.

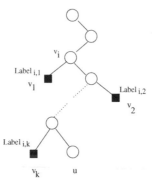

Fig. 7. Labels associated to nodes hanging off the path from v_i to user u

As for the total number of labels stored by receiver u, each tree T_i of depth k that contains u contributes $k-1$ labels; so the total is

$$\sum_{k=1}^{\log n+1} (k-1) = \frac{(\log n + 1)\log n}{2} = O((\log n)^2).$$

For a given set $\mathcal{R}$ of revoked receivers, let $\{u_1, \ldots, u_r\}$ be the leaves corresponding to the elements in $\mathcal{R}$. The method to partition $\mathcal{N} \setminus \mathcal{R}$ into disjoint subsets is as follows. Consider maximal chains of nodes with outdegree 1 in the Steiner tree $ST(\mathcal{R})$. Each such chain is of the form $[v_{i_1}, \ldots, v_{i_\ell}]$ where all of $v_{i_1}, \ldots, v_{i_{\ell-1}}$, have outdegree 1 in $ST(\mathcal{R})$, v_{i_ℓ} is either a leaf or a node with outdegree 2, and the parent of v_{i_1} is either a node of outdegree 2 or the root. For all such chains where $\ell \geq 2$ add a subset S_{i_1,i_ℓ} to the cover.

Layered Subset Difference Method (LSD, for short). The SD scheme covers any privileged set P defined as the complement of r revoked users by the union of $O(r)$ subsets $S_{i,j}$. The LSD scheme [HS02] shows that a small subcollection of subsets $S_{i,j}$ from the collection used by SD suffices to represent any set P as the union of $O(r)$ of the remaining sets, with a slightly larger constant.

The key observation to prune the collection of subsets used by SD is the following: if v_i, v_k and v_j are vertices which occur in this order on some root-to-leaf path in the tree, then $S_{i,j}$ can be described as the disjoint union $S_{i,j} = S_{i,k} \cup S_{k,j}$. LSD retains a subcollection of subsets $S_{i,j}$ of SD such that, whenever the center wants to use a discarded set in his set cover, he replaces it by the union of two smaller sets which are in the subcollection.

The subcollection of sets $S_{i,j}$ in the LSD scheme is defined by restricting the levels in which the vertices v_i and v_j can occur in the tree. More precisely, in the tree are identified $\sqrt{\log n}$ *special levels*. The levels between (and including) two special levels form a *layer*. Then $S_{i,j}$ is a set of the LSD collection if it is not empty and at least one of the following conditions is true: both v_i and v_j belong to the same layer, or v_i is at a special level. Subsets $S_{i,j}$ in the LSD collection are said *useful*.

The only labels user u has to store are those that correspond to useful sets $S_{i,j}$ in which v_i is an ancestor of u and v_j is just hanging off the path from v_i to u. It is not difficult to see by a counting argument that, since each layer contains $\sqrt{\log n}$ levels, then the number of labels corresponding to a layer is $O((\sqrt{\log n})^2) = O(\log n)$. Since there are $\sqrt{\log n}$ layers, the total number is $O((\log n)^{\frac{3}{2}})$. Moreover, each vertex v_i in a special level, can be associated to any one of the $O(\log n)$ levels underneath it. Since there are $\sqrt{\log n}$ special levels, the total number of labels of this type is $O((\log n)^{\frac{3}{2}})$.

Security. The security of the CS scheme and of the SD scheme was shown in [NNL01]. CS is unconditionally secure w.r.t. coalitions of users of any size (see Claim 1 of [NNL01]). SD is computationally secure, according to an indistinguishability definition, and based on some assumptions on the encryption scheme and the generator used in the scheme (see Theorem 16 of [NNL01]). The security of LSD follows from the security of SD.

Remark. Notice that a LKH scheme and the CS scheme are similar in terms of key assignment, i.e., a key is assigned to each node in the binary tree, and every user store all keys along the path from the leaf to the root. However, these keys are used quite differently: in the LKH scheme some of these keys change at every revocation. In the CS scheme keys do not change, what changes is only the session key. In the CS scheme the tree is over-sized in order to accommodate users who join the group later on. However, it is easy to see that, given a set of n users, the problem of how to minimise user key storage in the CS scheme in presence of a non-uniform probability distribution of user revocation is the same of LKH schemes, which has been studied in [PB01].

4   Optimisation Problems and Coding Theory

The CS, SD, and LSD schemes are based on full binary trees with n leaves. From the analysis of the CS, SD and LSD schemes, it comes up that the number of keys/labels each user has to store *depends on the depth of the leaf* to which the user is associated in the tree. Therein, each leaf has depth $\log n$ (uniform probabilities of revocation). However, as we have discussed in the introduction, it might be of some interest to optimise SD and LSD for settings in which the probabilities of revocation for the receivers are not all the same. If the probability distribution of user revocation is non-uniform, leaves could have different depths, since we would like to give less keys to some users than to others. The problem, hence, is *how to construct a tree which minimises the average number of keys/labels a user has to store* in such settings.

Let T be a tree with n leaves. Then, for $i = 1, \ldots, n$, let p_i be the revocation probability for user i, and let ℓ_i be the length of the path from the i-th leaf to the root node.

At this point notice that in an implementation of the CS scheme over a tree where user u is associated to a leaf at distance ℓ_i from the root, depending on the revocation probability p_i, user u gets $\ell_i + 1$ keys. Similarly, in an implementation of the SD scheme u gets $O(\ell_i^2)$ labels, while in an implementation of the LSD he gets $O(\frac{\ell_i^2}{\sqrt{\log n}})$ labels. Hence, with some approximation, the problem we have to solve is to find trees such that are minimised:

$$\sum_{i=1}^n p_i \cdot \ell_i \text{ (CS Scheme) }, \sum_{i=1}^n p_i \cdot \ell_i^2 \text{ (SD Scheme) }, \sum_{i=1}^n p_i \cdot \frac{\ell_i^2}{\sqrt{\log n}} \text{ (LSD Scheme) .}$$

We can re-state the above problems in coding theory problems has follows: assume that, starting from the root of the tree, to each left edge is associated a bit b, and to each right edge is associated $1 - b$. Then, each path can be seen as a binary codeword associated to the leaf. Due to the structure of the tree, the set of codewords is prefix-free, and the path lengths satisfy the Kraft inequality [CT91]. Hence, the problem of constructing a full binary tree with n leaves, minimising a certain cost measure, *coincides* with the problem of constructing an optimal set of n binary prefix-free codewords, satisfying Kraft's inequality, according to the cost measure.

Notice that, if the cost measure is the average length, i.e., $\sum_{i=1}^n p_i \cdot \ell_i$, then, as pointed out in [PB01], the coding theory problem is well known in the literature and efficiently solvable by means of Huffmann's algorithm.

The coding problems associated to the second and third measures belong to a family of coding problems referred to in the literature as coding with Campbell's penalties [Cam66]. Recently in [Bae06], an efficient solution to the coding problem in presence of penalties defined by a function $f(p_i, \ell_i)$ satisfying certain constraints has been described. Our measures are particular cases of this function. Hence, we have efficient solutions also for the other two tree optimisation problems.

Remark. *The scheme SD was introduced to get a revoking scheme in which the size of the broadcast message does not depend on n, the total number of users, but on r, the number of revoked users. We emphasize that, by optimising the tree structure in terms of the non-uniform probabilities of revocation, the performance of SD (resp., LSD) in terms of broadcast message size stays the same. For details see the proof of Lemma 3 in [NNL01].*

5   Source Coding for Campbell's Penalties

In this section we briefly describe the approach used in [Bae06] in order to find minimum penalty codes. However, for details, the reader is referred to [Bae06].

Codes and Cost Measures. Let $\mathcal{X} = \{1, 2, \ldots, n\}$ be an alphabet. For $i = 1, \ldots, n$, symbol i has probability p_i to be drawn from the alphabet. The symbols from $\mathcal{X}$ are coded into binary codewords. The codeword c_i, corresponding to symbol i, has length ℓ_i.

Huffman algorithm yields a prefix code minimizing $\sum_{i=1}^n p_i \ell_i$, given the natural coding constraints: ℓ_i integer values, and the Kraft inequality $\sum_{i=1}^n 2^{-\ell_i} \leq 1$.

Campbell introduced a variant of this problem in [Cam66] where, given a continuous (strictly) monotonic increasing cost function $\phi(\ell) : R_+ \to R_+$, the value to minimize is

$$L(p, \ell, \phi) = \phi^{-1}(\sum_i p_i \phi(\ell_i)).$$

The value $L(p, \ell, \phi)$ was called the *mean length for the cost function* ϕ or, for brevity, the *penalty*. In [Bae06] the concept was generalised by using a two-argument cost function $f(\ell, p)$ instead of $\phi(\ell)$. The following definitions were given:

Definition 5. *[Bae06] A cost function $f(\ell, p)$ and its associated penalty L^* are differentially monotonic in p if, for every $\ell > 1$, whenever $f(\ell - 1, p_i)$ is finite and $p_i > p_j$, then $(f(\ell, p_i) - f(\ell - 1, p_i)) > (f(\ell, p_j) - f(\ell - 1, p_j))$.*

Definition 6. *[Bae06] Let $f(\ell, p) : R_+ \times [0, 1] \to R_+ \cup \{\infty\}$ be a function nondecreasing in ℓ and p, and differentially monotonic in p. Then,*

$$L^*(p, \ell, f) = \sum_i^n f(\ell_i, p_i) \tag{1}$$

is called a generalised quasilinear penalty. Further, if f is convex in ℓ, it is called a generalised quasilinear convex penalty.

Baer's work provides algorithms for general penalties given by (1).

It is easy to see that both functions $f(\ell_i, p_i)$ of our interest belong to the generalised penalty family defined by (1). Hence, the algorithms proposed in [Bae06] can be used to find sets of codeword lengths $\{\ell_1, \ldots, \ell_n\}$ satisfying Kraft's and minimising $\sum_{i=1}^n p_i \cdot \ell_i^2$ or $\sum_{i=1}^n p_i \cdot \frac{\ell_i^2}{\sqrt{\log n}}$.

6   Conclusions

We have provided a characterisation for key assignments in LKH schemes, and we have shown that the key assignment given in [CWSP98, CEK+99] is optimal in terms of number of distinct keys generated by GC for 1-secure key-trees. Then, we have shown that the problem of realising efficient implementations, in terms of user key storage, of SD and LSD in presence of non-uniform probabilities of revocation, can be posed as optimisation problems which correspond to optimal codeword length selection problems in coding theory i.e., to find the lengths of the codewords of prefix-free codes minimising certain cost measures. We have also pointed out that, for such problems, efficient algorithms are available.

References

[Bae06]   Baer, M.: Source coding for campbell's penalties. IEEE Transactions on Information Theory 52(10), 4380–4393 (2006)

[Ber91]   Berkovits, S.: How to broadcast a secret. In: Davies, D.W. (ed.) EURO-CRYPT 1991. LNCS, vol. 547, pp. 535–541. Springer, Heidelberg (1991)

[Cam66]   Campbell, L.L.: Definition of entropy by means of a coding problem. Zeitschrift fur Wahrscheinlichkeitstheorie und wandte Gebiete 6, 113–118 (1966)

[CEK+99]   Chang, I., Engel, R., Kandlur, D., Pendarakis, D., Saha, D.: Key management for secure internet multicast using boolean function minimization techniques. In: Proceedings of IEEE INFOCOMM 1999, vol. 2, pp. 689–698 (1999)

[CGI+99]   Canetti, R., Garay, J., Itkis, G., Micciancio, D., Naor, M., Pinkas, B.: Multicast security: A taxonomy and some efficient constructions. In: Proceedings of INFOCOMM 1999, pp. 708–716 (1999)

[CMN99]   Canetti, R., Malkin, T., Nissim, K.: Efficient communication-storage tradeoffs for multicast encryption. In: Stern, J. (ed.) EUROCRYPT 1999. LNCS, vol. 1592, pp. 459–474. Springer, Heidelberg (1999)

[CT91]   Cover, T., Thomas, J.: Elements of Information Theory. Wiley, Chichester (1991)

[CWSP98]   Caronni, G., Waldvogel, M., Sun, D., Plattner, B.: Efficient security for large and dynamic multicast groups. In: IEEE 7th Workshop on Enabling Technologies: Infrastructure for Collaborative Enterprises (WET ICE 1998) (1998)

[EFF85]   Erdos, P., Frankl, P., Furedi, Z.: Families of finite subsets in which no set is covered by the union of r others. Israel Journal of Mathematics (51), 75–89 (1985)

[FN94]   Fiat, A., Naor, M.: Broadcast encryption. In: Stinson, D.R. (ed.) CRYPTO 1993. LNCS, vol. 773, pp. 480–491. Springer, Heidelberg (1994)

[GST04]   Goodrich, M.T., Sun, J.Z., Tamassia, R.: Efficient tree-based revocation in groups of low-state devices. In: Franklin, M. (ed.) CRYPTO 2004. LNCS, vol. 3152, pp. 511–527. Springer, Heidelberg (2004)

[HL06]   Hwang, Y.H., Lee, P.J.: Efficient broadcast encryption scheme with log-key storage. In: Di Crescenzo, G., Rubin, A. (eds.) FC 2006. LNCS, vol. 4107, pp. 281–295. Springer, Heidelberg (2006)

[HLL05]   Hwang, J.Y., Lee, D.H., Lim, J.: Generic transformation for scalable broadcast encryption schemes. In: Shoup, V. (ed.) CRYPTO 2005. LNCS, vol. 3621, pp. 276–292. Springer, Heidelberg (2005)

[HS02]   Halevy, D., Shamir, A.: The LSD broadcast encryption scheme. In: Yung, M. (ed.) CRYPTO 2002. LNCS, vol. 2442, pp. 47–60. Springer, Heidelberg (2002)

[JHC+05]   Jho, N., Hwang, J.Y., Cheon, J.H., Kim, M., Lee, D.H., Yoo, E.S.: One-way chain based broadcast encryption schemes. In: Cramer, R. (ed.) EUROCRYPT 2005. LNCS, vol. 3494, pp. 559–574. Springer, Heidelberg (2005)

[LH90]   Larmore, L.L., Hirschberg, D.S.: A fast algorithm for optimal length-limited Huffman codes. Journal of Association for Computing Machinery 37(2), 464–473 (1990)

[MP04]   Micciancio, D., Panjwani, S.: Optimal communication complexity of generic multicast key distribution. In: Cachin, C., Camenisch, J.L. (eds.) EUROCRYPT 2004. LNCS, vol. 3027, pp. 153–170. Springer, Heidelberg (2004)

[NNL01]   Naor, D., Naor, M., Lotspiech, J.: Revocation and tracing schemes for stateless receivers. In: Kilian, J. (ed.) CRYPTO 2001. LNCS, vol. 2139, pp. 41–62. Springer, Heidelberg (2001), Full version, http://www.wisdom.weizmann.ac.il/~naor/

[PB01]   Poovendran, R., Baras, J.S.: An information theoretic analysis of rooted-
           tree based secure multicast key distribution schemes. IEEE Transactions
           on Information Theory 47(7), 2824–2834 (2001); Preliminary version In:
           Wiener, M. (ed.) CRYPTO 1999. LNCS, vol. 1666, p. 624. Springer, Hei-
           delberg (1999)
[SM03]   Sherman, A.T., McGrew, D.A.: Key establishment in large dynamic groups
           using one-way function trees. IEEE Transactions on Software Engineer-
           ing 29(5), 444–458 (2003)
[SSV01]   Snoeyink, J., Suri, S., Varghese, G.: A lower bound for multicast key dis-
           tribution. In: Proceedings of IEEE INFOCOMM 2001, pp. 422–431 (2001)
[WGL98]   Wong, C., Gouda, M., Lam, S.: Secure group communications using key
           graphs. In: Proceedings ACM SIGCOMM 1998. ACM, New York (1998)
[WHA99]   Wallner, D., Hardler, E., Agee, R.: Key management for multicast: Issues
           and architectures. RFC 2627, National Security Agency (June 1999)

A   Algorithms for Finding Minimum Penalty Codes

As we have pointed out before, there is a natural representation of prefix-free
codes satisfying Kraft's in terms of full binary trees. The key idea of [Bae06]
is to use a *different representation* which makes possible reducing the minimum
penalty code problem to an efficiently solvable problem, the Coin Collector's
problem.

Definition 7. *[Bae06] A node is an ordered pair of integers (i, ℓ) such that
$i \in \{1, \ldots, n\}$ and $\ell \in \{1, \ldots, \ell_{max}\}$. We call the set of all $n\ell_{max}$ possible nodes
I. Usually I is arranged in a grid. The set of nodes, or nodeset, corresponding
to item i (assigned codeword c_i with length ℓ_i) is the set of the first ℓ_i nodes of
column i, that is $\eta_\ell(i) = \{(j, \ell) | j = i, \ell \in \{1, \ldots, \ell_i\}\}$. The nodeset corresponding
to length vector ℓ is $\eta(\ell) = \cup_i \eta_\ell(i)$. This corresponds to a set of n codewords, a
code. We say a node (i, ℓ) has width $\rho(i, \ell) = 2^{-\ell}$ and weight $\mu(i, \ell) = f(\ell, p_i) -
f(\ell - 1, p_i)$.*

Each node (i, ℓ) represents both the share of the penalty $L^*(\mathbf{p}, \ell, f)$ (weight) and
the share of the Kraft's sum (width). If I has a subset N that is a nodeset, then
it is straightforward to find the corresponding length vector and thus a code.
Moreover, it can be shown that an optimal nodeset can be found using the Coin
Collector's problem.

The Coin Collector's problem of size m considers m coins with width $\rho_i \in 2^Z$
(the set of powers of 2) and weight $\mu_i \in R$. The final problem parameter is the
total width, denoted t. The problem is then

$$\text{minimize}_{\{B \subset \{1,\ldots,m\}\}} \sum_{i \in B} \mu_i$$
$$\text{subject to} \qquad \sum_{i \in B} \rho_i = t$$

Roughly speaking, it consists in fitting into a minimum weight container coins
with total width exactly t. It was shown that any optimal solution N of the Coin

Collector's problem for $t = n - 1$ on coins I is a nodeset for an optimal solution of the coding problem (see Section VII of [Bae06] for the formal reduction). More precisely, defining $\mu(N) = \sum_{(i,\ell) \in N} \mu(i, \ell)$, it holds that:

Theorem 4. *Any N that is a solution of the Coin Collector's problem for $t = n - 1$ has a corresponding length vector ℓ such that $\eta(\ell) = N$ and $\min_\ell L^*(\mathbf{p}, \ell, f) = \mu(N)$.*

Notice that the Coin Collector's problem is an input-restricted case of the knapsack problem, which, in general, is NP-hard. A linear-time algorithm, referred to as *Package-Merge Algorithm*, which solves the Coin Collector's problem, was proposed in [LH90].

Trade-Offs in Information-Theoretic Multi-party One-Way Key Agreement

Renato Renner[1], Stefan Wolf[2], and Jürg Wullschleger[2]

[1] Centre for Quantum Computation, University of Cambridge, UK
r.renner@damtp.cam.ac.uk
[2] Computer Science Department, ETH Zürich, Switzerland
{wolf,wjuerg}@inf.ethz.ch

Abstract. We consider the following scenario involving three honest parties, Alice, Bob, and Carol, as well as an adversary, Eve. Each party has access to a single piece of information, jointly distributed according to some distribution P. Additionally, authentic public communication is possible from Alice to Carol and from Bob to Carol. Their goal is to establish two information-theoretically secret keys, one known to Alice and Carol, and one known to Bob and Carol. We derive joint bounds on the lengths of these keys. Our protocols combine distributed variants of Slepian-Wolf coding and the leftover hash lemma. The obtained bounds are expressed in terms of smooth Rényi entropies and show that these quantities are useful in this—single-serving—context as well.

1 Introduction

Consider the following scenario: Three parties, Alice, Bob, and Carol, as well as an adversary, Eve, each have access to a *single* realization of random variables X, Y, W, and Z, respectively, jointly distributed according to P_{XYWZ}. Furthermore, both Alice and Bob can send messages to Carol, but no other communication is possible between the parties (in particular, Alice and Bob cannot communicate). The goal of Alice, Bob, and Carol is to generate two *secret keys*, one of them known to Alice and Carol, and the other known to Bob and Carol. Secrecy means that Eve, who is assumed to have access to the entire communication between the parties, has almost no information about the two keys. In a nutshell, our result shows that there is a direct trade-off between the lengths of the keys generated by Alice and Bob, respectively.

Our scenario is an extension of the two-party settings considered in [AC93, CK78, Mau93, RW05], and also partly fits into the general framework on information-theoretic key agreement with a helper proposed in [CN04]. An important distinction to the treatment in [AC93, CK78, Mau93, CN04], however, is that—similarly to [RW05]—we are concerned with the *single-serving* case, where only *single* realizations—in contrast to infinitely many independent and identically distributed (i.i.d.) realizations—of the random variables are available.

Our result is based on multi-party extensions of two known techniques, called *privacy amplification* (or *randomness extraction*) and *information reconciliation*

Y. Desmedt (Ed.): ICITS 2007, LNCS 4883, pp. 65–75, 2009.

(or *compression*). The first can be seen as a direct application of the *leftover hash lemma* [ILL89]. A first extension of a similar statement to multiple parties has been proposed in [MKM03], but is restricted to the case of i.i.d. random variables. For our purpose, we need the full (single-serving) generalization of the leftover hash lemma as proposed in [Wul07] (Section 3). The second technique used for our proof is a novel single-serving version of the well-known *Slepian-Wolf coding* result [SW73] that acts as a distributed *information-reconciliation* protocol (Section 4).

The quantitative results are expressed in terms of *smooth (Rényi) entropies*. These entropy measures have been introduced as generalizations of the Shannon entropy in order to deal with single-serving scenarios [RW05] (see Section 2).[1] For the special case of i.i.d. distributions (i.e., n-fold product distributions $P^{\times n} = P \times P \times \cdots \times P$), smooth entropies asymptotically approach Shannon entropy. In particular, if the distribution P_{XYWZ} describing our scenario is of the i.i.d. form $(P_{X'Y'W'Z'})^{\times n}$, for some large n, then the smooth entropies in our results can be replaced by the corresponding Shannon entropies (thus reproducing i.i.d. results as in [CN04]).

2 Smooth Entropies

2.1 Motivation

Traditionally, operational quantities in information theory, i.e., quantities describing information-theoretic tasks such as channel coding, are defined asymptotically. More precisely, it is typically assumed that a certain functionality, e.g., a (memoryless) communication channel $P_{Y|X}$, can be invoked *many times independently*. The functionality is then characterized in terms of *asymptotic rates*. For example, the *capacity* $C^{\mathrm{asym}}(P_{Y|X})$ of a channel $P_{Y|X}$ is defined as the maximum rate at which bits can be transmitted per channel use such that the probability of a decoding error vanishes asymptotically as the number of channel uses approaches infinity. As shown in [Sha48], $C^{\mathrm{asym}}(P_{Y|X})$ can be expressed in terms of Shannon entropy,

$$C^{\mathrm{asym}}(P_{Y|X}) = \max_{P_X}(I(X;Y)) = \max_{P_X}(H(X) - H(X|Y)) . \tag{1}$$

Another example, situated in the area of cryptography, is *key agreement from correlated information* [AC93, CK78, Mau93]. Assume that two parties, Alice and Bob, as well as an adversary, Eve, have access to a source providing them with random variables X, Y, and Z, respectively. The goal of Alice and Bob is to generate a secret key, using only communication over an authentic, but otherwise fully insecure, communication channel. Under the assumption that the source emits *many independent* triples (X, Y, Z), the *key rate* $K^{\mathrm{asym}}(P_{XYZ})$, i.e., the asymptotic rate at which key bits can be generated per invocation of the source, is bounded by an expression which only involves Shannon entropy,

$$K^{\mathrm{asym}}(P_{XYZ}) \geq H(X|Z) - H(X|Y) . \tag{2}$$

---

[1] See also [Ren05] for a quantum information-theoretic version of smooth entropies.

In a realistic scenario, however, such an asymptotic viewpoint might not be fully satisfying. Firstly, any realistic device can only be accessed a finite number of times; this number might be smaller than the (usually unknown) minimum threshold which is needed for the asymptotic results to apply. Secondly, and even more importantly, the assumption of *independence* might not hold or, at least, be hard to justify. For instance, in cryptography, such an assumption typically translates to a condition on the behavior of the adversary.[2] Results depending on such assumptions are thus usually not sufficient for realistic applications. It is, therefore, natural to ask what happens *if the assumptions of independence and asymptoticity are dropped*. Ideally, one might want to completely eliminate the assumption that a resource is invoked many times. *Smooth (Rényi) entropies* are designed to deal with such general *single-serving* settings.

Recently, a variety of information-theoretic results have been generalized to the single-serving case. For instance, it has been shown in [RWW06] that the number $C^\varepsilon(P_{Y|X})$ of bits that can be sent by *one single use* of a communication channel $P_{Y|X}$ such that a decoding error occurs with probability at most ε is given in terms of smooth entropies,[3]

$$C^\varepsilon(P_{Y|X}) \approx \max_{P_X}\left(H_{\min}^\varepsilon(X) - H_{\max}^\varepsilon(X|Y)\right) , \qquad (3)$$

which is analogous to (1). Similarly, the number $K^\varepsilon(P_{XYZ})$ of ε-secure key bits[4] that Alice and Bob can generate in the cryptographic scenario described above is bounded by

$$K^\varepsilon(P_{XYZ}) \gtrsim H_{\min}^\varepsilon(X|Z) - H_{\max}^\varepsilon(X|Y) , \qquad (4)$$

which is analogous to (2).

As indicated above, Shannon entropy can be seen as a special case of smooth entropy. In fact, any result involving smooth entropies can be specialised to a result for Shannon entropy by virtue of the relation

$$H(X|Y) = \lim_{\varepsilon \to 0} \lim_{n \to \infty} \frac{1}{n} H_{\min}^\varepsilon(X^n|Y^n) = \lim_{\varepsilon \to 0} \lim_{n \to \infty} \frac{1}{n} H_{\max}^\varepsilon(X^n|Y^n) , \qquad (5)$$

where (X^n, Y^n) denotes n independent pairs (X_i, Y_i) of random variables jointly distributed according to P_{XY}. For example, using this identity, it is easy to see that expressions (1) and (2) are indeed special cases of (3) and (4), respectively.

2.2   Definition and Properties

Let X be a random variable with distribution P_X. The *max-entropy* of X is defined as the (binary) logarithm of the size of the support of P_X, i.e.,

$$H_{\max}(X) = \log\left|\{x \in \mathcal{X} : P_X(x) > 0\}\right| .$$

---

[2] E.g., in quantum key distribution, perfect independence of the distributed data is only guaranteed if the adversary does not introduce any correlations during her attack on the quantum channel.

[3] See Section 2.2 for a formal definition of smooth entropies.

[4] See Section 5 for a definition of ε-*security*.

Similarly, the *min-entropy* of X is given by the negative logarithm of the maximum probability of P_X, i.e.,

$$H_{\min}(X) = -\log \max_x P_X(x) .$$

Note that $H_{\min}(X) \leq H(X) \leq H_{\max}(X)$, i.e., the min- and max-entropies are lower and upper bounds for Shannon entropy (and also for any Rényi entropy H_α), respectively.

For random variables X and Y with joint distribution P_{XY}, the "conditional" versions of these entropic quantities are defined by

$$H_{\max}(X|Y) = \max_y H_{\max}(X|Y = y) ,$$
$$H_{\min}(X|Y) = \min_y H_{\min}(X|Y = y) ,$$

where $H_{\max}(X|Y = y)$ (and $H_{\min}(X|Y = y)$) denote the max-entropy (min-entropy) of a random variable distributed according to the conditional distribution $P_{X|Y=y}$.[5]

In [RW05], max- and min-entropies have been generalized to so-called *smooth entropies*. Smooth entropies can be expressed in terms of an optimization over events $\mathcal{E}$ with probability at least $1 - \varepsilon$. Let $P_{X\mathcal{E}|Y=y}(x)$ be the probability that $\{X = x\}$ *and* $\mathcal{E}$ occur, conditioned on $Y = y$. We then have

$$H^\varepsilon_{\max}(X|Y) = \min_{\mathcal{E}:\Pr(\mathcal{E})\geq 1-\varepsilon} \max_y \log |\{x : P_{X\mathcal{E}|Y=y}(x) > 0\}|$$
$$H^\varepsilon_{\min}(X|Y) = \max_{\mathcal{E}:\Pr(\mathcal{E})\geq 1-\varepsilon} \min_y \min_x (-\log P_{X\mathcal{E}|Y=y}(x)) .$$

Smooth entropies have properties similar to Shannon entropy [RW05].[6] For example, the *chain rule* $H(X|Y) = H(XY) - H(Y)$ translates to[7]

$$H^{\varepsilon+\varepsilon'}_{\max}(XY) - H^{\varepsilon'}_{\max}(Y) \leq H^\varepsilon_{\max}(X|Y) ,$$
$$\leq H^{\varepsilon_1}_{\max}(XY) - H^{\varepsilon_2}_{\min}(Y) + \log(1/(\varepsilon - \varepsilon_1 - \varepsilon_2))$$

and

$$H^{\varepsilon_1}_{\min}(XY) - H^{\varepsilon_2}_{\max}(Y) - \log(1/(\varepsilon - \varepsilon_1 - \varepsilon_2))$$
$$\leq H^\varepsilon_{\min}(X|Y) \leq H^{\varepsilon+\varepsilon'}_{\min}(XY) - H^{\varepsilon'}_{\min}(Y) ,$$

for any $\varepsilon, \varepsilon', \varepsilon_1, \varepsilon_2 > 0$.

Note that these rules also hold conditioned on an additional random variable Z. For instance, we have

$$H^{\varepsilon_1}_{\min}(XY|Z) - H^{\varepsilon_2}_{\max}(Y|Z) - \log(1/(\varepsilon - \varepsilon_1 - \varepsilon_2)) \leq H^\varepsilon_{\min}(X|YZ) . \quad (6)$$

---

[5] See [DRS04] for an alternative definition of conditional min-entropy.

[6] This is in contrast the the usual, "non-smooth" min- and max-entropies which have many counterintuitive properties that make them less useful in many contexts.

[7] Note that, because of (5), the chain rule $H(X|Y) = H(XY) - H(Y)$ for Shannon entropy can be seen as a special case of the chain rules for smooth entropies.

Because $H_{\max}^{\varepsilon_2}(Y|Z) \leq \log|\mathcal{Y}|$, where $\mathcal{Y}$ denotes the alphabet of Y, this inequality is a generalization of the fact that, by conditioning on an additional random variable Y, with high probability, the min-entropy decreases by at most the logarithm of the alphabet size of Y [Cac97, MW97].

2.3   Operational Interpretation

In [SW73] it was shown that the rate at which many independent realizations of X can be compressed is asymptotically equal to $H(X|Y)$ if the decoder is provided with side-information Y. It is easy to see that $H(X|Y)$ can also be interpreted as the rate at which uniform randomness can be extracted from X in such a way that it is independent of Y. In [RW05], these operational interpretations of the Shannon entropy have been generalized to the *single-serving* case, i.e., it was shown that the smooth entropies $H_{\max}^{\varepsilon}$ and $H_{\min}^{\varepsilon}$ quantify compression and randomness extraction, respectively. More precisely, let $H_{\text{comp}}^{\varepsilon}(X|Y)$ be the length of a bit string needed to store *one* instance of X such that X can later be recovered with an error of at most ε using this string and Y. This quantity is then roughly equal to $H_{\max}^{\varepsilon}$, i.e.,

$$H_{\max}^{\varepsilon}(X|Y) \leq H_{\text{comp}}^{\varepsilon}(X|Y) \leq H_{\max}^{\varepsilon'}(X|Y) + \log(1/(\varepsilon - \varepsilon')) \ .$$

Similarly, let $H_{\text{ext}}^{\varepsilon}(X|Y)$ be the maximum length of a string that can be computed from X, such that this string is uniformly distributed and independent of Y, with an error of at most ε. We then have

$$H_{\min}^{\varepsilon'}(X|Y) - 2\log(1/(\varepsilon - \varepsilon')) \leq H_{\text{ext}}^{\varepsilon}(X|Y) \leq H_{\min}^{\varepsilon}(X|Y) \ .$$

3   Distributed Randomness Extraction

The *statistical distance* of two random variables X and Y (or two distribution P_X and P_Y) over the same alphabet $\mathcal{U}$ is defined as

$$\Delta(X, Y) := \frac{1}{2} \sum_{u \in \mathcal{U}} \Big| \Pr[X = u] - \Pr[Y = u] \Big| \ .$$

We say that a random variable X *over* $\mathcal{X}$ *is ε-close to uniform with respect to* Y if $\Delta(P_{XY}, P_U \times P_Y) \leq \varepsilon$, where P_U is the uniform distribution over $\mathcal{X}$.

A function $h : \mathcal{S} \times \mathcal{X} \to \{0,1\}^m$ is called a *two-universal hash function* [CW79], if for all $x_0 \neq x_1 \in \mathcal{X}$ and for S uniform over $\mathcal{S}$, we have

$$\Pr[h(S, x_0) = h(S, x_1)] \leq 2^{-m} \ .$$

Lemma 1, first stated in [ILL89] (see also [BBR88]), gives us a bound on the amount of randomness that can be extracted from a random variable X (which might depend on another random variable Z) such that the extracted randomness is (almost) uniform and independent of Z. It has a wide range of applications, e.g., in cryptology, it can directly be used for *privacy amplification* [BBR88, BBCM95].

Lemma 1 (Leftover hash lemma [BBR88, ILL89]). *Let $\varepsilon > 0$ and let $h : \mathcal{S} \times \mathcal{X} \to \{0,1\}^m$ be a two-universal hash function. For any random variable X over $\mathcal{X}$ satisfying*

$$H_{\min}(X \mid Z) \geq m + 2\log(1/\varepsilon) \,,$$

and for S uniform over $\mathcal{X}$ and independent of X, the value $h(S, X)$ is ε-close to uniform with respect to (S, Z).

A *distributed* version of the leftover hash lemma has recently been proposed in [Wul07] (see Lemma 2 below). It can be applied to settings where two players independently extract randomness from two (possibly correlated) random variables. Lemma 1 implies that if the lengths of the extracted strings are smaller than the smooth min-entropies of these random variables, then each of them is close to uniform. However, the two strings might still be correlated. Lemma 2 states that if, in addition, the sum of the lengths of the extracted strings is smaller than the overall min-entropy, then they are almost independent of each other. The obtained bound is optimal.

Lemma 2 (Distributed leftover hash lemma [Wul07]). *Let $\varepsilon > 0$ and let $g : \mathcal{S} \times \mathcal{X} \to \{0,1\}^m$ and $h : \mathcal{R} \times \mathcal{Y} \to \{0,1\}^n$ be two-universal hash functions. For any random variables X and Y over $\mathcal{X}$ and $\mathcal{Y}$, respectively, such that*

$$H_{\min}(X \mid Z) \geq m + 2\log(1/\varepsilon) \,,$$
$$H_{\min}(Y \mid Z) \geq n + 2\log(1/\varepsilon) \,,$$
$$H_{\min}(XY \mid Z) \geq m + n + 2\log(1/\varepsilon) \,,$$

and for (S, R) uniform over $\mathcal{S} \times \mathcal{R}$ and independent of (X, Y), the pair $(g(S, X), h(R, Y))$ is ε-close to uniform with respect to (S, R, Z).

The proof of Lemma 2 is very similar to the proof of the leftover hash lemma (Lemma 1). For our purposes, we will need a variant of this lemma formulated in terms of *smooth* entropies.

Lemma 3 ("Smoothed" distributed leftover hash lemma). *Let $\varepsilon > 0$, $\varepsilon' \geq 0$, and let $g : \mathcal{S} \times \mathcal{X} \to \{0,1\}^m$ and $h : \mathcal{R} \times \mathcal{Y} \to \{0,1\}^n$ be two-universal hash functions. For any random variables X and Y over $\mathcal{X}$ and $\mathcal{Y}$, respectively, such that*

$$H_{\min}^{\varepsilon'}(X \mid Z) \geq m + 2\log(1/\varepsilon) \,,$$
$$H_{\min}^{\varepsilon'}(Y \mid Z) \geq n + 2\log(1/\varepsilon) \,,$$
$$H_{\min}^{\varepsilon'}(XY \mid Z) \geq m + n + 2\log(1/\varepsilon) \,,$$

and for (S, R) uniform over $\mathcal{S} \times \mathcal{R}$ and independent of (X, Y), the pair $(g(S, X), h(R, Y))$ is $(\varepsilon + 3\varepsilon')$-close to uniform with respect to (S, R, Z).

Proof. The claim follows immediately from Lemma 2 and the union bound.

4   Distributed Compression

Lemma 4 is the single-serving variant of the famous *Slepian-Wolf compression* [SW73]. The proof is very similar to the proof in [Cov75]. In cryptography, it can be used for so-called *information reconciliation* [BS94]. Unfortunately, the decoding in our schemes is generally not computationally efficient.

Lemma 4 (Single-serving Slepian-Wolf compression). *Let $\varepsilon > 0$, $\varepsilon' \geq 0$, and let X, Y, and Z be random variables over $\mathcal{X}$, $\mathcal{Y}$, and $\mathcal{Z}$, respectively. Let* encx $: \mathcal{R} \times \mathcal{X} \to \{0,1\}^m$ *and* ency $: \mathcal{S} \times \mathcal{Y} \to \{0,1\}^n$ *be two-universal hash functions, where*

$$m \geq H_{\max}^{\varepsilon'}(X \mid YZ) + \log(1/\varepsilon) \ ,$$
$$n \geq H_{\max}^{\varepsilon'}(Y \mid XZ) + \log(1/\varepsilon) \ ,$$
$$m + n \geq H_{\max}^{\varepsilon'}(XY \mid Z) + \log(1/\varepsilon) \ ,$$

and let (R, S) be uniform over $\mathcal{R} \times \mathcal{S}$. There exists a function dec $: \mathcal{R} \times \mathcal{S} \times \{0,1\}^m \times \{0,1\}^n \times \mathcal{Z} \to \mathcal{X} \times \mathcal{Y}$, *such that*

$$\Pr[\text{dec}(R, S, \text{encx}(R, X), \text{ency}(S, Y), Z) \neq (X, Y)] \leq 3(\varepsilon + \varepsilon') \ .$$

Proof. Assume first that $\varepsilon' = 0$. Every $x \in \mathcal{X}$ is mapped to any value $e_x \in \{0,1\}^m$ with probability 2^{-m}, and every $y \in \mathcal{Y}$ is mapped to any value $e_y \in \{0,1\}^n$ with probability 2^{-n}. Given a pair (x, y), the corresponding encoding (e_x, e_y) can be decoded if there does not exist another pair (x', y') which is mapped to the same encoding (e_x, e_y), too. For every y, there are at most $2^{H_{\max}(X|YZ)}$ different possible values for x'. Hence, the probability that there exists $x' \neq x$ such that (x', y) is mapped to the pair (e_x, e_y) is at most $2^{-m} \cdot 2^{H_{\max}(X|YZ)} \leq \varepsilon$. Similarly, the probability that there exists $y' \neq y$ such that (x, y') is mapped to the pair (e_x, e_y) is at most $2^{-n} \cdot 2^{H_{\max}(Y|XZ)} \leq \varepsilon$. The probability that a pair (x', y') with $x' \neq x$ and $y' \neq y$ is mapped to (e_x, e_y) is at most $2^{-(m+n)} \cdot 2^{H_{\max}(XY|Z)} \leq \varepsilon$. By the union bound, we get an error of at most 3ε. For $\varepsilon' > 0$, the claim follows by the union bound.

5   Distributed One-Way Secret Key Agreement

In this section, we put together the previous results in order to derive our main claims. Basically, our protocol for key agreement follows the same steps as "usual" one-way key agreement, namely information reconciliation followed by privacy amplification. The difference is that we now use the distributed versions of these tools.

For the following, let X, Y, W, and Z be random variables known to the parties Alice, Bob, and Carol, as well as to the adversary, Eve, respectively. In a *(one way) key agreement protocol*, Alice and Bob both send messages, A and B, respectively, to Carol. Then, Alice and Bob compute keys $K_A \in \{0,1\}^{k_A}$ and $K_B \in \{0,1\}^{k_B}$ of length k_A and k_B, respectively. The protocol is said to be

ε-secure if Carol can guess the pair (K_A, K_B) with probability at least $1 - \varepsilon$, given her information (W, A, B) and, in addition, the pair (K_A, K_B) is ε-close to uniform with respect to Eve's information (Z, A, B).

Theorem 1. *Let X, Y, W, and Z be random variables, and let $\varepsilon > 0$, $\varepsilon' \geq 0$. For any k_A, k_B satisfying*

$$k_A \leq H_{\min}^{\varepsilon'}(X \mid Z) - m - 5\log(1/\varepsilon) \ ,$$
$$k_B \leq H_{\min}^{\varepsilon'}(Y \mid Z) - m - 5\log(1/\varepsilon) \ ,$$
$$k_A + k_B \leq H_{\min}^{\varepsilon'}(XY \mid Z) - m - 5\log(1/\varepsilon)$$

where

$$m = \max(H_{\max}^{\varepsilon'}(X \mid YW) + H_{\max}^{\varepsilon'}(Y \mid XW), H_{\max}^{\varepsilon'}(XY \mid W)) \ ,$$

there exists a $(4\varepsilon + 3\varepsilon')$-secure key agreement protocol generating keys of length k_A and k_B.

Proof. Lemma 4 implies that Carol can decode X and Y with an error probability of at most $3(\varepsilon + \varepsilon')$ if Alice sends a hash value A of length a, and Bob sends a hash value B of length b, where

$$a \geq H_{\max}^{\varepsilon'}(X \mid YW) + \log(1/\varepsilon)$$
$$b \geq H_{\max}^{\varepsilon'}(Y \mid XW) + \log(1/\varepsilon)$$
$$a + b \geq H_{\max}^{\varepsilon'}(XY \mid W) + \log(1/\varepsilon) \ .$$

(Note that Alice and Bob additionally need to send the uniform randomness used for the hashing to Carol. However, for the secrecy considerations below, we can ignore it as it is independent of the rest.) It is easy to see that a and b can always be chosen such that

$$a + b = \max(H_{\max}^{\varepsilon'}(X \mid YW) + H_{\max}^{\varepsilon'}(Y \mid XW), H_{\max}^{\varepsilon'}(XY \mid W)) + 2\log(1/\varepsilon) \ .$$

The chain rule (6) yields a bound on the amount of uncertainty Eve has over X and Y,

$$H_{\min}^{\varepsilon+\varepsilon'}(X \mid ABZ) \geq H_{\min}^{\varepsilon'}(X \mid Z) - a - b - \log(1/\varepsilon)$$
$$H_{\min}^{\varepsilon+\varepsilon'}(Y \mid ABZ) \geq H_{\min}^{\varepsilon'}(Y \mid Z) - a - b - \log(1/\varepsilon)$$
$$H_{\min}^{\varepsilon+\varepsilon'}(XY \mid ABZ) \geq H_{\min}^{\varepsilon'}(XY \mid Z) - a - b - \log(1/\varepsilon) \ .$$

Now, using two-universal hashing, Alice extracts a key K_A of length k_A from X, and Bob extracts a key K_B of length k_B from Y. (Again, they use additional randomness which they send to Carol as well.) With the choice

$$k_A \leq H_{\min}^{\varepsilon+\varepsilon'}(X \mid ABZ) - 2\log(1/\varepsilon)$$
$$k_B \leq H_{\min}^{\varepsilon+\varepsilon'}(Y \mid ABZ) - 2\log(1/\varepsilon)$$
$$k_A + k_B \leq H_{\min}^{\varepsilon+\varepsilon'}(XY \mid ABZ) - 2\log(1/\varepsilon) \ .$$

Lemma 3 guarantees that (K_A, K_B) is $(4\varepsilon + 3\varepsilon')$-close to uniform with respect to the information held by Eve.

As in two-party key-agreement, the length of the keys that can be generated might be increased if Alice and Bob pre-process their values as follows. Given X and Y, Alice and Bob generate new pairs (U_A, V_A) and (U_B, V_B), respectively, according to certain conditional distributions $P_{U_A V_A|X}$ and $P_{U_B V_B|Y}$. Then they send V_A and V_B to Carol and apply the key agreement protocol described above to U_A and U_B instead of X and Y. Carol now has (W, V_A, V_B), and Eve (Z, V_A, V_B). Applying Theorem 1 to this situation, we get the following statement.

Corollary 1. *Let X, Y, W, and Z be random variables, and let $\varepsilon > 0$, $\varepsilon' \geq 0$. For any k_A, k_B such that there exist conditional probability distributions $P_{U_A V_A|X}$ and $P_{U_B V_B|Y}$ satisfying*

$$k_A \leq H_{\min}^{\varepsilon'}(U_A \mid ZV_AV_B) - m - 5\log(1/\varepsilon) ,$$
$$k_B \leq H_{\min}^{\varepsilon'}(U_B \mid ZV_AV_B) - m - 5\log(1/\varepsilon) ,$$
$$k_A + k_B \leq H_{\min}^{\varepsilon'}(U_AU_B \mid ZV_AV_B) - m - 5\log(1/\varepsilon) ,$$

where

$$m = \max\big(H_{\max}^{\varepsilon'}(U_A \mid U_BWV_AV_B) + H_{\max}^{\varepsilon'}(U_B \mid U_AWV_AV_B),$$
$$H_{\max}^{\varepsilon'}(U_AU_B \mid WV_AV_B)\big) ,$$

there exists a $(4\varepsilon + 3\varepsilon')$-secure key agreement protocol generating keys of length k_A and k_B.

We will now show that Corollary 1 is almost optimal.

Theorem 2. *Let X, Y, W, and Z be random variables, and let $\varepsilon > 0$. If there exists an ε-secure key agreement protocol generating keys of length k_A and k_B then there exist conditional probability distributions $P_{U_A V_A|X}$ and $P_{U_B V_B|Y}$ such that*

$$k_A \leq H_{\min}^{\varepsilon}(U_A \mid ZV_AV_B) - m ,$$
$$k_B \leq H_{\min}^{\varepsilon}(U_B \mid ZV_AV_B) - m ,$$
$$k_A + k_B \leq H_{\min}^{\varepsilon}(U_AU_B \mid ZV_AV_B) - m ,$$

where

$$m = \max\big(H_{\max}^{\varepsilon}(U_A \mid U_BWV_AV_B) + H_{\max}^{\varepsilon}(U_B \mid U_AWV_AV_B),$$
$$H_{\max}^{\varepsilon}(U_AU_B \mid WV_AV_B)\big) .$$

Proof. (Sketch) Let us assume that we have a protocol, where Alice receives the key K_A, and Bob the key K_B. Furthermore, let M_A and M_B be the messages sent by Alice and Bob to Carol.

Since Carol can calculate K_A and K_B with an error of at most ε, we have $H_{\max}^\varepsilon(K_A \mid K_B W M_A M_B) = 0$, $H_{\max}^\varepsilon(K_B \mid K_A W M_A M_B) = 0$, and $H_{\max}^\varepsilon(K_A K_B \mid W M_A M_B) = 0$. Since (K_A, K_B) is ε-close to uniform with respect to (Z, M_A, M_B), we also have $H_{\min}^\varepsilon(K_A \mid Z, M_A, M_B) \geq k_A$, $H_{\min}^\varepsilon(K_B \mid Z, M_A, M_B) \geq k_B$, and $H_{\min}^\varepsilon(K_A K_B \mid Z, M_A, M_B) \geq k_A + k_B$. The statement follows now for $(U_A, V_A) := (K_A, M_A)$, and $(U_B, V_B) := (K_B, M_B)$.

References

[AC93]   Ahlswede, R., Csiszár, I.: Common randomness in information theory and cryptography – part I: Secret sharing. IEEE Transactions on Information Theory 39(4), 1121–1132 (1993)

[BBCM95]   Bennett, C.H., Brassard, G., Crépeau, C., Maurer, U.: Generalized privacy amplification. IEEE Transactions on Information Theory 41(6), 1915–1923 (1995)

[BBR88]   Bennett, C.H., Brassard, G., Robert, J.-M.: Privacy amplification by public discussion. SIAM Journal on Computing 17(2), 210–229 (1988)

[BS94]   Brassard, G., Salvail, L.: Secret-key reconciliation by public discussion. In: Helleseth, T. (ed.) EUROCRYPT 1993. LNCS, vol. 765, pp. 410–423. Springer, Heidelberg (1994)

[Cac97]   Cachin, C.: Entropy Measures and Unconditional Security in Cryptography. PhD thesis, ETH Zurich, Switzerland (1997)

[CK78]   Csiszár, I., Körner, J.: Broadcast channels with confidential messages. IEEE Transactions on Information Theory 24, 339–348 (1978)

[CN04]   Csiszár, I., Narayan, P.: Secrecy capacities for multiple terminals. IEEE Transactions on Information Theory 50(12), 3047–3061 (2004)

[Cov75]   Cover, T.: A proof of the data compression theorem of Slepian and Wolf for ergodic sources. IEEE Transactions on Information Theory 21, 226–228 (1975)

[CW79]   Carter, J.L., Wegman, M.N.: Universal classes of hash functions. Journal of Computer and System Sciences 18, 143–154 (1979)

[DRS04]   Dodis, Y., Reyzin, L., Smith, A.: Fuzzy extractors: How to generate strong keys from biometrics and other noisy data. In: Cachin, C., Camenisch, J.L. (eds.) EUROCRYPT 2004. LNCS, vol. 3027, pp. 523–540. Springer, Heidelberg (2004)

[ILL89]   Impagliazzo, R., Levin, L.A., Luby, M.: Pseudo-random generation from one-way functions. In: Proceedings of the 21st Annual ACM Symposium on Theory of Computing (STOC 1989), pp. 12–24. ACM Press, New York (1989)

[Mau93]   Maurer, U.: Secret key agreement by public discussion. IEEE Transaction on Information Theory 39(3), 733–742 (1993)

[MKM03]   Muramatsu, J., Koga, H., Mukouchi, T.: On the problem of generating mutually independent random sequences. IEICE Transactions on Fundamentals of Electronics, Communications and Computer Sciences 86(5), 1275–1284 (2003)

[MW97]   Maurer, U., Wolf, S.: Privacy amplification secure against active adversaries. In: Kaliski Jr., B.S. (ed.) CRYPTO 1997. LNCS, vol. 1294, pp. 307–321. Springer, Heidelberg (1997)

[Ren05]   Renner, R.: Security of Quantum Key Distribution. PhD thesis, ETH
           Zurich, Switzerland (2005), http://arxiv.org/abs/quant-ph/0512258
[RW05]   Renner, R., Wolf, S.: Simple and tight bounds for information reconcil-
           iation and privacy amplification. In: Roy, B. (ed.) ASIACRYPT 2005.
           LNCS, vol. 3788, pp. 199–216. Springer, Heidelberg (2005)
[RWW06]   Renner, R., Wolf, S., Wullschleger, J.: The single-serving channel capac-
           ity. In: Proceedings of the IEEE International Symposium on Information
           Theory, ISIT 2006 (2006)
[Sha48]   Shannon, C.E.: A mathematical theory of communication. Bell System
           Tech. Journal 27, 379–423, 623–656 (1948)
[SW73]   Slepian, D., Wolf, J.K.: Noiseless coding of correlated information sources.
           IEEE Transactions on Information Theory IT-19, 471–480 (1973)
[Wul07]   Wullschleger, J.: Oblivious-transfer amplification. In: Naor, M. (ed.) EU-
           ROCRYPT 2007. LNCS, vol. 4515, pp. 555–572. Springer, Heidelberg
           (2007)

Improvement of Collusion Secure Convolutional Fingerprinting Information Codes*

Joan Tomàs-Buliart[1], Marcel Fernandez[1], and Miguel Soriano[1,2]

[1] Department of Telematics Engineering, Universitat Politècnica de Catalunya,
C/ Jordi Girona 1 i 3, Campus Nord, Mod C3, UPC. 08034 Barcelona, Spain
[2] CTTC: Centre Tecnològic de Telecomunicacions de Catalunya
Parc Mediterrani de la Tecnologia (PMT), Av. Canal Olímpic S/N,
08860 - Castelldefels, Barcelona, Spain
{jtomas,marcel,soriano}@entel.upc.edu

Abstract. This paper presents, analyzes and improves the false positive problem detected in Convolutional Fingerprinting Information Codes presented by Zhu *et al.* The codes are a concatenation of a convolutional code and a Boneh-Shaw code. In their paper Zhu *et al.* present a code construction that is not necessarily c-secure with ϵ-error because in their modified detection algorithm the standard Viterbi error probability analysis cannot be directly applied. In this case we show that false positives appear, that is to say, the problem of accusing an innocent and legal user of an illegal redistribution. In this paper, we give a bound on the probability of false positives and justify it analytically and by simulations. Moreover, some guidelines for a correct design of this family of codes is also given.

Keywords: digital fingerprinting, collusion security, tracing traitor, convolutinal code, false positive.

1 Introduction

The distribution and playback of digital images and other multimedia products is easy due to the digital nature of the content. Achieving satisfactory copyright protection has become a challenging problem for the research community. Encrypting the data only offers protection as long as the data remains encrypted, since once an authorized but fraudulent user decrypts it, nothing stops him from redistributing the data without having to worry about being caught.

The concept of fingerprinting was introduced by Wagner in [1] as a method to protect intellectual property in multimedia contents. The fingerprinting technique consists in making the copies of a digital object unique by embedding a different set of marks in each copy. Having unique copies of an object clearly

---

* This work has been supported partially by the Spanish Research Council (CICYT) Project TSI2005-07293-C02-01 (SECONNET), by the Spanish Ministry of Science and Education with CONSOLIDER CSD2007-00004 (ARES) and by Generalitat de Catalunya with the grant 2005 SGR 01015 to consolidated research groups.

Y. Desmedt (Ed.): ICITS 2007, LNCS 4883, pp. 76–88, 2009.

rules out plain redistribution, but still a coalition of dishonest users can collude. A collusion attack consist in comparing the copies of the coalition members and by changing the marks where their copies differ, they create a pirate copy that tries to disguise their identities. In this situation they can also frame an innocent user. Thus, the fingerprinting problem consists in finding, for each copy of the object, the right set of marks that help to prevent collusion attacks.

The construction of collusion secure codes was first addressed in [2]. In that paper, Boneh and Shaw obtain $(c > 1)$-secure codes, which are capable of identifying a guilty user in a coalition of c users over N with a probability ϵ of failing. The construction composes an inner binary code with an outer random code. Therefore, the identification algorithm involves decoding of a random code, that is known to be a NP-hard problem [3].

The Collusion Secure Convolutional Fingerprinting Information Codes presented in [4] have shorter information encoding length and achieve optimal traitor searching in larger number of buyers. Unfortunately, these codes suffer from an important drawback in the form of false positives, in other words, they can frame an innocent user with high probability. In this paper we analyse in depth the work in [4] and quantify the probability of false positives.

The paper is organized as follows. In Section 2 we provide some definitions on fingerprinting and error correcting codes. Section 3 presents the well known Boneh-Shaw fingerprinting codes. Section 4 discusses the Collusion Secure Convolutional Fingerprinting Information Codes presented by Zhu *et al.* and carefully explains the encoding and decoding mechanisms. In Section 5 we deal with the false positive problem and give a bound on the false positive probability. Some guidelines for the correct construction of this family of codes with low false positive probability are presented in Section 6. Finally, some conclusions are given in Section 7.

2   Definitions

We begin by defining some concepts which will be needed throughout this paper.

Definition 1. *(Error Correcting Code) A set C of N words of length L over an alphabet of p letters is said to be an $(L, N, D)_p$-Error-Correcting Code or in short, an $(L, N, D)_p$-ECC, if the Hamming distance[1] between every pair of words in C is at least D.*

Other important definitions needed below are:

Definition 2. *(Convolutional Code) A convolutional code is a type of error-correcting code in which each k-bit information symbol (each k-bit string) to be encoded is transformed into an n-bit symbol, where k/n is the code rate $(n \geq k)$ and the transformation is a function of the last m information symbols, where m is the constraint length of the code. Or more formally [6], an (n, k) convolutional*

---

[1] The Hamming distance $d(y; x)$ [5] between two sequences of equal length can be defined as the number of positions in which the two sequences differ.

encoder over a finite field F is a k-input n-output constant linear causal finite-state sequential circuit. And a rate k/n convolutional code C over F is the set of outputs of the sequential circuit.

An important concept in fingerprinting environments is the *Marking Assumption.*

Definition 3. *(Codebook [2]) A set $\Gamma = \{W^{(1)}, W^{(2)}, \cdots, W^{(n)}\} \subseteq \Sigma^l$, where Σ^l will denote some alphabet of size s, will be called an $l(l, n)$-code. The codeword $w^{(i)}$ will be assigned to user u_i, for $1 \leq i \leq n$. We refer to the set of words in Γ as the* **codebook***.*

Definition 4. *(Undetectable Position) Let $\Gamma = \{W^{(1)}, W^{(2)}, \cdots, W^{(n)}\}$ is an (l,n)-code and $C = \{u_1, u_2, \cdots, u_c\}$ is a coalition of c-traitors. Let position i be* **undetectable** *for C, i.e. the words assigned to users in C match in i'th position, that is $w_i^{(u_1)} = \cdots = w_i^{(u_c)}$.*

Definition 5. *(Feasible set) Let $\Gamma = \{W^{(1)}, W^{(2)}, \cdots, W^{(n)}\}$ is an (l,n)-code and $C = \{u_1, u_2, \cdots, u_c\}$ is a coalition of c-traitors. We define the* **feasible set** *Γ of C as*

$$\Gamma(C) = \{x = (x_1, \cdots, x_l) \in \Sigma^l \mid x_j \in w_j, 1 \leq j \leq l\}$$

where

$$w_j = \begin{cases} \{w_j^{(u_1)}\} & w_j^{(u_1)} = \cdots = w_j^{(u_c)} \\ \{w_j^{(u_i)} \mid 1 \leq i \leq c\} \cup \{?\} & otherwise \end{cases}$$

where ? denotes an erased position.

Now we are in position to define the *Marking Assumption* that establishes the rules that the attacking coalition are subjected to. This definition sets the work environment of many actual fingerprinting systems.

Definition 6. *(Marking Assumption) Let $\Gamma = \{W^{(1)}, W^{(2)}, \cdots, W^{(n)}\}$ be an (l,n)-code, $C = \{u_1, u_2, \cdots, u_c\}$ a coalition of c-traitors and $\Gamma(C)$ the feasible set of C. The coalition C is only capable of creating an object whose fingerprinting lies in $\Gamma(C)$.*

The main idea of this definition is that a coalition of c-traitors can not detect the positions in the document in which their mark holds the same value. Many of the fingerprinting schemes in the literature base their tracing algorithms in trying to estimated the positions that are changed by the attackers.

As example, a (3,4)-code can be defined as:

Positions: 1 2 3
$A : 1\ 1\ 1$
$B : 0\ 1\ 1$
$C : 0\ 0\ 1$
$D : 0\ 0\ 0$

Suppose that users B and C collude, for this collusion the positions 1 and 3 will be **undetectable positions**. And the **Feasible set** for this collusion will be:

$$0\ 1\ 1$$
$$0\ ?\ 1$$
$$0\ 0\ 1$$

And, taking into account the marking assumption, the coluders are only capable of creating an object whose fingerprinting lies in this set of words. Note that, as well as putting one of their value in the position 2, they can erase this position which is represented by?.

3   Boneh-Shaw Fingerprinting Model

In 1995, Dan Boneh and James Shaw presented in [2] a seminal paper about the collusion secure fingerprinting problem. First of all, we need to define what is a fingerprinting scheme.

Definition 7. *(Fingerprinting scheme [2,4]) An (l, n)-fingerprinting scheme is a function $\Gamma(u, r)$ which maps a user identifier $1 \geq u \geq n$ and a string of random bits $r \in \{0, 1\}^*$ to a codeword Σ^l. The random string r is the set of random bits used by the distributor and kept hidden from the user. We denote a fingerprinting scheme by Γ_r.*

3.1   c-Secure Codes

We now define c-secure codes, see [2] for a more detailed description.

Definition 8. *A fingerprinting scheme Γ_r is a c-secure code with ϵ-error if there exists a tracing algorithm A which from a word x, that has been generated by a coalition C of at most c users, satisfies the following condition $Pr[A(x) \in C] > 1 - \epsilon$ where the probability is taken over random choices made by the coalition.*

Now, we define the code and its decoding algorithm:

1. Construct an n-secure (l, n)-code with length $l = n^{O(1)}$.
2. Construct an $\Gamma_0(n, d)$-fingerprinting scheme by replicating each column of an (l, n)-code d times. For example, suppose a $(3, 4)$-code $\{111,011,001,000\}$. We can construct a $\Gamma_0(4, 3)$ for four users A,B,C and D as follows:

$$A : 111111111$$
$$B : 000111111$$
$$C : 000000111$$
$$D : 000000000$$

3. When the code has been defined, the next step is to define the appropriate decoding algorithm. For instance

Algorithm 1. *From [2], given $x \in \{0,1\}^l$, find a subset of the coalition that produced x. Note that B_m is the set of all bit positions in which the column m is replicated, $R_m = B_{m-1} \cup B_m$ and weight denotes the number of bits that are set to 1.*
(a) If weight $(x \mid B_1) > 0$ then output "User 1 is guilty"
(b) If weight $(x \mid B_{n-1}) < d$ then output "User n is guilty"
(c) For all $s = 2$ to $n - 1$ do:
Let $k = weight\ (x \mid R_s)$. if

$$weight(x \mid B_{s-1}) < \frac{k}{2} - \sqrt{\frac{k}{2}log\frac{2n}{\epsilon}}$$

then output "User s is guilty"

Finally, the only thing left is to find a relationship between the error ϵ and the replication factor d. This relation is given in the next theorem,

Theorem 1. *For $n \geq 3$ and $\epsilon > 0$ let $d = 2n^2 log(2n/\epsilon)$. The fingerprinting scheme $\Gamma_0(n, d)$ is n-secure with ϵ-error and has length $d(n-1) = O(n^3 log(n/\epsilon))$.*

4   Collusion Secure Convolutional Fingerprinting Information Codes

In [4], Yan Zhu *et al.* presented a fingerprinting scheme with the aim of obtaining a c-secure with ϵ-error fingerprinting schemes for N-users that improve BS in run-time and storage capacity. Mainly, their scheme composes an inner Boneh-Shaw code with an outer Convolutional code. In the decoding process, they propose a modified Viterbi algorithm that works with more than one symbol in each step or 'Optional Code Subset' as the authors term it. In the next subsections we explain in detail the original workflow of this scheme.

4.1   Convolutional Fingerprinting Encoding

The fingerprinting code presented in [4] has a two-layer concatenated structure (the Convolutional Error-Correcting Layer and the Fingerprinting Layer) and we denote it as $\Phi(L, N, l, n)$-Fingerprinting code where N is the number of users, L is the convolutional code length and l and n are the parameters of an $\Gamma(l, n)$ code. The encoding process of a $\Phi(L, N, l, n)$-fingerprinting code consists in the following 3 steps:

1. A codeword $m^{(u_i)}$ of length N is randomly assigned to each user u_i.
2. **Convolutional error-correcting layer encoding:** The codeword $m^{(u_i)}$, divided into blocks of k_0 bits, is used as input to a (n_0, k_0, m_0)-Convolutional encoder
3. **Fingerprinting layer encoding:** Each group of n_0 output bits is mapped to a $\Gamma(l, n)$-code.

To construct a $\Phi(L, N, l, n)$-code we need two codes. The first code must be a c-secure code with ϵ-error. For this purpose, the authors use the Boneh-Shaw $\Gamma_0(n, d)$ code [2].

As it has been discussed before, this code consist of all columns $(c_1, c_2, \cdots, c_{n-1})$ each duplicated d times. The value of c_i can be expressed as:

$$c_i = \begin{cases} 1 \; \text{if input } x \geq i \\ 0 \;\; otherwise \end{cases}$$

For example, when the input is 1 all c_i take the binary value 1, and when the input is n all c_i take the binary value 0. The value of d depends on ϵ as is shown in Theorem 1.

The other code that we need for an implementation of the Convolutional Fingerprinting Scheme is a $\Im(n_0, k_0, m_0)$-Convolutional code. The only requirement that the code $\Im(n_0, k_0, m_0)$ must satisfy is that $n \geq 2^{k_0 m_0}$, in other words, the number of symbols in the alphabet of the code $\Im(n_0, k_0, m_0)$ must not be larger than the number of symbols in the alphabet of code $\Gamma_0(n, d)$.

Algorithm 2 presents the encoding process. Finally, the result of this process must be randomly permuted by a permutation denoted by π. The result of this permutation is embedded into the original document to obtain a copy of this document customized for user u_i.

Algorithm 2. *From [4], Fingerprinting-Information-Encoding (original-document X, message $m^{(u_i)}$, permutation π)*

Let $v = Convolutional\text{-}Encoding(m^{(u_i)}, i)$
For each $1 \leq k \leq L$
  $w^{(v_k)} = Fingerprinting\text{-}Encoding(v_k)$
Let $W^{(v)} = \pi(W^{(v_1)} \parallel W^{(v_2)} \parallel \cdots \parallel W^{(v_L)} \parallel)$
Embed $W^{(v)}$ into document X to obtain $X^{(u_i)}$
Return marked copy $X^{(u_i)}$

End

4.2 Convolutional Fingerprinting Decoding

The main objective of fingerprinting decoding is to obtain a tracing algorithm that can retrieve with a very low error probability a group of traitors that created an illegal document. Of course, this group of traitors should not contain an innocent user, at least with high probability.

First of all, the fingerprinting layer is decoded using algorithm 1. As a result of this, an 'Optional Code Set' is retrieved from each position. An 'Optional Code Set' is the set of codewords from an $(L, N, D)_p$-ECC that must collude to obtain a pirate codeword.

In this way, in [4] the Viterbi algorithm has been modified by using as input an 'Optional Code Set' from the fingerprinting layer decoder output instead of a corrupted codeword for each state. This modification is shown in algorithm 3. In the classic implementation of the Viterbi algorithm, the decoder receives from the channel a set $R = (r_1, r_2, \cdots, r_L)$ where each r_i is a codeword of an ECC that contains errors. Now the decoder receives, from the Fingerprinting Layer, a set $R = (r_1, r_2, \cdots, r_L)$ where each r_i is a set of all suspicious codewords of an ECC, i.e. $r_i = \{r_{i,1}, r_{i,2}, \cdots, r_{i,t}\}$ where $t \in N$.

Algorithm 3. *From [4], Convolutional-Fingerprinting-Decoding (suspect-document Y, original-document X)*

> *Let $d_{0,i} = \infty$, $sp_{0,i} = \{\}$ for $(1 \leq k \leq n)$ except $d_{0,1} = 0$*
> *Let $W = \pi^{-1}(X)$*
> *For each $1 \leq k \leq L$*
> > *Let $r_k = $ Fingerprinting-Layer-Decoding (Y_k, X_k)*
> > *For each state s_j*
> > > *For each the incoming branch $e_{i,j}$*
> > > > *For each the element $r_{k,l} \in r_k$ $(1 \leq l \leq m)$*
> > > > > $c_{k,l} = D(r_{k,l} \mid e_{i,j})$
> > > > *Let $sq_{i,j} = (sp_{k,i}, e_{i,j})$, $t_{i,j} = d_{k-1,i} + min_{1 \leq l \leq m} c_{k,l}$*
> > > *Let $d_{k,j} = min_i(t_{i,j})$ for exist $e_{i,j}$*
> > > *Let $sp_{k,j} = sq_{l,j}$ for all $d_{k,j} == t_{l,j}$*
> *Let $d_{L,l} = min_{1 \leq j \leq n}(d_{L,j})$*
> *Return $M(sp_{L,l})$*

End

Maximum-likelihood (ML) decoding is modified to keep, for each state, the path that has minimum Hamming distance for each codeword in 'Optional Code Set'. For example, suppose that in the j-th step the fingerprinting layer retrieves as fraudulent binary codewords $r_j = \{1011, 0011\}$. Suppose that at the entry to state S_1 there exist two input path, one from state S_1 and other from S_2 labelled as $P1 = 0000, P2 = 1111$ and represented in the algorithm by $e_{1,1} = 0000$ and $e_{2,1} = 0000$. The next step will be to calculate the Hamming distance between the values in r_j (there are $r_{j,1} = 1011$ and $r_{j,2} = 0011$) and the values of $e_{1,1}$ and $e_{2,1}$. The paths that arrives to state S_1 in step j are stored in $sq_{i,j}$ and the associated total costs are stored in $t_{i,j}$. The next step in the algorithm is to search in the array $t_{i,j}$ the minimum value and this value is stored in $d_{k,j}$ as minimum distance in order to arrive to step j at state S_1. Finally, all path that arrive to state S_1 at step j with an associated cost equal to $d_{k,j}$ are stored in $sp_{k,j}$. The algorithm keeps as the ML path $P2$, with input codeword being 1011.

5   A New Critical Performance Analysis

In [4] two theorems were presented. These theorems are briefly detailed in this section with examples of their drawbacks. Some desirable characteristics to be added will be explained in depth throughout the next sections.

Theorem 2. *The survivor path is the maximum likelihood path in the improved Viterbi decoding algorithm 3, namely, there exist a survivor path sp for all candidate paths $sq \neq sp$, $D(R \mid sp) \geq D(R \mid sq)$.*

Let $SC(R)$ be the set of all possible combinations of suspicious codewords retrieved in each step by the Fingerprinting Layer, or more formally,

$$SC(R) = \{x = (x_1, x_2, \cdots, x_L) \mid x_j \in r_j, 1 \geq j \geq \#(r_j)\}$$

where r_j is the set of suspicious codeword retrieved by Fingerprinting Layer for the jth position in R. According to algorithm 3 the entry to each step consists in codewords. This idea can be seen as processing each element of $SC(R)$ with a classical Viterbi algorithm. If the fingerprinting decoding process is correct, this system will find at most c combinations all of which have zero Hamming distance with a path in the trellis diagram (2). The main problem is that Theorem 2 does not guarantee that only these c combinations are the ones to have zero Hamming distance with a path in the trellis diagram.

For example, suppose that, at random, we assign to users u_1 and u_2 the identification information $M_1 = \{0110100\}$ and $M_2 = \{1010000\}$ respectively, where the last two bits are the ending symbol for a Convolutional encoder with two memory positions. If the diagram state of [4] shown in the following figure 1 is used as (2,1,2)-Convolutional encoder, the codified symbols are $R^{(1)} = (00, 11, 01, 01, 00, 10, 11)$ and $R^{(2)} = (11, 10, 00, 10, 11, 00, 00)$.

The next step must be to encode $R^{(1)}$ and $R^{(2)}$ with well constructed Fingerprinting Layer, in other words, with an appropriate value of d that is robust against a coalition of two users over an alphabet of four words. After a random collusion attack of users u_1 and u_2, the resultant copy must contain a mark that the Fingerprinting Layer can retrieve

$$R' = (\{00, 11\}, \{11, 10\}, \{01, 00\}, \{01, 10\}, \{00, 11\}, \{10, 00\}, \{11, 00\})$$

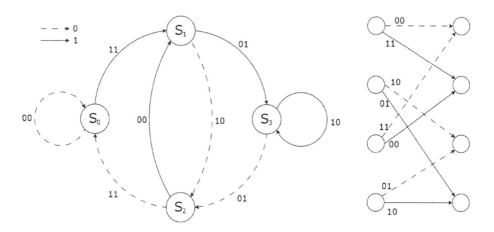

Fig. 1. State diagram for (2,1,2) Convolutional code

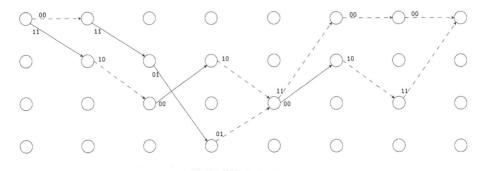

Fig. 2. Paths in a trellis diagram corresponding to two colluders that can create false positives

If algorithm 3 is applied to R', the trellis structure of Figure 2 is obtained. From this structure, the algorithm 3 retrieves as illegal users the ones with identification $M_1 = \{0110100\}$, $M_2 = \{1010000\}$, $M_3 = \{0110000\}$ and $M_4 = \{1010100\}$. And, in this case, users u_3 and u_4 have not done any illegal action.

Note that now is obvious that enforcing a false positive bound is necessary to design an appropriate coding scheme. Note that the problem lies in the Convolutional Error-Correcting layer not in the fingerprinting layer. In other words, we need tools to choose a correct Convolutional code for each application requirement.

Theorem 3. *Given integers N,c and $\epsilon > 0$, set $n = 2c$, $d = 2n^2(log(8n) + r)$, $r = (2/d_f)log(A_{d_f}/\epsilon)$, where d_f (free distance) is the minimum distance between any two code words in the convolutional code, A_{d_f} is the number of code words with weight d_f. Then the convolutional fingerprinting code $\Phi(L, N, l, n)$ is a code which is c-secure with ϵ-error. The code contains N codewords. Let x be a word which was produced by a coalition C of at most c users. Then algorithm 3 will output a codeword of C with probability at least 1-ϵ.*

The authors in [4] prove theorem 3, assuming the well know error probability P_e of Viterbi decoders in BSC channels (for references in error probability of Viterbi decoders in BSC channels [7,8,9]). The basic problem lies in the fact that a set C_1 is obtained as output of this algorithm and really, C_1 contains a codeword of C with probability at least 1-ϵ but can also contain other codewords that are not contained in C. For example, suppose that we can define $SC(R')$ with 128 possible codewords. Imagine that we take alternatively one symbol of each original codeword $R^{(3)} = (11, 11, 00, 01, 11, 10, 00)$. In this case, we can consider that channel error probability is close to 0,28 because 4 errors have occurred over the 14 bits transmitted (suppose that we are comparing to $R^{(1)}$).

5.1 False Positive Probability

It has been shown above, that a Convolutional Fingerprinting Information code exists with a non negligible false positive probability. Our approximation only takes into account the probability that a false positive can be generated when two paths have one common state in a single step i. First of all we can suppose that we have a system such as in all of the trellis states there are two input arcs and two output arcs as in Figure 1. On the other hand, we can suppose that there exist two colluders. Let $P(S_i^{u_1} = S_i^{u_2} = s)$ be the probability that the state of the associated path to user u_1 in step i is s and it is the same that the associated path to user u_2. This probability can be expressed formally as:

$$P(S_i^{u_1} = S_i^{u_2} = s) = P(S_{i-1}^{u_1} = s_n \cap X_i^{u_1} = x^{u_1})$$

$$+ P(S_{i-1}^{u_2} = s_m \cap X_i^{u_2} = x^{u_2}) = \frac{1}{S^2 2^2} + \frac{1}{S^2 2^2} = \frac{1}{S^2 2} \tag{1}$$

This expression can be generalized for c colluders, a trellis with a input arcs for each state and 2^k input symbols as:

$$P(S_i^{u_x} = S_i^{u_y} = s) = \frac{a!}{(a-2)!}\binom{c}{2}\frac{1}{S^2 2^{2k}} = \frac{ac(a-1)(c-1)}{S^2 2^{2k+1}} \tag{2}$$

The probability that two paths stay in the same state as in step i can be expressed as:

$$P_{T_i} = \sum_{j=1}^{S} P(S_i^{u_x} = S_i^{u_y} = s_j) = S\frac{ac(a-1)(c-1)}{S^2 2^{2k+1}}$$

$$= \frac{ac(a-1)(c-1)}{S 2^{2k+1}} \tag{3}$$

It is obvious that the probability that two paths do not stay in the same state is:

$$P_{NT_i} = 1 - P_{T_i} = 1 - \frac{ac(a-1)(c-1)}{S 2^{2k+1}} \tag{4}$$

And finally, taking into account the considerations presented above, the false positive probability can be approximated as:

$$P_{FP} = 1 - P_{NT_i}^{N-M-log_{a_O} S} = 1 - \left\{1 - \frac{ac(a-1)(c-1)}{S 2^{2k+1}}\right\}^{N-M-log_{a_O} S} \tag{5}$$

where P_{NT_i} is the probability that to paths do not stay in the same state, c is the number of colluders, M is the memory of convolutional encoder, N is the number of output symbols of the convolutional encoder, 2^k is the number of symbols of the input alphabet, a is the number of input arcs for each state, a_O is the number of output arcs for each state.

Note that a false positive can only be generated in the inner states, in other words, two paths which are crossed in the memory padding states or in the start states can not cause false positives. For example the state 0 is the last state for all paths.

5.2   Simulation Results

Figure 3 shows the simulation results of the behaviour of a CSCFI code with the convolutional code being the one shown in figure 1 after 5000 iterations for each number of users. The parameters of the BS code are $d = 331$, $\epsilon = 0.0001$ and $n = 4$. As we can imagine, when the number of users in the system increases, the number input bits increases and the false positive probability goes to 1.

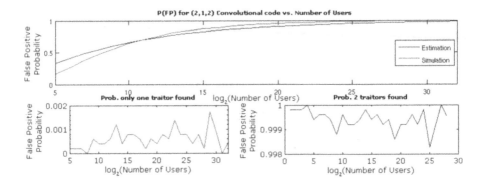

Fig. 3. False Positive Probability *vs.* Number of users

On the other hand, as figure 4 shows, when the complexity of the trellis increases (in this simulation we use Convolutional codes from table 11.1 in [7] with ratio 1/4) the false positive probability goes to 0.

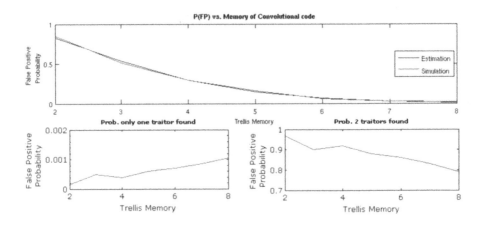

Fig. 4. False Positive Probability *vs.* Memory of Convolutional Code

6   Guidelines for Minimizing the Effect of False Positives

Basically, false positives can be caused by two reasons:

- **Decoding error in the Fingerprinting Layer:** This type of errors can be avoided by a good design of this layer. If the Boneh-Shaw Fingerprinting code is used, the parameter d will be dimensioned with an appropriate error probability. Normally, the inner code will have a low number of codewords and, for this reason, it will be easy to configure the system to obtain a very low error probability in this layer. After this, we can consider that the origin of false positives is the following item.

- **Path Crossing in the Convolutional Layer:** In [4], Zhu et. al. discuss an error probability condition. This condition has to be satisfied by equation 5. With this two conditions in mind we can design an effective Collusion Secure Convolutional Fingerprinting Information Code with ϵ-error probability. As we notice in equation 5, convolutional encoders that are used for the outer codes need a big complexity in their trellis structure in order to offer protection against Path Crossing. In the same way, Convolutional encoders with high ratios and a large number of symbols are more appropriate.

On the other hand, when a system with a complex convolutional encoder is designed, the coding and decoding time increases. This situation defines a relationship between the trellis complexity and the computational complexity. It will need to prioritize one of them.

7   Conclusions

The work presented in this paper shows a new problem in Collusion Secure Convolutional Fingerprinting Information Codes: False positives. As a result of the analysis of the work by Zhu *et al.* in [4], the drawbacks of not considering false positive have been enlightened. The original results in [4] are revisited from the point of view of the false positive problem. Moreover the probability of false positives has been quantified formally and contrasted with simulations. Finally some guidelines for a correct design of Collusion Secure Convolutional Fingerprinting Information Codes are given.

References

1. Wagner, N.R.: Fingerprinting. In: SP 1983: Proceedings of the 1983 IEEE Symposium on Security and Privacy, Washington, DC, USA, p. 18. IEEE Computer Society, Los Alamitos (1983)
2. Boneh, D., Shaw, J.: Collusion-secure fingerprinting for digital data (extended abstract). In: Coppersmith, D. (ed.) CRYPTO 1995. LNCS, vol. 963, pp. 452–465. Springer, Heidelberg (1995)

3. Barg, A., Blakley, G.R., Kabatiansky, G.A.: Digital fingerprinting codes: problem statements, constructions, identification of traitors. IEEE Transactions on Information Theory 49(4), 852–865 (2003)
4. Zhu, Y., Zou, W., Zhu, X.: Collusion secure convolutional fingerprinting information codes. In: ASIACCS 2006: Proceedings of the 2006 ACM Symposium on Information, computer and communications security, pp. 266–274. ACM Press, New York (2006)
5. Hamming, R.W.: Error detecting and error correcting codes. Bell System Techincal Journal 29, 147–160 (1950)
6. Forney Jr., G.: Convolutional codes i: Algebraic structure. IEEE Transactions on Information Theory 16(6), 720–738 (1970)
7. Lin, S., Costello Jr., D.J.: Error Control Coding: Fundamentals and Applications. Prentice-Hall, Englewood Cliffs (1983)
8. Viterbi, A.J.: CDMA: principles of spread spectrum communication. Addison Wesley Longman Publishing Co., Inc., Redwood City (1995)
9. Viterbi, A.J., Omura, J.K.: Principles of Digital Communication and Coding. McGraw-Hill, Inc., New York (1979)

On Exponential Lower Bound for Protocols for Reliable Communication in Networks

K. Srinathan[1], C. Pandu Rangan[2,*], and R. Kumaresan[3,**]

[1] Center for Security, Theory and Algorithmic Research
International Institute of Information Technology
Hyderabad India 500032
srinathan@iiit.ac.in
[2] Indian Institute of Technology
Chennai India
rangan@cs.iitm.ernet.in
[3] Dept of Computer Science
University of Maryland
ranjit@cs.umd.edu

Abstract. This work deals with the problem of fault-tolerant communication over networks, some of whose nodes are corrupted by a centralized byzantine adversary. The extant literature's perspective of the problem of reliable communication, especially in networks whose topology is known, is that of a simple problem to which even some naive solutions (like message-flooding etc.) turn out to be reasonably efficient. In this paper, we give an example of a directed graph and a non threshold adversary structure, which will require every protocol for perfect reliable unicast to transmit exponential number of bits in order to *reliably* transmit a single bit.

Keywords: Perfect Reliable Unicast; Byzantine non threshold adversary; Efficiency.

1   Introduction

The problem of perfect reliable unicast is a fundamental problem in distributed networks ([5]). It deals with information transfer between a sender and a receiver in a network without any error. The network might have some faults, either in the form of link failures or node failures, which might interfere with the functioning of a protocol trying to achieve perfect reliable unicast. In this paper we consider only node failures. The failures are modeled by means of an adversary. We consider non-threshold adaptive adversaries for our analysis. By adaptive, we mean that the adversary fixes the set to be corrupted before the execution

---

[*] Work Supported by Project No. CSE/05-06/076/DITX/CPAN on Protocols for Secure Communication and Computation, Sponsored by Department of Information Technology, Govt. of India.
[**] The work was done when the author was an under graduate student at IIT Madras.

Y. Desmedt (Ed.): ICITS 2007, LNCS 4883, pp. 89–98, 2009.

of the protocol but chooses the nodes that he would corrupt from the set as the protocol proceeds.

The extent to which these faults can affect the existence of a protocol for achieving reliable transfer is characterized in terms of graph structure in [3,4]. In this work, we study how these faults can affect the efficiency of a protocol which tries to achieve reliable communication. We have given an example of a directed graph and an adversary structure for which all protocols for reliably transmitting a single bit need to transmit exponential number of bits. This shows that reliable communication is not always feasible even if it is possible.

2   Communication Model and Known Results

The network $\mathcal{N}$ is modeled as a graph $\mathcal{G} = (V, E)$, where V denotes the node set (nodes are also known as players) and E refers to the links between the nodes. The faults in the network have been modeled as a centralized *Byzantine* adversary whose aim is to disrupt the functioning of any protocol for reliable communication to the maximum achievable level. Given below is the definition of the adversary structure ([4]), which explicitly denotes the set of sets that the adversary can corrupt.

DEFINITION. *The* **adversary structure** $\mathcal{A}_{adv}$ *is a monotone set of subsets of the player set* V. *The maximal basis of* $\mathcal{A}_{adv}$ *denoted by* $\mathcal{A}$ *is defined as the collection* $\{A | A \in \mathcal{A}_{adv}, \nexists X \in \mathcal{A}_{adv}, X \supset A\}$.

It is assumed that all the nodes in the network know the network topology as well as the adversary structure. We further assume that the adversary chooses one of the sets from $\mathcal{A}_{adv}$ for corrupting before the execution of the protocol but the protocol does not know the chosen set.

Reliable communication between the sender S and the receiver R is not always possible. The necessary and sufficient conditions for the existence of a protocol for reliable (secure) communication in this model is given by the following theorem([2]):

Theorem 1. *Perfectly secure message transmission from the sender* **S** *to the receiver* **R** *in the network* $\mathcal{N}$ *is possible if and only if for any two sets* $X, Y \in \mathcal{A}$, *the deletion of the nodes in* $X \cup Y$ *from the network does not disconnect* **S** *and* **R**.

The possibility of the protocol is shown by a construction in [2]. The protocol given, is polynomial in the number of paths from S to R. In dense graphs, such a protocol is not feasible. However this does not rule out efficient protocols in such graphs. For example, consider a graph which is $(2t+1)-(S, R)-connected$ and $\mathcal{A}$ consists of sets, all of which have cardinality t(threshold adversary). Irrespective of the number of paths in the graph, an efficient protocol exists([1]). One example of an efficient protocol would be to locate $2t+1$ disjoint paths by using a standard max-flow algorithm ([2]) and asking S to send the message along all the paths to R. Since there can be a maximum of t distorted versions of the message, the

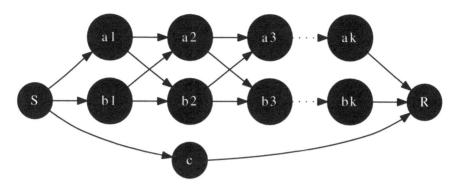

Fig. 1. An example graph where an efficient protocol for reliable communication exists

receiver obtains the original message by taking majority among the messages received along the $2t + 1$ paths.

Another example graph is presented in Fig. 1. Consider the graph $\mathcal{G}_1$ in Fig. 1. We define the adversary structure $\mathcal{A} = \{\{x_1, x_2, \ldots, x_k | x_i \in \{a_i, b_i\}\}, \{c\}\}$. Note that in the top layer, there are 2^k paths.

However, there exists an efficient protocol in this case too, as given in Fig. 2.

Protocol for reliable unicast in $\mathcal{G}_1$

1. S sends the message m to a_1, b_1 and c.
2. c forwards m to R.
   a_1 and b_1 forward m to both a_2 and b_2, if $k > 1$, else to R.
3. a_i, b_i forward m' if they receive m' from both their neighbors $\{a_{i-1}, b_{i-1}\}$ or *null* if they receive different or no messages from their neighbors.
4. R receives three messages, say m_a from a_k, m_b from b_k and m_c from c. R recovers m as follows:

$$m = \begin{cases} m_a & m_a = m_b \text{ and } m_a \neq null \\ m_c & \text{otherwise} \end{cases}.$$

Fig. 2. Protocol for the graph given in Fig. 1

Lemma 1. *The protocol given in Fig. 2 is correct.*

Proof. There are two cases to be considered.

Case 1. The adversary chooses to corrupt $\{x_1, x_2, \ldots, x_k | x_i \in \{a_i, b_i\}\}$. In this case, if there is no disruption at any stage, then $m_a = m_b = m_c$ and hence R recovers m. Suppose the first disruption of the message occurs at some layer i, x_i changes the message from m to m', then the honest player at layer $i + 1$

will get different messages and hence will forward *null*. Note that *null* will get forwarded by all the honest players through to R. On receiving *null*, R recovers m from m_c.

Case 2. The adversary chooses to corrupt c.
Since the top layer is not corrupted, $m = m_a = m_b$ and $m_a \neq null$ and R accepts m_a as the original message.   □

3   Reliable Unicast Is Not Always Efficient Whenever Possible

Consider the directed graph $\mathcal{G}$ shown in Fig. 3. The 6-tuple $\{a_i, b_i, c_i, d_i, e_i, f_i\}$ is referred to as *layer i* and the network $\mathcal{H}$ (Fig. 4) consisting of only a_i's and b_i's is referred to as the *top band* (denoted by T) and the rest is referred to as the *bottom band* (denoted by B). Specifically the notation B_i is used to represent the set $\{c_i, d_i, e_i, f_i\}$. S is connected to R through each node in B_i. In T, for $1 \leq i < k$, there is a directed edge between a_i and a_{i+1}, b_{i+1} and the same holds for b_i. The graph consists of k layers. This makes a total of 2^k paths between S and R in T. The adversary structure for $\mathcal{G}$ is introduced by presenting an instance of it. Define $\mathcal{B}_i = \{ \{a_i, c_i, d_i\}, \{b_i, c_i, e_i\}, \{a_i, e_i, f_i\}, \{b_i, d_i, f_i\} \}$ to be the adversary structure at layer i. Then the adversary structure for the graph $\mathcal{G}$ is given as $\mathcal{A} = \{ A | A = \{A_1, A_2, \ldots, A_k\}, A_i \in \mathcal{B}_i, 1 \leq i \leq k \}$.

Lemma 2. *There exist a protocol for reliable unicast between S and R in $\mathcal{G}$.*

Proof (PROOF). By Theorem 1, if the adversary could choose two sets X, Y such that $X, Y \in \mathcal{A}$ and removal of nodes belonging to $X \cup Y$ from $\mathcal{G}$ disconnect S and R, then no protocol will exist. Let $X = \{X_1, X_2, \ldots, X_k\}$ and $Y = \{Y_1, Y_2, \ldots, Y_k\}$ with $X_i, Y_i \in \mathcal{B}_i$. To disconnect S and R, adversary has to remove all the nodes in B since otherwise there will be a direct path from S to R through one of them. Hence $X_i = \{a_i, c_i, d_i\}, Y_i = \{a_i, e_i, f_i\}$ or $X_i = \{b_i, c_i, e_i\}, Y_i = \{b_i, d_i, f_i\}$ or vice versa. In all these cases $\{a_i, b_i\} - (X_i \cup Y_i) \neq \phi$. Hence, there exists a path from S to R through T and adversary can never disconnect S and R. Hence, by Theorem 1, there exist a protocol.   □

Lemma 3. *For any adversarial strategy, R can identify in polynomial time and space either*

1. *message m transmitted by S, or*
2. *the set of corrupted nodes in T.*

Proof. Consider the following protocol for reliable unicast of m. Let S send m along B to R. Let m_x^i denote the message that R obtained from node $x_i, x_i \in B_i$. Let M_i be the 4-tuple $\{m_c^i, m_d^i, m_e^i, m_f^i\}$. If all the elements of M_i are equal for some i, then R receives m. Also, if any 3 of the 4 elements are equal, R can still find out m, since there is no $A \in \mathcal{A}_{adv}$ such that $|A \cap \{c_i, d_i, e_i, f_i\}| > 2$, for $1 \leq i \leq k$. Hence corrupting less than 2 elements in each layer of the bottom band,

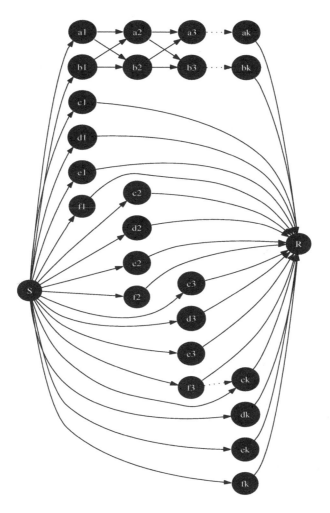

Fig. 3. The graph for which no efficient protocol exists given the adversary structure $\mathcal{A}$

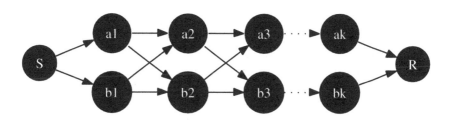

Fig. 4. Top layer of the graph given in Fig. 3. Every protocol for the reliable transmission of a bit require transmission of exponential number of bits through the network.

leads to an unsuccessful adversarial strategy. The only strategy that would not allow R to know m would be to disrupt the message from both the nodes in each B_i. This would result in a $2 - partition$ of B_i, say B_i^1 and B_i^2. Now R can learn the set of corrupt nodes in each layer of T as $\mathcal{B}_i \cap \{\{a_i, b_i\} \times B_i^1\} \cap \{\{a_i, b_i\} \times B_i^2\}$. Hence R can learn either m or the set of corrupt nodes in T after receiving one message from each of polynomial number of paths from B in a single phase. □

Lemma 4. *Atleast 1 bit must be transmitted through T for reliable unicast to be possible in $\mathcal{G}$.*

Proof. For the purpose of giving a proof by contradiction, assume that no bit is transmitted through T during a successful protocol for reliable unicast in $\mathcal{G}$. This would imply that all the messages pass only through B. Denote the subgraph induced by B on $\mathcal{G}$ as $\mathcal{G}_B$. Consider $X = \{c_i, d_i\}, Y = \{e_i, f_i\}$. Clearly $X, Y \in \mathcal{A}_{adv}$ and removal of nodes belonging to $X \cup Y$ from $\mathcal{G}$ disconnects S and R in $\mathcal{G}_B$. Hence by Theorem 1, there is no protocol for reliable unicast between S and R in $\mathcal{G}_B$. But by lemma 2, a protocol is possible in $\mathcal{G}$. Therefore, atleast 1 bit must be transmitted through T for reliable unicast to be possible in $\mathcal{G}$. □

Lemma 5. *Given that only R knows the corrupted nodes in T, there exists no polynomial protocol for reliable unicast in $\mathcal{H}$.*

Proof. The proof proceeds by induction on k. The induction hypothesis is that "R receives at least 2^{k-1} bits in every protocol for reliable unicast in $\mathcal{H}$". For purposes of clarity, m is assumed to be a single bit message. The base cases of $k = 1, 2$ have been discussed in detail.

$k = 1$: S simply sends m along both a_1 and b_1. R knows the honest player and obtains m from him. R receives 1 bit and hence this base case is true.

$k = 2$: S sends m along both a_1 and b_1. Assuming b_1 is a corrupt player, he sends to the honest player in the next layer (say b_2), whatever a_1 would send him if the message was $\bar{m}$. Player b_2 cannot distinguish between the case when a_1 is corrupt and the message is $\bar{m}$ and the case when b_1 is corrupt and the message is m. This happens because b_2 does not have information on the corrupt nodes in T. Hence b_2 must send both the possibilities to R, who is able to distinguish between the two cases. Hence b_2 sends at least 2 bits and this base case is also true.

Assuming that the induction hypothesis is true for a graph $\mathcal{H}$ with $1, 2, \ldots,$ $k - 1$ layers, the proof that the induction hypothesis remains valid when the number of layers is k is as follows. First, note that in the worst case that the adversary chooses not to send any message to R via the corrupt player at layer k. Hence a perfectly reliable unicast protocol from S to R must essentially consist of a perfectly reliable unicast protocol from S to a_k, assuming b_k is the corrupt node at the kth layer. Suppose b_{k-1} is the honest neighbor of a_k, then the strategy for a_{k-1} would be to transmit to a_k whatever b_{k-1} would transmit if the message was $\bar{m}$ and not m. Since a_k cannot differentiate between the case when b_{k-1} is corrupt and m is the message and the case when a_{k-1} is corrupt and $\bar{m}$ is the message, he has to send information on both the possibilities to R.

By induction assumption, we have 2^{k-2} bits received by a_k in the transmission of m and another 2^{k-2} bits received in the transmission of $\bar{m}$. Hence a_k needs to send a total of 2^{k-1} bits to R.   □

Theorem 2. *Any protocol for reliable unicast in $\mathcal{G}$ is infeasible.*

Proof. By lemma 3, there exists an adversarial strategy which allows R to know only the set of corrupt nodes in T without knowing anything about m. This implies that the precondition for lemma 4 is satisfied, and hence, along with lemma 5, it can be easily seen that there exists no polynomial protocol for reliable unicast in $\mathcal{G}$.   □

4   Efficient Protocols in Undirected Graphs

The graph $\mathcal{G}$ in the previous section is directed. This leads us to the question whether there exists undirected graphs where every protocol for reliable unicast is of exponential space or time complexity. The notation $\mathcal{G}_u$ and $\mathcal{H}_u$ is used to denote the undirected versions of $\mathcal{G}$ and $\mathcal{H}$. In general the subscript u is used to denote the corresponding undirected version.

Undirected graphs usually help in providing greater interaction. It is known that interaction, by itself cannot help in making *possible* a protocol for reliable unicast exist in a given network and an adversarial structure. But protocols using interaction (i.e. protocols which are not single phase), can be more efficient than those which do without it ([6]). For example, consider the graph $\mathcal{G}_1$ given in Fig. 5.

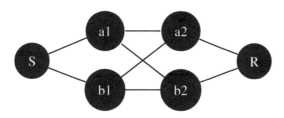

Fig. 5. Undirected graph with 2 layers

Let the honest player at i^{th} layer be denoted by $h_i, h_i \in \{a_i, b_i\}$. The power of interaction comes when in $\mathcal{G}_u$, R is able to tell h_k, who h_{k-1} is, and hence avoid doubling of messages at h_k. h_k simply forwards the message obtained from h_{k-1} to R. Presented in Fig. 6 is a protocol in $\mathcal{G}_1$ which makes use of $2 - way$ communication. It assumes that R knows the honest nodes h_i at each layer.

In the above protocol, we have outlined the roles of all the honest nodes. The proof that the protocol works is also trivial. Also note that there is no possibility of doubling of messages at any stage in the protocol. Note that lemmas 2-4 hold for $\mathcal{G}_u$. In addition to these, we have the following lemma too.

Protocol for reliable unicast in $\mathcal{G}_1$

1. S sends the message m to a_1, b_1.
2. R sends id of h_1 to h_2.
3. h_1 forwards m to a_2, b_2.
4. h_2 forwards whatever it receives from h_1 to R and discards whatever was received from $\{a_1, b_1\} - \{h_1\}$.

Fig. 6. A reliable unicast protocol for the graph given in Fig. 5

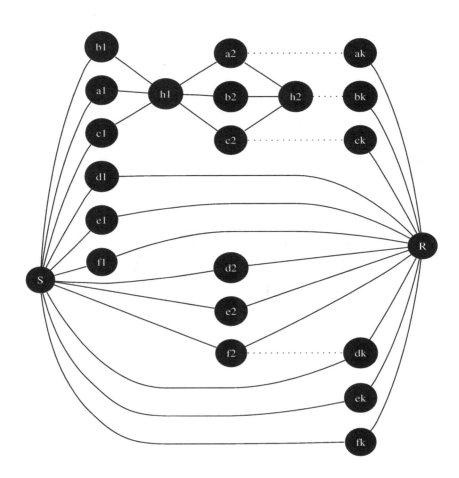

Fig. 7. Another graph in which no efficient PRU protocol may exist

Lemma 6. *If R knows the set of corrupted nodes in T, then S can learn this information.*

Proof. The above lemma is similar to lemma 3. Note that the graph is symmetric with respect to S and R. Replacing m by m' (which denotes the set of corrupted nodes in T), S by R and vice versa, will complete the proof.   □

We hope that like its directed counterpart, $\mathcal{G}_u$ too will require every protocol for PRU to transmit exponential number of bits.

Conjecture 1. In the graph $\mathcal{G}_u$, every protocol for reliable unicast will need to transmit atleast 2^{k-1} bits to transmit a single bit reliably between S and R.

Note that the conjecture takes into account both the forward and backward transmissions within a link.

4.1   Another Example Graph

We now give another example of a graph (Fig. 7) for which no efficient protocol might exist. The adversary structure for $\mathcal{G}$ is introduced by presenting an instance of it.
    Define

$$\mathcal{B}_i = \{\{a_i, b_i, d_i\}, \{a_i, c_i, f_i\}, \{a_i, d_i, e_i\},$$
$$\{b_i, c_i, e_i\}, \{b_i, e_i, f_i\}, \{c_i, d_i, f_i\}\}$$

to be the adversary structure at layer i. Then the adversary structure for the graph $\mathcal{G}$ is given as $\mathcal{A} = \{ A | A = \{A_1, A_2, \ldots, A_k\}, A_i \in \mathcal{B}_i, 1 \leq i \leq k \}$.

5   Conclusions and Open Problems

Efficiency of Reliable Communication is an important problem as it finds every-day use widespread across the internet in the form of e-mails. Hence, there is a need for characterizing graphs which have efficient protocols and for an algo-rithm that determines whether the input graph has an efficient protocol or not. In most of the cases, just eliminating distorted messages, with the help of fault knowledge may lead to a efficient protocol. Note that any adversary structure with polynomial number of possibilities or a graph with polynomial number of paths has an efficient protocol (by brute force) if the adversary structure satisfies Theorem 1.

    We have shown an exponential lower bound for the communication complexity of the reliable communication problem in a directed network. A natural question that arises is whether there exists an undirected graph, in which all protocols for reliable unicast are infeasible.

    Other closely related problems are finding the necessary and sufficient condi-tions for the existence of a polynomial protocol in graphs whose network topology is only partially known. Solutions under different models have been posed to this problem in [1,7] but the general problem still remains open.

References

1. Burmester, M., Desmedt, Y.: Secure communication in an unknown network using certificates. In: Lam, K.-Y., Okamoto, E., Xing, C. (eds.) ASIACRYPT 1999. LNCS, vol. 1716, pp. 274–287. Springer, Heidelberg (1999)
2. Cormen, T.H., Leiserson, C.E., Rivest, R.L., Stein, C.: Introduction to Algorithms Second Edition. The MIT Press and McGraw-Hill Book Company (2001)
3. Dolev, D., Dwork, C., Waarts, O., Yung, M.: Perfectly secure message transmission. J. ACM 40(1), 17–47 (1993)
4. Ashwin Kumar, M.V.N., Goundan, P.R., Srinathan, K., Pandu Rangan, C.: On perfectly secure communication over arbitrary networks. In: PODC 2002: Proceedings of the twenty-first annual symposium on Principles of distributed computing, pp. 193–202. ACM Press, New York (2002)
5. Lynch, N.: Distributed algorithms. Morgan Kaufmann, San Francisco (1996)
6. Sayeed, H.M., Abu-Amara, H.: Efficient perfectly secure message transmission in synchronous networks. Inf. Comput. 126(1), 53–61 (1996)
7. Subramanian, L., Katz, R.H., Roth, V., Shenker, S., Stoica, I.: Reliable broadcast in unknown fixed-identity networks. In: PODC 2005: Proceedings of the twenty-fourth annual ACM SIGACT-SIGOPS symposium on Principles of distributed computing, pp. 342–351. ACM Press, New York (2005)

Almost Secure (1-Round, n-Channel) Message Transmission Scheme

Kaoru Kurosawa[1] and Kazuhiro Suzuki[2]

[1] Department of Computer and Information Sciences,
Ibaraki University, Japan
`kurosawa@mx.ibaraki.ac.jp`
[2] Venture Business Laboratory, Ibaraki University, Japan
`tutetuti@dream.com`

Abstract. It is known that perfectly secure (1-round, n-channel) message transmission (MT) schemes exist if and only if $n \geq 3t+1$, where t is the number of channels that the adversary can corrupt. Then does there exist an *almost* secure MT scheme for $n = 2t + 1$? In this paper, we first sum up a number flaws of the previous *almost* secure MT scheme presented at Crypto 2004[1]. We next show an equivalence between almost secure MT schemes and secret sharing schemes with cheaters. By using our equivalence, we derive a lower bound on the communication complexity of almost secure MT schemes. Finally, we present a near optimum scheme which meets our bound approximately. This is the first construction of provably secure almost secure (1-round, n-channel) MT schemes for $n = 2t + 1$.

Keywords: Private and reliable transmission, information theoretic security, communication efficiency.

1 Introduction

1.1 Message Transmission Scheme

The model of (r-round, n-channel) message transmission schemes was introduced by Dolev et al. [2]. In this model, there are n channels between a sender and a receiver while they share no keys. The sender wishes to send a secret s to the receiver in r-rounds securely and reliably. An adversary $\mathbf{A}$ can observe and forge the messages sent through t out of n channels.

We say that a (r-round, n-channel) message transmission scheme is perfectly t-secure if $\mathbf{A}$ learns no information on s (perfect privacy), and the receiver can output $\hat{s} = s$ correctly (perfect reliability) for any infinitely powerful adversary $\mathbf{A}$ who can corrupt at most t channels (in information theoretic sense).[2] Dolev et al. showed that [2]

---

[1] The authors already noted in thier presentation at Crypto'2004 that their scheme was flawed. It was Ronald Cramer who informed the authors of the flaw.

[2] Dolev et al. called it a perfectly secure message transmission scheme [2].

Y. Desmedt (Ed.): ICITS 2007, LNCS 4883, pp. 99–112, 2009.

- $n \geq 3t + 1$ is necessary and sufficient for $r = 1$, and
- $n \geq 2t + 1$ is necessary and sufficient for $r = 2$

to achieve perfect t-security.

A perfectly t-secure scheme with optimum communication complexity is known for $r = 1$ and $n = 3t + 1$ [2,6]. Based on the work of [5,6], Agarwal et al. showed an asymptotically optimum perfectly t-secure scheme for $r = 2$ and $n = 2t + 1$ [1].

1.2 Secret Sharing Scheme with Cheaters

Tompa and Woll introduced a problem of cheating in (k, n) threshold secret sharing schemes [7]. In this problem $k - 1$ malicious participants aim to cheat an honest one by opening forged shares and causing the honest participant to reconstruct the wrong secret.

Ogata et al. derived a tight lower bound on the size of shares $|\mathcal{V}_i|$ for secret sharing schemes that protects against this type of attack: $|\mathcal{V}_i| \geq (|\mathcal{S}| - 1)/\delta + 1$, where $\mathcal{V}_i$ denotes the set of shares of participant P_i, $\mathcal{S}$ denotes the set of secrets, and δ denotes the cheating probability [4].[3]

They also presented an optimum scheme, which meets the equality of their bound by using "difference sets" [4].

1.3 Our Contribution

As we mentioned, it is known that perfectly secure (1-round, n-channel) message transmission schemes exist if and only if $n \geq 3t + 1$, where t is the number of channels that adversary can corrupt. Then does there exist an *almost* secure scheme for $n = 2t + 1$? At Crypto 2004, Srinathan et al. [6, Sec.5] proposed an almost secure (1-round, n-channel) message transmission scheme for $n = 2t + 1$. However, the authors already noted in thier presentation at Crypto'2004 that their scheme was flawed.

In this paper, we first sum up a number of flaws of the above scheme. (Actually, they showed two schemes in [6], a perfectly t-secure scheme and an almost secure scheme. Agarwal et al. showed a flaw of the former one [1].)

Table 1. Previous Work and Our Contribution

	Perfectly t-secure	Almost secure
$r = 1$	$n \geq 3t + 1$	$n = 2t + 1$ This paper
$r = 2$	$n \geq 2t + 1$	–

---

[3] $|\mathcal{X}|$ denotes the cardinality of a set $\mathcal{X}$.

We next show an equivalence between almost secure (1-round, n-channel) message transmission schemes with $n = 2t + 1$ and secret sharing schemes with cheaters. By using our equivalence, we derive a lower bound on the communication complexity of almost secure (1-round, n-channel) message transmission schemes (in the above sense) such that

$$|\mathcal{X}_i| \geq (|\mathcal{S}| - 1)/\delta + 1,$$

where $\mathcal{X}_i$ denotes the set of messages sent through the ith channel and $\mathcal{S}$ denotes the set of secrets which the sender wishes to send to the receiver.

We finally show a near optimum scheme which meets our bound approximately. This is the first construction of almost secure (1-round, n-channel) message transmission schemes for $n = 2t + 1$.

Our results imply that $n \geq 2t + 1$ is necessary and sufficient for almost secure (1-round, n-channel) message transmission schemes.

2   Flaw of the Previous Almost Secure MT Scheme

In this section, we sum up a number of flaws of the previous almost secure (1-round, n-channel) message transmission scheme [6, Sec.5].[4] Let $n = 2t + 1$ in what follows.

2.1   Previous Almost Secure Message Transmission Scheme

Their scheme [6, Sec.5] is described is as follows. For simplicity, let $\mathbb{F}$ be a finite field $GF(q)$ such that q is a prime, and assume that the sender wishes to send a secret $s = (s_1, \ldots, s_{t+1})$ to the receiver, where each s_i is an element of $\mathbb{F}$.[5]

 - **Enc.** The sender computes a ciphertext $(x_1, \cdots, x_n)$ from $s = (s_1, \ldots, s_{t+1})$ as follows.
    1. Randomly select n polynomials $p_1(x), \cdots, p_n(x)$ of degree at most t over $\mathbb{F}$ such that
       $$Q(1) = s_1, \cdots, Q(t + 1) = s_{t+1}, \tag{1}$$
       where[6] $Q(x) = p_1(0) + p_2(0)x + p_3(0)x^2 + \cdots + p_n(0)x^{n-1}$.
    2. For each (i, j) with $i \neq j$, randomly select one of the t points of intersection of p_i and p_j so that $r_{ij} \neq r_{ji}$ (denote the selected point by r_{ij}).
    3. For each i, let $x_i = (p_i(x), r_{ij}$ for all $j \neq i)$.
    4. Output $(x_1, x_2, \ldots, x_n)$.
 - **Dec.** The receiver computes $s = (s_1, \ldots, s_{t+1})$ or $\perp$ from $(\hat{x}_1, \hat{x}_2, \ldots, \hat{x}_n)$ as follows, where $\hat{x}_i = (\hat{p}_i(x), \hat{r}_{ij}$ for all $j \neq i)$.

---

[4] They called it a Las Vegas scheme.
[5] In [6, Sec.5], the sender sends a message $m = (m_1, \cdots, m_{t+1})$ to the receiver by broadcasting $y = m + s$ through all the channels.
[6] In [6, Sec.5], they wrote this as $s = \text{EXTRAND}(p_1(0), \cdots, p_n(0))$.

1. Set $\Lambda = \{1, 2, \ldots, n\}$.
2. We say that the i-th channel ch_i *contradicts* the j-th channel ch_j if $\hat{p}_i$ and $\hat{p}_j$ do not intersect at $\hat{r}_{ij}$.
3. For each i, if ch_i is contradicted by at least $t + 1$ channels then remove i from Λ.
4. If ch_i contradicts ch_j for some $i, j \in \Lambda$ then output **failure**.
5. If $|\Lambda| \leq t$, then output **failure**.
6. At this point, $\hat{p}_i = p_i$ for all $i \in \Lambda$ and $|\Lambda| \geq t + 1$.
   Derive all the polynomials $p_1, \ldots, p_n$ from $\hat{p}_i$ and $\hat{r}_{ij}$ $(i \in \Lambda)$.
7. Compute s as $s = [Q(1), \ldots, Q(t + 1)]$.

Srinathan et al. claimed the following lemmas for adversaries who can corrupts at most t out of n channels [6, Sec.5].

Lemma 1. *[6, Lemma 11]* **Reliability.** *The receiver will never output an incorrect value.*

Lemma 2. *[6, Lemma 13]* **Perfect Privacy.** *The adversary gains no information about the secret.*

2.2   Flaws

We show that the above two lemmas do not hold. In the above scheme, it is important to choose $p_1, \cdots, p_n$ randomly because otherwise we cannot ensure the perfect privacy. However, if the sender chooses $p_1, \cdots, p_n$ randomly, it has the following problems. For simplicity, suppose that $t = 2$ and $n = 2t + 1 = 5$. (It is easy to generalize the following argument to any $t \geq 2$.)

- **Sender's problem:** Since the polynomials $p_1, \ldots, p_5$ are randomly chosen, it can happen that some p_i and p_j do not intersect or intersect at one point. In these cases, the sender cannot execute Step 2 of **Enc**.
- **Perfect Privacy:** Suppose that the adversary **A** corrupts $t = 2$ channels 1 and 2. In most cases, **A** has no information on s_1, s_2, s_3 because eq.(1) has $t + 1 = 3$ equations and 3 unknown variables $p_3(0), p_4(0)$ and $p_5(0)$, where $p_3(0), p_4(0)$ and $p_5(0)$ are randomly chosen.
  However, with nonzero probability, it happens that $p_1(x)$ and $p_3(x)$ intersect at $x = 0$ and hence $r_{1,3} = 0$. In this case, **A** can compute $p_3(0)$, and she knows 3 values, $p_1(0), p_2(0)$ and $p_3(0)$. Consequently, **A** has only 2 unknown variables $p_4(0)$ and $p_5(0)$ in eq.(1). This means that **A** can learn some information on $s = (s_1, s_2, s_3)$ with nonzero probability. Therefore Lemma 2 (perfect privacy) does not hold.
- **Reliability:** Since the polynomials $p_1(x), \ldots, p_5(x)$ are all randomly chosen, it can happen that

$$b_1 = p_1(a_1) = \cdots = p_5(a_1)$$
$$b_2 = p_1(a_2) = \cdots = p_5(a_2)$$

with nonzero probability. That is, all polynomials go through (a_1, b_1) and (a_2, b_2). In this case, the sender will set $r_{ij} = a_1$ and $r_{ji} = a_2$ for each pair $i < j$.

Now consider an adversary **A** who corrupts channel 1 and replaces $p_1(x)$ with a random polynomial $p'_1(x)$. Then it can still happen that p'_1 passes through (a_1, b_1) and (a_2, b_2) with nonzero probability. In this case, the receiver accepts p'_1. Hence the receiver outputs $\hat{s} \neq s$ because $p'_1(0) \neq p_1(0)$. After all, the receiver outputs $\hat{s} \neq s$ with nonzero probability. Therefore, Lemma 1 does not hold.

We cannot fix these flaws. To correct these flaws, **Enc** must choose $p_1, \cdots, p_5$ in such a way that

- p_i and p_j intersect at at least two points,
- $r_{ij} \neq 0$,
- and all intersection points are distinct

for each pair of (i, j). However, if so, the perfect privacy does not hold because $p_1, \cdots, p_5$ are not random.

Suppose that the adversary **A** corrupts $t = 2$ channels 1 and 2. Then she learns the values of $p_1(0), p_2(0)$. Hence she knows that $p_3(0), \ldots, p_5(0)$ are not elements of $\{p_1(0), p_2(0)\}$. That is, $p_3(0), \ldots, p_5(0)$ are not randomly chosen from $\mathbb{F}$. Hence she can learn some information on s from eq.(1).

3   Model

In this section, we define a model of Almost Secure (1-round, n-channel) message transmission schemes formally. In the model, there are n channels between a sender and a receiver. The sender wishes to send a secret s to the receiver secretly and reliably in one-round without sharing any keys. An adversary can observe and forge the messages sent through at most t out of n channels.

A (1-round, n-channel) message transmission scheme consists of a pair of algorithms (**Enc**, **Dec**) as follows. Let $\mathcal{S}$ denote the set of secrets.

- **Enc** is a probabilistic encryption algorithm which takes a secret $s \in \mathcal{S}$ as an input, and outputs a ciphertext $(x_1, \cdots, x_n)$, where x_i is the i-th channel's message.
- **Dec** is a deterministic decryption algorithm which takes an alleged ciphertext $(\hat{x}_1, \cdots, \hat{x}_n)$ and outputs $\hat{s} \in \mathcal{S}$ or **failure**.

We require that **Dec**(**Enc**(s)) $= s$ for any $s \in \mathcal{S}$. We assume a certain probability distribution over $\mathcal{S}$, and let S denote the random variable. Let X_i denote the random variable induced by x_i, and $\mathcal{X}_i$ denote the possible set of x_i for $1 \leq i \leq n$.

To define the security, we consider the following game among the sender, the receiver and an adversary **A**, where **A** is a (infinitely powerful) probabilistic Turing machine.

1. **A** chooses t channels, $i_1, \cdots, i_t$.
2. The sender chooses $s \in \mathcal{S}$ according to the distribution over $\mathcal{S}$, and uses **Enc** to compute $x_1, \cdots, x_n$. Then x_i is sent to the receiver through channel i for $1 \le i \le n$.
3. **A** observes $x_{i_1}, \cdots, x_{i_t}$, and forges them to $x'_{i_1}, \cdots, x'_{i_t}$. We allow x'_{i_j} to be the null string for $1 \le j \le t$.
4. The receiver receives $\hat{x}_i$ through channel i for $1 \le i \le n$, and uses **Dec** to compute
$$\mathbf{Dec}(\hat{x}_1, \cdots, \hat{x}_n) = \hat{s} \text{ or } \mathbf{failure}.$$

Definition 1. *We say that a (1-round, n-channel) message transmission scheme is (t, δ)-secure if the following conditions are satisfied for any adversary* **A** *who can corrupt at most t out of n channels.*

Privacy. **A** *learns no information on s. More precisely,*
$$\Pr(S = s \mid X_{i_1} = x_{i_1}, \cdots, X_{i_t} = x_{i_t}) = \Pr(S = s)$$
for any $s \in \mathcal{S}$ and any possible $x_{i_1}, \cdots, x_{i_t}$.

General Reliability. *The receiver outputs $\hat{s} = s$ or* **failure**. *(He never outputs a wrong secret.)*

Trivial Reliability. *If the t forged messages $x'_{i_1}, \cdots, x'_{i_t}$ are all null strings, then* **Dec** *outputs $\hat{s} = s$.*

Failure.
$$\Pr(\mathbf{Dec} \text{ outputs } \mathbf{failure}) < \delta. \tag{2}$$

(The trivial reliability means that if t channel fail to deliver messages, then **Dec** outputs $\hat{s} = s$. Hence this is a reasonable requirement.)

4   Secret Sharing Scheme with Cheaters

In the model of secret sharing schemes, there is a probabilistic Turing machine D called a dealer. S denotes a random variable distributed over a finite set $\mathcal{S}$, and $s \in \mathcal{S}$ is called a secret. On input $s \in \mathcal{S}$, D outputs $(v_1, \ldots, v_n)$ according to some fixed probability distribution. For $1 \le i \le n$, each participant P_i holds v_i as his share. V_i denotes the random variable induced by v_i. Let $\mathcal{V}_i = \{v_i \mid \Pr[V_i = v_i] > 0\}$. $\mathcal{V}_i$ is the set of possible shares held by P_i.

Definition 2. *We say that D is a (k, n) threshold secret sharing scheme for S if the following two requirements hold:*

(A1) *Let $j \ge k$. Then there exists a unique $s \in \mathcal{S}$ such that*
$$\Pr[S = s \mid V_{i_1} = v_{i_1}, \ldots, V_{i_j} = v_{i_j}] = 1$$
for any $\{i_1, \ldots, i_j\} \subseteq \{1, \ldots, n\}$ and any $(v_{i_1}, \ldots, v_{i_j})$ with $\Pr[V_{i_1} = v_{i_1}, \ldots, V_{i_j} = v_{i_j}] > 0$.

(A2) *Let $j < k$. Then for each $s \in \mathcal{S}$,*

$$\Pr[S = s \mid V_{i_1} = v_{i_1}, \ldots, V_{i_j} = v_{i_j}] = \Pr[S = s]$$

for any $\{i_1, \ldots, i_j\} \subseteq \{1, \ldots, n\}$ and any $(v_{i_1}, \ldots, v_{i_j})$ with $\Pr[V_{i_1} = v_{i_1}, \ldots, V_{i_j} = v_{i_j}] > 0$.

Now we consider $k - 1$ malicious participants who aim to cheat an honest one by opening forged shares and causing the honest participant to reconstruct the wrong secret.

Definition 3. *For $A = \{i_1, \cdots, i_k\}$ and $v_{i_1} \in \mathcal{V}_{i_1}, \ldots, v_{i_k} \in \mathcal{V}_{i_k}$, define*

$$\mathsf{Sec}_I(v_{i_1}, \ldots, v_{i_k}) = \begin{cases} s & \text{if } \exists s \in \mathcal{S} \text{ s.t. } \Pr[S = s \mid V_{i_1} = v_{i_1}, \cdots, V_{i_k} = v_{i_k}] = 1, \\ \bot & \text{otherwise.} \end{cases}$$

That is, $\mathsf{Sec}_I(v_{i_1}, \ldots, v_{i_k})$ denotes the secret reconstructed from the k possible shares $(v_{i_1}, \ldots, v_{i_k})$ associated with $(P_{i_1}, \ldots, P_{i_k})$, respectively. The symbol $\bot$ is used to indicate when no secret can be reconstructed from the k shares. We will often aggregate the first $k - 1$ arguments of Sec_I into a vector, by defining $\mathbf{b} = (v_{i_1}, \ldots, v_{i_{k-1}})$ and $\mathsf{Sec}_I(\mathbf{b}, v_{i_k}) = \mathsf{Sec}_I(v_{i_1}, \ldots, v_{i_k})$.

Definition 4. *Suppose that $k - 1$ cheaters $P_{i_1}, \ldots, P_{i_{k-1}}$ possesses the list of shares $\mathbf{b} = (v_{i_1}, \ldots, v_{i_{k-1}})$. Let $\mathbf{b}' = (v'_{i_1}, \ldots, v'_{i_{k-1}}) \neq \mathbf{b}$ be a list of $k - 1$ forged shares. Then we say that P_{i_k} is cheated by $\mathbf{b}'$ if*

$$\mathsf{Sec}_I(\mathbf{b}', v_{i_k}) \notin \{\mathsf{Sec}_I(\mathbf{b}, v_{i_k}), \bot\}, \tag{3}$$

where v_{i_k} denotes the share of P_{i_k}.

To define a secure secret sharing scheme clearly, we consider the following game.

1. $k - 1$ cheaters and the target participant are fixed. That is, we fix $i_1, \ldots, i_{k-1}$ and i_k.
2. The dealer picks $s \in \mathcal{S}$ according to distribution S, and uses D to compute shares $v_1, \ldots, v_n$ for the n participants. v_i is given to P_i for $i \in \{1, \ldots, n\}$.
3. Let $\mathbf{b} = (v_{i_1}, \ldots, v_{i_{k-1}})$. The cheaters jointly use a *probabilistic* algorithm A to compute forged shares $\mathbf{b}' = (v'_{i_1}, \ldots, v'_{i_{k-1}})$ from $\mathbf{b}$.
4. The cheaters open the forged shares $\mathbf{b}'$. If P_{i_k} is cheated by $\mathbf{b}'$ (as defined above), then we say that the cheaters win the cheating game.

Definition 5. *We say that a (k, n) threshold secret sharing scheme D is a (k, n, δ) secure secret sharing scheme if*

$$\Pr(\text{cheaters win}) \leq \delta \tag{4}$$

for any $k - 1$ cheaters $P_{i_1}, \ldots, P_{i_{k-1}}$, any target P_{i_k} and any cheating strategy.

Ogata et al. derived a lower bound on $|\mathcal{V}_i|$ of (k, n, δ) secure secret sharing schemes as follows [4].

Proposition 1. *[4] In a (k, n, δ) secure secret sharing scheme,*

$$|\mathcal{V}_i| \geq \frac{|\mathcal{S}| - 1}{\delta} + 1 \tag{5}$$

for any i.

We say that a (k, n, δ) secure secret sharing scheme is optimal if the above equality is satisfied for all i.

5   Equivalence

In this section, we show an equivalence between (t, δ)-secure (1-round, n-channel) message transmission schemes and $(t + 1, n, \delta)$ secure secret sharing schemes.

5.1   From Secret Sharing to Message Transmission

Theorem 1. *Suppose that $n \geq 2t + 1$. If there exists a $(t + 1, n, \delta)$ secure secret sharing scheme D for S, then there exists a (t, ϵ)-secure (1-round, n-channel) message transmission scheme* (**Enc, Dec**) *for the same S such that*

$$\epsilon = (\binom{n}{t+1} - \binom{n-t}{t+1})\delta$$

Further it holds that $\mathcal{X}_i = \mathcal{V}_i$ for $1 \leq i \leq n$.

Proof. We construct (**Enc, Dec**) from D as follows. **Enc** is the same as D. That is, on input $s \in \mathcal{S}$, **Enc** runs $D(s)$ to generate $(x_1, \cdots, x_n) = (v_1, \cdots, v_n)$.

Our **Dec** is constructed as follows. On input $(\hat{x}_1, \cdots, \hat{x}_n)$, **Dec** computes $\mathsf{Sec}_I(\hat{x}_{i_1}, \cdots, \hat{x}_{i_{t+1}})$ for all $I = (i_1, \cdots, i_{t+1})$, where I is a subset of $\{1, \cdots, n\}$. If there exists some $\hat{s} \in \mathcal{S}$ such that

$$\mathsf{Sec}_I(\hat{x}_{i_1}, \cdots, \hat{x}_{i_{t+1}}) = \hat{s} \text{ or } \perp$$

for all $I = (i_1, \cdots, i_{t+1})$, then **Dec** outputs $\hat{s}$. Otherwise, **Dec** outputs **failure**.

We prove that the conditions of Def. 1 are satisfied. The privacy condition holds from (A1) of Def. 2.

Next note that

$$n - t \geq (2t + 1) - t = t + 1. \tag{6}$$

Therefore, the trivial reliability holds from (A2) of Def. 2. We next show the general reliability. From eq.(6), there exists a $J = \{j_1, \cdots, j_{t+1}\}$ such that $\hat{x}_{j_1} = x_{j_1}, \cdots, \hat{x}_{j_{t+1}} = x_{j_{t+1}}$. For this J, it holds that

$$\mathsf{Sec}_J(\hat{x}_{j_1}, \cdots, \hat{x}_{j_{t+1}}) = s$$

from (A2) of Def. 2, where s is the original secret. Therefore, **Dec** outputs **failure** if there exists some $I = (i_1, \cdots, i_{t+1}) \neq J$ such that

$$\mathsf{Sec}_I(\hat{x}_{i_1}, \cdots, \hat{x}_{i_{t+1}}) = s' \in \mathcal{S}$$

with $s' \neq s$. This means that if **Dec** does not output **failure**, then there is no such I. Hence **Dec** outputs $\hat{s} = s$.

Finally we show

$$\Pr(\textbf{Dec outputs failure}) < \left(\binom{n}{t+1} - \binom{n-t}{t+1} \right) \delta.$$

For simplicity, suppose that an adversary **A** corrupts channels $1, \cdots, t$ and forges $\mathbf{b}' = (x'_1, \cdots, x'_t)$. Then the number of subsets I of size $t+1$ such that $I \cap \{1, \cdots, t\} \neq \emptyset$ is given by $\binom{n}{t+1} - \binom{n-t}{t+1}$. $\qquad\square$

5.2   From Message Transmission to Secret Sharing

Suppose that there exists a (t, δ)-secure (1-round, n-channel) message transmission scheme such that $n = 2t + 1$. Then $n - t = (2t + 1) - t = t + 1$. Hence from the trivial reliability condition, we can define a function F_I such that

$$F_I(\hat{x}_{i_1}, \cdots, \hat{x}_{i_{t+1}}) = s_I \text{ or } \perp \qquad (7)$$

for each $(t+1)$-subset $I = (i_1, \cdots, i_{t+1}) \subset \{1, \cdots, n\}$, where $s_I \in \mathcal{S}$. We say that a (t, δ)-secure (1-round, n-channel) message transmission scheme with $n = 2t+1$ is canonical if

$$\mathbf{Dec}(\hat{x}_1, \cdots, \hat{x}_n) = \begin{cases} \hat{s} & \text{if } F_I(\hat{x}_{i_1}, \cdots, \hat{x}_{i_{t+1}}) = \hat{s} \text{ or } \perp \text{ for each } (t+1)\text{-subset } I \\ \textbf{failure} & \text{otherwise} \end{cases}$$

Theorem 2. *If there exists a canonical (t, δ)-secure (1-round, n-channel) message transmission scheme* (**Enc**, **Dec**) *with $n = 2t + 1$ for S, then there exists a $(t + 1, n, \delta)$ secure secret sharing scheme D for the same S. Further it holds that $\mathcal{X}_i = \mathcal{V}_i$ for $1 \leq i \leq n$.*

Proof. We construct D from (**Enc**, **Dec**) as $D = \textbf{Enc}$. That is, on input $s \in \mathcal{S}$, D runs **Enc**(s) to generate $(v_1, \cdots, v_n) = (x_1, \cdots, x_n)$.

We prove that the conditions of Def. 2 are satisfied. (A1) holds from the privacy condition of Def. 1. (A2) holds from the trivial reliability since $n - t = 2t + 1 - t = t + 1$.

We finally show eq.(4). Suppose that eq.(4) does not hold in the $(t + 1, n, \delta)$ secure secret sharing scheme. Then there exist some $\{i_1, \cdots, i_t\}$, a target i_{t+1} and some cheating strategy such that

$$\mathsf{Sec}_I(\mathbf{b}', v_{i_k}) \notin \{\mathsf{Sec}_I(\mathbf{b}, v_{i_k}), \perp\}$$

with probability more than δ.

For simplicity, suppose that $\{i_1, \cdots, i_t\} = \{1, 2, \cdots, t\}$ and $i_{t+1} = t+1$. Now in the attack game of the (t, δ)-secure (1-round, n-channel) message transmission scheme, consider an adversary **A** which chooses the corresponding t channels $\{1, 2, \cdots, t\}$ and forges $x_1, \cdots, x_t$ to $x'_1, \cdots, x'_t$ according to the cheating strategy above. Then

$$\mathsf{Sec}_I(x'_1, \cdots, x'_t, x_{t+1}) = s' \qquad (8)$$

with probability more than δ for some $s' \neq s$, where $I = \{1, \cdots, t, t+1\}$. On the other hand, we have

$$\mathsf{Sec}_J(x_{t+1}, \cdots, x_{2t+1}) = s \qquad (9)$$

for $J = \{t+1, \cdots, 2t+1\}$. In this case, **Dec** outputs **failure** from our definition of *canonical*. Hence

$$\Pr(\textbf{Dec outputs failure}) > \delta.$$

However, this is against eq.(2). Therefore, eq.(4) must hold.   □

5.3   Discussion

We show that *canonical* is a natural property that (t, δ)-secure (1-round, n-channel) message transmission schemes with $n = 2t + 1$ should satisfy. First from the proof of Theorem 1, we have the following corollary.

Corollary 1. *In Theorem 1, if $n = 2t+1$, then the message transmission scheme is canonical.*

Next suppose that there exists a (t, δ)-secure (1-round, n-channel) message transmission scheme with $n = 2t + 1$. Remember that the sender sends a ciphertext $(x_1, \cdots, x_{2t+1})$ for a secret s, and the receiver receives $\hat{X} = (\hat{x}_1, \cdots, \hat{x}_n)$. For a $(t + 1)$-subset $I = (i_1, \cdots, i_{t+1}) \subset \{1, \cdots, n\}$, define

$$G(I, \hat{X}) = F_I(\hat{x}_{i_1}, \cdots, \hat{x}_{i_{t+1}}).$$

(See eq.(7) for F_I.)

Definition 6. *We say that a $(t + 1)$-subset I is an acceptable (sub)set for $\hat{X}$ if $G(I, \hat{X}) \neq \perp$.*

In a canonical scheme, it is easy to see that **Dec** outputs **failure** if and only if there exist two acceptable $(t+1)$-subsets I and J such that $G(I, \hat{X}) \neq G(J, \hat{X})$. We will show that this is a natural property that (t, δ)-secure (1-round, n-channel) message transmission schemes with $n = 2t + 1$ should satisfy.

Consider an adversary **A** who corrupts channels $1, \cdots, t$, and replaces x_i to a random x'_i for $1 \leq i \leq t$.

1. We first show that
   - there are only two acceptable sets I and J, and $G(I, \hat{X}) \neq G(J, \hat{X})$ with nonzero probability. In this case, the receiver cannot see if $G(I, \hat{X}) = s$ or $G(J, \hat{X}) = s$. Hence he must output **failure** to satisfy the general reliability condition.

   The proof is as follows. From the trivial reliability, it holds that

$$G(I, \hat{X}) = s \qquad (10)$$

   for $I = \{t+1, \cdots, 2t+1\}$. Further there exists another acceptable set $J \neq I$ such that $G(I, \hat{X}) \neq G(J, \hat{X})$ with nonzero probability. Because otherwise we have a perfectly t-secure (1-round, n-channel) message transmission scheme with $n = 2t + 1$, which is a contradiction.

Finally, there exist no other acceptable sets with high probability because x'_i is chosen randomly for $1 \leq i \leq t$.

2. Next we show that there exists a case such that the majority vote does not work. That is, we show that there exist acceptable sets I and $J_1, \cdots, J_{\binom{2t}{t+1}}$ such that

   − $G(I, \hat{X}) = s$ and
   − $G(J_1, \hat{X}) = \cdots, G(J_{\binom{2t}{t+1}}, \hat{X}) = s' \neq s$

with nonzero probability. In this case, the receiver must output **failure** too to satisfy the general reliability condition.

The proof is as follows. From the privacy condition, we have no information on s from $(x_{t+1}, \cdots, x_{2t})$. Therefore for $s' \neq s$, it holds that

$$\Pr[S = s', X_{t+1} = x_{t+1}, \cdots, X_{2t} = x_{2t}] > 0.$$

Hence there exist some $b_1, \cdots, b_t, c_{2t+1}$ such that

$$\Pr[S = s', X_1 = b_1, \cdots, X_t = b_t, X_{t+1} = x_{t+1}, \cdots, X_{2t} = x_{2t}, X_{2t+1} = c_{2t+1}] > 0. \tag{11}$$

Further it holds that $x'_i = b_i$ for $1 \leq i \leq t$ with nonzero probability because the adversary **A** chooses x'_i randomly. In this case, we have

$$\hat{x}_1 = b_1, \cdots, \hat{x}_t = b_t, \ \hat{x}_{t+1} = x_{t+1}, \cdots, \hat{x}_{2t} = x_{2t}, \ \hat{x}_{2t+1} = x_{2t+1}.$$

Therefore from eq.(11), for any $(t + 1)$-subset $J \subset \{1, \cdots, 2t\}$, we obtain that

$$G(J, \hat{X}) = s'.$$

The number of such J is $\binom{2t}{t+1}$. Finally, it is clear that $G(I, \hat{X}) = s$ for $I = \{t + 1, \cdots, 2t + 1\}$.

So the scheme must be canonical in the above two cases. Hence we consider that *canonical* is a natural property for $n = 2t + 1$.

6   Lower Bound

In this section, we derive a lower bound on $|\mathcal{X}_i|$ of (t, δ)-secure (1-round, n-channel) message transmission schemes with $n = 2t + 1$ by using our equivalence. Indeed, we obtain the following bound immediately from Proposition 1 and Theorem 2.

Corollary 2. *In a canonical (t, δ)-secure (1-round, n-channel) message transmission scheme with $n = 2t + 1$, it holds that*

$$|\mathcal{X}_i| \geq \frac{|S| - 1}{\delta} + 1 \tag{12}$$

for any i.

7 Near Optimum Almost Secure MT Scheme

Ogata et al. showed a construction of optimum (k, n, δ) secure secret sharing schemes by using "difference sets" [4].

7.1 Optimum Robust Secret Sharing Scheme

Definition 7. *[3, p.397] A planar difference set modulo $N = \ell(\ell - 1) + 1$ is a set $B = \{d_0, d_1, \ldots, d_{\ell-1}\} \subseteq \mathbb{Z}_N$ with the property that the $\ell(\ell - 1)$ differences $d_i - d_j$ ($d_i \neq d_j$), when reduced modulo N, are exactly the numbers $1, 2, \ldots, N-1$ in some order.*

For example, $\{d_0 = 0, d_1 = 1, d_2 = 3\}$ is a planar difference set modulo 7 with $\ell = 3$. Indeed, the differences modulo 7 are

$$1 - 0 = 1, \ 3 - 0 = 3, \ 3 - 1 = 2, \ 0 - 1 = 6, \ 0 - 3 = 4, \ 1 - 3 = 5.$$

Proposition 2. *[3, p.398, Theorem 22] Let Π be a projective plane $PG(2, q)$. A point in Π can be represented as $(\beta_1, \beta_2, \beta_3) \in (\mathbb{F}_q)^3$, or $\alpha^i \in \mathbb{F}_{q^3}$ for some i, where α is a generator of $\mathbb{F}_{q^3}$. If $\ell = q + 1$ points $\alpha^{d_0}, \ldots, \alpha^{d_{\ell-1}}$ are the points on a line in Π, then $\{d_0, \ldots, d_{\ell-1}\}$ is a planar difference set modulo $q^2 + q + 1$.*

Let $\{d_0, \ldots, d_q\}$ be a planar difference set modulo $p = q^2 + q + 1$. Then a (k, n, δ) secure secret sharing scheme is obtained by applying Shamir's (k, n)-threshold secret sharing scheme to $\mathcal{S} = \{d_0, \ldots, d_q\}$ over $GF(p)$, where the secret s is uniformly distributed over $\mathcal{S}$ and $\delta = 1/(q + 1)$. In the reconstructoin phase, an honest participant outputs a reconstructed secret s' if $s' \in \mathcal{S}$, and $\perp$ otherwise.

Proposition 3. *[4, Corollary 4.5] Let q be a prime power that makes $q^2 + q + 1$ a prime. Then, there exists a (k, n, δ) secure secret sharing scheme for a uniform distribution over $\mathcal{S}$ which meets the bound (5) such that $|\mathcal{S}| = q + 1, \delta = 1/(q+1)$ and $n < q^2 + q + 1$.*

From Proposition 1, this construction is optimum.

7.2 Near Optimum Almost Secure MT Scheme

From the above proposition, Theorem 1 and Corollary 1, we can obtain the following construction of (t, ϵ)-secure (1-round, n-channel) message transmission schemes.

Corollary 3. *Let q be a prime power that makes $q^2 + q + 1$ a prime. Then, there exists a (t, ϵ)-secure (1-round, n-channel) message transmission scheme with $n \geq 2t + 1$ for a uniform distribution over $\mathcal{S}$ such that $|\mathcal{S}| = q + 1, \delta = 1/(q + 1), 2t + 1 \leq n < q^2 + q + 1$ and*

$$|\mathcal{X}_i| = \frac{|\mathcal{S}| - 1}{\delta} + 1,$$

where

$$\epsilon = \left(\binom{n}{t+1} - \binom{n-t}{t+1}\right)\delta.$$

Further if $n = 2t + 1$, the message transmission scheme is canonical.

Our (t, ϵ)-secure (1-round, n-channel) message transmission scheme is described as follows. Let $\{d_0, \ldots, d_q\}$ be a planar difference set modulo $p = q^2 + q + 1$. We assume that a message s is uniformly distributed over $\{0, 1, \cdots, q\}$.

1. For a message $s \in \{0, 1, \ldots, q\}$, let $y = d_s$. The sender applies Shamir's $(t + 1, n)$-threshold secret sharing scheme to the secret $y = d_s$ over $GF(p)$ to obtain the shares $(v_1, \cdots, v_n)$. She then sends $x_i = v_i$ to the receiver through the ith channel for $i = 1, \cdots, n$.
2. Suppose that the receiver received $(\hat{x}_1, \cdots, \hat{x}_n)$. He first reconstructs the secret y_I by applying Lagrange formula to $(\hat{x}_{i_1}, \cdots, \hat{x}_{i_{t+1}})$ for each subset $I = (i_1, \cdots, i_{t+1})$ of $\{1, \cdots, n\}$. If there exists some $\hat{s} \in \{0, 1, \ldots, q\}$ such that for all subset I,

$$y_I = d_{\hat{s}} \text{ or } y_I \notin \{d_0, \ldots, d_q\},$$

then he outputs $\hat{s}$. Otherwise the receiver outputs **failure**.

7.3 Generalization

Ogata et al. also showed another construction of optimum (k, n, δ) secure secret sharing schemes by using general "difference sets" [4].

Proposition 4. *[4, Corollary 4.5] For a positive integer u such that $4u - 1$ is a prime power, there exists a (k, n, δ) secure secret sharing scheme which meets the equality of our bound (5), such that $|\mathcal{S}| = 2u-1, \delta = (u-1)/(2u-1), n < 4u-1$.*

From the above proposition, Theorem 1 and Corollary 1, we can obtain another construction of (t, ϵ)-secure (1-round, n-channel) message transmission schemes as follows.

Corollary 4. *[4, Corollary 4.5] For a positive integer u such that $4u - 1$ is a prime power, there exists (t, ϵ)-secure (1-round, n-channel) message transmission scheme with $n \geq 2t + 1$ for a uniform distribution over $\mathcal{S}$ such that $|\mathcal{S}| = 2u - 1, \delta = (u - 1)/(2u - 1), n < 4u - 1$ and*

$$|\mathcal{X}_i| = \frac{|\mathcal{S}| - 1}{\delta} + 1,$$

where

$$\epsilon = \left(\binom{n}{t+1} - \binom{n-t}{t+1}\right)\delta.$$

Further if $n = 2t + 1$, the message transmission scheme is canonical.

In these constructions, there is a gap of $\log_2(\binom{n}{t+1} - \binom{n-t}{t+1})$ bits from our lower bound of Corollary 2. This gap is, however, small enough for small t.

Our results imply that $n \geq 2t + 1$ is necessary and sufficient for (t, ϵ)-secure (1-round, n-channel) message transmission schemes.

Theorem 3. (t, ϵ)-secure (1-round, n-channel) message transmission schemes exist if and only if $n \geq 2t + 1$.

Proof. It is enough to prove that there exist no (t, ϵ)-secure (1-round, n-channel) message transmission schemes for $n \leq 2t$. Suppose that there exists a (t, ϵ)-secure (1-round, n-channel) message transmission scheme with $n \leq 2t$. Consider an adversary **A** who replaces $x_1, \cdots, x_t$ with null strings. Then the receiver receives $n - t$ messages $x_{t+1}, \cdots, x_n$, where $n - t \leq 2t - t = t$. Then from the privacy condition, the receiver obtains no information on s. On the other hand, from the trivial reliability condition, he must output s. This is a contradiction.
□

8   Conclusion

In this paper, we first summed up a number of flaw of the previous almost secure (1-round, n-channel) message transmission scheme for $n = 2t + 1$ which was presented at Crypto 2004. We next showed an equivalence between (t, δ)-secure (1-round, n-channel) message transmission scheme for $n = 2t + 1$ and secret sharing schemes with cheaters. By using our equivalence, we derived a lower bound on the communication complexity. Finally, we presented a near optimum scheme which meets our bound approximately. This is the first construction of provably secure (t, δ)-secure (1-round, n-channel) message transmission schemes for $n = 2t + 1$.

Our results imply that $n \geq 2t + 1$ is necessary and sufficient for (t, ϵ)-secure (1-round, n-channel) message transmission schemes.

References

1. Agarwal, S., Cramer, R., de Haan, R.: Asymptotically Optimal Two-Round Perfectly Secure Message Transmission. In: Dwork, C. (ed.) CRYPTO 2006. LNCS, vol. 4117, pp. 394–408. Springer, Heidelberg (2006)
2. Dolev, D., Dwork, C., Waarts, O., Yung, M.: Perfectly Secure Message Transmission. J. ACM 40(1), 17–47 (1993)
3. MacWilliams, F.J., Sloanem, N.J.A.: The Theory of Error-correcting Codes. North-Holland, Amsterdam (1981)
4. Ogata, W., Kurosawa, K., Stinson, D.: Optimum Secret Sharing Scheme Secure against Cheating. SIAM J. Discrete Math. 20(1), 79–95 (2006)
5. Sayeed, H.M., Abu-Amara, H.: Efficient Perfectly Secure Message Transmission in Synchronous Networks. Inf. Comput. 126(1), 53–61 (1996)
6. Srinathan, K., Narayanan, A., Pandu Rangan, C.: Optimal Perfectly Secure Message Transmission. In: Franklin, M. (ed.) CRYPTO 2004. LNCS, vol. 3152, pp. 545–561. Springer, Heidelberg (2004)
7. Tompa, M., Woll, H.: How to share a secret with cheaters. Journal of Cryptology 1, 133–138 (1988)

Construction Methodology of Unconditionally Secure Signature Schemes

Junji Shikata

Graduate School of Environment and Information Sciences,
Yokohama National University, Japan

Abstract. In this talk, we survey: the models of unconditionally secure authentication and signature schemes; and the construction methodology for them. We also propose a construction of the unconditionally secure signature scheme by using universal hash families.

(I) Unconditionally Secure Authentication and Signature Schemes. In traditional unconditionally secure authentication codes (A-codes), there are a transmitter, a receiver, and an adversary (opponent). The receiver can check the validity of the message sent from the transmitter by using shared secret key. In this model it is assumed that they are trustworthy, and security under consideration is robustness for impersonation, substitution and more generally spoofing of order $L(\geq 0)$ by the adversary. In A^2-codes, one additional entity, called the arbiter, is included and assumed to be honest. If a dispute between the transmitter and receiver occurs, the arbiter resolves the dispute according to the resolution-rule. Furthermore, in A^3-codes, the arbiter is not necessarily trusted by the transmitter and receiver. The MRA-code (multireceiver authentication code) is the broadcast authentication system with multiple receivers. Any receiver can check the validity of the message sent from the honest transmitter by using his secret key. In this model, security under consideration is robustness for impersonation, substitution, and more generally spoofing of order $L(\geq 0)$, by a set of colluding receivers. Also, the MRA^2-code (resp. MRA^3-code) can be defined as a variant of the MRA-code such that the model of MRA^2-code (resp. MRA^3-code) is analogue of that of the A^2-code (resp. A^3-code). Although there have been several attempts to model signature schemes with unconditional security (e.g. [2]), we prefer the model of unconditionally secure signature schemes in [4], since it is much more similar to computationally secure ones than any other models: the (unconditionally secure) signature scheme is the point-to-point authentication system with multiple verifiers (receivers); any verifier can check the validity of the message by using his secret key; it is allowed to transfer the message among verifiers without compromising the security; and the security is formalized as EAUF-CMA&CSA.

(II) Construction Methodology. What we hope to achieve in construction of unconditionally secure authentication systems is: (i) efficiency; and/or (ii) flexibility and wide-range construction. From (i), we require efficient algorithms of the key generation, signature (authenticator, or tag) generation, and verification for it. Also, we require shorter sizes of keys and signatures (authenticator,

Y. Desmedt (Ed.): ICITS 2007, LNCS 4883, pp. 113–114, 2009.

or tag). In terms of key sizes, the ultimate is to reveal an optimal construction (i.e., a construction which meets lower bounds with equality). From (ii), it would be of interest to provide general settings of parameters and to utilize well-known primitives as building blocks to construct authentication systems. For A-codes, A^2-codes, A^3-codes, MRA-codes, and MRA^2-codes, there are various kinds of elegant constructions by using algebra (e.g. polynomials over finite fields/rings), geometry (e.g. projective spaces in finite geometry), combinatorics (e.g. orthogonal arrays, balanced incomplete block designs, cover-free families), universal hash families, and error-correcting codes. On the other hands, only a few constructions of unconditionally secure signature schemes are known: in [4], the construction based on multivariate polynomials over finite fields is proposed; and in [3], a systematic construction methodology based on multivariate polynomials over finite fields is proposed.

We now propose a construction of the unconditionally secure signature scheme by using universal hash families [1]. We first construct $\mathcal{F} = \{F : X \times Y \to Z(= Z_1 \times Z_2)\}$ as follows: Let $\mathcal{F}_1 = \{f : X \to Z_1\}$ be an ϵ_1-$ASU(N_1; l, n_1, \omega)$ and $\bar{Y} = \{\phi : \mathcal{F}_2 \to Z_2\}$ be an ϵ_2-$ASU(m; N_2, n_2, 2)$. Also, let $\Theta_1 : \mathcal{F}_1 \to GF(N_1)$ be a bijective map, $\Theta_2 : \bar{Y} \to GF(N_1)$ an injective map. We define $Y := \{(\phi_1, \phi_2) | \phi_1, \phi_2 \in \bar{Y}$ and the first components are all distinct$\}$, and $\mathcal{F} := \{\varphi_{f_1^{(0)}, f_1^{(1)}, ..., f_1^{(\kappa)}, f_2} : X \times Y \to Z_1 \times Z_2 | f_1^{(i)} \in \mathcal{F}_1 (0 \le i \le \kappa), f_2 \in \mathcal{F}_2\}$, where $\varphi_{f_1^{(0)}, f_1^{(1)}, ..., f_1^{(\kappa)}, f_2}(x, \phi_1, \phi_2) := (f(x), \phi_2(f_2))$ and $f = \Theta_1^{-1}(\Theta_1(f_1^{(0)}) + \sum_{i=1}^{\kappa} \Theta_2(\phi_1)^i \Theta_1(f_1^{(i)}))$. Then, we can obtain a signature scheme consisting of the following key generation algorithm Gen, signing algorithm Sig, and verification algorithm Ver. Gen chooses $F(\cdot, \cdot) \in \mathcal{F}$ uniformly at random. Also, it picks up $v_j \in Y$ at random, and computes $h_j(\cdot) := F(\cdot, v_j)$ for $j = 1, 2, \ldots, k$, where k is the number of verifiers. Then, a signing-key of the signer is $F(\cdot, \cdot)$ and a verification-key of the verifier V_j is $(v_j, h_j(\cdot))$ $(1 \le j \le k)$; Sig takes a message $m \in X$ and a signing-key $F(\cdot, \cdot) \in \mathcal{F}$ as input, and computes $g_m(\cdot) := F(m, \cdot)$. Then, the message-signature pair is $(m, g_m(\cdot))$; Ver takes a message-signature pair $(m, g_m(\cdot))$ and a verification-key $(v_j, h_j(\cdot))$ as input, and it outputs 1 if $g_m(v_j) = h_j(m)$ and 0 otherwise. Although this is the outline of construction, the details including security proofs will be provided in a full paper.

References

1. Atici, M., Stinson, D.: Universal hashing and multiple authentication. In: Koblitz, N. (ed.) CRYPTO 1996. LNCS, vol. 1109, pp. 16–30. Springer, Heidelberg (1996)
2. Chaum, D., Roijakkers, S.: Unconditionally secure digital signatures. In: Menezes, A., Vanstone, S.A. (eds.) CRYPTO 1990. LNCS, vol. 537, pp. 206–214. Springer, Heidelberg (1991)
3. Safavi-Naini, R., McAven, L., Yung, M.: General group authentication codes and their relation to "unconditionally-secure signatures". In: Bao, F., Deng, R., Zhou, J. (eds.) PKC 2004. LNCS, vol. 2947, pp. 231–247. Springer, Heidelberg (2004)
4. Shikata, J., Hanaoka, G., Zheng, Y., Imai, H.: Security notions for unconditionally secure signature schemes. In: Knudsen, L.R. (ed.) EUROCRYPT 2002. LNCS, vol. 2332, pp. 434–449. Springer, Heidelberg (2002)

New Results on Unconditionally Secure Multi-receiver Manual Authentication*

Shuhong Wang and Reihaneh Safavi-Naini

Center for Computer and Information Security Research
TITR, University of Wollongong, Australia
{shuhong,rei@uow.edu.au}

Abstract. Manual authentication is a recently proposed model of communication motivated by the settings where the only trusted infrastructure is a low bandwidth authenticated channel, possibly realized by the aid of a human, that connects the sender and the receiver who are otherwise connected through an insecure channel and do not have any shared key or public key infrastructure. A good example of such scenarios is pairing of devices in Bluetooth. Manual authentication systems are studied in computational and information theoretic security model and protocols with provable security have been proposed. In this paper we extend the results in information theoretic model in two directions. Firstly, we extend a single receiver scenario to multireceiver case where the sender wants to authenticate the same message to a group of receivers. We show new attacks (compared to single receiver case) that can launched in this model and demonstrate that the single receiver lower bound $2\log(1/\epsilon) + O(1)$ on the bandwidth of manual channel stays valid in the multireceiver scenario. We further propose a protocol that achieves this bound and provides security, in the sense that we define, if up to c receivers are corrupted. The second direction is the study of non-interactive protocols in unconditionally secure model. We prove that unlike computational security framework, without interaction a secure authentication protocol requires the bandwidth of the manual channel to be at least the same as the message size, hence non-trivial protocols do not exist.

Keywords: manual channel, (interactive) multireceiver authentication, security.

1 Introduction

Message authentication systems provide assurance for the receiver about the authenticity of a received message. Unconditionally secure authentication systems in symmetric key and asymmetric key models were introduced by Simmons [1] and later studied and extended to by a number of authors [2,3]. Information

---

* This work is in part supported by the Australian Research Council under Discovery Project grant DP0558490.

Y. Desmedt (Ed.): ICITS 2007, LNCS 4883, pp. 115–132, 2009.

theoretic bounds on the success probability of an adversary relates the success chance to the key entropy [4] and provides a lower bound on number of key bits that are required for achieving a certain level of protection. Gemmell and Naor [5] proposed an interactive protocol for authentication and showed that the key length can be reduced for the same level of protection[1].

As an extension of two-party authentication, MRA (multi-receiver authentication) aims at providing the integrity of a message sent from one sender to $n > 1$ receivers. MRA is very important for many applications, such as network control, TV broadcast, and other distributed systems. A trivial yet inefficient approach for MRA might be to run n copies of the two-party authentication protocol. Significant efforts have been made to construct nontrivial (more efficient and/or more secure) MRAs. Existing work on them in the information theoretic model includes [8,9,10], providing unconditional security. Note that all the existing MRAs were done in the shared key communication model where secrets are pre-distributed to participants.

Recently a new communication model for message authentication, motivated by scenarios such as pairing of devices in Bluetooth protocol [11], has been proposed. In this model sender and receiver do not have a shared key but in addition to the insecure channel that they are using for communication of messages, they are also connected through a low bandwidth authenticated channel, called *manual channel*. Messages sent over the manual channel cannot be modified. Also the attacker cannot inject a new message over this channel. However the attacker can change the synchronization of the channel and can delay or replay a sent message over this channel. The bandwidth of the manual channel is a scarce resource and has the same role as the key length in a symmetric or asymmetric key model and efficiency analysis of the protocols shows how efficiently the bandwidth has been used for providing protection against forgery.

Authentication in manual channel model has been studied in both computational and unconditionally secure frameworks [12,13]. Vaudenay proposed a formal model for analysis of protocols in this model. Naor, Sergev and Smith studied protocols in this model using unconditionally secure framework. Naor et al's protocol is interactive and is shown to limit the success chance of the forger to ϵ by using a manual channel with bandwidth $2\log\epsilon + O(1)$.

In computational model there are also non-interactive protocols, referred to as NIMAP (Non-interactive Manual Authentication Protocol). NIMAPs [14,15] are particularly interesting because they do not require the receive to be live and as long as what is received through the public channel *matches* what is received over the manual channel, the received message is considered authentic.

Our contribution

In this paper we extend the two party manual authentication scenario of [13] to a *multireceiver manual authentication* (MRMA), i.e., a scenario where there is one sender and multiple receivers, some possibly corrupted, and the sender does not have shared secret with receivers. The sender however has a low bandwidth

---

[1] The original version of their protocol was shown insecure [6]. The corrected version in [7] provides the claimed security.

manual channel with each receiver. We assume receivers are connected through a trusted infrastructure. In particular we assume there is a trusted initializer that provides key information to receivers. The adversary can corrupt up to c receivers. We will show that in the above MRMA system the $2\log(1/\epsilon) + O(1)$ lower bound on manual channel bandwidth holds for constant c. More specifically, we propose an interactive protocol for multireceiver case that limits the success chance of the forger to ϵ by using a manual channel with bandwidth $2\log(1/\epsilon) + O(\log c)$.

We also consider NIMAPs in unconditionally secure framework and show a lower bound on the bandwidth of the manual channel that effectively implies secure NIMAPs can only exist if the message is directly sent over the manual channel, i.e. trivial case. This demonstrates that unlike computational security framework interaction is necessary for secure manual authentication.

The paper is organized as follows. In Section 2 we present a communication model and a definition for multireceiver manual authentication (MRMA) under the model. We assume the strongest adversary in our model. In Section 3 we extend the Naor et al's protocol to multireceiver case. We first show that a straightforward extension cannot be secure in our strong adversary model, and then propose an secure extension, resulting in an interactive multireceiver manual authentication protocol. In Section 4 we show that non-interactive manual authentication in the unconditionally secure setting is not possible unless the message itself is sent over the manual channel. There, interaction is necessary in for unconditionally secure manual authentication. Finally, the paper is concluded in Section 5.

2   A Model for Multi-receiver Manual Authentication

We consider a setting where there are a sender $\mathcal{S}$ and a group of receivers denoted by $\mathcal{R} =: \{\mathcal{R}_1, \mathcal{R}_2, \cdots, \mathcal{R}_n\}$. The sender and receivers are connected via two types of channels (insecure and manual). Receivers are connected among themselves via one type of channels (insecure). However there is a trusted infrastructure among receivers. A motivating scenario is when a group leader is connected to each group member through a manual channel, and group members have some secret key information that enables them to have secure communication among themselves.

Communication between sender and receivers
The sender is connected to the receivers through an *insecure multicast* channel that is used to transmit the same message to all the receivers. Such an insecure multicast channel could be implemented by letting each receiver has a point to point channel to the sender. All these channels are insecure and are controlled by the adversary. In particular the adversary can control the link between the sender and each receiver independently, and read, inject, modify, remove and delay traffic as he wishes (similar to multicast over the Internet).

In addition to the public channel, we assume that there is a *manual multicast channel* that connects the sender to the receivers. This channel can be seen as n (unidirectional) manual channels, each connecting the sender to a receiver, that can be individually controlled by the adversary. The sender uses the multicast channel to send the same message to all receivers but the adversary's control can result in the message to have different synchronisation tampering for different receivers.

An example of a manual multicast channel is a display that is visible by all group members (e.g a classroom) and is used to show a short string to all group members (although in this example the tampering will be the same on all individual manual channels). Following the terminology in A-codes, such a short string is called as *manual tag* and sometimes *tag* without making confusion.

Communication among receivers

Receivers can communicate with each other through insecure point-to-point public channels. We assume there is a trusted initializer that securely distribute keys to receivers, hence allowing them to use traditional cryptographic primitives.

The adversary

Adversary has full control over public channels can target one or more channels (but not all). He can can read, modify or delay messages; he can prevent them from being delivered; he can also replay old messages or insert new ones at any time. The adversary can control one or more manual channels between the sender and receivers. He is however restricted to tampering with synchronisation information; i.e. read, remove, delay, reply of sent messages.

The adversary can also corrupt up to c receivers and have them deviate from the protocol in anyway he defines, but of course subject to restrictions in the communication model.

2.1   Extending Naor *et al* Protocol to MRMA

Our aim is to extend Naor *et al* protocol to allow a sender to authenticate a message m to a group of receivers when the communication structure is defined as above.

A basic approach would be to use the trusted infrastructure to reduce the group of receivers $\mathcal{R}$ into a single entity (i.e., a single receiver) and use the single receiver protocol of Naor *et al* [13] between the sender and this *combined receiver*.

We first show that without assuming a trusted infrastructure and using a direct application of the protocol, a single dishonest receiver can subvert the system. In Subsection 3.1 we describe two attacks that show how an adversary can use a man-in-middle strategy to forge a message with or without manipulating synchronization of messages. We next consider a model assuming receivers can be initialized by a *trusted initializer* who can provide some secret information (hence a trusted infrastructure) to them. Hence our model can be viewed as a combination of manual channel model between sender and receiver, and a trusted initializer model among receivers. See also Figure 1.

Similar to the single receiver model of [13], the input of the sender $\mathcal{S}$ is a message m, which she wishes to authenticate to the set of receivers $\mathcal{R}$. In the first round, $\mathcal{S}$ sends the message and an authentication tag $A_{\mathcal{S}}^1$ over the insecure

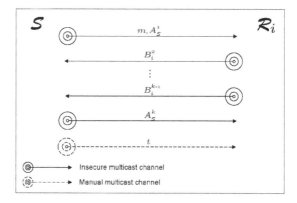

Fig. 1. The multireceiver manual authentication (MRMA) model

multicast channel. In the following rounds only a tag $A_{\mathcal{S}}^j$ (or B_i^j) is sent over the insecure channel, meaning that the tag is from $\mathcal{S}$ (or from $\mathcal{R}_i$). All communications over public channel can be controlled by the adversary. He can inject or modify the input message m. The replaced message $\widehat{m}_i$ is received by the receiver $\mathcal{R}_i, i = 1, 2, \cdots, n$. He receives all of the tags $A_{\mathcal{S}}^j$ and can replace them with $\widehat{A}_i^j$ of his choice intending for $\mathcal{R}_i$. The adversary also receives each of the tags B_i^j and can replace them with $\widehat{B}_i^j$ before they arrive $\mathcal{S}$. Finally, $\mathcal{S}$ manually authenticates a short *manual tag* t, i.e., sent over the manual channel.

For reading ease, we list the notations represent what are sent and received at each player's end in Table 1.

Table 1. Notations reflects changes. j specifies the round

$\mathcal{S}$ side sending/receiving $\mathcal{R}_i$ side		
m	$\longrightarrow$	$\widehat{m}_i$
$A_{\mathcal{S}}^j$	$\longrightarrow$	$\widehat{A}_i^j$
$\widehat{B}_i^j$	$\longleftarrow$	B_i^j

Notice that in the presence of a computationally unbounded adversary, we can assume w.l.g that the manually authenticated string is sent in the last round. As being pointed out in [13], this is true also in the computational setting, under the assumption that distributively one-way functions do not exit. And similarly, we also allow the adversary to control the synchronization of the protocol's execution. That is, the adversary can carry on two separate, possibly asynchronous conversations, one with the sender and one with the receivers. However, the party that is supposed to send a message waits until it receives the adversary's message from the previous round. For example, the sender $\mathcal{S}$ will only send his $A_{\mathcal{S}}^{j+1}$ after he has obtained all the $\widehat{B}_i^j$ ($i = 1, 2, \cdots, n$) from the receivers.

We assume the adversary can corrupt a subset $\mathcal{C} \subset \mathcal{R}$ of the receivers and $c = |\mathcal{C}|$.

Definition 1. *An unconditionally (n, c)-secure (a, b, k, ϵ)-manual authentication protocol is a k-round protocol in the communication model described above, in which the sender wishes to authenticate an a-bit input message to n receivers, while manually authenticating at most b-bits to over a multireceiver manual channel. The following requirement must hold:*

- *Completeness: For all input message m, when there is no interference by the adversary in the execution and all the players honestly follow, every receiver accepts with probability at least $1/2$.*
- *Unforgeability: For any computationally unbounded adversary, for any $\mathcal{C}$ of size c receivers corrupted by the adversary, and for all input messages m, if the adversary replaces m with a different message $\widehat{m}_i$ for any $\mathcal{R}_i \notin \mathcal{C}$, then $\mathcal{R}_i$ accepts $\widehat{m}_i$ with probability at most ϵ.*

Lower bound on bandwidth

Obviously when $n = 1$, our model reduces to the basic model of Naor *et al* [13] and so the lower bound for our model cannot be less than that. By constructing a protocol that uses a manual channel with bandwidth being only $2 \log(1/\epsilon) + O(\log c)$, we show that the lower bound for the our MRMA model is in fact equal to $2 \log(1/\epsilon) + O(1)$ for constant c, the same lower bound of the basic model. This is particularly the case for small groups.

3   Interactive MRMA Protocols

At first, we show that a straightforward extension of a single-receiver scheme is not secure in the multi-receiver setting due to existence of strong attacks. This result is consistent to other known results on multi-receiver authentications in the shared-key communication model. More precisely, that is a straightforward extension of a single receiver scheme (A-code) is not secure in the multi-receiver setting. We note that this consistence is however due to different reasons (of course both due to distrust among receivers). In the shared-key model, the insecurity is due to the difference that the sender and receiver in A-codes is symmetric while in secure MRA-codes should be asymmetric. But in the manual channel model (always asymmetric), the insecurity is due to the difference that a single-receiver will generate a truly random for himself, while a group of receivers may not voluntarily generate a truly random for the group (traitors exist).

Then we present two attacks to show that a single traitor is enough to subvert the protocol completely and thus new technique must employed to secure the protocol. And in Subsection 3.2 we show that by using commitment schemes, the group of receivers can be forced to play honestly, in the sense that dishonest behavior (of up to $c = n - 1$ corrupted receivers) can cheat no honest receiver.

3.1   A Straightforward Extension

In the following, we present a straightforward extension of the interactive protocol P_k of [13], from the single receiver setting to the multi-receiver setting. A brief description of the P_k [13] is given in the Appendix A. Denote the resulting protocol by P_k^n. We show how an inside attacker (e.g., corrupted by the adversary) can fool the other receivers in P_k^n. Note that P_k^n is quite efficient in the sense that generating and sending a message to all the receivers is once-off in every round. It is obvious that a trivial multi-receiver solution by repeating a single-receiver protocol multiple times does not enjoy this computation and communication efficiency.

For simplicity, let $n = 2$ and $k = 2$, thus the round index j can be omitted. The $P_{n=2}^{k=2}$ protocol is described as below, where f (more exactly f^j) is defined in Section 3.2, which is the function C^j in [13]. Note that for any equivalent tasks of R_1 and of R_2, the order of performing them can be either.

The protocol $P_{n=2}^{k=2}$

1. S multicasts m to the receivers through the insecure channel.
2. R_1 receives the message as $\widehat{m}_1$ and R_2 receives the message as $\widehat{m}_2$.
   (a) S chooses $A_S \in_R GF[Q]$ and multicasts it to R_1, R_2.
   (b) R_1 receives $\widehat{A}_1$, then chooses $B_1 \in_R GF[Q]$ and sends it to S and R_2.
   (c) R_2 receives $\widehat{A}_2$, then chooses $B_2 \in_R GF[Q]$ and sends it to S and R_1.
   (d) After receiving the $\widehat{B}_1$ and $\widehat{B}_2$, S computes $\widehat{B} = \widehat{B}_1 + \widehat{B}_2$ and computes $m_S = \langle \widehat{B}, f_{\widehat{B}}(m) + A_S \rangle$.
   (e) R_1 receives B_2, then computes $B = B_1 + B_2$ and $m_1 = \langle B, f_B(\widehat{m}_1) + \widehat{A}_1 \rangle$.
   (f) R_2 receives B_1, then computes $B = B_1 + B_2$ and $m_2 = \langle B, f_B(\widehat{m}_2) + \widehat{A}_2 \rangle$.
3. S multicasts m_S to R_1, R_2 through the manual multicast channel.
4. R_1 accepts if and only if $m_S = m_1$; R_2 accepts if and only if $m_S = m_2$.

Fig. 2. An insecure extension of Naor et al's P_k to MRMA model

Clearly the sum B (resp. $\widehat{B}$) plays exactly the role of the random number selected by the single receiver (resp. what received by the sender) of P_k. The protocol P_k is proved to be secure, but P_k^n is not secure any more. In order to better understand our construction, in the following we show two attacks on the protocol P_k^n below.

As illustrated in Figure 3, the *asynchronous* attack is named from that the dishonest R_2 (or considering that he is corrupted by an adversary) runs the protocol *non-synchronically* (i.e., separately) with the sender S and the other receiver R_1 who are both honest. When running the protocol with S, R_2 impersonates R_1 sending an arbitrary $\widehat{B}_1$ and also sending his own $\widehat{B}_2$. Then S will send the supposed manual tag $t = \langle \widehat{B}, f_{\widehat{B}}(m) + A \rangle$ through the manual channel. Now R_2 delays the manual tag, and impersonates S to run the protocol with R_1.

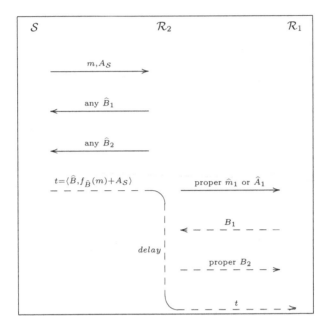

Fig. 3. An attack with manipulating synchronization

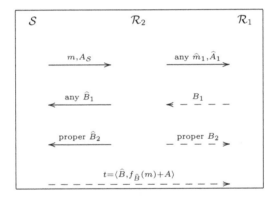

Fig. 4. An attack without manipulating synchronization

He can choose a proper $\widehat{A}_1$ for an arbitrary message $\widehat{m}_1$ or vice versa such that $f_{\widehat{B}}(\widehat{m}_1) + \widehat{A}_1 = f_{\widehat{B}}(m) + A$. On receiving $\widehat{m}_1, \widehat{A}_1$ the receiver $\mathcal{R}_1$ sends B_1 to $\mathcal{R}_2$ and thus $\mathcal{R}_2$ can simply sends $B_2 = \widehat{B}_1 + \widehat{B}_2 - B_1$ to $\mathcal{R}_1$. And then $\mathcal{R}_2$ let the tag t get through to $\mathcal{R}_1$ (recall that $\mathcal{R}_2$ is not able to modify the manual tag over the manual channel). It is easy to see that $\mathcal{R}_1$ will accept $\widehat{m}_1$ as authentic from $\mathcal{S}$.

As illustrated in Figure 4, the *dependent* attack does not use an asynchronous conversation, instead, it merely make use of the fact that $\widehat{B}_2$ and B_2 can be *dependent* on $\widehat{B}_1$ and B_1 (i.e. $\mathcal{R}_2$ can choose the former after he knows the latter). In fact, for any $m, A_{\mathcal{S}}$ and any $\widehat{m}_1, \widehat{A}_1$, $F(x) := (f_x(m) + A_{\mathcal{S}}) - (f_x(\widehat{m}_1) + \widehat{A}_1)$ is a polynomial of the variable x. Denote x_0 a root of $F(x)$, then $\mathcal{R}_2$ can simply compute and send $\widehat{B}_2 = x_0 - \widehat{B}_1$ and $B_2 = x_0 - B_1$. One can easily verify that $\mathcal{R}_1$ would accept the tag t sent by $\mathcal{S}$.

3.2   An Interactive Protocol

In a multireceiver manual authentication system the sender is trusted but some of the receivers can be corrupted by the adversary. Our protocol, Π_k, as described below is secure against such a strong adversary.

The main observation from the above section is that to ensure security of the protocol, one needs to ensure the sum $B^j = \sum_{i=1}^{n} B_i^j$ remains unpredictable (cannot be engineered by the adversary). We use unconditionally secure non-interactive commitment schemes (USNIC) to achieve this goal. Examples of such commitment schemes include the ones by Rivest [16] and by Blundo *et al* [17].

We denote the USNIC scheme working in finite field GF$[Q]$ by USNIC$[Q]$ and choose it to be the scheme of Blundo *et al*. To make the paper self-contained, we briefly review their scheme in Appendix B.

The commitment scheme is used in each round, by each receiver to commit to a random value of his choice to all the other receivers[2] to provide assurance for other receivers that their random values are not captured for subverting the protocol (See the dependent attack in Subsection 3.1, Figure 4 for detail). In other words the sum $B^j = \sum_{i=1}^{n} B_i^j$ is unpredictable (has full entropy). We note that this can be achieved even if only one receiver is honest, i.e., if one B_i^j is truly randomly. This lets us to treat the group of the receivers as one entity and thus the security of our MRMA protocol reduces to the security of Naor et al's protocol P_k [13].

To reduce the length of manual tag, similar to the protocol in [13], we use a sequence of compression function families $f^1, f^2, \cdots, f^{k-1}$ in an k-round interactive protocol. More precisely, given the length, a, of the input message and the upper bound, $(c+1)\epsilon$, on the adversary's forgery probability, $k-1$ finite fields $Q_j, j = 1, \cdots k-1$, are chosen such that $\frac{2^{k-j}a_j}{\epsilon} \leq Q_j < \frac{2^{k-j+1}a_j}{\epsilon}$, where $a_1 = a$ and $a_{j+1} = \lceil 2 \log Q_j \rceil$. Then each f_x^j chosen from the family f^j maps an a_j-bit message m into GF$[Q_j]$ in the following way: firstly the message is split as $m = m_1 m_2 \cdots m_d$ (concatenation of d strings) with each $m_i \in$ GF$[Q_j]$, and then the function is evaluated as $f_x^j(m) = m_1 x + m_2 x^2 + \cdots + m_d x^d \mod Q_j$. The splitting methods, and equivalently the function family f^j, is public known for all $j = 1, 2, \cdots, k-1$.

The protocol Π_k:

1. S multicasts $m_{\mathcal{S}}^1 = m$ to the receivers through the insecure channel.

---

[2] It is an interesting open problem to construct more sophistic schemes for committing to multiple messages, so that the trusted initializer is invoked only once.

2. For $i = \{1, 2, \cdots, n\}$, $\mathcal{R}_i$ obtains the message $m_i^1 = \widehat{m}_i$.
3. For $j = 1$ to $k - 1$.
   (a) If j is odd, then
       i. $\mathcal{S}$ chooses $A_\mathcal{S}^j \in_R \mathrm{GF}[Q_j]$ and multicasts it to $\mathcal{R}$, through the insecure multicast channel.
       ii. For $i = \{1, 2, \cdots, n\}$, $\mathcal{R}_i$ receives $\widehat{A}_i^j$. Then he chooses and commits to (using USNIC$[Q_j]$) a random $B_i^j \in_R \mathrm{GF}[Q_j]$ all the other receivers $\mathcal{R} \setminus \mathcal{R}_i$. After receiving all the commitments from other receivers, he sends B_i^j to $\mathcal{S}$ and opens the his commitment to other receivers.
       iii. After receiving all the $\widehat{B}_i^j$, $\mathcal{S}$ computes $\widehat{B}^j = \sum_{i=1}^n \widehat{B}_i^j$ and $m_\mathcal{S}^{j+1} = \langle \widehat{B}^j, f_{\widehat{B}^j}^j(m_\mathcal{S}^j) + A_\mathcal{S}^j \rangle$.
       iv. When all the commitments are correctly opened, $\mathcal{R}_i$ computes $B^j = \sum_{i=1}^n B_i^j$ and $m_i^{j+1} = \langle B^j, f_{B^j}^j(m_i^j) + \widehat{A}_i^j \rangle$.
   (b) If j is even, then
       i. For $i = \{1, 2, \cdots, n\}$, $\mathcal{R}_i$ chooses $B_i^j \in \mathrm{GF}[Q_j]$ and commits to it to other receivers using USNIC$[Q_j]$ scheme. After received all the commitments, he sends B_i^j to $\mathcal{S}$ and reveals his commitment.
       ii. After receiving all the $\widehat{B}_i^j$, $\mathcal{S}$ chooses $A_\mathcal{S}^j \in_R \mathrm{GF}[Q_j]$ and multicasts it to $\mathcal{R}$. Then he computes $\widehat{B}^j = \sum_{i=1}^n \widehat{B}_i^j$ and $m_\mathcal{S}^{j+1} = \langle A_\mathcal{S}^j, \widehat{B}^j, f_{A_\mathcal{S}^j}^j(m_\mathcal{S}^j) + \widehat{B}^j \rangle$.
       iii. For $i = \{1, 2, \cdots, n\}$, $\mathcal{R}_i$ computes $B^j = \sum_{i=1}^n B_i^j$ when all the commitments are correctly opened and then computes $m_i^{j+1} = \langle \widehat{A}_i^j, f_{\widehat{A}_i^j}^j(m_i^j) + B^j \rangle$ on receiving $\widehat{A}_i^j$.
4. $\mathcal{S}$ multicasts $m_\mathcal{S}^k$ to $\mathcal{R}$ through the manual multicast channel.
5. For $i = \{1, 2, \cdots, n\}$, $\mathcal{R}_i$ accepts if and only if $m_\mathcal{S}^k = m_i^k$.

Theorem 1. *For any $1 \leq c < n$ colluders, the above protocol Π_k is an (n, c)-secure $(a, b, k, (c+1)\epsilon)$-manual authentication protocol in the MRMA model, with $b \leq 2\log(1/\epsilon) + 2\log^{k-1} a + O(1)$.*

Proof (sketch). See Appendix C for the detailed proof.
The proof is analogous to that of the protocol P_k in [13] where the B^j is randomly chosen by a single receiver after receiving $\widehat{A}^j$. In our protocol B^j is the sum (or any function depending on all) of the random variables B_i^j chosen by $\mathcal{R}_i$, $i = 1, 2, \cdots, n$. Thus to prove the security of our protocol, it is sufficient to prove that the B^j that $\mathcal{R}_i \notin \mathcal{C}$ computes is truly random and plays the same role of B^j in the single receiver protocol. For instance in case of j odd, to prove that the sum B^j, after $\mathcal{R}_i$ received $\widehat{A}_i^j$ from the adversary, is truly random we note that since B^j depends on B_i^j which is chosen after $\mathcal{R}_i$ received $\widehat{A}_i^j$, it is sufficient to prove that the adversary can not control B^j. This is obviously true (except with a probability $\leq c/Q_j$) because the security of underlying commitment scheme USNIC$[Q_j]$ (see Appendix C), For the case of even j, the conclusion holds similarly. So the total cheating probability is bounded by $\sum_{j=1}^{k-1} (\frac{c}{Q_j} + \frac{\epsilon}{2^{k-j}}) \leq (c+1)\epsilon$.

Since by using USNIC schemes, we are able to handle a group $\mathcal{R}$ of receiver as a single receiver, thus the number of bits sent over the manual channel is actually same to the single receiver case, that is $b \leq 2\log(1/\epsilon) + 2\log^{k-1} a + O(1)$ by claim 17 in [13]. And if there exists some $1 \leq j \leq k-2$ such that $a_j \leq \frac{2^{k-j}}{\epsilon}$, we can choose $Q_{k-1} = \Theta(1/\epsilon)$ instead of $Q_{k-1} = \Theta((1/\epsilon)\log(1/\epsilon))$ and achieves $b = 2\log(1/\epsilon) + O(1)$. □

Corollary 1. *An (n, c)-secure (a, b, k, ϵ)-manual authentication protocol in the MRMA model exists for all $a, k, 1 \leq c \leq n-1$, $0 < \epsilon < 1$ and $b \leq 2\log(1/\epsilon) + 2\log^{k-1} a + O(\log c)$.*

Proof. By replacing $(c+1)\epsilon$ with ϵ in Theorem 1, we have $b \leq 2\log((c+1)/\epsilon) + 2\log^{k-1} a + O(1) = 2\log(1/\epsilon) + 2\log^{k-1} a + 2\log(c+1) + O(1)$. □

In case $a_j \leq \frac{(c+1)2^{k-j}}{\epsilon}$ for some $j = 1, \cdots, k-2$, we immediately have a lower bound for the MRMA model $2\log(1/\epsilon) + O(\log c)$. This is the same bound as the single receiver model for constant c, that is $2\log(1/\epsilon) + O(1)$. It is however not known for large c, whether $2\log(1/\epsilon) + O(\log c)$ is the tight bound.

4   Impossibility of Noninteraction

Non-interactive Manual Authentication Protocols (NIMAPs) [14,15] are particularly interesting in computational model because they do not require the receive to be live and as long as what is received through the public channel *matches* what is received over the manual channel, the received message is considered authentic. In this section we show a negative result that non-trivial NIMAPs do not exist in information theoretic model.

THE INFORMATION THEORETIC NIMAP MODEL: The sender $\mathcal{S}$ sends the message m and some x over the insecure public channel, and a tag t over the manual channel. The receiver $\mathcal{R}$ decides wether or not accepts m as authentic from $\mathcal{S}$.

ADVANTAGE: The non-interactive protocol (if exists) has an obvious advantage over interactive protocol, that is, it is simple and efficient in communication. More importantly, there is an advantage that non-interactive protocol for single receiver also works for multiple receivers by replacing the unicast channels with multicast ones. The intrinsic reason is that non-interactive protocol needs no information from the receiver, no matter it is a single entity or a group. For this reason, we thereafter consider $\mathcal{R}$ as a single entity.

IMPOSSIBILITY: We, however, notice that non-interactive manual authentication protocol does not exists in the "pure" manual channel model (i.e., without secrets between sender and receiver, and without requirements such as stall-free on the manual channel) *unless* the manual channel has enough bandwidth to transmit the whole message. This can be roughly argued as follows.

Suppose now $|m| > |t|$, then there definitely exists some other message $\widehat{m}$ which is authenticated under the same manual tag t (under some $\widehat{x}$). Therefore, on observing the authentication transcripts (m, x, t), the adversary simply replaces (m, x) with $(\widehat{m}, \widehat{x})$. The adversary can do so "online" by removing m, x and delaying t until he figures out such $(\widehat{m}, \widehat{x})$ and then inserts it into the insecure channel.

To formally prove the impossibility, we need the following formal definition of non-interactive manual authentication protocol.

Definition 2. *Let M, X, T denote the random variables overs the sets $\mathcal{M}, \mathcal{X}, \mathcal{T}$, respectively. A non-interactive manual protocol is given by a joint conditional distribution $P_{XT|M} : (\mathcal{X}, \mathcal{T}, \mathcal{M}) \to [0, 1]$, where the input message m is chosen according to the distribution $P_M : \mathcal{M} \to [0, 1]$ (by either the adversary or $\mathcal{S}$). The values (m, x) of (M, X) are sent over the insecure channel and the value t of T is sent over the manual channel. Finally, $\mathcal{R}$ receives $\widehat{m}, \widehat{x}, t$ and accepts $\widehat{m}$ as authentic if and only if $P_M(\widehat{m}) > 0$ [3] and $V(\widehat{m}, \widehat{x}, t) = 1$, where $V(\cdot)$ is a boolean-valued function $V(m, x, t) \in \{0, 1\}$ over $\mathcal{M} \times \mathcal{X} \times \mathcal{T}$.*

Typically, the distribution P_M is chosen to be the uniform distribution; the joint conditional distribution $P_{XT|M}$ is given in terms of efficiently computable randomized function $f : \mathcal{M} \times \Gamma \to \mathcal{X} \times \mathcal{T}$, where Γ is some finite se, such that $P_{..|M}$ is the distribution of $f(m, \gamma))$ for a uniformly random chosen $\gamma \in \Gamma$. This is often directly used as the definition of a manual authentication protocol, such as [19,15], although they are in computational setting. The protocol of Naor *et al* [13] and ours in previous sections are also described in this typical manner. Note that this definition can be extended to cover the interactive manual authentication protocol by defining a series of joint conditional distributions. Due to the time and space limitation, we leave the extension as our future work.

We use the term "an input message m" to mean a message $m \in \mathcal{M}$ satisfying $P_M(m) > 0$, and denote the set of input messages by $\mathcal{M}^+$. Then for every $m \in \mathcal{M}^+$, define $\mathcal{T}_m = \{t \in \mathcal{T} : \exists x \in \mathcal{X}, s.t., P_{XT|M}(x, t|m) > 0\}$ and $\Delta_m = \{t \in \mathcal{T} : \exists x \in \mathcal{X}, s.t., V(m, x, t) = 1\}$. $\mathcal{T}_m$ is called the set of correct manual tags with regard to an input message m, and Δ_m is called the acceptable manual tags with regard to an input message m. Then we can use $t \in \mathcal{T}_m$ (resp. $t \in \Delta_m$) to refer to the event that "there exists an $x \in \mathcal{X}$ such that $P_{XT|M}(x, t|m) > 0$ (resp. $V(m, x, t) = 1$) holds for the input message m". Let $1/2 \leq \xi \leq 1$ and $0 \leq \epsilon < 1$ be two real number constants, and let $\epsilon(\widehat{m}|m, t)$ be the chance of an adversary, who observes the authentication transcripts[4] (m, x, t), in deceiving $\mathcal{R}$ into accepting a different message $\widehat{m}$ using his best strategy. We have the following definition for security of a non-interactive manual authentication protocol.

Definition 3. *A non-interactive manual authentication protocol is said to be information theoretically (ξ, ϵ)-secure if the following properties hold.*

---

[3] This can be looked as the message redundancy verification that excludes the messages meaningless. However, one can assume $P_M(m) > 0$ holds for all $m \in \mathcal{M}$ to omit this verification without impact on our impossibility result since, adding m with $P_M(m) = 0$ to $\mathcal{M}$ only increase its size, has no effect on its entropy $H(M)$.

[4] Which, by the definition of $\mathcal{T}_m$, implies $t \in \mathcal{T}_m$.

Completeness. *The joint conditional distribution satisfies for every $m \in \mathcal{M}^+$, $\sum_{x,t:V(m,x,t)=1} P_{XT|M}(x,t|m) \geq \xi$. In other words, for all input message m, when there is no interference by the adversary in the execution, the receiver accepts m with probability at least ξ.*

Unforgeability. *The joint conditional distribution satisfies $\epsilon(\widehat{m}|m,t) \leq \epsilon$, for all $m \neq \widehat{m} \in \mathcal{M}^+$ and $t \in \mathcal{T}_m$. In other words, for any computationally unbounded adversary, and for all input message m, if the adversary replaces m with a different message $\widehat{m}$, then $\mathcal{R}$ accepts $\widehat{m}$ with probability at most ϵ.*

By the definitions, the property of *perfect completeness* (i.e., $\xi = 1$) in Section 2 is guaranteed if and only if $V(m,x,t) = 1$ holds whenever $P_{XT|M}(x,t,m) > 0$.

For a fixed protocol, i.e., a fixed joint conditional distribution $P_{XT|M}(x,t|m)$, the maximal chance ϵ of success of an adversary could be calculated as

$$\epsilon = \max_{m,t \in \mathcal{T}_m} \max_{\widehat{m} \neq m} \epsilon(\widehat{m}|m,t).$$

Since the adversary has computationally unbounded power, then

$$\begin{aligned}
\epsilon(\widehat{m}|m,t) &= \Pr[V(\widehat{m}, *, t) = 1 | t \in \mathcal{T}_m] \\
&= \Pr[t \in \Delta_{\widehat{m}} | t \in \mathcal{T}_m] = \Pr[t \in \mathcal{T}_m \cap \Delta_{\widehat{m}}] \\
&= \begin{cases} 1 & \text{if } t \in \Delta_{\widehat{m}}, \\ 0 & \text{if } t \notin \Delta_{\widehat{m}}. \end{cases}
\end{aligned}$$

is a boolean-valued function and is only defined for $m, \widehat{m} \in \mathcal{M}^+$.

Theorem 2. *For any information theoretically secure (ξ, ϵ) non-interactive manual authentication protocol, $|\mathcal{M}^+| \leq |\mathcal{T}|$. Furthermore, if $\xi = 1$, then $H(M) \leq H(T)$, where $H(\cdot)$ denotes the Shannon entropy function.*

Proof. We observe that $\Pr[t \in \mathcal{T}_m \cap \Delta_{\widehat{m}}] \leq \epsilon < 1$ is equivalent to $\Pr[t \in \mathcal{T}_m \cap \Delta_{\widehat{m}}] = 0$ since it is a boolean function. That is to say $\mathcal{T}_m \cap \Delta_{\widehat{m}} = \emptyset$ for all $m \neq \widehat{m} \in \mathcal{M}^+$. Because $\Delta_m \subseteq \mathcal{T}_m$, we further have $\Delta_m \cap \Delta_{\widehat{m}} = \emptyset$ for all $m \neq \widehat{m} \in \mathcal{M}^+$. And, thanks to the completeness property, we know $\Delta_m \neq \emptyset$ for all $P_M(m) > 0$. Together, we can claim that $\{\Delta_m\}_{m \in \mathcal{M}^+}$ forms a partition of a subset of $\mathcal{T}$. So we immediately have $|\mathcal{M}^+| \leq |\mathcal{T}|$. But $|\mathcal{M}| \leq |\mathcal{T}|$ is not necessarily true if there exist some messages m with $P_M(m) = 0$. Instead, we show $H(M) \leq H(T)$ as below.

Denote by P_{MXT} the joint distribution over $\mathcal{M}, \mathcal{X}, \mathcal{T}$ determined by P_M and $P_{XT|M}$. Then $P_{MXT}(m,x,t)$ is computed as $P_M(m) \cdot P_{XT|M}(x,t|m)$. Artificially define a conditional probability

$$\Pr[m|t] = \begin{cases} 1 & \text{if } t \in \Delta_m; \\ 0 & \text{otherwise,} \end{cases}$$

then $H(M|t) = -\sum_{\Pr[m|t]>0} \Pr[m|t] \cdot \log_2 \Pr[m|t] = 0$, which implies $H(M,T) = H(T)$. Following the fact that the joint entropy of two variables is not smaller than the entropy of either variable, i.e., $H(M,T) \geq H(M)$, we easily arrive at the conclusion $H(T) \geq H(M)$. If $\Pr[m|t]$ matches the conditional distribution $P_{M|T}$ deducted from P_{MXT}, then the conclusion also holds for the protocol.

In the following, we show that for perfect complete non-interactive protocol, $\Pr[m|t]$ does match the conditional distribution $P_{M|T}$ defined by the protocol. In fact, we have for the general case that,

$$
P_{M|T}(m,t) = \sum_{x \in \mathcal{X}} \frac{P_{MXT}(m,x,t)}{P_T(t)} = \frac{\sum_{x \in \mathcal{X}} P_M(m) \cdot P_{XT|M}(x,t,m)}{\sum_{m \in \mathcal{M}} \sum_{x \in \mathcal{X}} P_M(m) \cdot P_{XT|M}(x,t|m)}
$$

$$
= \frac{\sum_{x \in \mathcal{X}} P_M(m) \cdot P_{XT|M}(x,t,m)}{\sum_{x \in \mathcal{X}} P_M(m) \cdot P_{XT|M}(x,t,m) + \sum_{m \neq \widehat{m} \in \mathcal{M}} \sum_{x \in \mathcal{X}} P_M(\widehat{m}) \cdot P_{XT|M}(x,t,\widehat{m})}
$$

$$
= \begin{cases} 0 & \text{if } m \notin \mathcal{M}^+ \text{ or } t \notin \mathcal{T}_m; \\ p \in (0,1) & \text{if } t \in \mathcal{T}_m \setminus \Delta_m; \\ 1 & \text{if } t \in \Delta_m. \end{cases}
$$

Then we can conclude the proof by noticing that $\mathcal{T}_m = \Delta_m$ for a perfect completeness protocol and thus $\mathcal{T}_m \setminus \Delta_m = \emptyset$.   □

5   Conclusions

Manual authentication captures numerous real life scenarios where a sender wants to send a message to a receiver with whom he does not have any pre-distribute keys, however he an use a low bandwidth auxiliary channel to send short strings authentically. We propose an extension of this model where the sender wants to send the message to a group of receivers. We introduce multireceiver manual channel to model devices such as a display used to display a short string to a group of people, or a speaker is used to send a short string to a group. Such a manual channel can be seen as a collection of manual channels, one for each receiver. Our model of adversary is the most powerful one, allowing the adversary to control independently each manual channel. We gave the construction of a protocol that achieves optimal security assuming a trusted infrastructure among receivers. We also showed nontrivial NIMAP in unconditionally secure framework does not exist. An interesting question is to consider extensions of multireceiver manual authentication systems where receivers are connected through other types of trusted mechanisms (e.g. manual channels).

References

1. Simmons, G.J.: Authentication theory/coding theory. In: Blakely, G.R., Chaum, D. (eds.) CRYPTO 1984. LNCS, vol. 196, pp. 411–431. Springer, Heidelberg (1985)
2. Simmons, G.J.: Message authentication with arbitration of transmitter/receiver disputes. In: Price, W.L., Chaum, D. (eds.) EUROCRYPT 1987. LNCS, vol. 304, pp. 151–165. Springer, Heidelberg (1988)

3. Simmons, G.J.: A survey of information authentication. In: Simmons, G.J. (ed.) Contemporary Cryptology, The Science of Information Integrity, pp. 379–419. IEEE Press, Los Alamitos (1992); Preliminary version appeared in Proceedings of the IEEE 76, 603–620 (1988)

4. Shannon, C.E.: A mathematical theory of communication. Mobile Computing and Communications Review 5(1), 3–55 (2001)

5. Gemmell, P., Naor, M.: Codes for interactive authentication. In: Stinson, D.R. (ed.) CRYPTO 1993. LNCS, vol. 773, pp. 355–367. Springer, Heidelberg (1994)

6. Gehrmann, C.: Cryptanalysis of the gemmell and naor multiround authentication protocol. In: Desmedt, Y.G. (ed.) CRYPTO 1994. LNCS, vol. 839, pp. 121–128. Springer, Heidelberg (1994)

7. Gehrmann, C.: Secure multiround authentication protocols. In: Guillou, L.C., Quisquater, J.-J. (eds.) EUROCRYPT 1995. LNCS, vol. 921, pp. 158–167. Springer, Heidelberg (1995)

8. Desmedt, Y., Frankel, Y., Yung, M.: Multi-receiver/multi-sender network security: Efficient authenticated multicast/feedback. In: INFOCOM, pp. 2045–2054 (1992)

9. Kurosawa, K., Obana, S.: Characterisation of (k, n) multi-receiver authentication. In: Mu, Y., Pieprzyk, J.P., Varadharajan, V. (eds.) ACISP 1997. LNCS, vol. 1270, pp. 204–215. Springer, Heidelberg (1997)

10. Safavi-Naini, R., Wang, H.: New results on multi-receiver authentication codes. In: Nyberg, K. (ed.) EUROCRYPT 1998. LNCS, vol. 1403, pp. 527–541. Springer, Heidelberg (1998)

11. Hoepman, J.H.: The ephemeral pairing problem. In: Juels, A. (ed.) FC 2004. LNCS, vol. 3110, pp. 212–226. Springer, Heidelberg (2004)

12. Vaudenay, S.: Secure communications over insecure channels based on short authenticated strings. In: Shoup, V. (ed.) CRYPTO 2005. LNCS, vol. 3621, pp. 309–326. Springer, Heidelberg (2005)

13. Naor, M., Segev, G., Smith, A.: Tight bounds for unconditional authentication protocols in the manual channel and shared key models. In: Dwork, C. (ed.) CRYPTO 2006. LNCS, vol. 4117, pp. 214–231. Springer, Heidelberg (2006)

14. Peyrin, T., Vaudenay, S.: The pairing problem with user interaction. In: Sasaki, R., Qing, S., Okamoto, E., Yoshiura, H. (eds.) SEC, pp. 251–266. Springer, Heidelberg (2005)

15. Pasini, S., Vaudenay, S.: An optimal non-interactive message authentication protocol. In: Pointcheval, D. (ed.) CT-RSA 2006. LNCS, vol. 3860, pp. 280–294. Springer, Heidelberg (2006)

16. Rivest, R.L.: Unconditionally secure commitment and oblivious transfer schemes using private channels and a trusted initializer (unpublished manuscript) (November 1999), http://citeseer.ifi.unizh.ch/rivest99unconditionally.html/

17. Blundo, C., Masucci, B., Stinson, D.R., Wei, R.: Constructions and bounds for unconditionally secure non-interactive commitment schemes. Design Codes and Cryptography 26(1-3), 97–110 (2002)

18. Wang, S.: Unconditionally secure multi-receiver commitment schemes (manuscript) (2007)

19. Mashatan, A., Stinson, D.R.: Noninteractive two-channel message authentication based on hybrid-collision resistant hash functions (2006)

Appendix

A   Description of P_k [13]

For ease of reading and self-completeness, we give a brief description of the single-receiver ($\mathcal{R}$) protocol P_k due to Naor, Segev and Smith [13]. To uniform the notations, we replace C^j with f^j, $i_{\mathcal{S}}^j$ with $A_{\mathcal{S}}^j$, and $i_{\mathcal{R}}^j$ with $B_{\mathcal{R}}^j$.

The protocol P_k:

1. $\mathcal{S}$ sends $m_{\mathcal{S}}^1 = m$.
2. For $j = 1$ to $k - 1$.
   (a) If j is odd, then
      i. $\mathcal{S}$ chooses $A_{\mathcal{S}}^j \in_R \mathrm{GF}[Q_j]$ and sends it to $\mathcal{R}$.
      ii. $\mathcal{R}$ receives $\widehat{A}_{\mathcal{S}}^j$, chooses $B_{\mathcal{R}}^j \in_R \mathrm{GF}[Q_j]$, and sends it to $\mathcal{S}$.
      iii. $\mathcal{S}$ receives $\widehat{B}_{\mathcal{R}}^j$, and computes $m_{\mathcal{S}}^{j+1} = \langle \widehat{B}_{\mathcal{R}}^j, f_{\widehat{B}_{\mathcal{R}}^j}^j (m_{\mathcal{S}}^j) + A_{\mathcal{S}}^j \rangle$.
      iv. $\mathcal{R}$ computes $m_{\mathcal{R}}^{j+1} = \langle B_{\mathcal{R}}^j, f_{B_{\mathcal{R}}^j}^j (m_{\mathcal{R}}^j) + \widehat{A}_{\mathcal{S}}^j \rangle$.
   (b) If j is even, then
      i. $\mathcal{R}$ chooses $B_{\mathcal{R}}^j \in_R \mathrm{GF}[Q_j]$ and sends it to $\mathcal{S}$.
      ii. $\mathcal{S}$ receives $\widehat{B}_{\mathcal{R}}^j$, chooses $A_{\mathcal{S}}^j \in_R \mathrm{GF}[Q_j]$, and sends it to $\mathcal{R}$.
      iii. $\mathcal{R}$ receives $\widehat{A}_{\mathcal{S}}^j$, and computes $m_{\mathcal{R}}^{j+1} = \langle \widehat{A}_{\mathcal{S}}^j, f_{\widehat{A}_{\mathcal{S}}^j}^j (m_{\mathcal{R}}^j) + B_{\mathcal{R}}^j \rangle$.
      iv. $\mathcal{S}$ computes $m_{\mathcal{S}}^{j+1} = \langle A_{\mathcal{S}}^j, f_{A_{\mathcal{S}}^j}^j (m_{\mathcal{S}}^j) + \widehat{B}_{\mathcal{R}}^j \rangle$.
3. $\mathcal{S}$ manually authenticates $m_{\mathcal{S}}^k$ to $\mathcal{R}$.
4. $\mathcal{R}$ accepts if and only if $m_{\mathcal{S}}^k = m_{\mathcal{R}}^k$.

Fig. 5. The k-round authentication protocol [13]

B   Description of USNIC[p] [17]

Unconditionally secure non-interactive commitment scheme is suggested by Revist [16] and then formally addressed by Blundo, Masucci, Stinson and Wei [17]. As commitment schemes in computational setting, a USNIM scheme provides also two aspects of security. That is *concealing* and *binding* properties. Roughly speaking, concealing means the receiver learns nothing about the committed value before the reveal/open phase and binding means the sender can not change this value after committed. But different to computational setting, USNIM schemes works only in trusted initializer (TI) model – TI trusted by both the sender $\mathcal{S}$ and the receiver $\mathcal{R}$. For more information, please refer to their original work.

Fig. 6 is a brief description of the Affine Plane Commitment Scheme working in $\mathrm{GF}[p] = \mathbb{Z}_p$. We use the notation USNIC[p] to imply that any similar commitment scheme is applicable for our MRMA protocol in Subsection 3.2.

USNIC[p] Scheme:

initialize TI chooses $a, b, x_1 \in_R \mathbb{Z}_p$.
        He computes $y_1 = (ax_1 + b) \mod p$.
        Then he privately sends (a, b) to $\mathcal{S}$ and (x_1, y_1) to $\mathcal{R}$.

commit Suppose $\mathcal{S}$ wants to commit to the value $x_0 \in \mathbb{Z}_p$.
        She computes $y_0 = (x_0 + a) \mod p$ and sends y_0 to $\mathcal{R}$.

reveal $\mathcal{S}$ sends (a, b) and x_0 to $\mathcal{R}$.
        $\mathcal{R}$ verifies that $ax_1 + by_1 \mod p$ and $x_0 + a = y_0 \mod p$.
        If both congruences hold, $\mathcal{R}$ accepts x_0 and otherwise rejects.

Fig. 6. The USNIC[p] commitment scheme from [17]

The following theorem shows that $\mathcal{R}$'s probability of guessing the value of x_0 after the commit protocol is the same as his probability of randomly guessing it.

Theorem 3 (THEOREM 4.1 of [17]). *The USNIC[p] scheme in Fig. 6 is concealing.*

The following theorem says that the probability of $\mathcal{S}$ cheating $\mathcal{R}$ into accepting a different x_0 is less that $1/p$.

Theorem 4 (THEOREM 4.2 of [17]). *In the USNIC[p] scheme in Fig. 6, the binding probability is equal to $1 - 1/p$.*

C   The Proof of Theorem 1

Proof. Given an uncorrupted receiver $\mathcal{R}_i \in \mathcal{R} \backslash \mathcal{C}$ who was cheated into accepting a fraudulent message $\widehat{m}_i(= m_i^1) \neq m(= m_{\mathcal{S}}^1)$, it holds that $m_i^j \neq m_{\mathcal{S}}^j$ but $m_i^{j+1} = m_{\mathcal{S}}^{j+1}$ for some $1 \leq j \leq k - 1$. As in [13], denote this event by D_j. We similarly prove $\Pr[D_j] \leq \frac{(c+1)\epsilon}{2^{k-j}}$ and therefore the cheating probability is bounded by $\sum_{j=1}^{k-1} \Pr[D_j] \leq \sum_{j=1}^{k-1} \frac{(c+1)\epsilon}{2^{k-j}} \leq (c+1)\epsilon$.

Let $T(x)$ be the time at which the variable x is fixed. Namely, $T(A_{\mathcal{S}}^j)$ denotes the time in which $\mathcal{S}$ sent the tag $A_{\mathcal{S}}^j$, and $T(\widehat{A}_i^j)$ denotes the time in which $\mathcal{R}_i$ received the tag $\widehat{A}_i^j$ from the adversary, corresponding to $A_{\mathcal{S}}^j$; Similarly, $T(\widehat{B}^j)$ denotes the time in which $\mathcal{S}$ received the last $\widehat{B}_l^j$, $l \in [n]$, and $T(B_i^j)$ denote the time in which $\mathcal{R}_i$ opened his commitment for B_i^j.

From the description of the protocol, it holds that all the B_l^j's were chosen before $T(B_i^j)$. So, thanks to the security of the commitment scheme, B_i^j is unchangeable except with a probability $1/Q_j$ (binding property of USNIC[Q_j]) and the other B_l^j's ($l \neq i$) were chosen *independently* to B_i^j (concealing property of USNIC[Q_j]). In the exception case we regard the adversary as being successful, which happens with a probability at most $c/Q_j \leq \frac{c\epsilon}{2^{k-j}}$ (accumulated among all the corrupted users).

In the following we assume the commitment scheme has zero probability for both binding and secrecy. Denote by $\overline{D}_j$ the event D_j under the assumption, the conclusion follows as long as $\Pr[\overline{D}_j] \leq \frac{\epsilon}{2^{k-j}}$ is proved. Under the assumption, we easily have $\Pr_{B_i^j \in_R \mathrm{GF}[Q_j]}[B^j \ (i.e., \sum_{l=1}^{n} B_l^j) = B] = \frac{1}{Q_j}$ for any constant $B \in \mathrm{GF}Q_j]$ and no matter how B_l^j's $(l \neq i)$ were chosen.

Now suppose j is odd, we have the following possible cases:

1. $\mathbf{T(\widehat{B}^j) < T(B_i^j)}$: In this case, the receiver $\mathcal{R}_i$ opens the randomly chosen B_i^j only after the adversary chooses $\widehat{B}^j$. Therefore,

$$\Pr[\overline{D}_j] \leq \Pr_{B_i^j \in_R \mathrm{GF}[Q_j]}[\widehat{B}^j = B^j] = \frac{1}{Q_j} \leq \frac{\epsilon}{2^{k-j}}.$$

2. $\mathbf{T(\widehat{B}^j) \geq T(B_i^j)}$ and $\mathbf{T(\widehat{A}_i^j) \geq T(A_{\mathcal{S}}^j)}$: In this case, the adversary chooses $\widehat{B}^j$ not before the receiver opens the random B_i^j. Then the sum B^j may be known to the adversary. If the adversary chooses $\widehat{B}^j \neq B^j$, then $m_{\mathcal{S}}^{j+1} \neq m_i^{j+1}$, i.e., $\Pr[D_j] = 0$. Now suppose that the adversary chooses $\widehat{B}^j = B^j$. Since j is odd, $\mathcal{R}_i$ chooses (and then opens) B_i^j only after he receives $\widehat{A}_i^j$ from the adversary, therefore $T(B_i^j) > T(\widehat{A}_i^j) \geq T(A_{\mathcal{S}}^j) > T(m_{\mathcal{S}}^j)$, and also $T(B_i^j) > T(m_i^j)$. This means that $m_i^j, m_{\mathcal{S}}^j, \widehat{A}_i^j$ and $A_{\mathcal{S}}^j$ are chosen independently to B_i^j. Define $F(x) := f_x^j(m_{\mathcal{S}}^j) + A_{\mathcal{S}}^j - f_x^j(m_i^j) - \widehat{A}_i^j$, which is a polynomial of degree $d \in [1, \lceil \frac{a_j}{\log Q_j} \rceil]$ (since by assumption $m_{\mathcal{S}}^j \neq m_i^j$). Therefore,

$$\Pr[\overline{D}_j] \leq \Pr_{B_i^j \in_R \mathrm{GF}[Q_j]}[f_{B^j}^j(m_{\mathcal{S}}^j) + A_{\mathcal{S}}^j = f_{B^j}^j(m_i^j) + \widehat{A}_i^j]$$

$$= \Pr_{B_i^j \in_R \mathrm{GF}[Q_j]}[B^j \text{ is a root of } F(x)] = \frac{d}{Q_j} \leq \frac{\epsilon}{2^{k-j}}.$$

3. $\mathbf{T(\widehat{B}^j) \geq T(B_i^j)}$ and $\mathbf{T(\widehat{A}_i^j) < T(A_{\mathcal{S}}^j)}$: As in the previous case, we can assume that the adversary chooses $\widehat{B}^j = B^j$. It always holds that $T(A_{\mathcal{S}}^j) > T(m_{\mathcal{S}}^j)$ and $T(B^j) > T(B_i^j) > T(m_i^j)$. Since j is odd, $\mathcal{R}_i$ sends (before he opens) B_i^j only after he receives $\widehat{A}_i^j$, therefore $T(\widehat{A}_i^j) < T(B_i^j)$. And we can assume $T(B_i^j) < T(A_{\mathcal{S}}^j)$ (otherwise we have $T(B_i^j) > \{T(A_{\mathcal{S}}^j), T(\widehat{A}_i^j), T(m_{\mathcal{S}}^j), T(m_i^j)\}$ as in case 2). This implies that $\mathcal{S}$ chooses $A_{\mathcal{S}}^j \in_R \mathrm{GF}[Q_j]$ when $m_{\mathcal{S}}^j, m_i^j, \widehat{A}_i^j$ and B^j are fixed. As a result,

$$\Pr[\overline{D}_j] = \Pr_{A_{\mathcal{S}}^j \in_R \mathrm{GF}[Q_j]}[A_{\mathcal{S}}^j = f_{B^j}^j(m_i^j) + \widehat{A}_i^j - f_{B^j}^j(m_{\mathcal{S}}^j)] = \frac{1}{Q_j} \leq \frac{\epsilon}{2^{k-j}}.$$

When j is even, the conclusion follows in the same way. We just need to change the roles of A and B in classifying the possible cases. That is, i) $T(\widehat{A}_i^j) < T(A_{\mathcal{S}}^j)$; ii) $T(\widehat{A}_i^j) \geq T(A_{\mathcal{S}}^j)$ and $T(\widehat{B}^j) \geq T(B_i^j)$; and iii) $T(\widehat{A}_i^j) \geq T(A_{\mathcal{S}}^j)$ and $T(\widehat{B}^j) < T(B_i^j)$. Also refer to [13] for more details. $\qquad\square$

Unconditionally Secure Chaffing-and-Winnowing for Multiple Use

Wataru Kitada[1], Goichiro Hanaoka[2], Kanta Matsuura[1], and Hideki Imai[2]

[1] The University of Tokyo, Japan
{kitada,kanta}@iis.u-tokyo.ac.jp
[2] National Institute of Advanced Industrial Science and Technology, Japan
{hanaoka-goichiro,h-imai}@aist.go.jp

Abstract. Chaffing-and-winnowing is a cryptographic technique which does not require encryption but instead use a message authentication code (MAC) to provide the same function as encryption. Hanaoka et al. showed that an unconditionally secure chaffing-and-winnowing *with one-time security* can be constructed from any authentication code (A-code) (with one-time security). In this paper, we show a construction of unconditionally secure chaffing-and-winnowing for multiple use and prove the security of perfect secrecy and non-malleability.

Additionally, we investigate a relation between encryption and authentication in more detail. Particularly, we show through chaffing-and-winnowing that a fully secure A-code with a specific property can be converted to a non-malleable one-time pad with a short ciphertext size. Interestingly, when applying this method to a known A-code, this becomes a known construction of a non-malleable one-time pad. This fact implies that the notions of authentication and encryption can be seamlessly connected by chaffing-and-winnowing mechanism.

Keywords: Authentication codes, chaffing-and-winnowing, unconditional security.

1 Introduction

1.1 Background: Chaffing-and-Winnowing

In 1998, Rivest proposed a novel and interesting cryptographic technique called *"chaffing-and-winnowing"* [16]. Remarkable property of this cryptographic technique is that it can provide data confidentiality by using authentication when sending data over an insecure channel. In other words, chaffing-and-winnowing is *an encryption scheme without encryption.* As Rivest also made the point that, as chaffing-and-winnowing is not categorized as an encryption, this may be one solution to getting a way around existing encryption legislation. Realistically, though, the efficiency of chaffing-and-winnowing still remains to be a problem, and if we leave out the merit of being able to bypass the law enforcement, chaffing-and-winnowing, for this moment, does not measure up to what conventional encryption schemes offer especially regarding its practicality. However, to

Y. Desmedt (Ed.): ICITS 2007, LNCS 4883, pp. 133–145, 2009.

the extent that encryption export regulations are going to be a long-term issue, chaffing-and-winnowing is still marked as an interesting development methodology which uses authentication mechanisms to send confidential data, and if you dig down a bit more, interesting relations between encryption and authentication through chaffing-and-winnowing can be found.

1.2   Our Motivation

In our paper, we discuss and introduce some new insights in the relationship between unconditionally secure authentication schemes and unconditionally secure encryption schemes through observing the mechanism of chaffing-and-winnowing. Particularly, we consider the case in which the security is guaranteed under multiple use. Namely, we show through chaffing-and-winnowing, in an unconditionally secure setting, an authentication scheme which is secure against (only) impersonation under n-time use, in fact, stands equivalently for an encryption scheme with perfect secrecy under n-time use, and a fully secure authentication scheme under n-time use implies an encryption scheme with both perfect secrecy and non-malleability under n-time use. In addition, we investigate the relation between encryption and authentication. Particularly, we show through chaffing-and-winnowing that a fully secure A-code with a specific property can be converted to a non-malleable one-time pad with a short ciphertext size. Interestingly, when applying this method to a known A-code, this becomes a known construction of non-malleable one-time pad. This fact implies that notions of authentication and encryption can be seamlessly connected by chaffing-and-winnowing mechanism.

1.3   Related Works

Bellare and Boldyreva analyzed the security for chaffing-and-winnowing from a computationally-secure context [1]. They have shown in their paper that, with a message authentication code (MAC) based on pseudo-random function (PRF) as an authentication scheme, combining an appropriately chosen *all-or-nothing transform* (AONT) [15] (e.g., OAEP [4,5]) gives a semantically secure encryption scheme [9]. It should be noticed that any PRF is a good MAC [8,3] and not vice versa. In contrast, in [10], Hanaoka et al. looked into the relation from an information-theoretically perspective, and showed that with an authentication code (A-code) [7,19] (which corresponds to MAC in the computationally-secure setting), it gives an encryption scheme with perfect secrecy even for a *weak* A-code. If we have a stronger (fully-secure) A-code, then in an information-theoretically-secure setting, an even stronger encryption scheme (i.e. with perfect secrecy and non-malleability) can be constructed. Stinson [21] improved this work, and showed that it is possible to construct an encryption scheme with perfect secrecy from an A-code with shorter tags. However, both [10] and [21] addressed only security under one-time use.

There have also been proposals of combining an A-code with information-theoretically secure encryption called *A-code with secrecy* [7,18]. Furthermore, the secrecy property of A-code has been discussed in [19,20].

2 Preliminaries

2.1 Unconditionally Secure Authentication Code (A-Code)

In an A-code [7,19], there are three participants, a sender S, a receiver R and a trusted initializer TI. TI generates secret information u and v for R and S, respectively. In order to send a plaintext m to R, S generates an authenticated message (m, α) from m by using u and transmits (m, α) to R. R verifies the validity of α using m and v. We note that S and/or R may generate u and v themselves to remove TI. In this paper, we consider n-time use of A-code. Hence the security notion is different from only one-time use. We use the notion of "spoofing" which generalizes the notions of "institution" and "substitution".

Definition 1. Let $\mathcal{U}, \mathcal{V}, \mathcal{M}$ and $\mathcal{A}$ denote the random variables induced by u, v, m and α, respectively. We say that $(\mathcal{U}, \mathcal{V}, \mathcal{M}, \mathcal{A})$ is (p, n)-*spoofing secure* ((p, n)-Spf) if

> Any set of outsiders can perform spoofing with probability at most p under n-time use. Namely, letting (m_i, α_i) $(i = 1, \ldots, n)$ be authenticated messages generated by S, then

$$\forall i \in \{0, \ldots, n\}, \quad \max_{\{(m_j, \alpha_j)\}_{0 \leq j \leq i}} \quad \max_{(m, \alpha)(\notin \{(m_j, \alpha_j)\}_{0 \leq j \leq i})}$$
$$\Pr[R \text{ accepts } (m, \alpha) | (m_0, \alpha_0), \ldots, (m_i, \alpha_i)] \leq p,$$

where (m_0, α_0) denote no authenticated message. Note that in the case of $i = 0$, this is also called *impersonation* security, and $i = 1$, this is called *substitution* security. Under n-time use, we consider $i = 0, \ldots, n$.

Construction methods for A-codes are given in, for example, [7,19,11,17]. In the rest of the paper, for simplicity, we let $f : \mathcal{M} \times \mathcal{U} \to \mathcal{A}$ denote a mapping such that $f(m, u) = \alpha$.

2.2 Unconditionally Secure Encryption

In the model of unconditionally secure encryption, there are three participants, a senders S, a receiver R and a trusted initializer TI. TI generates an encryption key e for S, and a decryption key d for R. TI, after distributing these keys, deletes them from his memory. For $1 \leq i \leq n$, to send a plaintext m_i to R with confidentiality, S encrypts m_i by using e and transmits the ciphertext c_i to R. R decrypts c_i by using d and recovers m_i. Throughout this paper, we let a random variable be $\mathcal{X}$ and $H(\mathcal{X})$ denote the entropy of $\mathcal{X}$. For $\mathcal{X}$, let $X := \{x | \Pr[\mathcal{X} = x] > 0\}$. $|X|$ is the cardinality of X. And $\mathcal{X}_i$ and $H(\mathcal{X}_i)$ denotes a random variable and its entropy at ith time.

Definition 2. Let $\mathcal{E}$, $\mathcal{D}$, $\mathcal{M}_i$ and $\mathcal{C}_i$ denote the random variables induced by e, d, m_i and c_i, respectively. We say that $(\mathcal{E}, \mathcal{D}, \{\mathcal{M}_i, \mathcal{C}_i\}_{1 \leq i \leq n})$ has n-*perfect secrecy* (n-PS) if

1. R correctly decrypts m_i from c_i for all i, that is, $\forall i \in \{1, \ldots, n\}$, $H(\mathcal{M}_i | \mathcal{C}_i, \mathcal{D})$ $= 0$.
2. No outsider obtain any information on m_i from c_i for any i, that is,

$$H(\mathcal{M}_1 | \mathcal{C}_1) = H(\mathcal{M}_1),$$

and

$\forall i \in \{2, \ldots, n\}$,
$$H(\mathcal{M}_i | \mathcal{C}_i, (\mathcal{M}_1, \mathcal{C}_1), \ldots, (\mathcal{M}_{i-1}, \mathcal{C}_{i-1})) = H(\mathcal{M}_i | (\mathcal{M}_1, \mathcal{C}_1), \ldots, (\mathcal{M}_{i-1}, \mathcal{C}_{i-1})).$$

It will also satisfy n-*perfect-non-malleability* (n-NM) if

3. No outsider can generate a ciphertext at each time whose plaintext is meaningfully related to m for all time, that is,

$\forall i \in \{1, \ldots, n\}$,
$$H(\hat{\mathcal{M}} | \hat{\mathcal{C}}, (\mathcal{M}_1, \mathcal{C}_1), \ldots, (\mathcal{M}_i, \mathcal{C}_i)) = H(\hat{\mathcal{M}} | (\mathcal{M}_1, \mathcal{C}_1), \ldots, (\mathcal{M}_i, \mathcal{C}_i)),$$

where $\hat{c} (\notin \{c_i\}_{1 \leq i \leq n})$ be another ciphertext which can be generated under the encryption key e, $\hat{m} (\notin \{m_i\}_{1 \leq i \leq n})$ be a plaintext corresponding $\hat{c}$, and $\hat{\mathcal{C}}$ and $\hat{\mathcal{M}}$ denote random variables induced by $\hat{c}$ and $\hat{m}$, respectively.

Then, we say that $(\mathcal{E}, \mathcal{D}, \{\mathcal{M}_i, \mathcal{C}_i\}_{1 \leq i \leq n})$ has n-PS&NM if it satisfies both n-PS and n-NM. Here, look at the definition of n-PS and n-NM, the statement of n-PS can be taken as $(n-1)$-NM except $H(\mathcal{M}_1 | \mathcal{C}_1) = H(\mathcal{M}_1)$. Hence, if we want to prove that $(\mathcal{E}, \mathcal{D}, \{\mathcal{M}_i, \mathcal{C}_i\}_{1 \leq i \leq n})$ has n-PS&NM, it is sufficient to prove $H(\mathcal{M}_1 | \mathcal{C}_1) = H(\mathcal{M}_1)$ and n-NM.

The notion of "non-malleability" is a concept proposed by Dolev, Dwork and Naor [6]. The discussion that followed after their original proposal was mainly given from a computationally secure perspective [2]. The first formalization of an information-theoretically secure scheme with non-malleability was given recently in [12] by Hanaoka, Shikata, Hanaoka and Imai, and the idea was then extended by McAven, Safavi-Naini and Yung [14]. It is obvious that a classical one-time pad does not provide perfect non-malleability.

2.3 Chaffing-and-Winnowing

In brief, chaffing-and-winnowing can be constructed as follows. Start by each sender S and receiver R prepare themselves each a key for message authentication. When S sends a plaintext m to R, S adds a "dummy" plaintext m' (with an invalid authentication tag) so that the "dummy" m' obscure the intended message m, so that only the authorized receiver R can distinguish the "real" from the "dummy". On receiving the message, R removes the dummy m' by checking its tag. As long as an adversary do not distinguish a valid tag from the invalid tag, the adversary cannot tell which one of m and m' is real and not real. Chaffing-and-winnowing is a technique which consists of adding dummy messages to a message, so that it becomes unintelligible for anyone to distinguish the message except for the authorized receiver. Chaffing-and-winnowing is not an encryption and is not a technique which tries to hide the plaintext itself (like encryption).

3   Unconditionally Secure Chaffing-and-Winnowing

Here, we show the construction of an unconditionally secure chaffing-and-winnowing (USCW) scheme which is secure in n-time use against any adversary with unlimited computational power by using an A-code. Take notice that straightforward construction (i.e. if the dummy is not generated appropriately) will not be secure and the information on the plaintext will be more likely to leak. We give careful consideration on this point when we construct our scheme.

We show (p,n)-Spf A-codes imply USCW with n-PS&NM. For simplicity, we consider only an *optimal* (p,n)-Spf A-code such that $p = 1/|A| = 1/|U|^{1/(n+1)}$. It should be noticed that if an A-code is (p,n)-Spf, then $|A| \geq 1/p$ and $|U| \geq 1/p^{(n+1)}$ [13].

Unconditionally Secure Chaffing-and-Winnowing with n-PS&NM

KEY GENERATION. For a given A-code $(\mathcal{U}, \mathcal{V}, \mathcal{M}, \mathcal{A})$, TI generates $u \in U$ and $v \in V$ as an encryption key and a decryption key, respectively. Let the plaintext space be M. TI gives u and v to S and R, respectively. S picks $|M|$ distinct keys $u_1, ..., u_{|M|}$ from $U \backslash \{u\}$ such that

$$\forall u_i, u_j (\neq u_i), \ \forall m \in M, \ f(m, u_i) \neq f(m, u_j).$$

ENCRYPTION. Let a plaintext be $m^* \in M$. S sets $\alpha := f(m^*, u)$ and finds u_i such that $f(m^*, u_i) = \alpha$. Then, S sends $c := (m || \alpha_m)_{m \in M}$ to R, where $\alpha_m := f(m, u_i)$.

DECRYPTION. On receiving c', R parses c' as $c' := (m || \alpha_m)_{m \in M}$ and selects m' such that m' is accepted as valid (by using v). Finally, R outputs m'.

Before we begin the security proof, we first show that the above $u_1, ..., u_{|M|}$ in fact always exist if the given A-code is $(1/|M|, n)$-Spf.

Lemma 1. *If $(\mathcal{U}, \mathcal{V}, \mathcal{M}, \mathcal{A})$ is $(1/|M|, n)$-Spf, then, for all $u \in U$ there exist $u_1, ..., u_{|M|} \in U \backslash \{u\}$ such that for all $u_i, u_j (\neq u_i) \in \{u_1, ..., u_{|M|}\}$ and $m \in M$, $f(m, u_i) \neq f(m, u_j)$.*

Proof. Here, we show how $\{u_1, ..., u_{|M|}\}$ is chosen for any given u. First, pick u_1 from $U \backslash \{u\}$ randomly, and set $U_{1,m} := \{u | f(m, u_1) = f(m, u)\}$ for all $m \in M$. Since the given A-code is $(1/|M|, n)$-Spf, it is clear that $|U_{1,m}| \leq |M|^n$. This implies that

$$|U \backslash \cup_{m \in M} U_{1,m}| \geq |M| - 1.$$

Next, pick distinct $u_2, ..., u_{|M|} \in U \backslash \cup_{m \in M} U_{1,m}$, and set $U_{i,m} := \{u | f(m, u_i) = f(m, u)\}$ for $i = 2, ..., |M|$ and $m \in M$. Assume that there exist $u_{i_0}, u_{i_1} (\neq u_{i_0}) \in \{u_2, ..., u_{|M|}\}$ such that $f(m_0, u_{i_0}) = f(m_0, u_{i_1})$ for some $m_0 \in M$, i.e. $U_{i_0, m_0} = U_{i_1, m_0}$. This implies that $| \cup_{2 \leq i \leq |M|} U_{i, m_0}| \leq (|M| - 2)|M|^n$. On the other hand, it is obvious that $U = \cup_{\alpha \in A} \{u | f(u, m_0) = \alpha\}$, and consequently, we have

$$|U| = | \cup_{\alpha \in A} \{u | f(u, m_0) = \alpha\}| = | \cup_{1 \leq i \leq |M|} U_{i, m_0}| \leq (|M| - 1)|M|^n.$$

This is a contradiction since $|U| = |M|^{(n+1)}$. Hence, for all $i_0, i_1(\neq i_0)$ and m, $f(m_0, u_{i_0}) \neq f(m_0, u_{i_1})$. □

Next, we prove for such $u_1, ..., u_{|M|}$ and any $m \in M$, only one u_i exists, such that $f(m, u) = f(m, u_i)$.

Lemma 2. *For any $u \in U$, any $u_1, ..., u_{|M|}$ chosen as in the above, and any $m \in M$, $|\{u_i | f(m, u_i) = f(m, u), u_i \in \{u_1, ..., u_{|M|}\}\}| = 1$.*

Proof. Assume this lemma is false. Then, there exist $u_{i_0}, u_{i_1} \in \{u_1, ..., u_{|M|}\}$ such that $f(m, u_{i_0}) = f(m, u_{i_1})$ which is a contradiction. □

Lemma 1 and 2 guarantee that the proposed USCW will always work properly for any u and m.

Finally, we prove the security. To prove the security, we show the USCW satisfies $H(\mathcal{M}_1) = H(\mathcal{M}_1 | \mathcal{C}_1)$ and n-NM.

Lemma 3. *The proposed USCW satisfies $H(\mathcal{M}_1) = H(\mathcal{M}_1 | \mathcal{C}_1)$, where $\mathcal{M}_1$ is a random variable induced by m_1.*

Proof. Let $\mathcal{U}_i$ denote a random variable induced by u_i such that $f(m_1, u) = f(m_1, u_i)$. Then, it is clear that $H(\mathcal{C}_1 | \mathcal{U}_i) = 0$. Consequently, we have that

$$H(\mathcal{M}_1 | \mathcal{U}_i) - H(\mathcal{M}_1 | \mathcal{C}_1, \mathcal{U}_i) = H(\mathcal{M}_1 | \mathcal{U}_i) - H(\mathcal{M}_1 | \mathcal{U}_i) = 0.$$

If $H(\mathcal{M}_1 | \mathcal{U}_i) = H(\mathcal{M}_1)$, then we have

$$\begin{aligned} H(\mathcal{M}_1) - H(\mathcal{M}_1 | \mathcal{C}_1) &\leq H(\mathcal{M}_1) - H(\mathcal{M}_1 | \mathcal{C}_1, \mathcal{U}_i) \\ &= H(\mathcal{M}_1 | \mathcal{U}_i) - H(\mathcal{M}_1 | \mathcal{C}_1, \mathcal{U}_i) \\ &= 0. \end{aligned}$$

This means that to prove the lemma, it will be sufficient to prove $H(\mathcal{M}_1 | \mathcal{U}_i) = H(\mathcal{M}_1)$.

For a given u_i, we have only that $u \notin \{u_1, ..., u_{|M|}\}$ and $f(m_1, u) = f(m_1, u_i)$ for some m_1, and therefore, $u \in \{u | \exists m \in M, \ f(m, u) = f(m, u_i), \ u \in U \backslash \{u_i\}\} = \cup_{m \in M} U_{i,m} \backslash \{u_i\}$. Since $|U_{i,m}| = |M|^n$ for all $m \in M$,

$$\max_{m_1, u_i} \max_{m'} \Pr[m' = m_1 | u_i] = \frac{|U_{i,m'} \backslash \{u_i\}|}{|\cup_{m \in M} U_{i,m} \backslash \{u_i\}|} = \frac{|M|^n - 1}{|M|(|M|^n - 1)} = \frac{1}{|M|}.$$

Hence, $H(\mathcal{M}_1 | \mathcal{U}_i) = H(\mathcal{M}_1)$.   □

Lemma 4. *The proposed USCW has n-NM, i.e.*

$\forall i \in \{1, \ldots, n\}$,
$$H(\hat{\mathcal{M}} | \hat{\mathcal{C}}, (\mathcal{M}_1, \mathcal{C}_1), \ldots, (\mathcal{M}_i, \mathcal{C}_i)) = H(\hat{\mathcal{M}} | (\mathcal{M}_1, \mathcal{C}_1), \ldots, (\mathcal{M}_i, \mathcal{C}_i)),$$

where $\hat{c}(\neq c_i)$ is another ciphertext which can be generated by S instead of c_i, $\hat{m}(\neq m_i)$ is a plaintext corresponding to $\hat{c}$, and $\hat{\mathcal{C}}$ and $\hat{\mathcal{M}}$ denote random variables induced by $\hat{c}$ and $\hat{m}$, respectively.

Proof. First, we prove that

$$H(\hat{\mathcal{M}} | \hat{\mathcal{C}}, (\mathcal{M}_1, \mathcal{C}_1), \ldots, (\mathcal{M}_k, \mathcal{C}_k)) = H(\hat{\mathcal{M}} | (\mathcal{M}_1, \mathcal{C}_1), \ldots, (\mathcal{M}_k, \mathcal{C}_k)),$$

for some $k \in \{1, \ldots, n\}$. Let M_k and C_k be a subset of given messages and ciphertexts i.e. $M_k = \{m_1, \ldots, m_k\}, C_k = \{c_1, \ldots, c_k\}$. From M_k and C_k, an adversary only knows that $u \in \cap_{m \in M_k} U_{i,m} \backslash \{u_i\}$. Now, we prove that all $\tilde{m} \in M \backslash \{M_k\}$ are equally possible even if it is known that $u \in \cap_{m \in M_k} U_{i,m} \backslash \{u_i\}$.

Let $\hat{c} := (m || f(m, u_j))_{m \in M \backslash M_k}$, then $\tilde{m} \in M$ can be the plaintext only if $|(\cap_{m \in M_k} U_{i,m}) \cap U_{j,\tilde{m}}| \neq 0$.

Claim 1. *For any $\tilde{m} \in M \backslash M_k$, $|(\cap_{m \in M_k} U_{i,m}) \cap U_{j,\tilde{m}}| = |M|^{n-k}$.*

Proof. First we prove the case of $k = 1$, i.e. for one given m^*, $|U_{i,m^*} \cap U_{j,\tilde{m}}| = |M|^{n-1}$.

Assume that $|U_{i,m^*} \cap U_{j,\tilde{m}}| < |M|^{n-1}$. Then, for an authenticated message (m^*, α^*) where $\alpha^* = f(m^*, u_i)$, an adversary can launch a spoofing attack by generating $(\tilde{m}, \tilde{\alpha})$ where $\tilde{\alpha}$ is randomly chosen from $A \backslash \{f(\tilde{m}, u_j)\}$. Notice that the adversary can generate $(\tilde{m}, \tilde{\alpha})$ if he knows only (m^*, α^*). It is clear that $|\cap_{1 \leq j' \leq |M|} U_{j', \tilde{m}}| = |U| = |M|^{n+1}$, $|\cap_{1 \leq j' \leq |M|} (U_{j', \tilde{m}} \cap U_{i,m^*})| = |U_{i,m^*}| = |M|^n$, and consequently, we have

$$\Pr[R \text{ accepts } (\tilde{m}, \tilde{\alpha}) | (m^*, \alpha^*)] \geq \frac{|\cap_{1 \leq j' \leq |M|, j' \neq j} (U_{j', \tilde{m}} \cap U_{i,m^*})|}{|\cap_{1 \leq j' \leq |M|, j' \neq j} U_{j', \tilde{m}}|}$$
$$= \frac{|M|^n - |U_{i,m^*} \cap U_{j,\tilde{m}}|}{|M|^{n+1} - |U_{j,\tilde{m}}|}$$
$$> \frac{|M|^n - |M|^{n-1}}{|M|^{n+1} - |M|^n} = \frac{1}{|M|}.$$

Since the given A-code is $(1/|M|, n)$-Spf, this is a contradiction.

Next, assume that $|U_{i,m^*} \cap U_{j,\tilde{m}}| > |M|^{n-1}$. Then, for an authenticated message (m^*, α^*) where $\alpha^* = f(m^*, u_i)$, an adversary can launch a spoofing attack by generating $(\tilde{m}, \tilde{\alpha})$ where $\tilde{\alpha} = f(\tilde{m}, u_j)$. It is clear that there is at least $|M|^{n-1} + 1$ keys in U_{i,m^*} such that the correct authentication tag for $\tilde{m}$ is determined as $f(\tilde{m}, u_j)$, and consequently, we have

$$\Pr[R \text{ accepts } (\tilde{m}, \tilde{\alpha})|(m^*, \alpha^*)] \geq \frac{|U_{i,m^*} \cap U_{j,\tilde{m}}|}{|U_{i,m^*}|} \geq \frac{|M|^{n-1} + 1}{|M|^n} > \frac{1}{|M|},$$

which is a contradiction. Hence, $|U_{i,m^*} \cap U_{j,\tilde{m}}| = |M|^{n-1}$.

Next, we prove the case of $k = \ell$ ($2 \leq \ell \leq n$) under the condition that the claim is true in $k = \ell - 1$, that is, we prove

$$|(\cap_{m \in M_{\ell-1}} U_{i,m}) \cap U_{j,\tilde{m}}| = |M|^{n-\ell+1}$$
$$\Rightarrow |(\cap_{m \in M_\ell} U_{i,m}) \cap U_{j,\tilde{m}}| = |M|^{n-\ell}.$$

Assume that $|(\cap_{m \in M_\ell} U_{i,m}) \cap U_{j,\tilde{m}}| > |M|^{n-\ell}$. Then, for an authenticated message $\forall(m_i^*, \alpha_i)$ where $\alpha_i = f(m_i^*, u_i)$, an adversary can launch a spoofing attack by generating $(\tilde{m}, \tilde{\alpha})$ where $\tilde{\alpha} = f(\tilde{m}, u_j)$. It is clear that there exist at least $|M|^{n-\ell} + 1$ keys in $\cap_{m \in M_\ell} U_{i,m}$ such that the correct authentication tag for $\tilde{m}$ is determined as $f(\tilde{m}, u_j)$. And from the assumption,

$$|\cap_{m \in M_\ell} U_{i,m}| = |(\cap_{m \in M_{\ell-1}} U_{i,m}) \cap U_{j,m'}|$$
$$= |M|^{n-\ell+1}.$$

Then consequently, we have

$$\Pr[R \text{ accepts } (\tilde{m}, \tilde{\alpha})|(m_1, \alpha_1), \dots, (m_\ell, \alpha_\ell)] \geq \frac{|(\cap_{m \in M_\ell} U_{i,m}) \cap U_{j,\tilde{m}}|}{|\cap_{m \in M_\ell} U_{i,m}|}$$
$$\geq \frac{|M|^{n-\ell} + 1}{|M|^{n-\ell+1}} > \frac{1}{|M|},$$

which is a contradiction.

Next, assume that $|(\cap_{m \in M_\ell} U_{i,m}) \cap U_{j,\tilde{m}}| < |M|^{n-\ell}$. From the assumption,

$$|\cap_{m \in M_\ell} U_{i,m}| = |M|^{n-\ell+1},$$

and consequently, there must exists $(U_{j^*,\tilde{m}})(j^* \neq j)$ such that

$$|(\cap_{m \in M_\ell} U_{i,m}) \cap U_{j^*,\tilde{m}}| > |M|^{n-\ell}.$$

Then, for an authenticated message $\forall m_i \in M_\ell(m_i, \alpha_i)$ where $\alpha_i = f(m_i, u_i)$, an adversary can launch a spoofing attack by generating $(\tilde{m}, \tilde{\alpha})$ where $\tilde{\alpha} = f(\tilde{m}, u_{j^*})$ for some $u_{j^*} \in U_{j^*,\tilde{m}}$, and consequently, as above, we have

$$\Pr[R \text{ accepts } (\tilde{m}, \tilde{\alpha})|(m_1, \alpha_1), \dots, (m_\ell, \alpha_\ell)] \geq \frac{|(\cap_{m \in M_\ell} U_{i,m}) \cap U_{j^*,\tilde{m}}|}{|\cap_{m \in M_\ell} U_{i,m}|}$$
$$\geq \frac{|M|^{n-\ell} + 1}{|M|^{n-\ell+1}} > \frac{1}{|M|},$$

which is a contradiction.

Hence, the claim 1 is true.   □

Claim 2. *For any $\tilde{m}_i \in M$, $|\cap_{\tilde{m}_0,\ldots,\tilde{m}_{n-k}} U_{j,\tilde{m}_i}| = |M|^k$.*

Proof. Let $\tilde{U}_k := \cap_{\tilde{m}_0,\ldots,\tilde{m}_{n-k}} U_{j,\tilde{m}_i}$. It is obvious that $|\tilde{U}_n| = |M|^n$ since $|\tilde{U}_n| = |U_{j,\tilde{m}_0}| = |M|^n$. Assume that $|\tilde{U}_k| = |M|^k$, then we prove that $|\tilde{U}_{k-1}| = |M|^{k-1}$,that is, we prove

$$|\tilde{U}_k| = |M|^k \Rightarrow |\tilde{U}_{k-1}| = |M|^{k-1}.$$

Assume that $|\tilde{U}_{k-1}| > |M|^{k-1}$. Then, an adversary can launch a spoofing attack by generating $(\tilde{m}_{n-k+1}, \tilde{\alpha}_{n-k+1})$ where $\tilde{\alpha}_{n-k+1} = f(\tilde{m}_{n-k+1}, \tilde{u})$ and $\tilde{u}$ is randomly chosen from $\tilde{U}_k$. It is clear that there exist at least $|M|^{k-1} + 1$ keys in $\tilde{U}_k$ such that the correct authentication tag for $\tilde{m}_{n-k+1}$ is determined as $f(\tilde{m}_{n-k+1}, u_j)$, and consequently, we have

$$\begin{aligned}\Pr[R \text{ accepts } (\tilde{m}_{n-k+1}, \tilde{\alpha}_{n-k+1})|(\tilde{m}_0, \tilde{\alpha}_0), \ldots, (\tilde{m}_{n-k}, \tilde{\alpha}_{n-k})] &\geq \frac{|\tilde{U}_k \cap U_{j,\tilde{m}_{n-k+1}}|}{|\tilde{U}_k|} \\ &\geq \frac{|M|^{k-1} + 1}{|M|^k} > \frac{1}{|M|},\end{aligned}$$

which is a contradiction.

Next, assume that $|\tilde{U}_{k-1}| < |M|^{k-1}$. There exist $\tilde{m}^*$ such that $|\tilde{U}_k \cap U_{j,\tilde{m}^*}| > |M|^{k-1}$ since $|\tilde{U}_k| = |M|^k$. Then ,as above, an adversary can launch a spoofing attack by generating $(\tilde{m}^*, \tilde{\alpha}^*)$ where $\tilde{\alpha}^* = f(\tilde{m}^*, \tilde{u})$ and $\tilde{u}$ is randomly chosen from $\tilde{U}_k$. Consequently, we have,

$$\begin{aligned}\Pr[R \text{ accepts } (\tilde{m}^*, \tilde{\alpha}^*)|(\tilde{m}_0, \tilde{\alpha}_0), \ldots, (\tilde{m}_{n-k}, \tilde{\alpha}_{n-k})] &\geq \frac{|\tilde{U}_k \cap U_{j,\tilde{m}^*}|}{|\tilde{U}_k|} \\ &> \frac{|M|^{k-1}}{|M|^k} = \frac{1}{|M|},\end{aligned}$$

which is a contradiction. Hence,

$$|\tilde{U}_k| = |M|^k \Rightarrow |\tilde{U}_{k-1}| = |M|^{k-1}.$$

and the claim 2 is true. □

From Claims 1 and 2, consider a maximum probability to achieve guessing a message under given k pair of (m_i, u_i). Here, we evaluate the probability in the number of keys, i.e. a numerator is the number of keys such that a correct authentication tag is derived, and a denominator is the number of nominations of possible keys. Consequently, we have that

$$\begin{aligned}&\max_{\hat{m}, \forall m_i \in M_k, (m_i, u_i)} \max_{\tilde{m}} \Pr[\tilde{m} = \hat{m}|(m_1, u_1), \ldots, (m_k, u_k)] \\ &= \frac{|U_{j,\hat{m}} \cap (\cap_{m \in M_k} U_{i,m}) \backslash (\cup_{m \in (M_k \cup \{\hat{m}\})} \{u_i\})|}{|\cup_{m' \in M \backslash M_k} (U_{j,m'} \cap (\cap_{m \in M_k} U_{i,m}) \backslash (\cup_{m \in (M_k \cup \{m'\})} \{u_i\}))|}\end{aligned}$$

$$= \frac{|M|^{n-k+1} - (k+1)}{(|M| - k)(|M|^{n-k+1} - (k+1))}$$

$$= \frac{1}{|M| - k},$$

and this is true for any $k \in \{1, \ldots, n\}$, which proves the lemma. $\qquad\square$

4　A Relationship between Encryption and Authentication

The above results show that an unconditionally secure encryption scheme with perfect secrecy and non-malleability for n-time use can be constructed from an A-code with n-time spoofing security. This result shows that the notions of unconditionally secure encryption and A-code are mutually related via the chaffing-and-winnowing mechanism.

In this section, we investigate the relation between encryption and authentication in more detail. Specifically, we show that it is possible to compress the ciphertext size of our scheme to be only *one authentication tag* if the underlying A-code has a certain property, and that a known A-code can be converted into a known construction of non-malleable one-time pad [12] via this transformation. (Note that, in the construction in Sec. 3, a ciphertext consists of $|M|$ pairs of messages and authentication tags.) In other words, *these A-codes and one-time pad are essentially the same primitive*, but viewed from different perspectives. This fact supports our claim that the methodology for constructing non-malleable encryption is closely related to that for A-codes.

4.1　Chaffing-and-Winnowing with One Authentication Tag

Here, we demonstrate a method for compressing the ciphertext size of our scheme to be only one authentication tag. Our compressing technique can be utilized only if the underlying A-code has the following property:

For all $\alpha \in A$, there exists at least one $u \in U$ such that for all messages $m \in M$, $f(m, u) = \alpha$, that is,

$$\forall \alpha \in A, \exists u \in U \ s.t. \ \forall m \in M, f(m, u) = \alpha.$$

Let $\hat{U}$ denote a subset of U such that $\hat{U} = \cup_{\alpha \in A} \{u | \forall m \in M, f(m, u) = \alpha\}$.

Here, we give an intuitive explanation of our sceme. For our proposed scheme in Sec. 3, assume that

$$\forall u, \exists u_1, \ldots, u_{|M|}, \forall m_0, m_1 \in M, f(m_0, u_i) = f(m_1, u_i).$$

Then, a ciphertext becomes $\{m_j || \alpha\}_{m_j \in M}$ where $\alpha = f(m_j, u_i)$, and therefore, a full ciphertext can be re-construct from only α. Hence, it is sufficient to send only one authentication tag α as a cipheretext. For implementing this idea, we pick u from $U \backslash \hat{U}$, and always use $\hat{U}$ as $\{u_1, \ldots, u_{|M|}\}$.

The concrete construction is as follows.

PS&NM Construction with One Authentication Tag

KEY GENERATION. For a given A-code $(\mathcal{U}, \mathcal{V}, \mathcal{M}, \mathcal{A})$, TI generates $u \in U \backslash \hat{U}$ and $v \in V$ as an encryption key and a decryption key, respectively. Let the plaintext space be M. TI gives u and v to S and R, respectively.

ENCRYPTION. Let a plaintext be $m^* \in M$. S sets $c := f(m^*, u)$, and sends c to R.

DECRYPTION. On receiving c', R selects m' such that c' is accepted as valid (by using m', v). Finally, R outputs m'.

Since the above construction is a special case of our construction in Sec. 3 with a specific type of A-codes, it also satisfies PS&NM.

4.2   An Example

In this section, we show an example of the above construction by using a well-known A-code. Let $M = A = GF(p)$ and $U = V = GF(p)^2$. Let an authentication tag for message m be $\alpha = k_1 m + k_2$, where $(k_1, k_2) \in GF(p)^2$ is a shared secret between S and R. Notice that this is the most well-known construction of A-codes. For simplicity, we assume that p is a prime. Then, we can set $\hat{U} = \{(0,0), \ldots, (0, p-1)\}$.

Based on the above A-code, we can construct a non-malleable one-time pad as follows:

An Example of PS&NM One-Time Pad

KEY GENERATION. TI generates $(k_1, k_2) \in (GF(p) \backslash \{0\}) \times GF(p)$. Let the plaintext space be $GF(p)$. TI gives (k_1, k_2) to both S and R.

ENCRYPTION. Let a plaintext be $m^* \in GF(p)$. S sets $c = k_1 m^* + k_2$, and sends c to R.

DECRYPTION. On receiving $c' (= \alpha)$, R computes $m' = (c' - k_2) \cdot k_1^{-1}$, and outputs m'.

We note that the above example is strikingly identical to the non-malleable one-time pad which is presented in [12]. Furthermore, it should be noticed that in [12] this construction is designed independently to the chaffing-and winnowing framework.

This observation implies that fundamental methodology for constructing PS&NM secure encryption schemes are closely related to that for A-codes which has already been intensively studied.

5   Comparison

In this section, we evaluate efficiency of our proposed schemes by comparing them with the straightforward extension of the previous scheme which consists of n independent copies of a one-time scheme [10]. We call the extended version of [10] as n-HHHWI. Notice that it is easy to construct a PS&NM secure encryption scheme for n-time use by using n copies of a PS&NM secure scheme for one-time use. However, as shown in Table 1, this construction is significantly more inefficient than our proposed schemes in terms of key size. Furthermore, when we can assume a specific property of the underlying A-code, ciphertext size can also be remarkably compressed.

Table 1. Comparison of Ours (Sec. 3), Ours (Sec. 4) and n-HHHWI, where $|M|$ is the cardinality of the plaintext space. Note that $\log_2 |M|$ is the size of a plaintext.

Construction	Key size [bits]	Ciphertext size [bits]	Need specific A-codes?
Ours (Sec. 3)	$(n + 1) \log_2 |M|$	$|M| \log_2 |M|$	No
Ours (Sec. 4)	$(n + 1) \log_2 |M|$	$\log_2 |M|$	Yes
n-HHHWI	$2n \log_2 |M|$	$|M| \log_2 |M|$	No

In our constructions, we assume that the underlying A-codes satisfy $|A| = |M|$. Similarly to [21], it seems possible to remove this restriction, and this will be our future work.

Acknowledgement

The authors would like to thank anonymous reviewers for their invaluable comments. The authors would also like to thank Nuttapong Attrapadung, Yang Cui, Jun Furukawa, Takahiro Matsuda, Thi Lan Anh Phan and Rui Zhang for their comments and helpful discussions, and Jacob C.N. Schuldt for his helpful comment in preparing this paper.

References

1. Bellare, M., Boldyreva, A.: The security of chaffing and winnowing. In: Okamoto, T. (ed.) ASIACRYPT 2000. LNCS, vol. 1976, pp. 517–530. Springer, Heidelberg (2000)
2. Bellare, M., Desai, A., Pointcheval, D., Rogaway, P.: Relations among notions of security for public-key encryption schemes. In: Krawczyk, H. (ed.) CRYPTO 1998. LNCS, vol. 1462, pp. 26–45. Springer, Heidelberg (1998)
3. Bellare, M., Killian, J., Rogaway, P.: The security of cipher block chaining. In: Desmedt, Y.G. (ed.) CRYPTO 1994. LNCS, vol. 839, pp. 341–358. Springer, Heidelberg (1994)

4. Bellare, M., Rogaway, P.: Optimal asymmetric encryption - How to encrypt with RSA. In: De Santis, A. (ed.) EUROCRYPT 1994. LNCS, vol. 950, pp. 92–111. Springer, Heidelberg (1995)
5. Boyko, V.: On the security properties of OAEP as an all-or-nothing transform. In: Wiener, M. (ed.) CRYPTO 1999. LNCS, vol. 1666, pp. 503–518. Springer, Heidelberg (1999)
6. Dolev, D., Dwork, C., Naor, M.: Non-malleable cryptography. In: Proc. of 23rd ACM Symposium on the Theory of Computing (STOC), pp. 542–552 (1991)
7. Gilbert, E.N., MacWilliams, F.J., Sloane, N.J.A.: Codes which detect deception. Bell System Technical Journal 53, 405–425 (1974)
8. Goldreich, O., Goldwasser, S., Micali, S.: How to construct random functions. Journal of the ACM 33(4), 210–217 (1986)
9. Goldwasser, S., Micali, S.: Probabilistic encryption. Journal of Computer and System Science 28, 270–299 (1984)
10. Hanaoka, G., Hanaoka, Y., Hagiwara, M., Watanabe, H., Imai, H.: Unconditionally secure chaffing-and-winnowing: a relationship between encryption and authentication. In: Fossorier, M.P.C., Imai, H., Lin, S., Poli, A. (eds.) AAECC 2006. LNCS, vol. 3857, pp. 154–162. Springer, Heidelberg (2006)
11. Hanaoka, G., Shikata, J., Zheng, Y., Imai, H.: Unconditionally secure digital signature schemes admitting transferability. In: Okamoto, T. (ed.) ASIACRYPT 2000. LNCS, vol. 1976, pp. 130–142. Springer, Heidelberg (2000)
12. Hanaoka, G., Shikata, J., Hanaoka, Y., Imai, H.: Unconditionally secure anonymous encryption and group authentication. In: Zheng, Y. (ed.) ASIACRYPT 2002. LNCS, vol. 2501, pp. 81–99. Springer, Heidelberg (2002)
13. Maurer, U.M.: A unified and generalized treatment of authentication theory. In: Puech, C., Reischuk, R. (eds.) STACS 1996. LNCS, vol. 1046, pp. 387–398. Springer, Heidelberg (1996)
14. McAven, L., Safavi-Naini, R., Yung, M.: Unconditionally secure encryption under strong attacks. In: Wang, H., Pieprzyk, J., Varadharajan, V. (eds.) ACISP 2004. LNCS, vol. 3108, pp. 427–439. Springer, Heidelberg (2004)
15. Rivest, R.: All-or-nothing encryption and the package transform. In: Biham, E. (ed.) FSE 1997. LNCS, vol. 1267, pp. 210–218. Springer, Heidelberg (1997)
16. Rivest, R.: Chaffing and winnowing: confidentiality without encryption, http://theory.lcs.mit.edu/~rivest/publication.html
17. Shikata, J., Hanaoka, G., Zheng, Y., Imai, H.: Security notions for unconditionally secure signature schemes. In: Knudsen, L.R. (ed.) EUROCRYPT 2002. LNCS, vol. 2332, pp. 434–449. Springer, Heidelberg (2002)
18. Shikata, J., Hanaoka, G., Zheng, Y., Matsumoto, T., Imai, H.: Unconditionally secure authenticated encryption. IEICE Trans. E87-A(5), 1119–1131 (2004)
19. Simmons, G.J.: Authentication theory/coding theory. In: Blakely, G.R., Chaum, D. (eds.) CRYPTO 1984. LNCS, vol. 196, pp. 411–431. Springer, Heidelberg (1985)
20. Stinson, D.R.: A construction for authentication/secrecy codes from Certain combinatorial designs. J. Cryptology 1(2), 119–127 (1988)
21. Stinson, D.R.: Unconditionally secure chaffing and winnowing with short authentication tags. Cryptology ePrint Archive, Report 2006/189 (2006)

Introduction to Quantum Information Theory

Iordanis Kerenidis

CNRS and LRI-Univ. de Paris-Sud

Quantum computation and information studies how information is encoded in nature according to the laws of quantum mechanics and what this means for its computational power. In this note, we present a short and rather schematic introduction to quantum information theory by drawing comparisons to classical probability theory. For more details on quantum information theory and computation we refer to [3].

A binary random variable X is a system with two possible states 0 and 1. Similarly, a quantum bit (qubit) is a quantum mechanical system, which can be in a state $|0\rangle$, $|1\rangle$ or any convex combination of these states. In other words, a quantum bit is a unit vector in a two dimensional Hilbert space $a_0|0\rangle + a_1|1\rangle$, where $a_0, a_1 \in C$ and $|a_0|^2 + |a_1|^2 = 1$. By tensoring such systems together we can define larger quantum states, for example over $\log n$ qubits as $|\phi\rangle = \sum_{i=0}^{n-1} a_i|i\rangle$, with $\sum_{i=0}^{n-1} |a_i|^2 = 1$.

A random variable X with probability distribution $P = \{p_0, p_1\}$ evolves by multiplying the probability vector by a stochastic matrix S, i.e. a matrix that preserves the ℓ_1-norm. The new probability vector is $P' = S \cdot P$. Moreover, a measurement of the random variable has $\Pr[X = b] = p_b$, $p_b \in [0, 1]$.

Let us see how a quantum bit evolves. A quantum bit $|\phi\rangle = a_0|0\rangle + a_1|1\rangle$ can evolve by a unitary matrix U, i.e. a matrix that preserves the ℓ_2-norm, and the new state becomes $|\phi'\rangle = U \cdot |\phi\rangle$. In addition, we can perform a projective measurement of a state $|\phi\rangle$ in an orthonormal basis $\{\mathbf{b_1}, \mathbf{b_2}, \ldots, \mathbf{b_n}\}$ and have $\Pr[\text{outcome is } b_i] = |\langle\phi|b_i\rangle|^2$.

More generally, we can define a mixed quantum state, i.e. a classical probability distribution over quantum states. For example, a mixed state ρ can be in an ensemble of states $\{|\phi_i\rangle\}$ with probabilities p_i. We can rewrite a mixed state as a hermitian, positive, trace-one matrix, called density matrix $\rho = \sum_{i=1}^{n} p_i|\phi_i\rangle\langle\phi_i|$. The density matrix contains all necessary information about a quantum state. More precisely, the quantum state ρ evolves by a unitary U to the state $\rho' = U\rho U^\dagger$ and a projective measurement has $\Pr[\text{outcome } b_i] = \sum p_i|\langle\phi_i|b_k\rangle|^2 = \sum p_i\langle b_k|\phi_i\rangle\langle\phi_i|b_k\rangle = \langle b_k| \left(\sum p_i|\phi_i\rangle\langle\phi_i| \right) |b_k\rangle = \langle b_k|\rho|b_k\rangle$. Let us note that two mixed states may look very different as an ensemble of quantum states, however they might correspond to the same density matrix. For example,

$$\rho = \begin{cases} \frac{1}{\sqrt{2}}(|0\rangle - |1\rangle), & \text{w.p. } 1/2 \\ |0\rangle, & \text{w.p. } 1/2 \end{cases} \quad \rho = \begin{cases} \frac{\sqrt{3}}{2}|0\rangle - \frac{1}{2}|1\rangle), & \text{w.p. } 1/\sqrt{3} \\ |0\rangle, & \text{w.p. } \frac{3}{4}(1 - \frac{1}{\sqrt{3}}) \\ |1\rangle, & \text{w.p. } \frac{1}{4}(1 - \frac{1}{\sqrt{3}}) \end{cases} \quad \rho = \begin{pmatrix} \frac{3}{4} & -\frac{1}{4} \\ -\frac{1}{4} & \frac{1}{4} \end{pmatrix}$$

We now introduce a notion of entropy of a mixed quantum state. Note that the Shannon entropy of a random variable X with distribution P is defined as $H(X) = -\sum p_i \log p_i$ and captures the randomness in a measurement of the variable. We

Y. Desmedt (Ed.): ICITS 2007, LNCS 4883, pp. 146–147, 2009.

define a similar notion for quantum states, however as we saw, a mixed state can be described as different distributions over ensembles of states. Hence, we look at the description of a state as a density matrix and define the von Neumann entropy of a quantum state as $S(\rho) = -\sum \lambda_i \log \lambda$, where λ_i are the eigenvalues of the matrix. Since the matrix is positive and has trace one, the eigenvalues play the role of a probability distribution. In fact, they represent the probabilities of outcomes of a measurment in the basis of the eigenvectors of the state, which is the measurement that minimizes the Shannon entropy.

The notions of Shannon and von Neumann entropy share many important properties, for example they are always positive and they are upper bounded by the size of the system. Moreover, we can define conditional von Neumann entropy and mutual information for quantum states similarly to the classical case. In addition, we can prove important properties like strong subadditivity and Fano's inequality. However, there are differences between the two measures, for example the conditional von Neumann entropy could take negative values.

Quantum Information theory is a powerful tool for the study of quantum information. A main question is whether quantum information is more powerful than classical information. A celebrated result by Holevo, shows that quantum information cannot be used to compress classical information. In other words, in order to transmit n random classical bits, one needs to transmit no less than n quantum bits. This might imply that quantum information is no more powerful than classical information. This however is wrong in many situations.

In the model of Communication Complexity, one can show that transmitting quantum information results to exponential savings on the communication needed to solve specific problems ([4,1]). Moreover, quantum information enables us to perform unconditionally secure cryptographic primitives, for example key distribution, which are impossible in the classical world. Last, quantum information can be used as a mathematical theory for the study classical information. For example, one can get optimal bounds for classical locally decodable codes by reducing the problem to a quantum encoding problem and using quantum information theory to resolve it ([2]).

References

1. Gavinsky, D., Kempe, J., Kerenidis, I., Raz, R., de Wolf, R.: Exponential separations for one-way quantum communication complexity, with applications to cryptography. In: Proceedings of the 39th ACM Symposium on Theory of Computing, STOC (2007)
2. Kerenidis, I., de Wolf, R.: Exponential lower bound for 2-query locally decodable codes via quantum argument. In: STOC 2003, pp. 106–115 (2003)
3. Nielsen, M.A., Chuang, I.L.: Quantum Computation and Quantum Information. Cambridge University Press, Cambridge (2000)
4. Raz, R.: Exponential separation of quantum and classical communication complexity. In: Proceedings of 31st ACM STOC, pp. 358–367 (1999)

Strongly Multiplicative Hierarchical Threshold Secret Sharing

Emilia Käsper[1], Ventzislav Nikov[2], and Svetla Nikova[1]

[1] K.U. Leuven, ESAT/COSIC
[2] TASS Belgium
{emilia.kasper,svetla.nikova}@esat.kuleuven.be,
venci.nikov@gmail.com

Abstract. We consider multi-party computation (MPC) in a hierarchical setting, where participants have different capabilities depending on their position in the hierarchy. First, we give necessary conditions for multiplication of secrets in a hierarchical threshold linear secret sharing scheme (LSSS). Starting with known ideal constructions, we then propose a modified scheme with improved multiplication properties. We give sufficient conditions for the new scheme to be (strongly) multiplicative and show that our construction is almost optimal in the number of required participants. Thus, we obtain a new class of strongly multiplicative LSSS with explicit ideal constructions. Such LSSS are also useful outside the MPC setting, since they have an efficient algorithm for reconstructing secrets in the presence of errors.

Keywords: Secret sharing schemes, multipartite access structures, multi-party computation, strong multiplicativity.

1   Introduction

1.1   Motivation

In threshold secret sharing, a secret is shared amongst n participants and can only be reconstructed by more than t of them together. Such schemes have found numerous applications such as key escrow, distributed file storage and distributed computation. However, in threshold schemes, all participants play an equal role and cannot be distinguished according to trust or authority, whereas in many real-life situations, hierarchies are required. Consider an example from the military. Let the secret be the "nuclear button" of a country and suppose that it can only be accessed by two ministers, or a minister and a general, but not by two generals. In this case, a 2-out-of-n threshold scheme is clearly not suitable, since any two generals could pool their shares together to bypass access control. Secret sharing schemes that take into account hierarchies were the first non-threshold schemes considered in the literature [10,11,1].

In this paper, we investigate the *multiplicativity* of hierarchical schemes. Multiplicativity allows participants, holding shares of two secrets s and s', to privately compute shares of the product ss' without revealing the original secrets.

Y. Desmedt (Ed.): ICITS 2007, LNCS 4883, pp. 148–168, 2009.

Strong multiplicativity further guarantees that in the presence of an active adversary, honest participants can still compute such shares. A simple solution for multiplication of secrets exists for the Shamir threshold scheme [6]. In general, however, it is not known how to efficiently construct a strongly multiplicative linear secret sharing scheme (LSSS) with the desired non-threshold access structure. Thus, we tackle a more specific problem and show how to achieve strong multiplicativity for a class of access structures.

Strongly multiplicative schemes turn out to be useful even outside the context of multiplying secrets, since they are resistant to errors in shares. Although in any LSSS with a $\mathcal{Q}_3$ access structure, the secret is uniquely determined even if the shares submitted by corrupted participants contain errors, it is not known how to locate such errors efficiently. An efficient secret reconstruction algorithm is only known for strongly multiplicative LSSS [4]. This implicit "built-in" verifiability makes strongly multiplicative schemes an attractive building block for multiparty computation (MPC) protocols.

1.2   Related Work

Hierarchical Secret Sharing. Hierarchical threshold secret sharing is a natural extension of simple threshold secret sharing and has been studied by several authors, using slightly different assumptions. Shamir proposed a threshold scheme and further introduced hierarchies by giving higher-level participants a greater number of shares [10]. This results in a weighted threshold access structure: if there are m levels and participants at level i hold w_i shares, then a subset of them can recover the secret if and only if $w_1 p_1 + \cdots + w_m p_m > t$, where p_i is the number of participants present at level i. Let $w = \max_i w_i$ be the highest weight; Shamir's hierarchical scheme then has information rate $1/w$.

Simmons and Brickell independently considered a different setting where participants are also divided into levels, but each level i is associated with a different threshold t_i [11,1]. A subset of participants can recover the secret if *for some i,* their total number at levels $1, \ldots, i$ exceeds the threshold t_i. The scheme proposed by Simmons has information rate $1/t$, where t is the highest threshold, whereas Brickell's solution is ideal. However, both schemes suffer from inefficiency, since the dealer is required to check possibly exponentially many matrices for non-singularity.

The schemes of Shamir, Simmons and Brickell allow a sufficient number of participants from even the lowest level to reconstruct the secret. Thus, they still do not address our "nuclear button" example, where at least one minister must always be present. Tassa recently proposed a third setting where each level is again associated with a different threshold t_i, but this time, *for every level i,* more than t_i participants from that or higher levels must be present in order to reconstruct the secret [12]. He notes that the threshold scheme provides a simple construction: the secret s is divided into m random parts, $s = s_1 + \cdots + s_m$, and part s_i is secret-shared with threshold t_i amongst the participants from levels $1, \ldots, i$. Again, the resulting scheme is not ideal: participants from level 1 receive m shares. More interestingly, Tassa also proposed efficient ideal constructions for his setting as well as for the setting of Simmons and Brickell. Both solutions are based on a generalization of Lagrange interpolation. In this paper, we use these two schemes to construct strongly multiplicative hierarchical threshold schemes.

Finally, hierarchical secret sharing has also been studied in the more general setting of multipartite access structures, where the set of participants is divided into several disjoint subsets and all participants in the same subset play an equivalent role. Farràs et al. give necessary and sufficient conditions for a multipartite access structure to be ideal and apply these results to characterize ideal tripartite structures [5]. While these results study the question whether an access structure can be realized with an ideal LSSS *at all*, for all practical purposes one is clearly interested in an *explicit* efficient construction. For all access structures that we consider in this paper, explicit ideal constructions have already been given. We proceed to study the (strong) multiplicativity of these particular constructions.

(Strongly) Multiplicative Secret Sharing. It is well known that a Shamir secret sharing scheme with n participants and threshold t is multiplicative if and only if $t < n/2$ and strongly multiplicative if and only if $t < n/3$. Moreover, Cramer et al. demonstrated an efficient construction that renders any LSSS with a $\mathcal{Q}_2$ access structure (i.e., any access structure for which multiplicativity is possible at all) into a multiplicative scheme that has the same access structure and has size at most twice the original scheme [3]. On the other hand, no similar result is known for achieving strong multiplicativity, where the general construction is exponential in the size of the original scheme. In fact, there are only two known families of access structures with an explicit construction that is both ideal and strongly multiplicative: the simple threshold scheme and a quasi-threshold construction recently proposed by Chen and Cramer [2].

1.3   Our Contributions

In this paper, we analyze the multiplicativity of two important families of hierarchical secret sharing schemes: threshold schemes based on conjunction and disjunction of conditions. First, we prove necessary conditions for multiplicativity. Then, we look at constructions based on Shamir threshold secret sharing and show that they are always (strongly) multiplicative whenever these necessary conditions are fulfilled. The constructions are not ideal but have a reasonable information rate when the number of levels in the hierarchy is small. Next, we investigate ideal constructions and propose a new conjunctive scheme based on the Tassa scheme [12]. We prove sufficient conditions for (strong) multiplicativity of the modified scheme. The conditions are not tight but we demonstrate that the gap is quite small, i.e, the construction is close to optimal. Finally, we note that our modified scheme actually has better multiplicative properties than the original scheme of Tassa. Thus, as a result of our analysis and our improvements to existing designs, we describe a big class of strongly multiplicative secret sharing schemes that have an efficient ideal construction.

Road Map. In Sect. 2 we review the basic theory of linear secret sharing schemes and monotone span programs. In Sect. 3 we introduce hierarchical threshold access structures and give necessary conditions for (strong) multiplicativity (Sect. 3.1). In Sect. 4, we describe non-ideal constructions and prove their multiplicativity (Theorems 3 and 4). In Sect. 5, we describe two ideal constructions and subsequently propose a modification that improves multiplication properties. The main result of this section is Theorem 6 that gives sufficient conditions for (strong) multiplicativity in the conjunctive case. Finally, in Sect. 6, we discuss some open problems. Technical details of proofs are given in appendices.

2 Preliminaries

Notations. For a set $A \subseteq S$, we denote its complement set by $A^c = \{b \in S : b \notin A\}$. The ith derivative of a polynomial $P(x)$ is denoted by $P^{(i)}(x)$.

Linear Secret Sharing Schemes. In a (linear) secret sharing scheme (LSSS), a *dealer* distributes shares of a secret s amongst n *participants*. The shares are computed in such a way that *qualified* groups of participants can completely reconstruct the secret (as a linear combination of their shares), while *forbidden* groups obtain no information about the secret whatsoever. An LSSS is *correct* if every qualified group can reconstruct the secret, and *private*, if no forbidden group can learn anything about the secret. In the multi-party computation setting, the scheme is *robust* if honest participants can correctly carry out computations. An LSSS is *ideal* if the share of every participant and the secret are equal in size. The first secret sharing schemes used a (t, n)-threshold setting, where the number of participants in a group needs to be strictly greater than a threshold t in order to become qualified. In general, as first put forth by Ito et al. [7], the set of qualified groups may be arbitrary, with the natural restriction that it is monotone: if $\mathcal{V}$ is qualified, then any $\mathcal{V}' \supset \mathcal{V}$ is also qualified.

Access and Adversary Structures. The set of qualified groups is called the access structure of the LSSS and is denoted by Γ. Conversely, the set of forbidden groups is the privacy structure $\Delta = \Gamma^c$. Notice that an adversary can fully corrupt any single set in Δ without violating privacy. Sometimes, we distinguish between passive and active corruption and also consider weaker active adversaries $\Delta_{\mathcal{A}} \subset \Delta$. In this case, we require privacy w.r.t. Δ and robustness w.r.t. $\Delta_{\mathcal{A}}$.

Monotone Span Programs. LSSS with arbitrary monotone access structures can conveniently be described by the following share dealing mechanism borrowed from linear algebra [8]:

Definition 1. *A monotone span program (MSP) $\mathcal{M}$ is a quadruple $(\mathbb{F}, M, \psi, \varepsilon)$, where $\mathbb{F}$ is a finite field, M is a matrix (with $d \geq n$ rows and $e \leq d$ columns), $\psi : \{1, \dots, d\} \to \{1, \dots, n\}$ is a surjective function and $\varepsilon \in \mathbb{F}^e$ is a target vector. The size of $\mathcal{M}$ is the number of rows d.*

Function ψ assigns each row to a participant. An MSP is called ideal if $d = n$, so each participant holds exactly one row. Unless explicitly stated otherwise, we assume that the target vector is $\varepsilon = (1, 0, \ldots, 0)$. Any MSP $\mathcal{M}$ can then be used to construct an LSSS as follows: to share $s \in \mathbb{F}$, the dealer chooses a random vector $\boldsymbol{r} \in \mathbb{F}^{e-1}$, computes a vector of d shares $\boldsymbol{s} = M(s, \boldsymbol{r})$ and gives share s_i to participant $\psi(i)$. That is, each participant receives shares corresponding to the rows he holds. For a subset of participants $\mathcal{V}$, we denote by $M_{\mathcal{V}}$ the matrix M restricted to the rows they hold. Participants in $\mathcal{V}$ can then reconstruct s if and only if the rows of $M_{\mathcal{V}}$ contain the target vector ε in their linear span. An MSP $\mathcal{M}$ *computes* access structure Γ if ε is in the linear span of $M_{\mathcal{V}}$ precisely if $\mathcal{V} \in \Gamma$. In what follows, we identify an LSSS with its underlying MSP. For example, in Shamir's (t, n)-threshold scheme, the dealer chooses a random degree t polynomial $P(x)$ subject to $P(0) = s$ and gives participant u a share $P(\alpha_u)$, where $0 \neq \alpha_u \in \mathbb{F}$ is a field element associated with u. In terms of MSPs, participant u then holds a row $(1, \alpha_u, \ldots, \alpha_u^t)$.

The *diamond product* of two matrices M_1, M_2 associated with MSPs $\mathcal{M}_1$, $\mathcal{M}_2$ is the matrix

$$M = M_1 \diamond M_2 = \begin{pmatrix} M_1^1 \otimes M_2^1 \\ M_1^2 \otimes M_2^2 \\ \ldots \\ M_1^n \otimes M_2^n \end{pmatrix} ,$$

where M_i^j is the matrix of rows owned by participant j in MSP $\mathcal{M}_i$; and $\otimes$ is the Kronecker product. Given two MSPs $\mathcal{M}_1 = (\mathbb{F}, M_1, \psi_1, \varepsilon_1)$, $\mathcal{M}_2 = (\mathbb{F}, M_2, \psi_2, \varepsilon_2)$, we now define the product MSP $\mathcal{M}_1 \diamond \mathcal{M}_2 = (\mathbb{F}, M_1 \diamond M_2, \psi, \varepsilon_1 \otimes \varepsilon_2)$, where $\psi(i, j) = p$ if and only if $\psi_1(i) = \psi_2(j) = p$. Product MSPs are useful in investigating the multiplication property of MSPs.

Multiplicativity. Informally, an MSP is multiplicative if participants, holding shares of secrets s and s', can compute shares of the product ss', using only their local shares. An MSP is strongly multiplicative if honest participants can compute shares of the product. More precisely, we require the product ss' to be a linear combination of such shares. Given two share-vectors $\boldsymbol{s} = M(s, \boldsymbol{r}) = (s_1, \ldots, s_d)$ and $\boldsymbol{s}' = M(s', \boldsymbol{r}') = (s_1', \ldots, s_d')$, we define $\boldsymbol{s} \diamond \boldsymbol{s}'$ to be the vector containing all entries $s_i s_j'$, where $\psi(i) = \psi(j)$. Then $\boldsymbol{s} \diamond \boldsymbol{s}'$ is computed by $\mathcal{M} \diamond \mathcal{M}$ as $\boldsymbol{s} \diamond \boldsymbol{s}' = M(s, \boldsymbol{r}) \diamond M(s', \boldsymbol{r}') = (M \diamond M)((s, \boldsymbol{r}) \otimes (s', \boldsymbol{r}'))$. Each component of $\boldsymbol{s} \diamond \boldsymbol{s}'$ can be computed locally by some participant, and we arrive at the following formal definition:

Definition 2. *A monotone span program $\mathcal{M}$ is multiplicative if there exists a recombination vector $\boldsymbol{\lambda}$ such that for any two secrets s and s' and any $\boldsymbol{r}, \boldsymbol{r}'$, it holds that*

$$s \cdot s' = \langle \boldsymbol{\lambda}, M(s, \boldsymbol{r}) \diamond M(s', \boldsymbol{r}') \rangle .$$

An MSP $\mathcal{M}$ is strongly multiplicative with respect to an adversary structure $\Delta_{\mathcal{A}}$ if for every $\mathcal{W} \in \Delta_{\mathcal{A}}$, $\mathcal{M}_{\mathcal{W}^c}$ is multiplicative.

If $\mathcal{M}$ is strongly multiplicative with respect to its privacy structure $\Delta = \Gamma^c$, then we say simply that $\mathcal{M}$ is strongly multiplicative. Shamir's (t, n)-scheme tolerates the corruption of t parties and requires an additional $2t + 1$ honest participants for multiplication, so it is strongly multiplicative for $n > 3t$. In general, multiplicativity is strongly related to the $\mathcal{Q}_\ell$ property of access structures:

Definition 3. *An adversary structure $\Delta_\mathcal{A}$ is $\mathcal{Q}_\ell$ if no ℓ sets in $\Delta_\mathcal{A}$ cover the full set of participants. An access structure Γ is $\mathcal{Q}_\ell$ if the corresponding privacy structure $\Delta = \Gamma^c$ is $\mathcal{Q}_\ell$.*

It is well known that multiplicative MSPs only exist for $\mathcal{Q}_2$ access structures and strongly multiplicative MSPs only exist for $\mathcal{Q}_3$ access structures [3].

3 Hierarchical Threshold Secret Sharing

In this section, we define two important families of hierarchical threshold access structures (HTAccS): the disjunctive HTAccS and the conjunctive HTAccS. We then give *necessary* conditions for schemes realizing these access structures to be (strongly) multiplicative. These conditions depend only on the underlying access structure and not on the specific construction of the LSSS. In Section 5, we analyze explicit constructions of schemes having such access structures and give *sufficient* conditions for those schemes to have the (strong) multiplicativity property.

The first family of access structures corresponds to the setting where at least one threshold must be met, so we call this the disjunctive access structure. The second definition captures our "nuclear button" example where all thresholds must be met, so this is the conjunctive access structure. We also define two adversary structures.

Definition 4. *Let $\mathcal{U}$ be a set of n participants divided into m disjoint levels, i.e., $\mathcal{U} = \bigcup_{i=1}^m \mathcal{U}_i$ where $\mathcal{U}_i \cap \mathcal{U}_j = \emptyset$ for all $1 \le i < j \le m$. Let $\boldsymbol{t} = \{t_i\}_{i=1}^m$ be a monotonically increasing sequence of integers, $0 \le t_1 < \cdots < t_m$. Then the $(\boldsymbol{t}, n)$-disjunctive hierarchical threshold access structure (HTAccS) is*

$$\Gamma^\exists = \left\{ \mathcal{V} \subseteq \mathcal{U} : \exists i \in \{1, \ldots, m\} \ \left| \mathcal{V} \cap \left(\cup_{j=1}^i \mathcal{U}_j \right) \right| > t_i \right\} \tag{1}$$

and the $(\boldsymbol{t}, n)$-conjunctive hierarchical threshold access structure is

$$\Gamma^\forall = \left\{ \mathcal{V} \subseteq \mathcal{U} : \forall i \in \{1, \ldots, m\} \ \left| \mathcal{V} \cap \left(\cup_{j=1}^i \mathcal{U}_j \right) \right| > t_i \right\}. \tag{2}$$

The $(\boldsymbol{t}, n)$-disjunctive hierarchical threshold adversary structure (HTAdS) is

$$\Delta^\exists = \left\{ \mathcal{W} \subseteq \mathcal{U} : \exists i \in \{1, \ldots, m\} \ \left| \mathcal{W} \cap \left(\cup_{j=1}^i \mathcal{U}_j \right) \right| \le t_i \right\} \tag{3}$$

and the $(\boldsymbol{t}, n)$-conjunctive hierarchical threshold adversary structure is

$$\Delta^\forall = \left\{ \mathcal{W} \subseteq \mathcal{U} : \forall i \in \{1, \ldots, m\} \ \left| \mathcal{W} \cap \left(\cup_{j=1}^i \mathcal{U}_j \right) \right| \le t_i \right\}. \tag{4}$$

The choice of adversary structures is not arbitrary: a (t, n)-disjunctive HTAdS coincides with the privacy structure of a (t, n)-conjunctive HTAccS and, vice versa, a (t, n)-conjunctive HTAdS coincides with the privacy structure of a (t, n)-disjunctive HTAccS. In other words, in the above definition, $\Delta^\exists = (\Gamma^\forall)^c$ and $\Delta^\forall = (\Gamma^\exists)^c$. Notice that for the same threshold vector t and the same set of participants $\mathcal{U}$, the conjunctive access structure is contained in the disjunctive structure. Conversely, the conjunctive adversary is weaker than the disjunctive adversary: $\Delta^\forall \subseteq \Delta^\exists$. A duality relation exists between conjunctive and disjunctive HTAccS [12].

3.1   Necessary Conditions for (Strong) Multiplicativity

Recall that an access structure is $\mathcal{Q}_\ell$ if no ℓ forbidden subsets cover the whole set of participants. It is well known that if an LSSS is multiplicative, then the corresponding access structure must be $\mathcal{Q}_2$, and if it is strongly multiplicative, then the access structure must be $\mathcal{Q}_3$. In the following, we give necessary and sufficient conditions for the two types of hierarchical access structures to be $\mathcal{Q}_2$ and $\mathcal{Q}_3$. Thus, we immediately obtain necessary conditions for (strong) multiplicativity. However, sufficient conditions for multiplicativity depend on the LSSS rather than just the access structure. In the Shamir setting, every scheme with a $\mathcal{Q}_2$ ($\mathcal{Q}_3$) access structure is also (strongly) multiplicative, but this is not the case in general. In particular, we can give counterexamples for the ideal hierarchical threshold constructions proposed by Tassa. Thus, we shall later look for stronger conditions that are sufficient for these particular schemes to have multiplication.

In order to be able to distinguish the possibly smaller (active) adversary structure from the privacy structure, we give all our results in terms of general adversary structures (for proofs of theorems in this section, see Appendix A). We begin with the conjunctive adversary that corresponds to the disjunctive access structure. From now on, we denote by $u_i = |\bigcup_{j=1}^i \mathcal{U}_i|$ the number of participants at levels $\mathcal{U}_1, \ldots, \mathcal{U}_i$ in a hierarchical threshold secret sharing scheme (HTSSS).

Theorem 1. *A (t, n)-conjunctive HTAdS $\Delta^\forall$ is $\mathcal{Q}_\ell$ if and only if*

$$\exists i \in \{1, \ldots, m\} \quad such \ that \quad u_i > \ell t_i . \tag{5}$$

Recalling that a disjunctive access structure $\Gamma^\exists$ is $\mathcal{Q}_\ell$ if its corresponding privacy structure $\Delta^\forall$ is $\mathcal{Q}_\ell$, we immediately conclude a necessary condition for multiplicativity.

Corollary 1. *If an HTSSS realizing a (t, n)-disjunctive HTAccS $\Gamma^\exists$ is multiplicative, then*

$$\exists i \in \{1, \ldots, m\} \quad such \ that \quad u_i > 2t_i . \tag{6}$$

If an HTSSS realizing $\Gamma^\exists$ is strongly multiplicative, then

$$\exists i \in \{1, \ldots, m\} \quad such \ that \quad u_i > 3t_i . \tag{7}$$

The result for the conjunctive case is slightly more complicated.

Theorem 2. *A (t, n)-disjunctive HTAdS $\Delta^{\exists}$ is $\mathcal{Q}_\ell$ if and only if*

$$\forall i \in \{1, \ldots, m\} \qquad u_i > t_i + (\ell - 1)t_m . \tag{8}$$

Corollary 2. *If an HTSSS realizing a (t, n)-conjunctive HTAccS $\Gamma^{\forall}$ is multiplicative, then*

$$\forall i \in \{1, \ldots, m\} \qquad u_i > t_i + t_m . \tag{9}$$

If an HTSSS realizing $\Gamma^{\forall}$ is strongly multiplicative, then

$$\forall i \in \{1, \ldots, m\} \qquad u_i > t_i + 2t_m . \tag{10}$$

Notice that if for some $i > 1$ we have $u_i - u_{i-1} = |\mathcal{U}_i| \leq t_i - t_{i-1}$, then for any allowed set $\mathcal{V}$ in the conjunctive setting, condition $\mathcal{V} \cap \cup_{j=1}^{i} \mathcal{U}_j > t_i$ implies $\mathcal{V} \cap \cup_{j=1}^{i-1} \mathcal{U}_j > t_{i-1}$, so the latter threshold is obsolete. Thus, we can collapse levels: the (t, n)-conjunctive HTSSS with sets $\mathcal{U}_1, \ldots, \mathcal{U}_m$ has the same access structure as the (t', n)-conjunctive HTSSS with $t' = (t_1, \ldots, t_{i-2}, t_i, t_{i+1}, \ldots, t_m)$ and sets $\mathcal{U}_1, \ldots, \mathcal{U}_{i-2}, \mathcal{U}_{i-1} \cup \mathcal{U}_i, \mathcal{U}_{i+1}, \ldots, \mathcal{U}_m$. Assuming now that $u_i - u_{i-1} > t_i - t_{i-1}$, $i \in \{2, \ldots, m\}$, we see that the first condition of (8) $u_1 > t_1 + (\ell - 1)t_m$ implies all the remaining conditions $u_i > t_i + (\ell - 1)t_m$.

Thus, we see that the necessary condition for the conjunctive hierarchical threshold access structure to be (strongly) multiplicative is essentially a lower bound on the number of participants of highest priority. This is unavoidable, since the adversary can by definition corrupt all participants at levels $2, \ldots, m$ without violating privacy. On the other hand, the strength of the bound is somewhat unnatural in real-life scenarios, where there are usually few top-level participants, be it company directors, ministers or program committee chairs.

An interesting question is to what extent the situation changes if we distinguish the passive adversary from the active adversary. That is, while the conjunctive HTAccS $\Gamma^{\forall}$ has privacy w.r.t. the disjunctive HTAdS $\Delta^{\exists}$, we only require that multiplication is robust w.r.t. a weaker adversary $\Delta_{\mathcal{A}} \subset \Delta^{\exists}$. A natural candidate for a weaker active adversary is the conjunctive adversary $\Delta_{\mathcal{A}} = \Delta^{\forall}$ from Eq. (4) of Definition 4. Consider a (t', n)-conjunctive adversary that can actively corrupt at most t'_i participants from any subset $\bigcup_{j=1}^{i} \mathcal{U}_j$. The next result gives necessary conditions on participant set sizes in order to preserve robustness of multiplication.

Corollary 3. *If an HTSSS realizing a (t, n)-conjunctive HTAccS $\Gamma^{\forall}$ is strongly multiplicative with respect to a (t', n)-conjunctive HTAdS $\Delta^{\forall}$, then*

$$\forall i \in \{1, \ldots, m\} \qquad u_i > t_i + t'_i + t_m . \tag{11}$$

Proof. If the scheme is strongly multiplicative w.r.t. $\Delta^{\forall}$, then for all $\mathcal{W} \in \Delta^{\forall}$, $\Gamma^{\forall}_{\mathcal{U} \setminus \mathcal{W}}$ is multiplicative and thus $\mathcal{Q}_2$. Assume now that for some k, $u_k \leq t_k +$

$t'_k + t_m$. As in the proof of Theorem 1, we can construct a set $\mathcal{W}$ such that $\forall i \in \{1, \ldots, m\}$ $|\mathcal{W} \cap \cup_{j=1}^i \mathcal{U}_j| \le t'_i$ and in particular, $|\mathcal{W} \cap \cup_{j=1}^k \mathcal{U}_j| = \min\{t'_k, u_k\}$. But then, $|(\cup_{j=1}^k \mathcal{U}_j) \setminus \mathcal{W}| \le u_k - t'_k \le t_k + t_m$, so by Theorem 2, $\Gamma_{\mathcal{U} \setminus \mathcal{W}}^{\forall}$ is not $\mathcal{Q}_2$, contradiction. $\square$

Notice that the threshold vectors may differ for the access structure and the adversary structure. In the simple case when they coincide, we require $u_i > 2t_i + t_m$. More than t_i participants from $\cup_{j=1}^i \mathcal{U}_j$ are then required to reconstruct the secret, while multiplication is possible when at most t_i participants from these levels are corrupt.

Example. If a $((1,3), n)$-conjunctive scheme is used, then the total number of top-level participants must be at least 5 to allow multiplication; on the other hand, it must be at least as much as 8 to allow multiplication in the presence of an adversary. At the same time, with 6 top-level participants, we can already hope to assure robustness of multiplication against the weaker, conjunctive adversary. In the next section, we look at constructions with optimal multiplication properties.

4   Non-ideal Constructions

In this section we analyze two simple explicit constructions, one for the conjunctive and one for the disjunctive HTAccS. Although these constructions are not ideal, they have the advantage that they are (strongly) multiplicative whenever the access structure permits multiplication at all. Since both constructions use Shamir secret sharing as the basic building-block, the results are not surprising. Note though that in the conjunctive case, usual care must be taken to assure compatibility of shares: every participant u must be associated with the same field element α_u in every Shamir block used to construct the scheme.

The notion of sum and product access structures is helpful in formalizing our results [9]:

Definition 5. *If Γ_1 and Γ_2 are access structures defined on sets $\mathcal{U}_1$ and $\mathcal{U}_2$, respectively, then the sum $\Gamma_1 + \Gamma_2$ and product $\Gamma_1 \times \Gamma_2$ access structures are defined on $\mathcal{U}_1 \cup \mathcal{U}_2$ such that for $\mathcal{V} \subseteq \mathcal{U}_1 \cup \mathcal{U}_2$,*

$$\mathcal{V} \in \Gamma_1 + \Gamma_2 \iff (\mathcal{V} \cap \mathcal{U}_1 \in \Gamma_1 \ \text{or} \ \mathcal{V} \cap \mathcal{U}_2 \in \Gamma_2) \ ,$$
$$\mathcal{V} \in \Gamma_1 \times \Gamma_2 \iff (\mathcal{V} \cap \mathcal{U}_1 \in \Gamma_1 \ \text{and} \ \mathcal{V} \cap \mathcal{U}_2 \in \Gamma_2) \ .$$

Now, let Γ_i be a (t_i, u_i)-threshold access structure on the set $\cup_{j=1}^i \mathcal{U}_j$. Clearly, every $(\boldsymbol{t}, n)$-disjunctive HTAccS is a sum access structure: $\Gamma = \Gamma_1 + \cdots + \Gamma_m$. Similarly, every $(\boldsymbol{t}, n)$-conjunctive HTAccS is a product access structure: $\Gamma = \Gamma_1 \times \cdots \times \Gamma_m$. We use the following well-known result to construct MSPs for the disjunctive and conjunctive HTAccS:

Lemma 1. *If MSPs $\mathcal{M}_1$ and $\mathcal{M}_2$ with matrices $M_1 = (\boldsymbol{v}_1 \ \overline{M_1})$ and $M_2 = (\boldsymbol{v}_2 \ \overline{M_2})$ (where $\boldsymbol{v}_1$ and $\boldsymbol{v}_2$ are the first columns of the matrices) and target* *vectors* $(1, 0, \ldots, 0)$ *compute access structures* Γ_1 *and* Γ_2, *then MSPs* $\mathcal{M}_1 + \mathcal{M}_2$ *and* $\mathcal{M}_1 \times \mathcal{M}_2$ *defined by*

$$M_1 + M_2 = \begin{pmatrix} v_1 & \overline{M_1} & \mathbf{0} \\ v_2 & \mathbf{0} & \overline{M_2} \end{pmatrix} \quad and \quad M_1 \times M_2 = \begin{pmatrix} v_1 & \mathbf{0} & \overline{M_1} & \mathbf{0} \\ \mathbf{0} & v_2 & \mathbf{0} & \overline{M_2} \end{pmatrix} \quad (12)$$

compute $\Gamma_1 + \Gamma_2$ *and* $\Gamma_1 \times \Gamma_2$, *respectively.*[1]

The first construction formalizes the situation where the same secret is shared twice using two different access structures; the second corresponds to the case where a secret is split into two parts and each part is shared according to a different access structure. Using this construction with Shamir secret sharing as the basic building block, we can give strongly multiplicative MSPs for the disjunctive and the conjunctive HTAccS. The corresponding schemes have information rate $1/m$.

The disjunctive construction is obtained by sharing the same secret in m different ways using m different thresholds $t_1, \ldots, t_m$. The multiplication property then follows from the multiplicativity of the underlying Shamir scheme. For the conjunctive case, we choose randomly m different secrets $s_1, \ldots, s_m$ such that they add up to the secret: $s = s_1 + \cdots + s_m$. Each s_i is then shared using a different threshold t_i. We give constructive proofs of the following results in Appendix B.

Theorem 3. *If* $\Gamma^\exists$ *is a* $\mathcal{Q}_2$ ($\mathcal{Q}_3$) *disjunctive HTAccS, then there exists a (strongly) multiplicative MSP of size* $u_1 + \cdots + u_m$ *computing* $\Gamma^\exists$.

Theorem 4. *If* $\Gamma^\forall$ *is a* $\mathcal{Q}_2$ ($\mathcal{Q}_3$) *conjunctive HTAccS, then there exists a (strongly) multiplicative MSP of size* $u_1 + \cdots + u_m$ *computing* $\Gamma^\forall$. *If* $\Gamma^\forall$ *is a conjunctive HTAccS that satisfies condition* (11) *of Corollary 3, then there exists an MSP of size* $u_1 + \cdots + u_m$ *computing* $\Gamma^\forall$ *that is strongly multiplicative with respect to the conjunctive adversary* $\Delta^\forall$ *of Corollary 3.*

Example. Suppose that a secure computation is carried out by 5 servers, and 3 of them are trusted more than the remaining two. If a $(1, 5)$-threshold scheme is used, then the two semi-trusted servers can jointly recover all secrets. If a $(2, 5)$-threshold scheme is used, then no errors are tolerated in multiplication. But if we use a two-level $((0, 1), 5)$-conjunctive scheme, then the presence of one trusted server is always required, while the failure of one trusted server is also tolerated. The maximum share size is still reasonable—it is double the size of the secret. However, when the hierarchy has more levels, it becomes important to look for ideal constructions.

5   Ideal Constructions

We proceed to analyze the multiplicativity of two ideal constructions proposed by Tassa [12]. Both schemes, one for the conjunctive and one for the disjunctive hierarchical threshold access structure, draw ideas from polynomial interpolation.

---

[1] The target vector of $\mathcal{M} \times \mathcal{M}$ is $(1, 1, 0, \ldots, 0)$.

5.1   The Conjunctive Construction

Tassa's key idea is to give participants in the top level of the hierarchy points on a polynomial, and participants in lower levels points on derivatives of the same polynomial. This way, shares of lower levels contain less information; in particular, when the secret is the free coefficient, points on derivatives contain no information about the secret, so a number of participants from the top level is always required to recover the secret. More precisely, in order to share a secret s according to a (t, n)-conjunctive HTAccS, the dealer (1) selects a random polynomial $P(x) = \sum_{i=0}^{t_m} a_i x^i$ subject to $a_0 = s$, where t_m is the highest threshold; and (2) gives participant $u \in \mathcal{U}_i$ a share $P^{(t_{i-1}+1)}(\alpha_u)$, i.e., the $(t_{i-1}+1)$th derivative of $P(x)$ at $x = \alpha_u$, where $t_0 = -1$ and α_u is the field element associated with participant u. Thus, in the corresponding MSP, participant $u \in \mathcal{U}_i$ holds a row

$$\left(0, \dots, 0, c_0, c_1 \alpha_u, c_2 \alpha_u^2, \dots, c_{t_m - t_{i-1} - 1} \alpha_u^{t_m - t_{i-1} - 1}\right) \tag{13}$$

with $t_{i-1} + 1$ leading zeroes (where $c_i = (t_{i-1} + i + 1)!/i!$).

Example. Consider a two-level scheme with thresholds $t_1 = 0$, $t_2 = 2$ and suppose that there are 4 participants at level $\mathcal{U}_1$ and 1 participant at level $\mathcal{U}_2$. The matrix of the MSP is then

$$M = \begin{pmatrix} 1 & \alpha_1 & \alpha_1^2 \\ 1 & \alpha_2 & \alpha_2^2 \\ 1 & \alpha_3 & \alpha_3^2 \\ 1 & \alpha_4 & \alpha_4^2 \\ 0 & 1 & 2\alpha_5 \end{pmatrix}, \tag{14}$$

where α_i are some distinct non-zero field elements. The first question that we need to ask is: does this construction indeed yield the desired hierarchical access structure? It turns out that some care must be taken in assigning field elements to participants, but that even a random allocation strategy is successful with an overwhelming probability [12]:

Theorem 5. *Assume a random allocation of participant identities in a field* $\mathbb{F}_q$. *Then the ideal HTSSS of* (13) *computes a* (t, n)-*conjunctive HTAccS with probability*

$$p \geq 1 - \frac{\binom{n+1}{t_m+1} t_m (t_m - 1)}{2(q - t_m - 1)}.$$

The secret space is normally very large compared to the threshold t_m and the number of participants n, hence the success probability $p = 1 - \Theta(1/q)$ is indeed overwhelming.

Next, we look at multiplication. While secret sharing based on polynomials is "naturally" multiplicative, derivatives bring trouble. Indeed, when participants from the top level multiply their shares of $P(x)$ and $Q(x)$, they obtain shares of

$(P \cdot Q)(x)$, but participants holding points on $P^{(i)}(x)$ and $Q^{(i)}(x)$ obtain shares of $(P^{(i)} \cdot Q^{(i)})(x) \neq (P \cdot Q)^{(j)}(x)$ for any j. Returning to Example (14), we see that the scheme is not multiplicative, even though the access structure is $\mathcal{Q}_2$. We get

$$
M \diamond M = \begin{pmatrix}
1 & \alpha_1 & \alpha_1^2 & \alpha_1^2 & \alpha_1^3 & \alpha_1^4 \\
1 & \alpha_2 & \alpha_2^2 & \alpha_2^2 & \alpha_2^3 & \alpha_2^4 \\
1 & \alpha_3 & \alpha_3^2 & \alpha_3^2 & \alpha_3^3 & \alpha_3^4 \\
1 & \alpha_4 & \alpha_4^2 & \alpha_4^2 & \alpha_4^3 & \alpha_4^4 \\
0 & 0 & 0 & 1 & 2\alpha_5 & 4\alpha_5^2
\end{pmatrix} .
$$

Clearly, the five participants in $\mathcal{U}_1 \bigcup \mathcal{U}_2$ can recover the secret only if the five last columns of the matrix are linearly dependent. However, expanding by the last row, we see that the corresponding determinant is a Vandermonde determinant (multiplied by $\alpha_1\alpha_2\alpha_3\alpha_4$), so it is always non-zero, regardless of the choice of field elements.

Before analyzing further the multiplicativity of the scheme, we modify the distribution of shares. Namely, we ignore the leading coefficients c_i in (13) and let participant $u \in \mathcal{U}_i$ hold a row

$$
(0, 0, \ldots, 0, 1, \alpha_u, \ldots, \alpha_u^{t_m - t_{i-1} - 1}) \tag{15}
$$

with $t_{i-1} + 1$ leading zeroes. In the example above, we let the fifth participant hold $(0, 1, \alpha_5)$ instead of $(0, 1, 2\alpha_5)$. This tweak simplifies the analysis and in fact even improves the multiplication property of the scheme. Since all arguments in the proof of Theorem 5 apply equally for the modified scheme, random allocation yields the correct access structure with an overwhelming probability. For completeness, we give the proof of Theorem 5 for the modified case in Appendix C.

Denote by p_i the number of participants at level $\mathcal{U}_i$, i.e., $p_i = |\mathcal{U}_i| = u_i - u_{i-1}$. The next theorem gives sufficient conditions for having an ideal HTSSS with multiplication for a conjunctive HTAccS:

Theorem 6. *If the (t, n)-conjunctive HTAccS computed by the HTSSS of (15) satisfies*

$$
\exists\, s,\ 0 = i_1 < i_2 < \cdots < i_s = m \quad \text{such that}
$$
$$
\forall j \in \{1, \ldots, s - 1\} \quad p_{i_j + 1} > t_{i_{j+1}} + t_m - 2(t_{i_j} + 1) , \tag{16}
$$

where $t_0 = -1$, then the scheme is multiplicative.

In order to understand condition (16), we note that taking $i_j = j - 1$ and $s = m + 1$ yields

$$
\forall i \in \{1, \ldots, m\} \quad p_i > t_i + t_m - 2(t_{i-1} + 1) .
$$

Proof. We prove the theorem for the general condition (16). The key idea is to prove that (1) there exists a set of participants $\mathcal{V}$ such that the corresponding product MSP $\mathcal{M}_{\mathcal{V}} \diamond \mathcal{M}_{\mathcal{V}}$ has a block-triangular matrix; and (2) the blocks on the diagonal of $M_{\mathcal{V}} \diamond M_{\mathcal{V}}$ are Vandermonde blocks, and its determinant is thus non-zero. Technical details of the proof are presented in Appendix D.   □

Example. Consider a $((1,2,4),n)$-scheme. Then, any one of the following sets of conditions is sufficient for the scheme to be multiplicative:

$$p_1 > 8 \text{ or } p_1 > 6 \ \& \ p_3 > 2 \text{ or } p_1 > 5 \ \& \ p_2 > 2 \ \& \ p_3 > 2 \text{ or } p_1 > 5 \ \& \ p_2 > 4 \ . \tag{17}$$

For example, a set $\mathcal{V}$ with 6 participants from level $\mathcal{U}_1$ and 5 participants from level $\mathcal{U}_2$ is allowed. In comparison, if we were using the original Tassa scheme, the same set $\mathcal{V}$ would always be forbidden. Thus, by deleting the leading coefficients in the lower-order shares, we have actually improved the multiplication property of the scheme (see Appendix D for details).

Finally, we also give sufficient conditions for strong multiplicativity. For simplicity, we consider only the case where participants from all levels are engaged.

Corollary 4. *If the (t,n)-conjunctive HTAccS computed by the HTSSS described above satisfies*

$$\forall i \in \{1,\ldots,m\} \qquad p_i > t_i + 2t_m - 2(t_{i-1}+1) \ , \tag{18}$$

where $t_0 = -1$, then the scheme is strongly multiplicative. If it satisfies

$$\forall i \in \{1,\ldots,m\} \qquad p_i > t_i + t_i' + t_m - 2(t_{i-1}+1) \ , \tag{19}$$

then it is strongly multiplicative with respect to a (t',n)-conjunctive HTAdS $\Delta^{\mathcal{V}}$.

Proof. We prove only the first claim. Let $\mathcal{W}$ be a corrupted set and assume (18). Again, there must exist an index for which $\mathcal{W}$ does not cross the threshold, i.e., $\exists k : |\mathcal{W} \cap \cup_{j=1}^{k} \mathcal{U}_j| \le t_k \le t_m$. But then

$$\forall i < k \quad |(\mathcal{U} \setminus \mathcal{W}) \cap \mathcal{U}_i| = |\mathcal{U}_i| - |\mathcal{W} \cap \mathcal{U}_i| \ge p_i - t_m > t_i + t_m - 2(t_{i-1}+1) \ ,$$
$$|(\mathcal{U} \setminus \mathcal{W}) \cap \mathcal{U}_k| = |\mathcal{U}_k| - |\mathcal{W} \cap \mathcal{U}_k| \ge p_k - t_k > 2t_m - 2(t_{k-1}+1) \ ,$$

so $s = k+1$ with index set $i_j = j-1$, $j = 1,\ldots,k$ satisfies the assumptions of Theorem 6 and the participants in $\bigcup_{j=1}^{k} \mathcal{U}_j \setminus \mathcal{W}$ can compute shares of the product.   □

Although there is a gap between necessary and sufficient conditions for (strong) multiplicativity, the positive implication of our results is the following: it is possible to achieve (strong) multiplicativity while keeping the number of top-level participants at the minimum required threshold. That is, if there are sufficiently many lower-level participants, then the scheme is multiplicative for $u_1 > t_1 + t_m$ and strongly multiplicative for $u_1 > t_1 + 2t_m$. Returning to Example (17) above, the minimum requirement for multiplicativity is $u_1 > 5$. Additionally, we require $u_2 > 6$ and $u_3 > 8$ (see Corollary 2). On the other hand, as we have seen, $p_1 > 5$, $p_2 > 2$ and $p_3 > 2$ is sufficient. Thus, we only need 3 extra participants from lower levels to fill the gap.

5.2   The Disjunctive Construction

Tassa's construction is again based on polynomial interpolation, only this time, participants from higher levels get lower-order derivatives. Also, the secret is the set to be the highest-power coefficient a_{t_m}, instead of the free coefficient a_0. So, to share a secret according to a (t, n)-disjunctive HTAccS, the dealer (1) selects a random polynomial $P(x) = \sum_{i=0}^{t_m} a_i x^i$, where t_m is the highest threshold and the secret is $s = a_{t_m}$; and (2) gives participant $u \in \mathcal{U}_i$ a share $P^{(t_m - t_i)}(\alpha_u)$. An analog of Theorem 5 again guarantees the desired access structure.

Recall from Corollary 1 that if the disjunctive scheme is (strongly) multiplicative, then there exists an index i for which $u_i > 2t_i$ $(u_i > 3t_i)$. On the other hand, it is easy to see that if the number of participants at some single level i is $p_i > 2t_i$ $(p_i > 3t_i)$, then the scheme is (strongly) multiplicative. However, if these conditions hold, then participants in $\mathcal{U}_i$ can compute shares of the product without engaging participants in other sets at all. In the following we show that strong multiplicativity is possible even if such an index i does not exist.

Theorem 7. *If the (t, n)-disjunctive HTAccS computed by the HTSSS described above satisfies*

$$\exists i \quad such \ that \quad u_i > 3t_i + 2\sum_{j=1}^{i-1} t_j \ , \tag{20}$$

then the scheme is strongly multiplicative.

Proof. Assume that (20) holds. The (t, n)-conjunctive hierarchical threshold adversary $\Delta^\vee$ can corrupt at most t_i participants from $\bigcup_{j=1}^{i} \mathcal{U}_i$. Consequently, there are more than $2\sum_{j=1}^{i} t_j$ honest participants in this set. But then at least one of the sets $\mathcal{U}_j$, $j \in \{1, \dots, i\}$ must have more than $2t_j$ honest participants, and they can compute shares of the product. □

Example. Consider a $((1, 2, 4), n)$-disjunctive HTAccS and let $p_1 = 3$, $p_2 = 5$ and $p_3 = 11$. Then the HTSSS computing the HTAccS is strongly multiplicative, even though $p_i \leq 3t_i$ for $i \in \{1, 2, 3\}$.

6   Concluding Remarks

Strongly multiplicative secret sharing schemes are used in multi-party computation to obtain error-free multiplication unconditionally secure against an active adversary. However, enforcing the multiplication property is in general expensive and few efficient non-threshold examples are known.

We have proposed two different solutions for obtaining strong multiplication in the hierarchical threshold setting. The constructions of Section 4 achieve robustness against the strongest possible adversary. These schemes are not ideal but have a reasonable information rate for hierarchies with few levels. The ideal constructions of Section 5 are strongly multiplicative under somewhat stronger, but still feasible assumptions. In particular, we have proposed a modification that improves the multiplication properties of the scheme. Our results are not tight and it is possible that better bounds can be obtained by more careful analysis. However, we have proven the modified scheme to be optimal with respect to the most crucial property—the number of required top-level participants.

The modified ideal scheme has a randomized identity allocation strategy with failure probability $p = \Theta(1/q)$, which is a safe bet for large field sizes q. Still, for the original conjunctive and disjunctive constructions, the author also proposed a deterministic allocation strategy, which has zero failure probability if the field is sufficiently large. The strategy allocates identities in a monotone fashion, so participants from higher levels get "smaller" field elements. It would be interesting to verify if the deterministic strategy also applies for the new scheme.

Acknowledgements. The authors thank Sven Laur and George Danezis for helpful comments. This work was supported in part by the Concerted Research Action (GOA) Ambiorics 2005/11 of the Flemish Government, by the European Commission through the IST Programme under Contract IST-2002-507932 ECRYPT and the IAPP–Belgian State–Belgian Science Policy BCRYPT. Svetla Nikova was also partially supported by the Flemish IWT SBO project ADAPID and Emilia Käsper by the FWO-Flanders project nr. G.0317.06 *Linear Codes and Cryptography.*

References

1. Brickell, E.F.: Some ideal secret sharing schemes. In: Quisquater, J.-J., Vandewalle, J. (eds.) EUROCRYPT 1989. LNCS, vol. 434, pp. 468–475. Springer, Heidelberg (1990)
2. Chen, H., Cramer, R.: Algebraic geometric secret sharing schemes and secure multiparty computations over small fields. In: Dwork, C. (ed.) CRYPTO 2006. LNCS, vol. 4117, pp. 521–536. Springer, Heidelberg (2006)
3. Cramer, R., Damgård, I., Maurer, U.M.: General secure multi-party computation from any linear secret-sharing scheme. In: Preneel, B. (ed.) EUROCRYPT 2000. LNCS, vol. 1807, pp. 316–334. Springer, Heidelberg (2000)
4. Cramer, R., Daza, V., Gracia, I., Urroz, J.J., Leander, G., Martí-Farré, J., Padró, C.: On codes, matroids and secure multi-party computation from linear secret sharing schemes. In: Shoup, V. (ed.) CRYPTO 2005. LNCS, vol. 3621, pp. 327–343. Springer, Heidelberg (2005)
5. Farràs, O., Martí-Farré, J., Padró, C.: Ideal multipartite secret sharing schemes. In: Naor, M. (ed.) EUROCRYPT 2007. LNCS, vol. 4515, pp. 448–465. Springer, Heidelberg (2007)
6. Gennaro, R., Rabin, M.O., Rabin, T.: Simplified VSS and fact-track multiparty computations with applications to threshold cryptography. In: ACM Symposium on Principles of Distributed Computing, pp. 101–111 (1998)
7. Ito, M., Saito, A., Nishizeki, T.: Secret sharing scheme realizing general access structure. In: IEEE Goblecom 1987 (1987)
8. Karchmer, M., Wigderson, A.: On span programs. In: Structure in Complexity Theory Conference, pp. 102–111 (1993)

9. Martin, K.M.: New secret sharing schemes from old. Journal of Combinatorial Mathematics and Combinatorial Computing 14, 65–77 (1993)
10. Shamir, A.: How to share a secret. Commun. ACM 22(11), 612–613 (1979)
11. Simmons, G.J.: How to (really) share a secret. In: Goldwasser, S. (ed.) CRYPTO 1988. LNCS, vol. 403, pp. 390–448. Springer, Heidelberg (1990)
12. Tassa, T.: Hierarchical threshold secret sharing. Journal of Cryptology 20(2), 237–264 (2007)

A $\mathcal{Q}_\ell$ Conditions (Theorems 1 and 2)

Proof (of Theorem 1). If (5) holds for some i, then no ℓ adversarial sets can cover all participants in $\bigcup_{j=1}^{i} \mathcal{U}_j$, so $\Delta^{\vee}$ is $\mathcal{Q}_\ell$. Assume now that (5) does not hold, so $\forall i \quad u_i \leq \ell t_i$. Clearly, it is possible to divide the u_1 participants of level $\mathcal{U}_1$ into ℓ sets $\mathcal{W}_1, \ldots, \mathcal{W}_\ell$ such that $|\mathcal{W}_k \cap \mathcal{U}_1| \leq t_1$ for $k \in \{1, \ldots, \ell\}$. We complete the proof by induction on levels. Suppose that all u_i participants from $\bigcup_{j=1}^{i} \mathcal{U}_j$ have been divided into ℓ sets such that $|\mathcal{W}_k \cap \bigcup_{j=1}^{i}\mathcal{U}_j| = w_k \leq t_i$ for $k \in \{1, \ldots, \ell\}$. Then, we can add $t_{i+1} - w_k$ participants from $\mathcal{U}_{i+1}$ into $\mathcal{W}_k$ without violating $|\mathcal{W}_k \cap \bigcup_{j=1}^{i+1}\mathcal{U}_j| \leq t_{i+1}$. On the other hand,

$$|\mathcal{U}_{i+1}| = u_{i+1} - u_i = u_{i+1} - \sum_{k=1}^{\ell} w_k \leq \ell t_{i+1} - \sum_{k=1}^{\ell} w_k = \sum_{k=1}^{\ell}(t_{i+1} - w_k) \ ,$$

so all u_{i+1} participants from $\bigcup_{j=1}^{i+1} \mathcal{U}_j$ can also be allocated. $\qquad \square$

Proof (of Theorem 2). Assume first that (8) holds and consider any ℓ corrupt sets $\mathcal{W}_1, \mathcal{W}_2, \ldots, \mathcal{W}_\ell \in \Delta^{\exists}$. For $k \in \{1, \ldots, \ell\}$, let i_k be the smallest index such that $\left|\mathcal{W}_k \cap \left(\cup_{j=1}^{i_k}\mathcal{U}_j\right)\right| \leq t_{i_k}$ and assume w.l.o.g. that $i_1 \leq i_2 \leq \cdots \leq i_\ell$. Then

$$\left|\left(\cup_{k=1}^{\ell}\mathcal{W}_k\right) \cap \left(\cup_{j=1}^{i_1}\mathcal{U}_j\right)\right| \leq \sum_{k=1}^{\ell}\left|\mathcal{W}_k \cap \left(\cup_{j=1}^{i_1}\mathcal{U}_j\right)\right| \leq \sum_{k=1}^{\ell}\left|\mathcal{W}_k \cap \left(\cup_{j=1}^{i_k}\mathcal{U}_j\right)\right|$$

$$\leq \sum_{k=1}^{\ell} t_{i_k} \leq t_{i_1} + (\ell - 1)t_m < u_{i_1} \ ,$$

implying that $\mathcal{W}_1, \mathcal{W}_2, \ldots, \mathcal{W}_\ell$ cannot cover all players in $\cup_{j=1}^{i_1}\mathcal{U}_j$, so $\Delta^{\exists}$ is $\mathcal{Q}_\ell$.

Assume now that condition (8) does not hold and let i be the smallest index such that $u_i \leq t_i + (\ell - 1)t_m$. Construct ℓ sets as follows. Let $\mathcal{W}_1, \ldots, \mathcal{W}_{\ell-1}$ be pairwise disjoint sets that each consist of some t_m participants from $\bigcup_{j=1}^{i} \mathcal{U}_j$. Clearly, $\mathcal{W}_k \in \Delta^{\exists}$, $k \in \{1, \ldots, \ell - 1\}$. Finally, let $\mathcal{W}_\ell$ consist of the remaining $u_i - (\ell - 1)t_m$ participants in $\bigcup_{j=1}^{i} \mathcal{U}_j$ and all the participants in $\bigcup_{j=i+1}^{m} \mathcal{U}_j$. Then $|\mathcal{W}_\ell \cap (\cup_{j=1}^{i}\mathcal{U}_j)| = u_i - (\ell - 1)t_m \leq t_i$, implying that $\mathcal{W}_\ell \in \Delta^{\exists}$. On the other hand, $\bigcup_{k=1}^{\ell} \mathcal{W}_k = \mathcal{U}$, so $\Delta^{\exists}$ is not $\mathcal{Q}_\ell$. $\qquad \square$

B   Non-ideal Constructions (Theorems 3 and 4)

Proof (of Theorem 3). We prove only the multiplicative case. Let $\mathcal{M}_i$ with $M_i = (1 \ \overline{M_i})$ be an MSP realizing the (t_i, u_i)-threshold access structure. Consider the MSP $\mathcal{M} = \mathcal{M}_1 + \cdots + \mathcal{M}_m$ with matrix

$$M = \begin{pmatrix} 1 \ \overline{M_1} & \mathbf{0} & \cdots & \mathbf{0} \\ 1 \ \mathbf{0} & \overline{M_1} & \cdots & \mathbf{0} \\ \vdots & & \ddots & \\ 1 \ \mathbf{0} & \mathbf{0} & \cdots & \overline{M_m} \end{pmatrix} \ ,$$

where participants in $\bigcup_{j=1}^{i} \mathcal{U}_j$ hold rows from $(1, 0, \ldots, 0, \overline{M_i}, 0, \ldots, 0)$. By Lemma 1, $\mathcal{M}$ computes the (t, n)-disjunctive HTAccS $\Gamma^{\exists}$. Now, if $\Gamma^{\exists}$ is $\mathcal{Q}_2$, then by Theorem 1, there exists an index i s.t. $u_i > 2t_i$. But then participants from $\mathcal{U}_{j=1}^{i}$ can clearly compute the product by using a recombination vector $(0, \ldots, 0, \boldsymbol{\lambda}_i, 0, \ldots, 0)$, where $\boldsymbol{\lambda}_i$ is a suitable recombination vector for the MSP $\mathcal{M}_i \diamond \mathcal{M}_i$. $\qquad\square$

Proof (of Theorem 4). We prove only the strongly multiplicative case. As before, let $\mathcal{M}_i$ with $M_i = (1 \ \overline{M_i})$ be the (t_i, u_i)-threshold MSP. Consider the MSP $\mathcal{M} = \mathcal{M}_1 \times \cdots \times \mathcal{M}_m$, where

$$M = \begin{pmatrix} 1 \ 0 \cdots 0 \ \overline{M_1} & \mathbf{0} & \cdots & \mathbf{0} \\ 0 \ 1 \cdots 0 \ \mathbf{0} & \overline{M_1} & \cdots & \mathbf{0} \\ \vdots & & \ddots & \\ 0 \ 0 \cdots 1 \ \mathbf{0} & \mathbf{0} & \cdots & \overline{M_m} \end{pmatrix} \ ,$$

where participants in $\bigcup_{j=1}^{i} \mathcal{U}_j$ hold rows from $(0, \ldots, 0, 1, 0, \ldots, 0, \overline{M_i}, 0, \ldots, 0)$. By Lemma 1, $\mathcal{M}$ computes the (t, n)-conjunctive HTAccS $\Gamma^{\forall}$ with a target vector $(1, \ldots, 1, 0, \ldots, 0)$ that has m leading 1-entries. Note that if the secret $s = s_1 + \cdots + s_m$ is shared using a vector $(s_1, \ldots, s_m, r)$, then the target vector corresponds to s. Next, it is easy to verify that for Shamir MSPs $\mathcal{M}_i$,

$$\mathcal{M} \diamond \mathcal{M} = (\mathcal{M}_1 \times \cdots \times \mathcal{M}_m) \diamond (\mathcal{M}_1 \times \cdots \times \mathcal{M}_m)$$
$$\equiv (\mathcal{M}_1 \diamond \mathcal{M}_1) \times \cdots \times (\mathcal{M}_1 \diamond \mathcal{M}_m) \times \cdots \times (\mathcal{M}_m \diamond \mathcal{M}_m) \ ,$$

where $\mathcal{M}_i \diamond \mathcal{M}_k$ is computed on $\bigcup_{j=1}^{i} \mathcal{U}_j$ for $i \le k$. By basic properties of Shamir secret sharing, $\mathcal{M}_i \diamond \mathcal{M}_k$ computes a $(t_i + t_k, u_i)$-threshold access structure. Thus, by Lemma 1, $\mathcal{M} \diamond \mathcal{M}$ computes a $(\bar{t}, n)$-conjunctive HTAccS $\bar{\Gamma}^{\forall}$, where $\bar{t} = (t_1 + t_m, \ldots, t_m + t_m)$. The target vector $(1, \ldots, 1, 0, \ldots, 0)$ of $\mathcal{M} \diamond \mathcal{M}$ has (after suitable reordering of columns) m^2 leading 1-entries and it corresponds to $ss' = s_1 s_1' + \cdots + s_1 s_m' + \cdots + s_m s_1' + \cdots + s_m s_m'$.

It only remains to show that if $\Gamma^{\forall}$ is $\mathcal{Q}_3$, then the number of honest participants at every level $\bigcup_{j=1}^{i} \mathcal{U}_i$, $i \in \{1, \ldots, m\}$, always exceeds the threshold $t_i + t_m$.

Let $\mathcal{W} \in \Delta^{\exists}$ be the set of corrupted participants. Then there must exist an index k for which $\mathcal{W}$ does not cross the threshold, i.e., $\exists k : |\mathcal{W} \cap \cup_{j=1}^k \mathcal{U}_j| \le t_k$. Next,

$$\forall i \ge k \ \left|\left(\cup_{j=1}^i \mathcal{U}_j\right) \setminus \mathcal{W}\right| \ge \left|\left(\cup_{j=1}^k \mathcal{U}_j\right) \setminus \mathcal{W}\right| \ge u_k - t_k > 2t_m \ge t_i + t_m,$$

$$\forall i < k \ \left|\left(\cup_{j=1}^i \mathcal{U}_j\right) \setminus \mathcal{W}\right| \ge u_i - t_k \ge u_i - t_m > t_i + t_m \ ,$$

where strict inequalities follow from condition (8).   □

C   Allocation of Participant Identities (Theorem 5)

Proof. Let D be the dealer holding the row $(1, 0, \ldots, 0)$ corresponding to the secret. Call a qualified subset $\mathcal{V}$ minimal if no proper subset $\mathcal{V}' \subset \mathcal{V}$ is qualified, and call a forbidden subset $\mathcal{W}$ maximal, if it has size $|\mathcal{W}| = t_m$ and is missing a single participant to become qualified. We divide the proof into two steps:

Claim 1. If for every minimal qualified subset $\mathcal{V}$ and for every maximal forbidden subset $\mathcal{W}$, matrices $M_{\mathcal{V}}$ and $M_{\mathcal{W} \cup \{D\}}$ are regular, then the scheme is correct and private.

Claim 2. When participant identities are allocated at random, then the probability that all such matrices $M_{\mathcal{V}}$ and $M_{\mathcal{W} \cup \{D\}}$ are regular is at least

$$p \ge 1 - \frac{\binom{n+1}{t_m+1} t_m (t_m - 1)}{2(q - t_m - 1)} \ .$$

Proof of Claim 1. If the matrix of every minimal qualified subset $\mathcal{V}$ is regular, then the scheme is clearly correct. If the matrix $M_{\mathcal{W} \cup \{D\}}$ of a maximal forbidden subset $\mathcal{W}$ is regular, then the row $(1, 0, \ldots, 0)$ corresponding to the dealer is independent of the rows of $\mathcal{W}$ and the linear span of the rows of $\mathcal{W}$ does not contain the target vector, so $\mathcal{W}$ can indeed learn nothing about the secret.

Consider now any forbidden set $\mathcal{W}$ of size $|\mathcal{W}| > t_m$. W.l.o.g. we may assume that $\mathcal{W}$ is missing a single participant from a level $\mathcal{U}_i$, i.e., $|\mathcal{W} \cap \cup_{j=1}^i \mathcal{U}_j| = t_i$. Consider the set $\mathcal{W} \cap \cup_{j=i+1}^m \mathcal{U}_j$. The rows belonging to participants in these levels begin with at least $t_i + 1$ leading zeroes, so we may select $t_m - t_i$ participants whose rows span the same space. Thus, these $t_m - t_i$ participants together with the t_i participants from $\mathcal{W} \cap \cup_{j=1}^i \mathcal{U}_j$ have the same information about the secret as $\mathcal{W}$. But the former set is a maximal forbidden subset, so we can repeat the above argument to conclude that they can learn nothing about the secret.

Proof of Claim 2. We prove that the probability of a single matrix M being singular is bounded by $\Pr[|M| = 0] \le \frac{t_m(t_m-1)}{2(q-t_m-1)}$. Since there are altogether at most $\binom{n}{t_m+1} + \binom{n}{t_m} = \binom{n+1}{t_m+1}$ such matrices, the claim follows.

The proof is by induction on t_m. Notice that when we delete the last column of the matrix of a $(\boldsymbol{t}, n)$-scheme, the dealer and the participants are holding rows according to a $(\boldsymbol{t}', n)$-scheme, where $\boldsymbol{t}' = (t_1, \ldots, t_{m-1}, t_m - 1)$. The matrices are clearly regular for $t_m = 0$. Assume now that $t_m > 0$ and let the rows in the matrix be ordered according to the hierarchy (the dealer having the highest priority). Let $\boldsymbol{r}$ be the last row in a matrix M. There are two cases to consider:

1. $r = (0, \ldots, 0, 1)$;
2. $r = (0, \ldots, 0, 1, \alpha_u, \ldots, \alpha_u^{t_m - t_i - 1})$.

The first case happens when $t_{m-1} = t_m - 1$. Clearly, in a minimal qualified subset or a maximal forbidden subset, there can be only one such row. Thus, we can solve for the last unknown a_{t_m}, delete the last row and the last column of the matrix and conclude by induction that $\Pr\left[|M| = 0\right] \leq \frac{(t_m-1)(t_m-2)}{2(q-t_m)} < \frac{t_m(t_m-1)}{2(q-t_m-1)}$.

In the second case, we write the determinant of M as a polynomial in α_u:

$$|M| = P(\alpha_u) = \sum_{j=0}^{t_m - t_i - 2} c_j \alpha_u^j + \mu \alpha_u^{t_m - t_i - 1} \ ,$$

where c_i are some coefficients and μ is the determinant of the upper-left $t_m \times t_m$ minor. Then

$$\Pr\left[|M| = 0\right] = \Pr\left[P(\alpha_u) = 0\right] \leq \Pr\left[\mu = 0\right] + \Pr\left[P(\alpha_u) = 0 | \mu \neq 0\right] \ .$$

In the first case, we can apply the induction argument to conclude that $\Pr\left[\mu = 0\right] \leq \frac{(t_m-1)(t_m-2)}{2(q-t_m)}$. In the second case when $\mu \neq 0$, $P(\alpha_u)$ vanishes for at most $t_m - t_i - 1$ of the $(q-1) - t_m$ possible values of α_u (there are $q-1$ nonzero elements in $\mathbb{F}_q$, and t_m of them are reserved for other rows of the matrix). Thus $\Pr\left[P(\alpha_u) = 0 | \mu \neq 0\right] \leq \frac{(t_m - t_i - 1)}{(q-1-t_m)}$. If $i = 0$ ($t_0 = -1$), then all participants belong to the highest level, so the matrix is a Vandermonde matrix and is regular. Thus, the worst case is $t_i = 0$ and we get

$$\Pr\left[|M| = 0\right] = \Pr\left[P(\alpha_u) = 0\right] \leq \frac{(t_m - 1)(t_m - 2)}{2(q - t_m)} + \frac{t_m - 1}{q - 1 - t_m} \leq \frac{t_m(t_m - 1)}{2(q - 1 - t_m)} \ ,$$

completing the induction step.   □

D   Multiplicativity of the Ideal Scheme (Theorem 6)

Proof. First, notice that if we multiply each row $(0, \ldots, 0, 1, \alpha_u, \ldots, \alpha_u^{t_m - t_i - 1})$ by $\alpha_u^{t_i + 1}$, then each column of M has the form $(\alpha_1^i, \alpha_2^i, \ldots, \alpha_k^i, 0, \ldots, 0)^T$ for some i and k. It then follows that also each column in $M \diamond M$ has the same form. We conclude that if lowest-level participants in some set $\mathcal{V}$ hold rows $(0, 0, \ldots, 1, \alpha_u, \ldots, \alpha_u^i, \ldots, \alpha_u^i, \ldots, \alpha_u^{t_m - t_i - 1})$ in $M_{\mathcal{V}} \diamond M_{\mathcal{V}}$, then the two columns containing the ith powers are linearly dependent in the whole matrix $M_{\mathcal{V}} \diamond M_{\mathcal{V}}$. We will use this observation to delete linearly dependent columns in $M_{\mathcal{V}} \diamond M_{\mathcal{V}}$.

Assume now that (16) holds and let $\mathcal{V} = \bigcup_{j=1}^{s-1} \mathcal{U}_{i_j + 1}$. We finish the proof by induction on j. Let $j = s - 1$ and let i_{s-1} be such that $p_{i_{s-1}+1} > t_{i_s} + t_m - 2(t_{i_{s-1}} + 1) = 2(t_m - t_{i_{s-1}} - 1)$ (recall that $i_s = m$ by definition).

Each player $u \in \mathcal{U}_{i_{s-1}+1}$ holds a row $(0, \ldots, 0, 1, \alpha_u, \ldots, \alpha_u^{t_m - t_{i_{s-1}} - 1})$ in M and a row
$(0, \ldots, 0, 1, \alpha_u, \ldots, \alpha_u^{2(t_m - t_{i_{s-1}} - 1)})$ in $M \diamond M$. In particular, since $\mathcal{U}_{i_{s-1}+1}$ is the

lowest level present in $\mathcal{V}$, we can delete linearly dependent columns in $M_{\mathcal{V}} \diamond M_{\mathcal{V}}$ and assume that each power α_u^i is present only once in the row. But then the block formed by any $2(t_m - t_{i_{s-1}} - 1) + 1$ participants from the lowest level is a Vandermonde block and its determinant is non-zero.

Let now $j < s - 1$ and assume that the lower-right minor obtained from the non-zero columns of lower levels in $\mathcal{V}$ is non-zero. In the original matrix $M_{\mathcal{V}}$, participant $u \in \mathcal{U}_{i_j+1}$ and participant $v \in \mathcal{U}_{i_{j+1}+1}$ hold rows

$$(0, \ldots, 0, 1, \alpha_u, \ldots, \alpha_u^{t_{i_{j+1}}-t_{i_j}-1}, \alpha_u^{t_{i_{j+1}}-t_{i_j}}, \ldots, \ldots, \alpha_u^{t_m-t_{i_j}-1}),$$
$$(0, \ldots, 0, 0, 0, \ldots, 0, 1, \alpha_v, \ldots, \alpha_v^{t_m-t_{i_{j+1}}-1}),$$

respectively. Thus, in $M_{\mathcal{V}} \diamond M_{\mathcal{V}}$, they hold rows

$$(0, \ldots, 0, 1, \alpha_u, \ldots, \alpha_u^{t_m+t_{i_{j+1}}-2t_{i_j}-2}, \alpha_u^{2(t_{i_{j+1}}-t_{i_j})}, \ldots, \ldots, \alpha_u^{2(t_m-t_{i_j}-1)}),$$
$$(0, \ldots, 0, 0, 0, \ldots, 0, 1, \alpha_v, \ldots, \alpha_v^{2(t_m-t_{i_{j+1}}-1)}).$$

By the induction assumption, the lower-right minor obtained from the $2(t_m - t_{j+1})$ non-zero columns of lower levels is non-zero. By applying our observation about deleting linearly dependent columns on the upper-left minor, we see that the next block on the diagonal contains rows $\left(1, \alpha_u, \ldots, \alpha_u^{t_m+t_{i_{j+1}}-2t_{i_j}-2}\right)$. Since the number of participants at level $\mathcal{U}_{i_j+1}$ is indeed $p_{i_j+1} > t_{i_{j+1}} + t_m - 2(t_{i_j}+1)$, we obtain another Vandermonde block. This completes the induction step.   □

Example. Consider a $((1,2,4), n)$-scheme. For a set $\mathcal{V}$ with 6 participants from level $\mathcal{U}_1$ and 5 participants from level $\mathcal{U}_2$, we get

$$M_{\mathcal{V}} \diamond M_{\mathcal{V}} = \begin{pmatrix} 1 & \alpha_1 & \alpha_1^2 & \alpha_1^3 & \alpha_1^4 & \alpha_1^5 & \alpha_1^4 & \alpha_1^5 & \alpha_1^6 & \alpha_1^7 & \alpha_1^8 \\ & & & & & \vdots & & & & & \\ 1 & \alpha_6 & \alpha_6^2 & \alpha_6^3 & \alpha_6^4 & \alpha_6^5 & \alpha_6^4 & \alpha_6^5 & \alpha_6^6 & \alpha_6^7 & \alpha_6^8 \\ 0 & 0 & 0 & 0 & 0 & 0 & 1 & \alpha_7 & \alpha_7^2 & \alpha_7^3 & \alpha_7^4 \\ & & & & & \vdots & & & & & \\ 0 & 0 & 0 & 0 & 0 & 0 & 1 & \alpha_{11} & \alpha_{11}^2 & \alpha_{11}^3 & \alpha_{11}^4 \end{pmatrix},$$

so the determinant is the product of two Vandermonde determinants and the set $\mathcal{V}$ is allowed. In comparison, if we were using the original Tassa scheme, we would have

$$M_{\mathcal{V}} \diamond M_{\mathcal{V}} = \begin{pmatrix} 1 & \alpha_1 & \alpha_1^2 & \alpha_1^3 & \alpha_1^4 & \alpha_1^5 & \alpha_1^4 & \alpha_1^5 & \alpha_1^6 & \alpha_1^6 & \alpha_1^7 & \alpha_1^8 \\ & & & & & & \vdots & & & & & \\ 1 & \alpha_6 & \alpha_6^2 & \alpha_6^3 & \alpha_6^4 & \alpha_6^5 & \alpha_6^4 & \alpha_6^5 & \alpha_6^6 & \alpha_6^6 & \alpha_6^7 & \alpha_6^8 \\ 0 & 0 & 0 & 0 & 0 & 0 & 4 & 12\alpha_7 & 24\alpha_7^2 & 36\alpha_7^2 & 72\alpha_7^3 & 144\alpha_7^4 \\ & & & & & & \vdots & & & & & \\ 0 & 0 & 0 & 0 & 0 & 0 & 4 & 12\alpha_{11} & 24\alpha_{11}^2 & 36\alpha_{11}^2 & 72\alpha_{11}^3 & 144\alpha_{11}^4 \end{pmatrix}.$$

It is easy to verify that the determinant of the matrix formed by the last 11 columns of $M_\mathcal{V} \diamond M_\mathcal{V}$ is non-zero, so the set $\mathcal{V}$ is forbidden in the original scheme. In general, by modifying the scheme, we introduce new linear dependencies in the columns of $M \diamond M$ and thus improve the multiplicative properties.

Secret Sharing Comparison by Transformation and Rotation

Tord Ingolf Reistad[1] and Tomas Toft[2],[*]

[1] NTNU, Dept. of Telematics,
N-7491 Trondheim, Norway
tordr@item.ntnu.no
[2] University of Aarhus, Dept. of Computer Science,
DK-8200 Aarhus N, Denmark
tomas@daimi.au.dk

Abstract. Given any linear secret sharing scheme with a multiplication protocol, we show that a given set of players holding shares of two values $a, b \in \mathbb{Z}_p$ for some prime p, it is possible to compute a sharing of ρ such that $\rho = (a < b)$ with only eight rounds and $29\ell + 36 \log_2(\ell)$ invocations of the multiplication protocol, where $\ell = \log(p)$. The protocol is unconditionally secure against active/adaptive adversaries when the underlying secret sharing scheme has these properties. The proposed protocol is an improvement in the sense that it requires fewer rounds and less invocations of the multiplication protocol than previous solutions.

Further, most of the work required is independent of a and b and may be performed in advance in a pre-processing phase before the inputs become available, this is important for practical implementations of multiparty computations, where one can have a set-up phase. Ignoring pre-processing in the analysis, only two rounds and 4ℓ invocations of the multiplication protocol are required.

1 Introduction

In multiparty computation (MPC) a number of parties $P_1, \ldots, P_n$ have *private* inputs for some function that they wish to evaluate. However, they are mutually mistrusting and do not wish to share their inputs with anyone. A great deal of work has been done on unconditionally secure constant round MPC with honest majority including but not limited to [1,9,4,10], indeed it has been demonstrated that any function can be computed securely using circuit based protocols.

However, when considering concrete applications, it is often more efficient to focus on secure arithmetic e.g. in the field $\mathbb{Z}_p$ for some odd prime p, which may then be used to simulate integer arithmetic. Unfortunately, many such applications require non-arithmetic operations as well; this provides motivation for constructing specialized, efficient, constant-rounds protocols for primitive tasks.

Access to the binary representation of values allows many operations to be performed relatively cheaply. Although constant-round bit-decomposition is possible as demonstrated by Damgård et al. [5], it is less efficient than desired.

---

[*] Supported by Simap.

Y. Desmedt (Ed.): ICITS 2007, LNCS 4883, pp. 169–180, 2009.
© Springer-Verlag Berlin Heidelberg 2009

Primitives may be used repeatedly and any improvement of these lead to improvements in the overall applications. This work focuses on one such primitive, namely comparison (less-than-testing) of secret shared values, i.e. obtaining a sharing of a bit stating whether one value is less than another without leaking any information.

Related work and contribution. Much research has focused on secure comparison in various settings as it is a quite useful primitive, though focus is often on some concrete application e.g. auctions. Often the setting differs from the present [2,7,13]. Through bit-decomposition, Damgård et al. provided the first constant rounds comparison in the present setting [5] – this required $\mathcal{O}(\ell \log(\ell))$ secure multiplications where $\ell = \log(p)$. Comparison was later improved by Nishide and Ohta [11] who reduced the complexity to $\mathcal{O}(\ell)$ multiplications.

A common streak in all of the above solutions is that the binary representation of the values is considered. Thus, unless a radically different approach is taken, improving on the $\mathcal{O}(\ell)$ bound does not seem feasible. The present work builds on sub-protocols and ideas of [5] and [11], but also uses ideas from [6] which considers comparison of bitwise stored values based on homomorphic encryption in a two-party setting.

Based on these papers, we construct a protocol with the aim of reducing the constants hidden under big-$\mathcal{O}$. In particular, when the protocol is split into pre-processing (secure computation independent of the inputs) and online computation, the online round complexity is extremely low; this split has not been considered in the related literature.

Table 1 compares the present solution to those of Damgård et al. and Nishide and Ohta. Type A refers to comparison of arbitrary values $[a], [b] \in \mathbb{Z}_p$, while R denotes values of restricted size, $[a], [b] < \lfloor \frac{p}{4} \rfloor$. When using $\mathbb{Z}_p$ to simulate integer computation, it is not unreasonable to choose p a few bits larger to accommodate this assumption.

With regard to the restricted comparison, in contrast to earlier papers (and the general comparison of Table 1), it is assumed that two rather than four attempts are needed to generate random bitwise shared values. When generating such values, the probability of failing may be as high as $1/2$ implying that multiple attempts may be needed. Earlier work used a Chernoff bound to bound the number of required attempts by a factor of four, ensuring that overall failure was negligible in the number of generated values.

In this paper we assume only a factor of two *plus* κ attempts, where κ is a security parameter much smaller than the number of values to be generated. It can be shown that in this case, the probability of failure (encountering too many failures) is negligible in κ. An alternative way of viewing the issue is that the random element generation is rerun. This does not compromise security, however, we only obtain an *expected* constant-rounds solution (with double round complexity), however, this only affects pre-processing. The issue only occurs when p may be arbitrary; if it is chosen sensibly, e.g. as a Mersenne prime, the failure probability may be reduced to negligible in the bit-length of p implying even greater efficiency.

Table 1. Complexities of comparison protocols

Presented in	Type	Rounds		Multiplications	
		overall	online	overall	online
[5]	A	44	37	$184\ell\log_2(\ell) + 209\ell$	$21\ell + 56\ell\log_2(\ell)$
[11]	A	15	8	$279\ell + 5$	$15\ell + 5$
This paper	A	10	4	$153\ell + 432\log_2(\ell) + 24$	$18\ell + 8$
[5]	R	44	37	$171\ell + 184\ell\log_2(\ell)$	$21\ell + 56\ell\log_2(\ell)$
[11]	R	13	6	$55\ell + 5$	$5\ell + 1$
This paper	R	11	2	$24\ell + 26\log_2(\ell) + 4$	$4\ell + 1$
This paper	R	8	2	$27\ell + 36log_2(\ell) + 5$	$4\ell + 1$

The structure of this article. Sections 2 and 3 introduce the setting as well as a number of primitives required. Most of these are well-known, and are included in order to provide detailed analysis of our protocol. Section 4 takes a high-level view of the computation required; it reduces the problem of comparison to a more manageable form similar to previous work. Section 5 introduces the DGK comparison protocol, while Sect. 6 shows how the DGK algorithm can be used to create random bitwise shared elements. Sections 7, 8 and 9 modifies DGK to avoid leaking information. Finally Sect. 10 gives an overall analysis and conclusion.

2   Preliminaries

We assume a linear secret sharing scheme with a multiplication protocol allowing values of the prime field $\mathbb{Z}_p$, $\ell = \lceil \log(p) \rceil$, to be shared among n parties. As as example, consider Shamir's scheme along with the protocols of Ben-Or et al. (or the improved protocols of Gennaro et al.) [12,3,8]. The properties of the scheme are inherited, i.e. if this is unconditionally secure against active/adaptive adversaries then so are the protocols proposed. In addition to sharing values and performing secure arithmetic of $\mathbb{Z}_p$, the parties may reveal (reconstruct) shared values, doing this ensures that the value becomes known by *all* parties.

We use $[a]$ to denote a secret sharing of $a \in \mathbb{Z}_p$. Secure computation is written using an infix notation. For shared values $[a]$ and $[b]$, and constant $c \in \mathbb{Z}_p$, computation of sums will be written as $[a] + c$ and $[a] + [b]$, while products will be written $c[a]$ and $[a][b]$. The initial three follow by the linearity of the scheme, while the fourth represents an invocation of the multiplication protocol.

Sharings of bits, $[b] \in \{0,1\} \subset \mathbb{Z}_p$ will also be considered. Boolean arithmetic is written using infix notation, though it must be realized using field arithmetic. Notably xor of two bits is constructed as $[b_1] \oplus [b_2] = [b_1] + [b_2] - 2[b_1][b_2]$ which is equivalent.

Values may also be *bitwise shared*, written $[a]_B$. Rather than having a sharing of a value itself, sharings of the bits of the binary representation of a are given, i.e. $[a_0], \ldots, [a_{\ell-1}] \in \{0,1\}$ such that

$$[a] = \sum_{i=0}^{\ell-1} 2^i [a_i]$$

for $\ell = \lceil \log(p) \rceil$, with the sum being viewed as occurring over the integers. Note that $[a]$ is easily obtained from $[a]_B$ by the linearity of the scheme.

When considering complexity, the focus will be on communication. Computation will be disregarded in the sense that polynomial time suffices. Similar to other work, focus will be placed on the number of invocations of the multiplication protocol as this is considered the most costly of the primitives. Addition and multiplication by constants require no interaction and is considered costless. The complexity of sharing and revealing is seen as negligible compared to that of multiplication and is ignored.

It is assumed that invocations of the multiplication protocol parallelize arbitrarily – multiplications are executed in parallel when possible. Round complexity is formally rounds-of-multiplications; rounds for reconstruction are disregarded as in other work.

3   Simple Primitives

This section introduces a number of simple primitives required below. Most of these sub-protocols are given in [5] but are are repeated here in order to provide a detailed analysis as well as for completeness. Most of these are related to the generation of random values unknown to all parties. It is important to note that these may fail, however, this does not compromise the privacy of the inputs – failure simply refers to the inability to generate a proper random value (which is detected). Generally the probability of failure will be of the order $1/p$, which for simplicity will be considered negligible, see [5] for further discussion.

Random element generation. A sharing of a uniformly random, unknown value $[r]$ may be generated by letting all parties share a uniformly random value. The sum of these is uniformly random and unknown to all, even in the face of an active adversary. The complexity of this is assumed to be equivalent to an invocation of the multiplication protocol.

Random non-zero values. A uniformly random, non-zero value may be obtained by generating two random values, $[r]$ and $[s]$ and revealing the product. If $rs = 0$ the protocol fails, however if not, $[r]$ is guaranteed non-zero and unknown as it is masked by $[s]$. The complexity is three multiplications in two rounds.

Random bits. The parties may create an uniformly random bit $[b] \in \{0, 1\}$. As described in [5] the parties may generate a random value $[r]$ and reveal its square, r^2. If this is 0 the protocol fails, otherwise they compute $[b] = 2^{-1}((\sqrt{r^2})^{-1})[r] + 1)$ where $\sqrt{r^2}$ is defined such that $0 \leq \sqrt{r^2} \leq \frac{p-1}{2}$. The complexity is two multiplications in two rounds.

Unbounded Fan-In Multiplications. It is possible to compute prefix-products of arbitrarily many non-zero values in constant rounds using the method of Bar-Ilan and Beaver [1]. Given $[a_1], \ldots, [a_k] \in \mathbb{Z}_p^*$, $[a_{1,i}] = [\prod_{j=1}^{i} a_j]$ may be computed for $i \in \{1, 2, \ldots, k\}$ as follows.

Let $r_0 = 1$ and generate k random non-zero values $[r_1], \ldots, [r_k]$ as described above, however, in parallel with the multiplication of $[r_j]$ and the mask $[s_j]$, compute $[r_{j-1}s_j]$ as well. Then $[r_{j-1}r_j^{-1}]$ may be computed at no cost as $[r_{j-1}s_j] \cdot (r_j s_j)^{-1}$. Each $[a_j]$ is then multiplied onto $[r_{j-1}r_j^{-1}]$ and all these are revealed. We then have

$$[a_{1,i}] = \prod_{j=1}^{i} (a_j r_{j-1} r_j^{-1}) \cdot [r_j] \ .$$

Privacy of the $[a_j]$ is ensured as they are masked by the $[r_j^{-1}]$, and complexity is $5k$ multiplications in three rounds. Regarding the preparation of the masking values as pre-prossessing, the online complexity is k multiplications in a single round.

Constructing a unary counter. Given a secret shared number $[a] < m < p - 1$ for some known m, the goal is to construct a vector of shared values $[V]$ of size m containing all zeros except for the a'th entry which should be 1. This may be constructed similarly to the evaluation of symmetric Boolean functions of [5].

Let $[A] = [a + 1]$ and for $i \in \{0, 1, \ldots, m - 1\}$ consider the set of functions: $f_i : \{1, 2, \ldots, m + 1\} \to \{0, 1\}$ mapping everything to 0 except for $i + 1$ which is mapped to 1. The goal is to evaluate these on input A. By Lagrange interpolation, each may be replaced by a *public* m-degree polynomial over $\mathbb{Z}_p$. Using a prefix-product, $[A], \ldots, [A^m]$ may be computed; once this is done, the computation of the entries of $[V]$ is costless. Thus, complexity is equivalent to prefix-product of m terms.

4   A High-Level View of Comparison

The overall idea behind the proposed protocol is similar to that of other comparison protocols, including that of [11]. The problem of comparing two secret shared numbers is first transformed to a comparison between shared values where sharings of the binary representations are present; this greatly simplifies the problem. The main difference between here and previous solutions is that we consider inputs of marginally bounded size: $[a], [b] < \lfloor \frac{p-1}{4} \rfloor$. This assumption reduces complexity but may be dropped; the section concludes with a sketch of the required alterations allowing a general comparison as in previous works. Once the problem is transformed to comparison of bitwise represented values, the novel secure computation of the following sections may be applied.

The goal is to compute a bit $[\rho] = ([a] < [b])$. The transformation of the problem proceeds as follows, first the comparison of $[a'] = 2[a] + 1 < \frac{p-1}{2}$ and $[b'] = 2[b] < \frac{p-1}{2}$ rather than that of $[a]$ and $[b]$ is considered. This does not alter the result, however, it ensures that the compared values are not equal, which will be required below.

As $[a'], [b'] < \frac{p-1}{2}$, comparing them is equivalent to determining whether $[z] = [a'] - [b'] \in \{1, 2, \ldots, (p-1)/2\}$. In turn this is equivalent to determining the least significant bit of $2[z]$, written $[(2z)_0]$. If $z < (p-1)/2$, then $2z \in \mathbb{Z}_p$ is even; if not then a reduction modulo p occurs and it is odd.

The computation of $[(2z)_0]$ is done by first computing and revealing $[c] = 2[z] + [r]_B$, where $[r]_B$ is uniformly random. Noting that $[(2z)_0]$ depends only on the least significant bits of c and $[r]_B$ (c_0 and $[r_0]$) and whether an overflow (a modulo p reduction) has occurred in the computation of c. The final result is simply the xor of these three Boolean values.

It can be verified that determining overflow is equivalent to computing $c < [r]_B$; the remainder of the article describes this computation. Privacy is immediate and follows from the security of the secret sharing scheme. Seeing c does not leak information, as $[r]_B$ is uniformly random then so is c. The full complexity analysis is postponed until Sect. 10.

Unbounded $[a]$ and $[b]$. If it is not ensured that $[a], [b] < \lfloor \frac{p-1}{4} \rfloor$ then further work must be performed in order to perform a comparison. Similarly to [11] bits $[t_=] = [a = b]$, as well as $[t_a] = [a < (p-1)/2]$, $[t_b] = [b < (p-1)/2]$, and $[t_\delta] = [a - b < (p-1)/2]$ may be computed. Based on these, the final result may be determined by a small Boolean circuit which translates to a simple secure computation over $\mathbb{Z}_p$. The result is either immediate (if $[a] = [b]$) or may be determined by the three latter bits.

5   The DGK Comparison Protocol

In [6] Damgård et al. proposed a two-party protocol for comparison based on a homomorphic encryption scheme. They consider a comparison between a publicly known and a bitwise encrypted value with the output becoming known. Though their setting is quite different, ideas may be applied in the present one. Initially, we consider comparison of two unknown, ℓ-bit, bitwise shared values $[a]_B$ and $[b]_B$, determining $[a] < [b]$ is done by considering a vector $[E] = [e_{\ell-1}], \ldots, [e_0]$ of length ℓ with

$$[e_i] = [s_i] \left(1 + [a_i] - [b_i] + \sum_{j=i+1}^{\ell-1} ([a_j] \oplus [b_j]) \right) \tag{1}$$

where the $[s_i]$ are uniformly random non-zero values.

Theorem 1 (DGK). *Given two bitwise secret shared values $[a]_B$ and $[b]_B$, the vector $[E]$, given by equation 1 will contain uniformly random non-zero values and at most one 0. Further, a 0 occurs exactly when $[a] < [b]$.*

Proof. The larger of two values is characterized by having a 1 at the most significant bit where the numbers differ. Letting m denote the most significant differing bit-position, the intuition behind the $[e_i]$ is that $[e_{\ell-1}], \ldots, [e_{m+1}]$ will equal their respective $[s_i]$, and $[e_{m-1}], \ldots, [e_0]$ will also be uniformly random and non-zero, as $1 \le \sum_{j=i+1}^{\ell-1}([a_j] \oplus [b_j]) \le \ell$ for $i < m$. Finally, $[e_m]$ will then be 0 exactly when $[b_m]$ is 1, i.e. when $[b]$ is larger than $[a]$, otherwise it is random as well.   □

Though the non-zero elements of vector $[E]$ are random, the location of the zero leaks information. In [6] this is solved by the two-party nature of the protocol – the $[e_i]$ are encrypted, with one party knowing the decryption key, while the other permutes them. The multiparty setting here requires this to be performed using arithmetic.

6   Creating Random Bitwise Shared Values

Based on the comparison of Sect. 5, a random, bitwise shared value $[r]_B$ may be generated such that it is less than some k-bit bound m. This is accomplished by generating the k bits $[r_{k-1}], \ldots, [r_0]$ and verifying that this represents a value less than m. Noting that information is only leaked when a 0 occurs in the $[e_i]$, ensuring that this coincides with the discarding of $[r]_B$ if it is too large suffices. Based on the above, the k $[e_i]$ are computed as

$$[e_i] = [s_i] \left(1 + (m-1)_i - [r_i] + \sum_{j=i+1}^{k-1} ((m-1)_j \oplus [r_j]) \right) \qquad (2)$$

where $(m-1)_i$ denotes the i'th bit of $m-1$. By Theorem 1 this will contain a 0 exactly when $m - 1 < [r]_B \Leftrightarrow [r]_B \ge m$.

   The complexity of generating random bitwise shared values consists of the generation of the k bits and the k masks, $[s_{k-1}], \ldots, [s_0]$, plus the k multiplications needed to perform the masking. Overall this amounts to $4k$ multiplications in three rounds as the $[r_i]$ and $[s_i]$ may be generated in parallel (and the $[s_i]$ need not be verified non-zero, this increases the probability of failure marginally). The probability of success depends heavily on m, though it is at least $1/2$. Note that this may be used to generate uniformly random elements of $\mathbb{Z}_p$.

7   Avoiding Information Leaks

Though Sect. 4 has reduced the problem of general comparison to that of comparing a public value to a bitwise shared one, $c < [r]_B$, two problems remain with regard to the DGK-protocol in the present setting. First off, the result is stored as the existence of a 0 in a vector $[E]$ of otherwise uniformly random non-zero values, rather than as a single shared bit $[\rho] \in \{0, 1\}$ which is required to conclude the computation. Second, the position of the 0 in $[E]$ (if it exists) leaks information.

Hiding the result. The former of the two problems may be solved by "masking the result" thereby allowing it to be revealed. Rather than attempting to hide the result, the comparison will be hidden. Formally, a uniformly random value $[s] \in \{-1, 1\}$ is generated, this is equivalent to generating a random bit. The $[e_i]$ of equation 1 are then replaced by

$$[e_i] = [s_i] \left(1 + (c_i - [r_i])[s] + \sum_{j=i+1}^{\ell-1} (c_j \oplus [r_j]) \right) .$$

As $[z]$ is non-zero, we have $c \neq [r]_B$, and thus the desired result is the one obtained, xor'ed with $-2^{-1}([s] - 1)$; if the comparison was flipped ($[s] = -1$) so is the output. Note that the observation made here implies that when considering comparison, it suffices to consider public results: Shared results are immediately available by randomly swapping the inputs.

Hiding the location of the 0. In order to hide the location of the 0, the $[e_i]$ must be permuted, however, as the non-zero entries are uniformly random, it suffices to *shift* $[E]$ by a unknown, random amount $v \in \{0, 1, \ldots, \ell - 1\}$. I.e. constructing a vector $[\tilde{E}]$ with $[\tilde{e}_i] = [e_{(i+v) \bmod \ell}]$.

Shifting an ℓ-term vector by some unknown amount $[v]$ may be done by encoding $[v]$ in a *shifting-vector* $[W]$ of length ℓ with entries

$$[w_i] = \begin{cases} 0 & i \neq [v] \\ 1 & i = [v] \end{cases}$$

Note that this is *exactly* the unary counter of Sect. 3. Given this, an entry of the shifted vector may be computed as:

$$[\tilde{e}_i] = [e_{(i+v) \bmod \ell}] = \sum_{j=0}^{\ell-1} [e_j] \cdot [w_{(j+i) \bmod \ell}] , \tag{3}$$

however, this implies quadratic complexity overall. Thus, rather than shifting the $[e_i]$, the $[\tilde{e}_i]$ will be computed based on already shifted values, i.e. we will consider $[\tilde{r}_i] = [r_{(i+v) \bmod \ell}]$ and $[\tilde{c}_i] = c_{(i+[v]) \bmod \ell}$ along with shifted sums of xor's (the masks $[s_i]$ need not be shifted). This leaves us with two distinct problems:

1. Obtain the shifted bits of $[r]_B$ and c.
2. Obtain the shifted sums of the xor'ed bits

The solutions to these problems are described in the following sections.

8   Shifting Bits

The first thing to note is that securely shifting *known* values is costless, though naturally the result is shared. This is immediate from equation 3, thus the shifted bits of c, $[\tilde{c}_{\ell-1}], \ldots, [\tilde{c}_0]$, are available at no cost.

Regarding $[r]$, shifting its bits is as difficult as shifting the $[e_i]$. Thus an alternative strategy must be employed, namely generating "shifted" bits and constructing the *unshifted* $[r]$ from these. Let $[v]$ denote the shifting-value and $[W]$ the shifting vector, and compute an ℓ-entry bit-vector $[K]$ as

$$[k_i] = 1 - \sum_{j=0}^{i} [w_j] \tag{4}$$

at no cost. Clearly $[k_i] = 1$ for $i < [v]$ and $[k_i] = 0$ for $i \geq [v]$. $[r]$ may then be computed based on random "shifted" bits as

$$[r] = [2^{-v}] \cdot \left(\sum_{i=0}^{\ell-1} 2^i [\tilde{r}_i] \left(1 + [k_i](2^\ell - 1) \right) \right) \; ,$$

where $[2^{-v}]$ is computed by the costless $\sum_{i=0}^{\ell-1} 2^{-i} [w_i]$. It can be verified that the above is correct, assuming that the bits represent a value in $\mathbb{Z}_p$. $[2^{-v}]$ performs the "unshifting," while the final parenthesis handles "underflow."

It remains to verify that the bits represent a shifted value of $\mathbb{Z}_p$. This may be done by performing the exact same computation as needed for the full comparison, i.e. shifting the bits of $p - 1$, computing the shifted sums of xors (as described below) and masking these. The shifting value $[v]$ is "hard-coded" into $[r]$, but it may be "reused" for this, as no information is leaked when no 0 occurs, i.e. when $[r] < p$. When information is leaked, the value is discarded anyway.[1]

Generating $[r]$ and the shifted bits $[\tilde{r}_i]$ involves creating a uniformly random value $[v] \in \{0, 1, \ldots, \ell - 1\}$ as described in Sect. 6. This requires 3 rounds and $8 \log_2(\ell)$ multiplications, as a factor of two attempts are needed when p may be arbitrary. $[W]$ may be computed from $[v]$ using $5 \log_2(\ell)$ multiplications, but only one additional round as pre-processing parallelizes. The shifted bits of $[r]$ and the masks $[s_i]$ may be generated concurrently using 3ℓ multiplications; these masks will not be ensured non-zero as this is unlikely to occur, this results in a slightly larger probability of aborting. Checking $[r]_B < p$ adds four rounds and 4ℓ multiplications, providing a total of 8 rounds, $7\ell + 13 \log_2(\ell)$ multiplications. A factor of two attempts of this implies $14\ell + 26 \log_2(\ell)$ multiplications in 8 rounds per random value generated.

Computing $[r]$ based on the shifted bits uses an additional round and 1 multiplication as the $[\tilde{r}_i k_i]$ are needed for the verification of $[r]$ anyway. Concurrently, a sharing of the least significant bit of $[r]$ may be obtained using ℓ multiplications as described by equation 3. This value is needed for the overall computation.

9   Shifting the Sums of Xor's

It remains to describe how to "shift" the sums of the xor's, $\sum_{j=i+1}^{\ell-1} [r_j] \oplus c_j$. The shifted xor's $[\tilde{c}_i \oplus \tilde{r}_i]$ may be computed directly based on the previous section. The

---

[1] Note that verifying $[r] < p$ is simple when p is chosen as a Mersenne prime. It must simply be ensured that not all $[r_i]$ are 1.

sum, however, consists of the terms from the *current* index to the *shifted* position of the most significant bit, which may or may not "wrap around." Focusing on a single $[\tilde{e}_i]$, we consider two cases: $i < [v]$ and $i \geq [v]$. Naturally, $[v]$ is unknown, however, the correct case is determined by $[k_i]$ of above.

When $i < [v]$ the terms have been shifted more than i, thus we must sum from $i + 1$ to $[v] - 1$, this equals:

$$[\sigma_i^<] = \sum_{j=i+1}^{\ell-1} [k_j] \cdot ([\tilde{r}_j \oplus \tilde{c}_j]) \ .$$

Multiplying by the $[k_j]$ ensures that only the relevant terms are included. For $i \geq [v]$ the terms are shifted less than i, thus the most significant bit does not pass the i'th entry. The sum must therefore be computed from i to $\ell - 1$ *and* from 0 to $[v] - 1$. Viewing this as the sum of all terms *minus* the sum from $[v]$ to i we get

$$[\sigma_i^\geq] = \left(\sum_{j=0}^{\ell-1} [\tilde{r}_j \oplus \tilde{c}_j] \right) - \left(\sum_{j=0}^{i} (1 - [k_j]) \cdot [\tilde{r}_j \oplus \tilde{c}_j] \right) \ .$$

Thus, as the computation of the two candidates $[\sigma_i^<]$ and $[\sigma_i^\geq]$ for each position i is linear, computing all sums simply require selecting the correct one for each entry based on $[k_i]$:

$$[k_i][\sigma_i^<] + (1 - [k_i]) [\sigma_i^\geq] \ .$$

All this requires 3 rounds and 4ℓ multiplications, however, noting that

$$[k_j] \cdot ([\tilde{r}_j] \oplus [\tilde{c}_j]) = [k_j \tilde{r}_j] + ([k_j] - 2[k_j \tilde{r}_j]) [\tilde{c}_j] \ ,$$

the $[k_j \tilde{r}_j]$ is pre-prossessed. This reduces the online complexity of calculating the sums to 1 round and 3ℓ multiplications.

10   Overall Analysis and Optimizations

Pre-processing. Initially a uniformly random value $[v] \in \{0, 1, \ldots, \ell - 1\}$ must be created. This value is used to construct a random shifting vector $[W]$ of length ℓ. Concurrently the *shifted* bits of $[r]$ are generated. It must then be verified that $[r] < p$. Once this is done the values $[r]$ and $[r_0]$ may be computed. In addition, the non-zero masks $[s_i]$, the sign bit $[s]$ must be generated, and $[s_i \cdot s]$ and $[s_i \cdot k_i]$ computed in order to reduce online complexity as described below.

The overall cost of creating the $[v]$, $[W]$ and shifted bits $[\tilde{r}_i]$ of $[r]$ is eight rounds, $14\ell + 26 \log_2(\ell)$ multiplications. In addition, creating $[r]$, $[r_0]$, $[s_i]$, $[s]$, $[s_i \cdot s]$, and $[s_i \cdot k_i]$ adds another round and $6\ell + 3$ multiplications (as $[k_i \tilde{r}]$ are already computed). The total pre-processing complexity is therefore nine rounds $20\ell + 26 \log_2(\ell) + 3$ multiplications.

Round complexity may be further reduced as $[v]$ and $[W]$ may be created in parallel, also $[r]$ and $[r_0]$ may be computed before $[r] < p$ is verified. Additionally, the verification of $[r] < p$ may be reduced by one round at the cost of ℓ additional multiplications by masking the sums of xor's and the remainder of Eq. 2 separately. The complexity of pre-processing is thereby changed to 6 rounds, though $23\ell + 36\log_2(\ell) + 4$ multiplications are required.

Online. The computation of $c = [r] + 2\left((2[a] + 1) - 2[b]\right)$ where $[a], [b] < \lfloor \frac{p}{4} \rfloor$ is costless. The intuition behind the online computation of the $[\tilde{e}_i]$ is

$$[\tilde{e}_i] = [s_i]\left(1 + ([\tilde{c}_i] - [\tilde{r}_i])\,[s] + \left([k_i][\sigma_i^{\geq}] + (1 - [k_i])\,[\sigma_i^{<}]\right)\right) \ ,$$

however, this is rephrased to reduce online round complexity:

$$[s_i] + [s_i \cdot s]\,([\tilde{c}_i] - [\tilde{r}_i]) + \left(([s_i \cdot k_i])[\sigma_i^{\geq}] + ([s_i] - [s_i \cdot k_i])\,[\sigma_i^{<}]\right) \ . \tag{5}$$

This implies two rounds and 4ℓ multiplications: First $[\sigma_i^{<}]$ and $[\sigma_i^{\geq}]$ are determined using ℓ multiplications, then three parallel multiplications are performed for each of the ℓ instances of Eq. 5. Letting e denote if a 0 was encountered in the $[\tilde{e}_i]$, the final result is

$$[\rho] = [r_0] \oplus c_0 \oplus \left(\left(-2^{-1}([s] - 1)\right) \oplus e\right) = [r_0 \oplus (-2^{-1}([s] - 1))] \oplus c_0 \oplus e \ ,$$

where the multiplication needed parallelizes with the above. Indeed it is even possible to perform this in pre-processing, though it adds another round.

The overall complexity is therefore $24\ell + 26\log_2(\ell) + 4$ multiplications in 11 rounds or 8 rounds $27\ell + 36\log_2(\ell) + 5$ if the pre-processing round complexity is optimized as described above.

Acknowledgements. The authors would like to thank Jesper Buus Nielsen for discussions as well as comments on the article. Further, the anonymous reviewers are thanked for their helpful comments, and Prof. Ivan Damgård and Prof. Stig Frode Mjølsnes for their support.

References

1. Bar-Ilan, J., Beaver, D.: Non-cryptographic fault-tolerant computing in a constant number of rounds of interaction. In: Rudnicki, P. (ed.) Proceedings of the eighth annual ACM Symposium on Principles of distributed computing, pp. 201–209. ACM Press, New York (1989)
2. Bogetoft, P., Damgård, I., Jakobsen, T., Nielsen, K., Pagter, J., Toft, T.: Secure computing, economy, and trust: A generic solution for secure auctions with real-world applications. BRICS Report Series RS-05-18, BRICS (2005), http://www.brics.dk/RS/05/18/
3. Ben-Or, M., Goldwasser, S., Wigderson, A.: Completeness theorems for noncryptographic fault-tolerant distributed computations. In: 20th ACM Annual ACM Symposium on Theory of Computing, pp. 1–10. ACM Press, New York (1988)

4. Cramer, R., Damgård, I.: Secure distributed linear algebra in a constant number of rounds. In: Kilian, J. (ed.) CRYPTO 2001. LNCS, vol. 2139, pp. 119–136. Springer, Heidelberg (2001)

5. Damgård, I., Fitzi, M., Kiltz, E., Nielsen, J., Toft, T.: Unconditionally secure constant-rounds multi-party computation for equality, comparison, bits and exponentiation. In: Halevi, S., Rabin, T. (eds.) TCC 2006. LNCS, vol. 3876, pp. 285–304. Springer, Heidelberg (2006)

6. Damgård, I., Geisler, M., Krøigaard, M.: Efficient and secure comparison for online auctions. In: Pieprzyk, J., Ghodosi, H., Dawson, E. (eds.) ACISP 2007. LNCS, vol. 4586, pp. 416–430. Springer, Heidelberg (2007)

7. Fischlin, M.: A cost-effective pay-per-multiplication comparison method for millionaires. In: Naccache, D. (ed.) CT-RSA 2001. LNCS, vol. 2020, pp. 457–471. Springer, Heidelberg (2001)

8. Gennaro, R., Rabin, M., Rabin, T.: Simplified vss and fast-track multiparty computations with applications to threshold cryptography. In: PODC 1998: Proceedings of the seventeenth annual ACM symposium on Principles of distributed computing, pp. 101–111. ACM Press, New York (1998)

9. Ishai, Y., Kushilevitz, E.: Randomizing polynomials: A new representation with applications to round-efficient secure computation. In: 41st Annual Symposium on Foundations of Computer Science, Las Vegas, Nevada, USA, pp. 294–304. IEEE Computer Society Press, Los Alamitos (2000)

10. Ishai, Y., Kushilevitz, E.: Perfect constant-round secure computation via perfect randomizing polynomials. In: Widmayer, P., Triguero, F., Morales, R., Hennessy, M., Eidenbenz, S., Conejo, R. (eds.) ICALP 2002. LNCS, vol. 2380, pp. 244–256. Springer, Heidelberg (2002)

11. Nishide, T., Ohta, K.: Multiparty computation for interval, equality, and comparison without bit-decomposition protocol. In: Okamoto, T., Wang, X. (eds.) PKC 2007. LNCS, vol. 4450, pp. 343–360. Springer, Heidelberg (2007)

12. Shamir, A.: How to share a secret. Communications of the ACM 22(11), 612–613 (1979)

13. Schoenmakers, B., Tuyls, P.: Practical two-party computation based on the conditional gate. In: Lee, P.J. (ed.) ASIACRYPT 2004. LNCS, vol. 3329, pp. 119–136. Springer, Heidelberg (2004)

Anonymous Quantum Communication

(Extended Abstract)

Gilles Brassard[1], Anne Broadbent[1], Joseph Fitzsimons[2],
Sébastien Gambs[1], and Alain Tapp[1]

[1] Université de Montréal
Département d'informatique et de recherche opérationnelle
C.P. 6128, Succursale Centre-Ville, Montréal (Québec), H3C 3J7 Canada
{brassard,broadbea,gambsseb,tappa}@iro.umontreal.ca
[2] University of Oxford
Department of Materials
Parks Road, Oxford, OX1 3PH United Kingdom
joe.fitzsimons@materials.ox.ac.uk

Abstract. We introduce the first protocol for the anonymous transmission of a quantum state that is information-theoretically secure against an active adversary, without any assumption on the number of corrupt participants. The anonymity of the sender and receiver is perfectly preserved, and the privacy of the quantum state is protected except with exponentially small probability. Even though a single corrupt participant can cause the protocol to abort, the quantum state can only be destroyed with exponentially small probability: if the protocol succeeds, the state is transferred to the receiver and otherwise it remains in the hands of the sender (provided the receiver is honest).

1   Introduction

We introduce the first information-theoretically secure protocol for the anonymous transmission of quantum messages, which tolerates an arbitrary number of corrupt participants. Our protocol allows Alice to send a quantum message to Bob such that both Alice and Bob remain anonymous (no participant learns the identity of Alice—even if Bob is corrupt—and the identity of Bob remains known only to Alice), and the quantum message remains private (nothing about it leaks to participants other than Bob, unless of course Bob is corrupt). The anonymity of the sender and receiver is perfect, and so is the privacy of the quantum message (except with exponentially small probability), regardless of the behaviour of cheating parties, with no need to rely on any assumptions other than the availability of a classical broadcast channel as well as private authenticated quantum channels between each pair of participants. (The latter requirement is easily achieved through unprotected quantum channels if each pair of participants share a sufficiently long secret random key.) Given that our protocol can tolerate an arbitrary number of corrupt participants, it is not surprising that any single one can cause the protocol to abort. However, no private information can be obtained by making the protocol abort.

Y. Desmedt (Ed.): ICITS 2007, LNCS 4883, pp. 181–182, 2009.

2   Sketch of the Protocol

Our protocol, which allows an anonymous sender Alice to transmit an m-qubit quantum message $|\psi\rangle$ to an anonymous receiver Bob, is described in complete detail in the full paper [1], where a formal proof of security is provided. Several ideas are taken from an earlier paper written by two of us [2], which solved the *classical* version of the anonymous message transmission problem. One subtle concern is unique to the transmission of *quantum* information, though: the state to be transmitted should never be destroyed *even if the protocol aborts*.

In the first step, the purely classical collision detection protocol of [2] is performed to make sure that exactly one participant wants to send an anonymous quantum message. In the next two steps, the participants collaborate to establish multiple instances of a shared state $|+_n\rangle = \frac{1}{\sqrt{2}}|0^n\rangle + \frac{1}{\sqrt{2}}|1^n\rangle$. Corrupt participants could prevent these states from being genuine instances of $|+_n\rangle$. However, a key contribution of our protocol is to introduce a verification step, which forces the resulting quantum states to be *symmetric* among all honest participants. This ensures sender and receiver anonymity. In the next step, Alice designates a receiver (Bob) by use of the notification protocol of [2]. If honest, Bob will act differently from the other participants, but in a way that is indistinguishable from them, so that his anonymity is preserved. The shared instances of $|+_n\rangle$ (if not corrupted) are then used to establish *anonymous entanglement* [3], which consists of Bell States $|\Phi^+\rangle = \frac{1}{\sqrt{2}}|00\rangle + \frac{1}{\sqrt{2}}|11\rangle$ shared between Alice and Bob, but in a way that Bob does not know with whom he is entangled (only Alice knows). Because there is no guarantee that these are genuine $|\Phi^+\rangle$'s if other participants misbehave, they cannot be used directly to teleport $|\psi\rangle$. Instead, Alice creates a sufficient number of genuine local $|\Phi^+\rangle$ states. The possibly imperfect anonymous entanglement is used by Alice to teleport an *authenticated* version of half of each of these $|\Phi^+\rangle$'s. If this teleportation is successful and if Bob accepts the authentication, Alice uses this newly established perfect anonymous entanglement with Bob to finally teleport the quantum message $|\psi\rangle$ itself. To complete the teleportation, Alice must use the classical anonymous message transmission protocol of [2] to transmit the teleportation bits. If *that* fails, due to corrupt participants, it may seem that the quantum message has been lost since the no-cloning theorem had prevented Alice from making a backup copy of it before entrusting it to the teleportation process. Fortunately, Bob (if honest) can bounce it back to Alice by use of our novel *fail-safe teleportation* feature [1].

References

1. Brassard, G., Broadbent, A., Fitzsimons, J., Gambs, S., Tapp, A.: Anonymous quantum communication. In: Kurosawa, K. (ed.) ASIACRYPT 2007. LNCS, vol. 4833, pp. 460–473. Springer, Heidelberg (2007), http://arxiv.org/abs/0706.2356
2. Broadbent, A., Tapp, A.: Information-theoretic security without an honest majority. In: Kurosawa, K. (ed.) ASIACRYPT 2007. LNCS, vol. 4833, pp. 410–426. Springer, Heidelberg (2007), http://arxiv.org/abs/0706.2010
3. Christandl, M., Wehner, S.: Quantum anonymous transmissions. In: Roy, B. (ed.) ASIACRYPT 2005. LNCS, vol. 3788, pp. 217–235. Springer, Heidelberg (2005)

Efficient Oblivious Transfer Protocols Achieving a Non-zero Rate from Any Non-trivial Noisy Correlation

Hideki Imai[1,2], Kirill Morozov[1], and Anderson C.A. Nascimento[3]

[1] RCIS, AIST, Japan
{h-imai,kirill.morozov}@aist.go.jp
[2] Department of Electrical, Electronic and Communication Engineering,
Chuo University, Japan
[3] Department of Electrical Engineering, University of Brasilia, Brazil
andclay@ene.unb.br

Abstract. Oblivious transfer (OT) is a two-party primitive which is one of the cornerstones of modern cryptography. We focus on providing information-theoretic security for both parties, hence building OT assuming noisy resources (channels or correlations) available to them. This primitive is about transmitting two strings such that the receiver can obtain one (and only one) of them, while the sender remains ignorant of this choice. Recently, Winter and Nascimento proved that oblivious transfer capacity is positive for any non-trivial discrete memoryless channel or correlation in the case of passive cheaters. Their construction was inefficient. The OT capacity characterizes the maximal efficiency of constructing OT using a particular noisy primitive. Building on their result, we extend it in two ways: 1) we construct efficient passively-secure protocols achieving the same rates; 2) we show that an important class of noisy correlations actually allows to build OT with non-zero rate secure against active cheating (before, positive rates were only achieved for the erasure channel).

Keywords: Information-theoretical security, oblivious transfer, noisy resources.

1 Introduction

Oblivious transfer (OT) [24,20,9] is an important and well-studied cryptographic primitive. Being one of the corner stones of modern cryptography, it implies any secure two-party computation [13]. It comes in many flavors, but all of them turned out to be equivalent [4]. Informally, OT is a means to transmit data such that the sender is guaranteed that the data will be partially lost during the transmission, but he does not know what exactly the receiver gets. It is impossible to obtain OT "from scratch", i.e., in the plain model when information-theoretical security is required for both the sender and the receiver. Hence, one needs additional assumptions. One of them is the use of noisy resources (channels or

Y. Desmedt (Ed.): ICITS 2007, LNCS 4883, pp. 183–194, 2009.

pre-distributed noisy data, i.e. noisy correlations). This assumption seems quite natural as the real communication channels are inherently noisy. Recently, the concept of oblivious transfer capacity was introduced by Nascimento and Winter [19] (following the manuscript [18]). The OT capacity is a measure of how efficient one can use a noisy resource in order to obtain oblivious transfer from it. In this paper, they proved that any non-trivial discrete memoryless noisy resource can be used for obtaining noisy channels (this was first independently proved in [18] and in [7]). Moreover, for the case of passive cheating, they proved that for any non-trivial noisy resource, its OT capacity is positive by presenting protocols achieving non-zero rate. However, those protocols were inefficient (as they relied on random coding arguments).

In this paper, we show that the results of [19] can be obtained using efficient protocols. For any non-trivial correlation, we present such efficient protocols with non-zero rate, hereby showing that oblivious transfer capacity of these correlations is bounded away from zero in the case of honest-but-curious sender but completely malicious receiver.

Additionally, for a wide class of noisy correlations (here called symmetric basic correlations (SBC)), we completely characterize the oblivious transfer capacity in the case of passive cheaters (with efficient protocols) and show protocols which are optimal up to a constant in the case of active adversaries. We emphasize that previously, all the reductions achieving non-zero rates and based on noisy channels [6,5,18,7] (with the exception of reductions to the erasure channel[1] [8]) always considered an honest-but-curious sender. Hereby, we enlarge the class of channels for which oblivious transfer is practical to SBC.

Symmetric basic correlations are important as many previous protocols for obtaining oblivious transfer from noisy resources used it as an intermediate step towards obtaining a fully secure OT. Thus, computationally efficient and rate-efficient constructions of SBC from noisy resources are of special relevance in noise-based cryptography.

Related work. Crépeau and Kilian [6] showed that any binary symmetric channel provides us with oblivious transfer. The efficiency of this result was consequently improved in [5]. Crepeau's result was extended to any non-trivial binary symmetric channel in   [23]. A general characterization of which noisy channels yield oblivious transfer was independently obtained in [14] (with efficient protocols) and in [18] (where the classification was also extended to noisy correlations).

Winter et al. [25] introduced the concept of cryptographic capacity of a channel for secure two-party computations. They derived a single-letter characterization of the commitment capacity of a discrete memoryless channel. Recently, Imai et al. [12], showed the OT capacity of the erasure channel to be equal to $1/2$ in the case of passive cheaters and presented a protocol achieving the rate $1/4$ for the case of active cheaters. Using the Interactive Hashing [17], Crépeau and Savvides [8] showed a reduction of string OT to bit OT achieves an optimal

---

[1] Which is the same as Rabin oblivious transfer [20].

rate of 1/2. We conjecture that their protocol can be changed to provide the reduction of the string OT to Rabin OT achieving the optimal rate of 1/2.

Structure of the paper. Section 2 establishes the notation and provides some useful facts from information theory and cryptography. In Section 3, oblivious transfer is formally described and its security definition is provided. The main results together with security proofs are contained in Section 4. Our concluding remarks and the open questions are given in Section 5.

2   Preliminaries

Here we introduce our notation and some tools that are useful in proving our main result.

Given a sample space (a set of events), a random variable X is a mapping from the sample space to a certain range $\mathcal{X}$ and it is characterized by its probability distribution P_X that assigns to every $x \in \mathcal{X}$ the probability $P_X(x)$ of the event that X takes on the value x.

We deal with two kinds of noise: a discrete memoryless channel, generated by the stochastic map $W : \mathcal{X} \longrightarrow \mathcal{Y}$; and secondly: independent, identically distributed (i.i.d.) realizations of a pair of random variables (X, Y) (range $\mathcal{X} \times \mathcal{Y}$ with distribution P_{XY}, in both cases with finite sets $\mathcal{X}, \mathcal{Y}$).

For elements of information theory, we refer the reader to the book by Thomas and Cover [22].

The Shannon entropy of a random variable is a measure of the uncertainty of a random variable X

$$H(X) = -\sum_{x} P_X(x) \log P_X(x)$$

assuming that $0 \log 0 = 0$. All the logarithms in this papers are to the base 2.

The mutual information between two random variables is defined as

$$I(X; Y) = \sum_{x,y} P(x, y) \log \frac{P(x, y)}{P(x) P(y)}$$

The min-entropy of X is

$$H_\infty(X) = \min_{y} \log(1/P_X(x))$$

The min-entropy of X conditioned on Y is

$$H_\infty(X) = \min_{y} H_\infty(X | Y = y)$$

We also will use the following quantities

$$H_0(X) = \log |\{x \in X | P_X(x) > 0\}|$$

and

$$H_0(X | Y) = \max_{y} H_0(X | Y = y)$$

We will use the so-called smooth entropies as defined by Renner and Wolf [21]. For $1 > \epsilon \geq 0$ the ϵ-smooth min-entropy is defined as

$$H_\infty^\epsilon(X) = \max_{X':\|P_{X'}-P_X\|\leq\epsilon} H_\infty(X)$$

where $\|P_{X'} - P_X\|$ denotes the statistical distance between the distributions $P_{X'}$ and P_X. The conditional min-entropies are defined similarly:

$$H_\infty^\epsilon(X|Y) = \max_{X'Y':\|P_{X'Y'}-P_{XY}\|\leq\epsilon} H_\infty(X|Y)$$

Analogous definitions exist for smooth entropy $H_0(X)$ and its conditioned version. Smooth entropies are of special importance since many nice properties of Shannon entropies (such as sub-additivity, chain rule and monotonicity), which are known to not hold for H_0 and H_∞, do hold in an approximated version for smooth entropies [21]. Two of these properties are important for our result.

For any $\epsilon, \epsilon' > 0$, and any distribution P_{XYZ} we have

$$H_\infty^{\epsilon+\epsilon'}(X|YZ) \geq H_\infty^\epsilon(XY|Z) - H_0(Y|Z) - \log(1/\epsilon') \tag{1}$$

$$H_\infty^{\epsilon+\epsilon'}(XY|Z) \geq H_\infty^\epsilon(X|Z) + H_\infty^{\epsilon'}(Y|XZ) \tag{2}$$

Assuming that Z is independent of XY, we obtain

$$H_\infty^{\epsilon+\epsilon'}(X|Y) \geq H_\infty^\epsilon(XY) - H_0(Y) - \log(1/\epsilon') \tag{3}$$

$$H_\infty^{\epsilon+\epsilon'}(XY) \geq H_\infty^\epsilon(X) + H_\infty^{\epsilon'}(Y|X) \tag{4}$$

The smooth min-entropy gives us the amount of randomness that can be extracted from a random variable X given some side information Y, as proved in [21]. We will make use of the Left-over Hash-Lemma [15] (also known as privacy amplification [2]). We state the version presented in [11].

Theorem 1. *Let X be a random variable over $\{0,1\}^n$. Let U^n and U^m be independent and uniform over $\{0,1\}^n$ and $\{0,1\}^m$, respectively. There exists an efficient function $Ext : \{0,1\}^n \times \{0,1\}^m$, such that, if $H_\infty(X|Y) \geq m + 2\log(1/\epsilon)$, then $\|(Ext(X,U^n),U^n,Y) - (U^m,U^n,Y)\| \leq \epsilon$.*

A particular example of such efficient function Ext is a two-universal hash function [3]. Finally, we need the following result originated from [10]. The basic idea is to concatenate a random linear code with the Reed-Solomon code.

Theorem 2. *There exists an error-correcting code, efficiently encodable and decodable, such that for any channel $W : \mathcal{X} \longrightarrow \mathcal{Y}$, it achieves the capacity of W.*

For the definition of triviality for noisy correlations see [25,19] for details.

3   Oblivious Transfer Protocols

In this section, we give the definition of security used in this paper. We closely follow [19] for this presentation. A two-party protocol consists of a program which describes a series of messages to be exchanged (over a noisy and/or a noiseless channel) and local computations to be performed by the two parties. The protocol is said to halt if no more local computations or message exchanges are required. At the end of an execution of a protocol, each party emits an accept/reject message, depending on the messages he/she received and on the result of local computations. In this paper we concentrate on 1-out-of-2 oblivious transfer protocols.

In an oblivious transfer protocol, there are two parties: a sender (Alice) and a receiver (Bob). The sender's inputs to the protocol consist of two strings of length k. We denote those strings by $U_i = b_0^{(i)} b_1^{(i)} \ldots b_{k-1}^{(i)}$, $i \in \{0,1\}$, where $b_j^{(i)} \in \{0,1\}$, $0 \le j \le k-1$. The receiver's input is a single bit c. At the end of the protocol Bob receives U_c as his output, while Alice receives nothing. Informally speaking, the protocol is correct, if for honest players, Bob receives his desired output and both players do not abort the protocol. It is said to be private if Alice has no information on Bob's choice and Bob learns information concerning at most one string.

The protocol (for honest players) or more generally any strategy (in the case of cheaters) defines random variables for all the messages exchanged and results of computations performed during an execution of the protocol, depending on their mutual inputs. For the sake of simplicity, we use the same notation for outcomes of a random experiment and their random variables. Denote by $V_A(V_B)$ the random variable which represents all the information in possession of Alice (Bob) at the end of the protocol (including the results of all local computations, local random samplings, local inputs and messages exchanged). This information is also known as the *view of a player*. We denote an execution of a program G by players A and B on inputs x_A and x_B which generates the outcomes y_A and y_B by $\mathsf{G}[A,B](x_A, x_B) = (y_A, y_B)$. A party receiving no output is represented by $y = \Delta$.

We restrict the following definition and analysis to the particular case where the inputs of the honest players are chosen at random. This does not compromise the generality of our results, as random instances of oblivious transfer can easily be converted into OT protocols with specific inputs without any further assumptions, as shown in [1].

Definition 1. *A protocol* $\mathsf{G}[A,B](x_A, x_B) = (y_A, y_B)$ *is an ϵ-correct implementation of a 1-out-of-2 string oblivious transfer protocol,* $\binom{2}{1} - OT^k$ *for short, if at the end of its execution for honest players Alice and Bob, we have that*

$$\Pr\{\mathsf{G}[A,B]((U_0, U_1), c) \neq (\Delta, U_c)\} \le \epsilon \tag{5}$$

for any $U_i \in \{0,1\}^k$, $i \in \{0,1\}$ *and* $c \in \{0,1\}$.
It is ϵ-private for Bob if for any possible behavior of Alice,

$$I(V_A; C) \le \epsilon \tag{6}$$

where $I(\cdot; \cdot)$ is Shannon's mutual information, V_A is the random variable which represents Alice's view after the completion of the protocol and C is the random variable which represents Bob's input c (assuming uniform distribution).

Consider the set of all possible pairs of k-bit strings τ, $\{\tau : (t_0, t_1), t_0, t_1 \in \{0,1\}^k\}$. Let T be a random variable uniformly distributed on τ and T_i be the random variable, corresponding to t_i, $i \in \{0,1\}$. The protocol is ϵ-private for Alice if for any behavior of Bob, for any T, there exists a random binary variable $\tilde{i}$ independent of T such that such that

$$I(T; V_B | T_{\tilde{i}}) \leq \epsilon, \tag{7}$$

where $\tilde{i} = c$ in the case of honest Bob.

A protocol is said to be ϵ-private if it ϵ-private for both Alice and Bob.

A protocol $\mathsf{G}[A,B](x_A, x_B) = (y_A, y_B)$ is said to be an ϵ-private, ϵ-correct 1-out-of-2 string oblivious transfer protocol secure against honest-but-curious Alice when in the above definitions Alice has to follow the protocol but tries to gather as much information as she can from her view of the protocol V_A.

Let $\mathsf{G}[A,B](x_A, x_B) = (y_A, y_B)$ be a protocol implementing ϵ-private, ϵ-correct $\binom{2}{1}$-OT^k, based on a noisy channel $W : \mathcal{X} \longrightarrow \mathcal{Y}$ or a noisy correlation P_{XY} on $\mathcal{X} \times \mathcal{Y}$. Let n be the number of invocations of the noisy channel/correlation. The 1-out-of-2 rate of $\mathsf{G}[A,B](x_A, x_B) = (y_A, y_B)$ is defined as: $R_2 = \frac{k}{n}$.

A rate R^* is said to be achievable if for any $\epsilon, \gamma > 0$, there exists a protocol $\mathsf{G}[A,B](x_A, x_B) = (y_A, y_B)$ implementing ϵ-private, ϵ-correct $\binom{2}{1}$-OT^k which, for sufficiently large n, has $R_2 \geq R^* - \gamma$. The supremum of all achievable rates is called the 1-out-of-2 OT capacity of the channel W or of the correlation P, denoted $C_{\binom{2}{1}\text{-OT}}(W)$ or $C_{\binom{2}{1}\text{-OT}}(P)$.

4   Main Result

According to the result of [19], in order to prove that the oblivious transfer capacity for the honest-but-curious sender and malicious receiver is positive for any non-trivial correlation, we just need to prove it is positive for a particular kind of correlation, called in [19] a *symmetric basic correlation (SBC)*. We assume that the players have access to an unlimited bi-directional noiseless channel.

There are three main settings for the considered protocols: 1) Both players can cheat actively; 2) Alice is passive and Bob is active; 3) Both players are passive. In Setting 1, secure OT can be achieved only based on SBC, while in Settings 2 and 3, our result works for any non-trivial noisy correlation.

Now, we formally define SBC, introduce our protocol (which is in the spirit of [4]) and argue its security for all the above cases.

Let p be a constant such that $0 < p < 1$. In SBC (X, Y), X is uniformly distributed on $\{0,1\}$ and the range $\mathcal{Y}$ of Y is partitioned into three sets: $\mathcal{Y} = \mathcal{U}_0 \cup \mathcal{E} \cup \mathcal{U}_1$, of non-zero probability under the distribution of Y, with the following properties.

- For all $y \in \mathcal{E}$, $\Pr\{Y = y | X = 0\} = \Pr\{Y = y | X = 1\}$.
- $\mathcal{U}_1 = \{ y' :$ for all $y \in \mathcal{U}_0$ we have

$$\Pr\{Y = y | X = x\} = \Pr\{Y = y' | X = \overline{x}\} \quad \wedge$$
$$\Pr\{Y = y | X = 1\} < \Pr\{Y = y | X = 0\} \quad \wedge$$
$$\Pr\{Y = y' | X = 1\} > \Pr\{Y = y' | X = 0\} \quad \}$$

- $\Pr\{Y \in \mathcal{E}\} = 1 - p$.

From Alice's point of view it looks like the uniform input to a binary channel, while for Bob it looks like the output of a distinguishable mixture of two channels: an erasure channel and a channel $W : \{0,1\} \longrightarrow \mathcal{U}_0 \cup \mathcal{U}_1$, with conditional probabilities $W(y|x) = \frac{1}{p} \Pr\{Y = y | X = x\}$. If Bob finds $y \in \mathcal{E}$ he has no information at all about the input (a perfect erasure), but for $y \in \mathcal{U}_i$ he has a (more or less weak) indication that $x = i \in \{0,1\}$ because the likelihood for $x = 1 - i$ is smaller.

It is clear that the correlation (X, Y) is completely characterized by p and W. Thus, we denote this distribution $\mathrm{SBC}_{p,W}$. For the sake of simplicity of this presentation, we analyze the case when $p = 1/2$. However, our protocols and proofs can be easily adapted for the case $0 < p < 1$.

Suppose Alice and Bob are given n identical, independent executions of $\mathrm{SBC}_{1/2,W}$. Thus, Alice and Bob receive n-tuples $(x_1, \ldots, x_n)$ and $(y_1, \ldots, y_n)$, respectively.

Remember that by Theorem 2, for any channel W there exists an efficient encodable and decodable error-correcting code $\mathcal{C}$ achieving the capacity of W.

Alice has inputs $U_0, U_1 \in \{0,1\}^k$ and Bob has input $c \in \{0,1\}$.

Protocol I

1. Bob chooses two sets $S_0, S_1 \subset \{1, 2, \ldots, n\}$, $S_0 \cap S_1 = \emptyset$, $|S_0| = |S_1| = (1/2 - \eta)n$, $0 < \eta < 1/2$, where $(1/2 - \eta)n$ is an integer. Define $q = (1/2 - \eta)n$. Bob chooses S_0 and S_1 so that, for any $i \in S_c$, y_i is not an erasure. Bob sends the sets S_0 and S_1 to Alice over the noiseless channel.
2. Denote the j-th element of S_i by $S_i(j)$. Alice computes tuples $\rho_0 = (x_{S_0(1)}, \ldots, x_{S_0(q)})$, $\rho_1 = (x_{S_1(1)}, \ldots, x_{S_1(q)})$. Alice then computes the syndromes of ρ_0 and ρ_1 by using an error correcting code $\mathcal{C}$ with rate $Cap(W) - \gamma$, where $\gamma > 0$ and $Cap(W)$ is the Shannon capacity of the channel W. She sends the syndromes to Bob.
3. Alice picks up a random matrix G dimension $(1/2 - \eta)n \times nR$, where R is the rate of the protocol. She computes the vectors $A_0 = \rho_0 * G$ and $A_1 = \rho_1 * G$ where "$*$" is the usual matrix multiplication, and then encrypts her inputs as follows: $B_0 = A_0 \oplus U_0$ and $B_1 = A_1 \oplus U_1$ where "$\oplus$" is a bit-wise exclusive-or. She sends G, B_0 and B_1 to Bob over the noiseless channel.
   Using its respective syndrome, Bob computes ρ_c and then calculates $A_c = \rho_c * G$. He obtains $U_c = A_c \oplus B_c$.
   If Bob experiences a decoding error when computing ρ_c, he defines U_c as the zero-vector.

Before analyzing the protocol security, we note that with exponentially bounded probability Bob sees between $(1/2 - \delta)\, n$ and $(1/2 + \delta)\, n$ non-erasures, for some positive constant δ, thus we assume that this is the case. Note also that, for the positions where Bob does not receive erasures his view is exactly like the output of the channel W with input X.

We state our main result. Let X and Z be random variables describing the input of $\mathrm{SBC}_{1/2,W}$ and the output of W, respectively.

Theorem 3. *Protocol I implements an ϵ-private, ϵ-correct 1-out-of-2 oblivious transfer protocol for any $R < I(X; Z)/4$ against active cheaters and $R < I(X; Z)/2$ against passive cheaters.*

Active cheating. We sketch here a proof of why this theorem holds, the complete proof is given in the full version of the paper.

Let's first analyze if the protocol is secure against a malicious Bob. We should prove that Bob obtains knowledge about at most one of Alice's strings.

Dishonest Bob who tries to obtain knowledge on both Alice's inputs U_0 and U_1 will distribute positions where he did not receive an erasure into both sets S_0 and S_1. The number of non-erasures that Bob sees is in between $(1/2 - \delta)\, n$ and $(1/2 + \delta)\, n$, for some positive constant δ. Thus, we can assume that in one of the sets, let's say S_1 we will have a number of non-erasures no larger than $(1/4 + \delta)\, n$. Denote the random variable associated with the syndrome of ρ_1 by Syn_1. We will slightly abuse the notation and denote by ρ_1 the string computed by Alice and, at the same time, its corresponding random variable.

We are interested in the following quantity $H_\infty^\varepsilon(\rho_1 | Y^n Syn_1)$ which gives us how much secret information Bob can extract from ρ_1. We first note that $q = (1/2 - \eta)n$ symbols of Y^n will not be related to ρ_1 at all, because they will be used for constructing ρ_0 and because of the i.i.d. assumption on (X, Y). Denote the remaining q symbols of Y^n which are possibly related to ρ_1 by Y^q. Also, note that ρ_1 will consist of q general instances of X, again because of the i.i.d. assumption on (X, Y). Thus, instead of ρ_1 we will just write X^q to denote the part of X^n that is used to compute ρ_1. Finally, observe that no more than just $(1/4 + \delta)\, n$ bits of the remaining Y^q bits related to ρ_0 will be non-erasures. Thus, we are left with

$$H_\infty^\varepsilon(\rho_1 | Y^n Syn_1) = H_\infty^\varepsilon(X^q | Y^q Syn_1) \tag{8}$$

By sequentially applying (1) and (2) we obtain

$$H_\infty^{2\varepsilon}(X^q | Y^q Syn_1) \geq H_\infty^{\varepsilon/2}(X^q | Y^q) + H_\infty^{\varepsilon/2}(Syn_1 | X^q Y^q) \\ - H_0(Syn_1) - \log(1/\varepsilon) \tag{9}$$

that gives us

$$H_\infty^{2\varepsilon}(X^q | Y^q Syn_1) \geq H_\infty^{\varepsilon/2}(X^q | Y^q) - H_0(Syn_1) - \log(1/\varepsilon) \tag{10}$$

Denote the equivocation of the channel W specified in $SBC_{p,W}$ by $H(X|Z)$. It is clear that $H_0(Syn_1) \leq \frac{n}{2}(H(X|Z) - \gamma)$. We state the following lemma whose proof appears in the full version of this paper.

Lemma 1. *For any $0 < \varepsilon' < \varepsilon < 1, \delta' > 0$ we have*

$$H_\infty^\varepsilon(X^q|Y^q) \geq H_\infty^{\varepsilon'/2}(X^{(1/4-\delta')n}) + H_\infty^{\varepsilon'/2}(X^{(1/4+\delta')n}|Z^{(1/4+\delta')n})$$

The intuition behind the lemma is that we can split Y^q in two random variables $Y_\Delta^{q'}$, where $q' = (1/4 - \delta')n$ which consists of the positions where, with an exponentially small (in n) probability, there will be only erasures and $Z^{q''}, q'' = (1/4 + \delta')n$ which consists of the positions where Bob receives X through the channel W. We then split the input random variable X^q accordingly in $X_\Delta^{q'}$ for those inputs where Bob received erasures and $X^{q''}$ for those inputs where Bob received them as through W. Note that, $Y_\Delta^{q'} Z^{q''}$, for large enough n is the typical space of Y^q, thus, the statistical difference of these two distributions goes to zero exponentially as n becomes large by the asymptotic equipartition property. Therefore, we can find appropriate $0 < \varepsilon' < \varepsilon < 1$ so that we have:

$$H_\infty^\varepsilon(X^q|Y^q) \geq H_\infty^{\varepsilon'}(X_\Delta^{q'} X^{q''}|Y_\Delta^{q'} Z^{q''})$$

As $Y_\Delta^{q'}$ is completely useless for Bob (it gives no information at all on X^q), we obtain

$$H_\infty^\varepsilon(X^q|Y^q) \geq H_\infty^{\varepsilon'}(X_\Delta^{q'} X^{q''}|Z^{q''})$$

By applying Equation (2), we get

$$H_\infty^{\varepsilon'}(X_\Delta^{q'} X^{q''}|Z^{q''}) \geq H_\infty^{\varepsilon'/2}(X_\Delta^{q'}|Z^{q''}) - H_\infty^{\varepsilon'/2}(X^{q''}|Z^{q''})$$

However, by definition, $Z^{q''}$ is independent from $X_\Delta^{q'}$, thus we obtain

$$H_\infty^\varepsilon(X^q|Y^q) \geq H_\infty^{\varepsilon'/2}(X_\Delta^{q'}) - H_\infty^{\varepsilon'/2}(X^{q''}|Z^{q''})$$

our desired result.

We then note that according to [11] for general random variables (X, Y), we have $H_\infty^\varepsilon(X^n|Y^n) \geq nH(X|Y) - 4\sqrt{n \log(1/\varepsilon)} \log(|\mathcal{X}|)$.

Putting everything together,

$$H_\infty^\varepsilon(\rho_1|Y^n Syn_1) \geq (1/4 - \delta')\, nH(X) + (1/4 + \delta')\, nH(X|Z) -$$
$$\frac{n}{2}(H(X|Z) - \gamma) - \log(1/\varepsilon) - 8\sqrt{n \log(1/\varepsilon)} \log(|\mathcal{X}|), \quad (11)$$

and by the definition of mutual information,

$$H_\infty^\varepsilon(\rho_1|Y^n Syn_1) \geq$$
$$n(I(X;Z)/4 - \delta'I(X;Z) - \gamma) - \log(1/\varepsilon) - 8\sqrt{n \log(1/\varepsilon)} \log(|\mathcal{X}|) \quad (12)$$

Noting that $\log(|\mathcal{X}|) = 1$, making $\varepsilon = 2^{-\alpha n}$, $\alpha > 0$ and choosing an appropriate constant $\epsilon' > 0$ satisfying simultaneously $\epsilon'/3 > \delta' I(X;Z) - \gamma$, $\epsilon'/3 > 8\sqrt{\alpha}$ and $\epsilon'/3 > \alpha$ we obtain

$$H_\infty^\varepsilon(\rho_1 | Y^n Syn_1) \geq n(I(X;Z)/4 - \epsilon')$$

Note that the random matrix G is, in fact, a two-universal hash function[2]. Hence, applying Theorem 1 with $m = (\frac{1}{4}I(X;Z) - \epsilon - 2\alpha)n = Rn$, we can see that Bob's amount of information on A_1 will be at most $2^{-\alpha n}$. Thus, a cheating Bob cannot obtain simultaneously knowledge on Alice's two inputs.

The correctness of the protocol follows from the fact that, with high probability, by using its respective syndrome, Bob can compute ρ_c and then calculate $A_c = \rho_c * G$. He obtains $U_c = A_c \oplus B_c$.

Security against malicious Alice: it is easy to see by inspecting the protocol that she has only two ways to cheat. First, she may try to distinguish the sets S_0 and S_1 as for which contains erasures and which does not. However, the probability to become erasure is equal for both inputs 0 and 1 of SBC, therefore, Alice's best strategy here is guessing at random. The second way is sending a random string instead of one of the syndromes. Indeed, this will lead Bob to a decoding error with high probability, if Alice spoils the syndrome Syn_c. In this case, Bob could complain but this would disclose his choice c. If he does not complain, then his output is undefined. When Alice happens to spoil Syn_{1-c}, honest Bob simply accepts the protocol, again disclosing his choice. Note that all the above cases contradict Definition 1.

It is easy to see that the last instruction of Step 3 makes this kind of cheating useless for Alice because even if she sends an incorrect syndrome, Bob's output is always well-defined. Besides, he may mark Alice as a cheating player for the higher order protocols.

Passive cheating. In the case of passive cheating, Bob would not split his erasures between S_0 and S_1, thus one can see that the achievable rate will be twice the one achieved in the previously stated analysis. Therefore, in the case of passive adversaries we have that any rate $R < I(X;Z)/2$ is achievable.

Upper bounds. In [26], it was proved that the mutual information between two noisy correlations is a secure monotone, in the sense it can not be increased by local computations and noiseless communications between the parties holding the correlations. This fact implies that the mutual information between the correlations is an upper bound on their oblivious transfer capacity. Thus, in the case of an $SBC_{p,W}$, its oblivious transfer capacity is upper bounded by its mutual information of $I(X;Y) = pI(X;Z)$. For $p = 1/2$ we obtain that $C_{OT}(SBC_{1/2,W}) < I(X;Z)/2$ thus showing that our protocols are optimal in the case of passive cheaters.

---

[2] In principle, any efficiently computable two-universal hash function can be used in our protocol.

5 Conclusions and Future Works

In this paper, we presented an efficient protocol for implementing oblivious transfer that achieves a non-zero rate for any non-trivial correlation. In the case of symmetric basic correlations, we show that for passive adversaries, the oblivious transfer capacity is efficiently achievable. In the case of active adversaries, our protocol is optimal up to a constant. An open question left by this work is to obtain the oblivious transfer capacity of symmetric noisy correlations in the case of active adversaries. A possible way of doing this is by using interactive hashing in order to prevent Bob from cheating, as proposed in [8] in the case of 1-out-of-2 bit OT. The problem of computing the oblivious transfer capacity for general correlations remains wide open.

Acknowledgement

The authors would like to thank the anonymous reviewers for their valuable comments and corrections.

References

1. Beaver, D.: Precomputing Oblivious Transfer. In: Coppersmith, D. (ed.) CRYPTO 1995. LNCS, vol. 963, pp. 97–109. Springer, Heidelberg (1995)
2. Bennett, C.H., Brassard, G., Crépeau, C., Maurer, U.: Generalized Privacy Amplification. IEEE Trans. Inf. Theory 41(6), 1915–1923 (1995)
3. Carter, J.L., Wegman, M.N.: Universal Classes of hash functions. J. of Computer and Syst. Sci. 18, 143–154 (1979)
4. Crépeau, C.: Equivalence between two flavors of oblivious transfers. In: Pomerance, C. (ed.) CRYPTO 1987. LNCS, vol. 293, pp. 350–354. Springer, Heidelberg (1988)
5. Crépeau, C.: Efficient Cryptographic Protocols Based on Noisy Channels. In: Fumy, W. (ed.) EUROCRYPT 1997. LNCS, vol. 1233, pp. 306–317. Springer, Heidelberg (1997)
6. Crépeau, C., Kilian, J.: Achieving oblivious transfer using weakened security assumptions. In: Proc. 29th FOCS, pp. 42–52. IEEE, Los Alamitos (1988)
7. Crépeau, C., Morozov, K., Wolf, S.: Efficient Unconditional Oblivious Transfer from Almost Any Noisy Channel. In: Blundo, C., Cimato, S. (eds.) SCN 2004. LNCS, vol. 3352, pp. 47–59. Springer, Heidelberg (2005)
8. Crépeau, C., Savvides, G.: Optimal Reductions Between Oblivious Transfers Using Interactive Hashing. In: Vaudenay, S. (ed.) EUROCRYPT 2006. LNCS, vol. 4004, pp. 201–221. Springer, Heidelberg (2006)
9. Even, S., Goldreich, O., Lempel, A.: A Randomized Protocol for Signing Contracts. Comm. ACM 28(6), 637–647 (1985)
10. Forney, G.D.: Concatenated codes. MIT Press, Cambridge (1966)
11. Holenstein, T., Renner, R.: One-Way Secret-Key Agreement and Applications to Circuit Polarization and Immunization of Public-Key Encryption. In: Shoup, V. (ed.) CRYPTO 2005. LNCS, vol. 3621, pp. 478–493. Springer, Heidelberg (2005)
12. Imai, H., Morozov, K., Nascimento, A.C.A.: On the Oblivious Transfer Capacity of the Erasure Channel. In: Proc. ISIT 2006, pp. 1428–1431. IEEE, Los Alamitos (2006)

13. Kilian, J.: Founding Cryptography on Oblivious Transfer. In: Proc. STOC 1988, pp. 20–31 (1988)
14. Korjik, V., Morozov, K.: Generalized Oblivious Transfer Protocols Based on Noisy Channels. In: Gorodetski, V.I., Skormin, V.A., Popyack, L.J. (eds.) MMM-ACNS 2001. LNCS, vol. 2052, pp. 219–229. Springer, Heidelberg (2001)
15. Håstad, J., Impagliazzo, R., Levin, L.A., Luby, M.: A Pseudorandom Generator from any one-way function. SIAM J. on Comp. 28(4), 1364–1396 (1999)
16. Maurer, U.: Secret Key Agreement by Public Discussion. IEEE Trans. Inf. Theory 39(3), 733–742 (1993)
17. Naor, M., Ostrovsky, R., Venkatesan, R., Yung, M.: Perfect Zero-Knowledge Arguments for NP using any one-way permutation. J. of Cryptology 11(2) (1998)
18. Nascimento, A., Winter, A.: Oblivious Transfer from any Genuine Noise, pre-print version (2004)
19. Nascimento, A., Winter, A.: On the Oblivious Transfer Capacity of Noisy Correlations. In: Proc. ISIT 2006, pp. 1871–1875. IEEE, Los Alamitos (2006)
20. Rabin, M.O.: How to exchange secrets by oblivious transfer. Technical Memo TR–81, Aiken Computation Laboratory, Harvard University (1981)
21. Renner, R., Wolf, S.: Simple and tight bounds for information reconciliation and privacy amplification. In: Roy, B. (ed.) ASIACRYPT 2005. LNCS, vol. 3788, pp. 199–216. Springer, Heidelberg (2005)
22. Cover, T.M., Thomas, J.A.: Elements of Information Theory. Wiley, Chichester (1991)
23. Stebila, D., Wolf, S.: Efficient oblivious transfer from any non-trivial binary-symmetric channel. In: Proc. ISIT 2002 (Lausanne), p. 293. IEEE, Los Alamitos (2002)
24. Wiesner, S.: Conjugate coding. Sigact News 15(1), 78–88 (1983); original manuscript written ca (1970)
25. Winter, A., Nascimento, A.C.A., Imai, H.: Commitment Capacity of Discrete Memoryless Channels. In: Paterson, K.G. (ed.) Cryptography and Coding 2003. LNCS, vol. 2898, pp. 35–51. Springer, Heidelberg (2003)
26. Wolf, S., Wullschleger, J.: New monotones and lower bounds in unconditional two-party computation. In: Shoup, V. (ed.) CRYPTO 2005. LNCS, vol. 3621, pp. 467–477. Springer, Heidelberg (2005)
27. Wolf, S., Wullschleger, J.: Oblivious transfer is symmetric. In: Vaudenay, S. (ed.) EUROCRYPT 2006. LNCS, vol. 4004, pp. 222–232. Springer, Heidelberg (2006)
28. Wyner, A.: The Wire Tap Channel. Bell System Tech. J. 54, 1355–1387 (1975)

Cryptographic Security of Individual Instances

L. Antunes[1], S. Laplante[2], A. Pinto[1], and L. Salvador[1,*]

[1] Departamento de Ciências de Computadores
Universidade do Porto, Portugal
[2] Université Paris-Sud
LRI, France

Abstract. There are two principal notions of security for cryptographic systems. For a few systems, they can be proven to have perfect secrecy against an opponent with unlimited computational power, in terms of information theory. However, the security of most systems, including public key cryptosystems, is based on complexity theoretic assumptions.

In both cases there is an implicit notion of average-case analysis. In the case of conditional security, the underlying assumption is usually average-case, not worst case hardness. And for unconditional security, entropy itself is an average case notion of encoding length.

Kolmogorov complexity (the size of the smallest program that generates a string) is a rigorous measure of the amount of information, or randomness, in an individual string x. By considering the time-bounded Kolmogorov complexity (program limited to run in time $t(|x|)$) we can take into account the computational difficulty of extracting information. We present a new notion of security based on Kolmogorov complexity. The first goal is to provide a formal definition of what it means for an individual instance to be secure. The second goal is to bridge the gap between information theoretic security, and computational security, by using time-bounded Kolmogorov complexity.

In this paper, we lay the groundwork of the study of cryptosystems from the point of view of security of individual instances by considering three types of information-theoretically secure cryptographic systems: cipher systems (such as the one-time pad), threshold secret sharing, and authentication schemes.

Keywords: Perfect secrecy, Kolmogorov complexity.

1 Introduction

Classical information theory originated in Shannon's 1948 paper "A mathematical theory of communication" [Sh49], where the author defined the notion of entropy and showed that it corresponds to the amount of information associated with any given statistical event. Another notion of information was proposed in the 60's, independently by Solomonoff, Kolmogorov and Chaitin [Sol64, Kol65, Cha66]. This quantity is now known as Kolmogorov complexity and is defined as the length of the shortest program

---

* Partially supported by KCrypt (POSC/EIA/60819/2004), the grant SFRH/BD/13124/2003 from FCT and funds granted to LIACC through the Programa de Financiamento Plurianual, FCT and Programa POSI, as well as ANR Blanc AlgoQP.

Y. Desmedt (Ed.): ICITS 2007, LNCS 4883, pp. 195–210, 2009.

that can produce a given string. Unlike entropy, this quantity depends exclusively on the string, and not on the probability with which it is sampled from some given distribution. As such, Kolmogorov complexity measures the intrinsic information in a given string.

Traditionally, information theory has been used in the analysis of unconditionally secure cryptographic systems. However, because of the inherent statistical nature of information theory, two distributions may have nil information about each other and yet particular instances of the plaintext and ciphertext have large mutual information in the individual sense. Even though such cases are probabilistically rare, and don't influence the information theoretic security, they still correspond to situations we'd rather avoid in practice.

In this paper, we give a notion of individual security, using Kolmogorov complexity to formalize what is meant by an *ad hoc* attack on an individual instance.

We believe this is a more realistic model of attack, since in practice, an attacker may not necessarily attempt to break all instances of a cryptosystem, but is likely to be willing to invest a lot of resources in breaking a single instance.

We then analyse some cryptographic protocols, in order to determine which are the truly secure instances of the cryptosystem. We consider three basic types of information theoretically secure cryptographic systems: cipher systems, threshold secret sharing schemes, and authentication schemes.

Our first goal is to provide a finer grained notion of security than the traditional information theoretic security. For each of the settings that we consider, we first give a Kolmogorov complexity based definition of security of an individual instance. Then we prove that security in this sense implies security in the traditional sense, by showing that if sufficiently many instances of a system are individually secure, then the system is also information theoretically secure. This implication is not perfect in the case of cypher systems and secret sharing, because we cannot avoid the existence of instances with very significant mutual information of the ciphertext about the plaintext (and equivalent notions for the secret sharing system). Finally, we identify the high-security instances of specific systems, using again properties derived from Kolmogorov complexity.

Our second goal in this work is to bridge the gap between information theoretic security, which does not take into account the resources necessary to extract information, and computational security. This paper takes a first step towards using tools from time-bounded Kolmogorov complexity to analyse cryptographic systems.

By providing a computable (though admittedly not efficient) method to establish the level of security of a particular instance of the system, we can guarantee that an instance of a cryptosystem is secure against a time-bounded adversary. We give such results for the one-time pad as well as for authentication schemes.

2   Preliminaries

2.1   Entropy

Information theory quantifies the *a priori* uncertainty about the results of an experiment. It is based on Shannon's entropy and corresponds to the number of bits necessary on average to describe an outcome from an ensemble.

Let X, Y be random variables. The probability that X takes on the value x from a finite or countably infinite set $\mathcal{X}$ is denoted by $p_X(x)$; the *mutual probability*, the probability that both x and y occur, by $p_{XY}(x, y)$ and the *conditional probability*, the probability that x occurs knowing that y has occurred by $p_{XY}(x|y)$. Two random variables X and Y are *independent* if and only if for all $x \in X$ and $y \in Y$ $p_{XY}(x, y) = p_X(x) \times p_Y(y)$. For convenience, $p_{XY}(x, y), p_{XY}(x|y)$ and $p_X(x)$ are denoted, respectively by $p(x, y), p(x|y)$ and $p(x)$.

Definition 1. *Let X and Y be random variables.*

- **Entropy:** $H(X) = -\sum_{x \in \mathcal{X}} p(x) \log p(x)$, *and* $H(X|Y) = \sum_{y \in \mathcal{Y}} p(y) H(X|Y = y)$.
- **Mutual information:** $I(X; Y) = H(X) - H(X|Y)$.

We recall a few properties of entropy.

Theorem 1. *Let X and Y be random variables.*

1. **Conditional entropy:** $H(Y|X) \leq H(Y)$ *and X and Y are independent if and only if equality holds.*
2. **Additivity:** $H(X, Y) = H(Y) + H(X|Y)$.
3. **Symmetry of information:** $I(X; Y) = I(Y; X)$.

2.2 Kolmogorov Complexity

We briefly introduce Kolmogorov complexity only at the level of generality needed. For more details, the textbook by Li and Vitányi [LV97] and Peter Gács' lecture notes [G88] are good references.

We consider only the binary alphabet $\Sigma = \{0, 1\}$. Our computation model will be *prefix free* Turing machines: Turing machines with a one-way input tape (the input head can only read from left to right), a one-way output tape and a two-way work tape. A set of strings A is prefix-free if there are no strings x and y in A where x is a proper prefix of y. The function log denotes $\log_2$, $|.|$ denotes the length of a string and $\#$ the cardinality of a set. A Turing Machine is prefix-free if its domain (set of inputs on which it halts) is prefix-free.

We present next the necessary definitions:

Definition 2 (Kolmogorov complexity). *Let U be a fixed universal prefix-free Turing machine.*

- **Conditional Kolmogorov complexity:** $K(x|y) = \min_p \{|p| : U(p, y) = x\}$.
- **Mutual information:** $I_K(x : y) = K(x) + K(y) - K(x, y)$.

The default value for y is the empty string ϵ. A different universal machine U may affect the program size $|p|$ by at most a constant additive factor.

We list the properties of Kolmogorov complexity that we need.

Theorem 2

1. **Upper bound:** *For each n, $\max\{K(x) : |x| = n\} = n + K(n) + O(1)$.*
2. **Incompressibility:** *For any string y, for each fixed constant r, the number of x of length n with $K(x|y) \leq n - r$ does not exceed 2^{n-r}.*

3. **Additivity:** *Up to an additive constant,* $K(x,y) = K(x) + K(y|x^*) = K(y) + K(x|y^*)$, *where* x^* *is the first shortest program that produces* x.
4. **Conditional additivity:** *Up to an additive constant,* $K(x,y|z) = K(x|z) + K(y|x, K(x|z), z) = K(y|z) + K(x|y, K(y|z), z)$.

2.3 Resource-Bounded Kolmogorov Complexity

The main disadvantage of using Kolmogorov complexity in many settings (including the one addressed in this paper) is that determining the Kolmogorov complexity of a given string is not a computable task. However, resource-bounded Kolmogorov complexity [Har83], where the programs considered always halt before expending their allocated resource bound, does not suffer from this drawback. More importantly, it gives a notion of information theory that takes complexity limitations into account, bridging the gap between complexity and information theory.

Definition 3 (Time-bounded Kolmogorov complexity). *Let* U *be a fixed universal Turing machine, and* t *be a fully-constructible time bound. Then for any string* $x, y \in \Sigma^*$, *the* t time-bounded complexity *is*
$K^t(x|y) = \min_p\{|p| : U(p,y) = x \text{ and } U(p,y) \text{ runs in at most } t(|x|+|y|) \text{ steps}\}.$

This definition corresponds to time-bounded computation, but one may also define other measures, for instance for space bounded computation, and so on. For this paper we require a variant where the program has the same computing ability as the class AM, where the computation is done in probabilistic polynomial time with bounded error (Arthur), with the help of nondeterminism (Merlin).

Definition 4 (CAM complexity). *Let* U *be a fixed universal nondeterministic Turing machine. Then for any string* $x, y \in \Sigma^*$, *for a polynomial* t, *the* t-time-bounded AM decision complexity $CAM^t(x|y)$ *is the length of the smallest program* p *such that*

1. $\forall r, U(p, y, r)$ *runs in at most* $t(|x|+|y|)$ *steps,*
2. *with probability at least* 2/3 *over the choice of* r, $U(p, y, r)$ *has at least one accepting path, and* $U(p, y, r) = x$ *on all of the accepting paths.*

We give a bound to the time that it takes to compute $K^t(x)$:

Theorem 3. *For* t *a fully-constructible time bound,* $K^t(x)$ *can be computed in time* $O(t(|x|) \cdot 2^{|x|})$.

Many facts about Kolmogorov complexity, such as existence and number of incompressible strings, are also true for resource bounded Kolmogorov complexity. However, one important property of Kolmogorov complexity that is believed to fail to hold in resource bounded models is symmetry of information. Symmetry of information states that information in x about y is the same as information in y about x. Note that this naturally comes into play in a cryptographic setting: consider the case where y is the result of applying a one-way permutation to x. Without any time bounds, the permutation can be inverted. However, this no longer works for time-bounded computation. Intuitively, for the same reason that one-way functions are believed to exist, it is believed that symmetry of information fails to hold for polynomial-time bounded computation.

However, weaker versions of symmetry of information are known to hold for resource bounded Kolmogorov complexity.

Theorem 4 (Time-bounded symmetry of information, [LR05]). *For any polynomial time bound t, there exists a polynomial time bound t' such that*

$$K^t(y) + K^t(x|y) \geq CAM^{t'}(x) + CAM^{t'}(y|x) - O(\log^3(|x| + |y|)).$$

2.4   Entropy vs Kolmogorov Complexity

There is a very close relation between these two measures: Shannon's entropy is the expected value of Kolmogorov complexity for computable distributions. In this sense, Kolmogorov complexity is a sharper notion than entropy. The following theorem follows from Corollary 4.3.2 and Theorem 8.1.1 in [LV97].

Theorem 5. *Let X,Y be random variables over $\mathcal{X}, \mathcal{Y}$. For any computable probability distribution $\mu(x, y)$ over $\mathcal{X} \times \mathcal{Y}$, $0 \leq \left(\sum_{x,y} \mu(x, y) K(x|y) - H(X|Y) \right) \leq K(\mu) + O(1)$.*

Proof. Let μ_Y and μ_X be the marginal probability distributions over $\mathcal{Y}$ and $\mathcal{X}$ respectively. Similarly, denote by $\mu_{X|Y}$ and $\mu_{Y|X}$ the conditional probability distributions. For the first inequality, $H(X|Y) = \sum_y \mu_Y(y)H(X|Y = y) \leq \sum_y \mu_Y(y) \sum_x \mu_{X|Y}(x)K(x|y) = \sum_{x,y} \mu(x, y)K(x|y)$ where the last inequality follows from the Noiseless Coding Theorem (see [LV97]) since y is a fixed string.

For the second direction, Corollary 4.3.2 in [LV97] states that $K(x|y) \leq \log 1/\mu_{X|Y}(x|y) + K(\mu) + O(1)$. Therefore,

$$\sum_y \mu_Y(y) \sum_x \mu_{X|Y}(x|y)K(x|y) \leq \sum_y \mu_Y(y) \sum_x \mu_{X|Y}(x|y)\log 1/\mu_{X|Y}(x|y) + K(\mu) + O(1)$$

$$= \sum_{x,y} \mu(x, y) \log 1/\mu_{X|Y}(x|y) + K(\mu) + O(1)$$

$$= H(X|Y) + K(\mu) + O(1).$$

By $K(\mu)$, we mean the length of the smallest probabilistic algorithm A that outputs x with probability $\mu(x)$. Note that $K(\mu)$ is a constant c_μ depending only on the (computable) conditional probability of X and Y, but not on the particular value of x [Cha75]. The $O(1)$ term depends only on the reference universal prefix machine.

An analogous result for mutual information holds.

Theorem 6 ([GV04]). *Let X,Y be random variables over $\mathcal{X}, \mathcal{Y}$. For any computable probability distribution $\mu(x, y)$ over $\mathcal{X} \times \mathcal{Y}$, $I(X;Y) - K(\mu) \leq \sum_{x,y} \mu(x, y)I_K(x : y) \leq I(X;Y) + 2K(\mu)$. When μ is given, then $I(X;Y) = \sum_{x,y} \mu(x, y)\hat{I}_K(x : y|\mu) + O(1)$.*

3   Cipher Systems

We begin this study by examining the simplest cryptographic systems: cipher systems. In this section, we show what makes a cipher system secure both with entropy and Kolmogorov complexity and give an example system that is secure under both definitions: the one-time pad.

3.1 Information Theoretic Security of Cipher Systems

A private key cipher system is a five tuple $(\mathcal{M}, \mathcal{C}, \mathcal{K}, e, d)$, where $\mathcal{M}$ is the plaintext space, $\mathcal{C}$ is the ciphertext space, $\mathcal{K}$ is the key space, $e : \mathcal{K} \times \mathcal{M} \to \mathcal{C}$ is the encryption algorithm, $d : \mathcal{K} \times \mathcal{C} \to \mathcal{M}$ is the decryption algorithm and $d(k, e(k, m)) = m$. We use uppercase M, C, K to denote random variables over the message, ciphertext, and key spaces, and lower case m, c, k for individual instances of the cipher system.

A system is called *computationally secure* if it is secure against an adversary with bounded resources and it is called *information-theoretically (or unconditionally) secure* if the ciphertext provides no information about the plaintext, regardless of the adversary's computational power.

Definition 5. *A private key cipher system has δ security if $I(M; C) \leq \delta$.*

When $\delta = 0$, the classical notion of perfect security states that the *a posteriori* probability that a message m was sent, given that we observe ciphertext c, is equal to the *a priori* probability that message m is sent.

3.2 Instance Security for Cipher Systems

We use Kolmogorov complexity to define what it means for an individual instance of a cryptographic system to be secure. Intuitively, an instance m, k is secure if there is no *ad hoc* attack that can find the plaintext, even when given this particlular ciphertext and full information about the distribution of the messages. Of course, we cannot rule out the *ad hoc* attack where the attacker already knows the message and prints it out. But we define security in such a way that the length of the *ad hoc* program that computes the plaintext, given the ciphertext, must be at least as long as any shortest program that prints the plaintext – so any *ad hoc* attack may as well have a description of the plaintext hard-coded into its program.

Definition 6. *Let $(\mathcal{M}, \mathcal{C}, \mathcal{K}, e, d)$ be a cipher system, and μ be a distribution over $\mathcal{M} \times \mathcal{K}$. An instance $m, k \in \Sigma^n$ of the cipher system is γ-secure if $I_K(m : e(k, m) | \mu) \leq \gamma$.*

We say that a γ-*secure* instance has γ secrecy. We now prove that if enough instances of a cipher system are secure, then the system is information theoretically secure. This result establishes that instance security is a sharper notion than information theoretic security.

Theorem 7. *For any private key cipher system $(\mathcal{M}, \mathcal{K}, \mathcal{C}, e, d)$, for any independent M, K over $\mathcal{M}, \mathcal{K}$ with distribution μ, if the probability that an instance is γ secure is at least $(1-\epsilon)$, then the system has $\gamma + \epsilon \log(\#\mathcal{M})$ secrecy, in the information theoretic sense.*

Furthermore, if for any $t, \gamma < t \leq n, \mu(\{m, k : I_K(m : e(k, m) | \mu) = t\}) = O(f(t))$, then the system has $\gamma + \sqrt{\epsilon \sum_{\gamma < t \leq n} t^2 O(f(t))}$ security.

Proof. Let M, K be independent random variables with computable distribution μ. By Theorem 6 we have that up to an additive constant, $I(M; C) \leq \sum_{m,k} \mu(k, m) I_K(m : e(m, k)|\mu)$. We separate the sum into two parts, the secure instances and the others. Let G be the set of γ-secure instances.

$$
\begin{aligned}
I(M; C) &\leq \sum_{m,k \in G} \mu(k, m) I_K(m : e(m, k)|\mu) + \sum_{m,k \notin G} \mu(k, m) I_K(m : e(m, k)|\mu) \\
&\leq \gamma \sum_{m,k \in G} \mu(k, m) + \sum_{m,k \notin G} \mu(k, m)[K(m|\mu) - K(m|e(m, k), \mu)] \\
&\leq \gamma + \sum_{m,k \notin G} \mu(k, m) K(m|\mu) \\
&\leq \gamma + \epsilon \log(\#\mathcal{M}).
\end{aligned}
$$

If in addition we have $\mu(\{m, k : I_K(m : e(k, m)|\mu) = t\}) = O(f(t))$, then as before,

$$
\begin{aligned}
I(M; C) &\leq \gamma + \sum_{m,k \notin G} \mu(k, m) I_K(m : e(m, k)|\mu) \\
&= \gamma + \sum_{\gamma < t \leq n} t \cdot \mu(\{m, k : I_K(m : e(k, m)|\mu) = t\}) \\
&\leq \gamma + \sum_{\gamma < t \leq n} t \sqrt{f(t)} \cdot \sqrt{\mu(\{m, k : I_K(m : e(k, m)|\mu) = t\})}.
\end{aligned}
$$

Recall that the Cauchy-Schwarz inequality states that $\sum_i a_i b_i \leq \sqrt{(\sum_i a_i^2)(\sum_i b_i^2)}$.

$$
\begin{aligned}
I(M; C) &\leq \gamma + \sqrt{\sum_{\gamma < t \leq n} t^2 f(t)} \sqrt{\sum_{\gamma < t \leq n} \mu(\{m, k : I_K(m : e(k, m)|\mu) = t\})} \\
&\leq \gamma + \sqrt{\sum_{\gamma < t \leq n} t^2 f(t)} \sqrt{\epsilon},
\end{aligned}
$$

since $\sum_{\gamma < t \leq n} \mu(\{m, k : I_K(m : e(k, m)|\mu) = t\}) = \sum_{m,k \notin G} \mu(m, k) \leq \epsilon$.

3.3   Instance Security of One-Time Pad

In the previous section, we have given a definition of security of individual instances of cipher systems, and shown that if sufficiently many instances are secure, then the system is secure in the traditional sense, thereby establishing that our definition is a refinement of the standard notion of security.

In this section, we illustrate this with a specific cipher system: the one-time pad. First (Theorem 8), we identify a set of secure instances according to our definition. These are the keys with maximum Kolmogorov complexity, together with messages that have no common information with the key. Then (Corollary 1), we show that this set is indeed large enough to imply security in the information theoretic sense.

Theorem 8. *Let μ be a distribution over $\Sigma^n \times \Sigma^n$. Let $m, k \in \Sigma^n$ and consider $e(k, m) = m \oplus k$, an instance of the one-time pad, with $K(k|\mu) \geq n - \alpha$, and $K(m, k|\mu) \geq K(m|\mu) + K(k|\mu) - \beta$. Then the instance has $\alpha + \beta$ secrecy.*

Proof. By Theorem 2 (item 4), up to an additive constant,

$$
\begin{aligned}
K(m|m \oplus k, \mu) &\geq K(m|m \oplus k, K(m \oplus k|\mu), \mu) \\
&= K(m|\mu) - K(m \oplus k|\mu) + K(m \oplus k|m, K(m|\mu), \mu) \\
&= K(m|\mu) - K(m \oplus k|\mu) + K(k|m, K(m|\mu), \mu) \\
&\geq K(m|\mu) - n + K(k|m, K(m|\mu), \mu) \quad \text{(using } |m \oplus k| = n) \\
&\geq K(m|\mu) - n + K(k, m|\mu) - K(m|\mu) \quad \text{(by Theorem 2 (item 4))} \\
&\geq K(m|\mu) - n + n - \alpha - \beta \quad \text{(by hypothesis)} \\
&= K(m|\mu) - \alpha - \beta.
\end{aligned}
$$

Combining this with Theorem 7, we have the following corollary.

Corollary 1. *Let μ_M be a computable distribution over $\mathcal{M}$, and μ_K be the uniform distribution. Then one-time pad is $O(1)$-secure in the information theoretic sense.*

Proof. Let $\mu(m, k) = \mu_M(m) \cdot \mu_K(k)$. Let $G_{\alpha,\beta} = \{(m, k) : K(k|\mu) \geq n - \alpha$ and $K(m, k|\mu) \geq K(m|\mu) + K(k|\mu) - \beta\}$. By Theorem 8, we know that all instances in $G_{\alpha,\beta}$ have $\alpha + \beta$ secrecy. We show that $\mu((\mathcal{M} \times \mathcal{K}) \setminus G) \leq (2^{-\alpha} + 2^{-\beta}))$.
    Observe that $\mathcal{M} \times \mathcal{K} \setminus G \subseteq B_\alpha \cup B_\beta$, where

$$
\begin{aligned}
B_\alpha &= \{(m, k) : K(k|\mu) < n - \alpha\} \\
B_\beta &= \{(m, k) : K(m, k|\mu) < K(m|\mu) + K(k|\mu) - \beta\}.
\end{aligned}
$$

By Theorem 2 (item 2), $\mu(B_\alpha) \leq 2^{-\alpha}$.

Claim. $\mu(B_\beta) \leq 2^{-\beta}$

By definition, $\mu(B_\beta) = \sum_{m,k \in B_\beta} \mu(m, k) = \sum_m \mu_M(m) \sum_{k:m,k \in B_\beta} \mu_K(k)$. By Theorem 2 (item 4), $K(m, k|\mu) = K(m|\mu) + K(k|m, K(m|\mu), \mu)$, so when m is fixed, the second summation runs over k with $K(k|m, K(m|\mu), \mu) < K(k|\mu) - \beta$. By Theorem 2 (item 2), there are at most $2^{K(k|\mu)-\beta}$ terms in the inner summation. Therefore, using $\mu_K(k) = 2^{-n}$ and $K(k|\mu) \leq n$, $\mu(B_\beta) \leq \sum_m \mu_M(m) 2^{K(k|\mu)-\beta} \mu_K(k) \leq 2^{-\beta}$, which concludes the proof of the claim.

Claim. For any $t, \gamma < t \leq n, \mu(\{m, k : I_K(m : e(k, m)|\mu) = t\}) \leq 2^{-t}$.

The claim follows from the fact that

$$
\begin{aligned}
I_K(m : e(k, m)|\mu) &= K(e(k, m)|\mu) - K(e(k, m)|m, K(m|\mu), \mu) \\
&\leq n - K(e(k, m)|m, K(m|\mu), \mu) \\
&= n - K(k|m, K(m|\mu), \mu)
\end{aligned}
$$

where the final equality holds in the case of the one-time pad. Therefore $\mu(\{m, k : I_K(m : e(k, m)|\mu) = t\}) \leq \mu(\{m, k : K(k|m, K(m|\mu), \mu) \leq n - t\}) \leq 2^{n-t} \cdot 2^{-n} = 2^{-t}$.

We can apply Theorem 7 with $\gamma = \alpha + \beta$ and $\epsilon = 2^{-\alpha} + 2^{-\beta}$. Therefore, the system has $\gamma + \sqrt{\epsilon \sum_{\gamma < t \leq n} t^2 2^{-t}} = \alpha + \beta + O(1)$ security since the series converges. If $\alpha = \beta = O(1)$, then we can conclude that the one-time pad is $O(1)$-secure.

3.4   Resource-Bounded Instance Security of One-Time Pad

Of more practical importance, we prove that if one is willing to expend the time necessary to produce a secure instance, then it is guaranteed to be secure against an adversary that is limited in the amount of time at its disposal to decrypt the instance.

Definition 7. *Let $(\mathcal{M}, \mathcal{C}, \mathcal{K}, e, d)$ be a cipher system. An instance m, k of the cipher system is γ-secure against a t-time-bounded adversary if $K^t(m|e(k, m)) \geq K^t(m) - \gamma$.*

Theorem 9. *For any polynomial time bound t, there is a time bound t' polynomial in t such that the following holds: if $m, k \in \Sigma^n$ and $e(k, m) = m \oplus k$ be an instance of a one time pad scheme, such that $CAM^{t'}(k, m) \geq n + K^t(m) - \alpha$, then the instance has $\log^{O(1)} n + \alpha$ secrecy against a t-time-bounded adversary.*

Proof. The proof is similar to Theorem 8, except for the application of time bounded symmetry of information, Theorem 4.

$$K^t(m|m \oplus k, \mu) \geq K^t(m|(m \oplus k, \mu)^*)$$
$$\geq CAM^{t'}(m) + CAM^{t'}(m \oplus k, \mu|m^*) - K^t(m \oplus k, \mu) - O(\log^3(|x| + |y|))$$
$$\geq CAM^{t'}(m, k) - n - O(\log^3(|x| + |y|))$$
$$\geq K^t(m) - \alpha - O(\log^3(|x| + |y|)).$$

To compute the CAM complexity of a key and message pair, one could simulate all CAM programs up to length $2n$ (an exponential number) to rule out the existence of a short program. This is by no means efficient; however, it is computable.

4   Threshold Secret Sharing Schemes

In this section, we revisit threshold secret sharing schemes, invented independently in 1979 by Shamir ([Sha79]) and Blakley ([Bla79], and analyse the security of individual instances.

4.1   Information Theoretic Secrecy of Secret Sharing Schemes

Let q, w be positive integers, $q \leq w$. $(\mathcal{K}, \mathcal{S}, d, r)$ is a (q, w) *threshold scheme* if $d : \mathcal{K} \to \mathcal{S}^w$ produces w shares of a key $K \in \mathcal{K}$ in such a way that any q participants can compute the value of K by using the reconstruction function r, but no group of at most $q - 1$ participants can do so.

Let $\mathcal{P} = \{P_i, 1 \leq i \leq w\}$ denote the set of participants, and let $D \notin \mathcal{P}$ be the dealer, that is a special participant who chooses the value of the key K.

Let $\mathcal{B} = (i_1, \cdots, i_j)$ be any set of participants that want to reconstruct the key, where $j \leq w$. Let $d(K) = \{(x_i, y_i) : 1 \leq i \leq w\}$ be the set of all shares distributed by the dealer, where the values x_i are public and each y_i is known only by its holder. The values y_i are determined from the secret information held by D, which includes at least the secret K. Let X be a random variable over the possible values for x_i, and Y be analogous for y_i. Then, Y is totally dependent of X, that is, $H(X, Y) = H(X)$.

Definition 8. *A (q, w) threshold scheme $(\mathcal{K}, \mathcal{S}, d, r)$ has δ security if:*

- *If $|\mathcal{B}| \geq q$ then $H(K | x_{i_1}, \ldots, x_{i_{|\mathcal{B}|}}, y_{i_1}, \ldots, y_{i_{|\mathcal{B}|}}) = 0$*
- *If $|\mathcal{B}| < q$ then $H(K | x_{i_1}, \ldots, x_{i_{|\mathcal{B}|}}, y_{i_1}, \ldots, y_{i_{|\mathcal{B}|}}) \geq H(K) - \delta$*

4.2 Individual Secrecy of Secret Sharing Schemes

We now give an individual analysis of perfect security based on Kolmogorov complexity.

To simplify reading, we use the following notation.

Definition 9. *Let $[w] = 1, 2, \ldots, w$ represent the set of all participants. Let $\mathbf{xy_w} = \langle (x_1, y_1), \ldots, (x_w, y_w) \rangle$ represent the concatenation of all shares in the same ordering as used for the participants. For any $\mathcal{B} \subseteq [w]$, let $\mathbf{xy}_\mathcal{B}^j = \mathbf{xy_w} | \mathcal{B}$ be the projection of $\mathbf{xy_w}$ onto the participants selected by $\mathcal{B}$, that is, $\mathbf{xy}_\mathcal{B}^j = \langle (x_{i_1}, y_{i_1}), \ldots, (x_{i_{|\mathcal{B}|}}, y_{i_{|\mathcal{B}|}}) \rangle$ where $\mathcal{B} = \{i_1, i_2, \ldots, i_j\}$ for some $j \leq w$. For any instance $(k, \mathbf{xy_w})$ and $\mathcal{B} \subseteq [w]$, $(k, \mathbf{xy}_\mathcal{B}^{q-1})$ is a $|\mathcal{B}|-$arrangement of the instance $(k, \mathbf{xy_w})$. We also write $\mathbf{xy_{q-1}}$ to represent any concatenation of some $q - 1$ distinct pairs of $\mathbf{xy_w}$, without considering which subset of $[w]$ originated it.*

We need a shorthand definition for the remainder of this section.

Definition 10. *Fix an integer w and another integer $q \leq w$. Then, the notation $\binom{[w]}{q-1}$ represents the set of subsets of $[w]$ that have $q - 1$ elements. Formally, $\binom{[w]}{q-1} = \{\mathcal{B} : \mathcal{B} \subseteq [w], \#\mathcal{B} = q - 1\}$.*

Definition 11. *Let $(\mathcal{K}, \mathcal{S}, d, r)$ be a (q, w) threshold scheme and μ a distribution over $\mathcal{K} \times \mathcal{S}^w$, and $(k, \mathbf{xy_w})$ an instance of this scheme.*

1. *$(k, \mathbf{xy}_\mathcal{B}^{q-1})$ is $\gamma-$secure against an attack from $\mathcal{B}$ if $I_K(k : \mathbf{xy}_\mathcal{B}^{q-1} | \mu) \leq \gamma$.*
2. *$(k, \mathbf{xy_w})$ is (γ, ϕ)-secure if $\Pr_{\mathcal{B} \in \binom{[w]}{q-1}}[I_K(k : \mathbf{xy}_\mathcal{B}^{q-1} | \mu) \leq \gamma] \geq 1 - \phi$ under the uniform distribution over $q-1$ arrangements.*

Theorem 10. *For any (q, w)-threshold scheme where $\mathcal{K}$ is the set of keys and $\mathcal{S} = \{(x_i, y_i) : 1 \leq i \leq w\}$ the set of all shares, for any variables $K, S^w = \underbrace{S \times \cdots \times S}_{w}$*

over $\mathcal{K}, \mathcal{S}^w$ with distribution $\mu(\mathbf{xy_w})$ over the total shares of the users, where the several public shares are i.i.d., if the probability that any given instance is (γ, ϕ)-secure is at least $(1 - \epsilon)$, then the system has $(\gamma + (\epsilon + \phi) \log \#\mathcal{K})$ secrecy, in the information theoretic sense.

Proof. 1. By definition of (q, w)-threshold secret sharing scheme, if $|\mathcal{B}| \geq q$ and all elements of $\mathcal{B}$ have different shares, the attackers can effectively compute the secret merely by pooling their private and public shares. This means there is a function that computes K from any set of q distinct points $\langle x_i, y_i \rangle$, and therefore $H(K|\mathbf{xy_w} \lceil \mathcal{B}) = 0$.

2. Let $\mathbf{xy_w} = \langle (x_1, y_1), \ldots, (x_w, y_w) \rangle$ represent a particular legal instance of the system. Since this includes all the shares, $\mathbf{xy_w}$ uniquely determines the secret and we can consider the complete instance $(k, \mathbf{xy_w})$.

We show that $I(K; X^{q-1}Y^{q-1})$ is bounded above by $\gamma + (\epsilon + \phi) \log \#\mathcal{K}$, using the upper bound given by Theorem 6, as the average of Kolmogorov mutual information. We first consider fixed instances of the scheme, then take the average over all instances.

For any instance $(k, \mathbf{xy_w})$, let

$$\tilde{I}(k : \mathbf{xy_w} | \mu) = E_{\mathcal{B} \sim U\left(\binom{[w]}{q-1}\right)} (I_K(k : \mathbf{xy_w} \lceil \mathcal{B} | \mu))$$

represent the average mutual information that an unqualified group of users can gain about the secret.

Let μ' be derived from μ as the marginal distribution of μ, with k being uniquely determined from $\mathbf{xy_w}$.

Let G be the set of instances that are (γ, ϕ) secure. Then, for all $(k, \mathbf{xy_w}) \in G$,

$$\tilde{I}(k : \mathbf{xy_w} | \mu) = \sum_{\mathcal{B}: I_K(k:\mathbf{xy_w} \lceil \mathcal{B}) \leq \gamma} \mu'(k, \mathbf{xy_w} \lceil \mathcal{B} | \mathbf{xy_w}) I(k : \mathbf{xy_w} \lceil \mathcal{B} | \mu)$$

$$+ \sum_{\mathcal{B}: I_K(k:\mathbf{xy_w} \lceil \mathcal{B}) > \gamma} \mu'(k, \mathbf{xy_w} \lceil \mathcal{B} | \mathbf{xy_w}) I(k : \mathbf{xy_w} \lceil \mathcal{B} | \mu)$$

$$\leq \gamma + \phi \cdot \log \#\mathcal{K}.$$

The average value of $\tilde{I}(k : \mathbf{xy_w} | \mu)$ over all instances is

$$E_{\mathbf{xy_w} \sim \mu} \tilde{I}(k : \mathbf{xy_w} | \mu) = E_{\mathbf{xy_w} \sim \mu} E_{\mathcal{B} \sim U\left(\binom{[w]}{q-1}\right)} I_K(k : \mathbf{xy_w} \lceil \mathcal{B} | \mu)$$

$$= E_{k, \mathbf{xy_{q-1}} \sim \mu'} I_K(k : \mathbf{xy_{q-1}} | \mu).$$

By Theorem 6,

$$I(K : X^{q-1}, Y^{q-1}) \leq E_{k, \mathbf{xy_{q-1}} \sim \mu'} I_K(k : \mathbf{xy_{q-1}} | \mu)$$

$$= E_{\mathbf{xy_w} \sim \mu} \tilde{I}(k : \mathbf{xy_w} | \mu)$$

$$= E_{\mathbf{xy_w} \sim \mu} \tilde{I}(k : \mathbf{xy_w} | \mu, \mathbf{xy_w} \in G)$$

$$+ E_{\mathbf{xy_w} \sim \mu} \tilde{I}(k : \mathbf{xy_w} | \mu, \mathbf{xy_w} \notin G)$$

$$\leq \gamma + \phi \cdot \log \#\mathcal{K} + \epsilon \cdot \log \#\mathcal{K}$$

$$= \gamma + (\phi + \epsilon) \log \#\mathcal{K}.$$

4.3 Instance Secrecy of Shamir's Scheme

The Shamir (q, w)-threshold scheme (see [Sha79]) in $\mathbb{Z}_p$, with $p \geq w + 1$ is constituted by two phases:

- **Initialization phase.** D publicly chooses w non-zero elements of $\mathbb{Z}_p$, denoted by $x_i, 1 \leq i \leq w$. For $1 \leq i \leq w$, D gives the value x_i to P_i.
- **Share distribution.** Suppose D wants to share a key $K \in \mathbb{Z}_p$. D secretly chooses independently at random $q - 1$ elements of $\mathbb{Z}_p$, $a_1, \ldots, a_{q-1}$ and constructs a random polynomial $a(x) = K + \sum_{j=1}^{q-1} a_j x^j \bmod p$, where $a(x) \in \mathbb{Z}_p[x]$ of degree at most $q - 1$.
- For $1 \leq i \leq w$, D computes the secret share $y_i = a(x_i)$ and gives it to participant P_i.

For $1 \leq i \leq w$, every participant P_i obtains a point (x_i, y_i) on this polynomial where all the coefficients $a_0, \ldots, a_{q-1}$ are unknown elements of $\mathbb{Z}_p$ and $a_0 = K$ is the key. A set $\mathcal{B} \subseteq \mathcal{P}, \mathcal{B} = \{P_{i_j}, 1 \leq i_j \leq w, 1 \leq j \leq q\}$ can reconstruct the key by means of polynomial interpolation like the Lagrange formula, which is an explicit formula to recover $a(x)$ given q points $(x_{i_1}, y_{i_1}), \ldots, (x_{i_q}, y_{i_q})$ on the polynomial.

We identify the secure instances of Shamir's scheme to be the ones where the key and the shares are independent according to Kolmogorov complexity.

Lemma 1. *Let $(k, \mathbf{xy_w})$ be an instance of the Shamir secret sharing scheme. For any set $\mathcal{B} \subseteq [w]$ with $|\mathcal{B}| = q - 1$, if $K(k, \mathbf{xy}_\mathcal{B}^{q-1}|\mu) \geq K(k|\mu) + |\mathbf{xy}_\mathcal{B}^{q-1}| - \alpha$ then $I(k : \mathbf{xy}_\mathcal{B}^{q-1}|\mu) \leq \alpha + O(1)$.*

Proof. By assumption,

$$K(k, \mathbf{xy}_\mathcal{B}^{q-1}|\mu) \geq K(k|\mu) + |\mathbf{xy}_\mathcal{B}^{q-1}| - \alpha,$$

and symmetry of information gives that

$$K(k, \mathbf{xy}_\mathcal{B}^{q-1}|\mu) = K(\mathbf{xy}_\mathcal{B}^{q-1}|\mu) + K(k|\mathbf{xy}_\mathcal{B}^{q-1}, K(\mathbf{xy}_\mathcal{B}^{q-1}|\mu), \mu)$$
$$\leq |\mathbf{xy}_\mathcal{B}^{q-1}| + K(k|\mathbf{xy}_\mathcal{B}^{q-1}, K(\mathbf{xy}_\mathcal{B}^{q-1}|\mu), \mu) + O(1).$$

Therefore,

$$K(k|\mu) + |\mathbf{xy}_\mathcal{B}^{q-1}| - \alpha - O(1) \leq K(k|\mathbf{xy}_\mathcal{B}^{q-1}, K(\mathbf{xy}_\mathcal{B}^{q-1}|\mu), \mu) + |\mathbf{xy}_\mathcal{B}^{q-1}|$$
$$\Leftrightarrow K(k|\mathbf{xy}_\mathcal{B}^{q-1}, K(\mathbf{xy}_\mathcal{B}^{q-1}|\mu), \mu) \geq K(k|\mu) - \alpha - O(1)$$
$$\Leftrightarrow I(k : \mathbf{xy}_\mathcal{B}^{q-1}|\mu) \leq \alpha + O(1).$$

For Shamir's scheme, we can infer information theoretic security from instance security, as follows.

Theorem 11. *Under the uniform distribution over the random shares and a computable distribution over the secret, Shamir's secret sharing scheme is $(\log \log p + 1)$ secure in the information theoretic sense.*

Proof. For a given instance $(k, \mathbf{xy_w})$, and any $\mathbf{xy}_{\mathcal{B}}^{q-1}$ arrangement derived from $\mathbf{xy_w}$, $K(k, \mathbf{xy_w}) \leq K(k, \mathbf{xy}_{\mathcal{B}}^{q-1}) + |\mathbf{x_{w-q+1}}|$ where $\mathbf{x_{w-q+1}} = \langle x_1, x_2, \ldots, x_w \rangle \upharpoonright ([w] \setminus \mathcal{B})$, that is, the public shares of all users not present in $\mathcal{B}$. This is because if we are given the description of $q-1$ private shares and the secret k we can recover the secret polynomial and from there, using the remaining public values, compute all the missing private shares.

Then,

$$K(\mathbf{xy_w}|\mu) = K(k, \mathbf{xy_w}|\mu) \leq \min_{\mathcal{B} \subseteq [w], |\mathcal{B}| = q-1} K(k, \mathbf{xy}_{\mathcal{B}}^{q-1}|\mu) + |\mathbf{x_{w-q+1}}|.$$

This means that if $K(k, \mathbf{xy_w}|\mu) \geq K(k|\mu) + |\mathbf{xy}_{\mathcal{B}}^{q-1}| + |\mathbf{x_{w-q+1}}| - \alpha$, then for all arrangements $\mathbf{xy}_{\mathcal{B}}^{q-1}$ of $q-1$ users made from $(k, \mathbf{xy_w})$

$$K(k|\mathbf{xy}_{\mathcal{B}}^{q-1}, \mu) \geq K(k|\mu) + |\mathbf{xy}_{\mathcal{B}}^{q-1}| + |\mathbf{x_{w-q+1}}| - \alpha - |\mathbf{x_{w-q+1}}|$$
$$\Leftrightarrow K(k|\mathbf{xy}_{\mathcal{B}}^{q-1}, \mu) \geq K(k|\mu) + |\mathbf{xy}_{\mathcal{B}}^{q-1}| - \alpha$$

which implies, by Theorem 1, $I(k : \mathbf{xy}_{\mathcal{B}}^{q-1}|\mu) \leq \alpha + O(1)$. Then, by definition, this instance will be $(\alpha, 0)$ secure.

Using $K(k, \mathbf{xy_w}|\mu) = K(\mathbf{xy_w}|\mu)$, the probability that $(k, \mathbf{xy_w})$ satisfies the above condition is:

$$\Pr_{(\mathbf{xy_w})}[K(\mathbf{xy_w}|\mu) \geq K(k|\mu) + |\mathbf{xy}_{\mathcal{B}}^{q-1}| + |\mathbf{x_{w-q+1}}| - \alpha]$$

$$= \sum_{\mathbf{xy_w} \in \mathcal{W}} \mathcal{U}_w(\mathbf{xy_w})$$

for $\mathcal{W} = \{\mathbf{xy_w} : K(\mathbf{xy_w}|\mu) \geq K(k|\mu) + |\mathbf{xy}_{\mathcal{B}}^{q-1}| + |\mathbf{x_{w-q+1}}| - \alpha\}$

In the Shamir scheme, the key and the public shares are all drawn independently from the same alphabet $\mathcal{K}$. Also, by construction, any q distinct private shares are also independent. So, a whole instance may be coded by a string with just $(w + q) \log p$ bits. Then, $|\mathbf{xy}_{\mathcal{B}}^{q-1}| = 2(q-1) \log p$, $|\mathbf{x_{w-q+1}}| = (w - q + 1) \log p$ and $|\mathbf{xy_w}| = (w + q) \log p$.

Now we apply Theorem 2, item 4, to find there is at least a fraction $1 - \frac{2^{(1+2(q-1)+(w-q+1)) \log p - \alpha}}{2^{(q+w) \log p}} = 1 - \frac{1}{2^{\alpha}}$ of secure instances, where we used the fact that $K(k|\mu) \leq \log p$.

Finally, let $\alpha = \log \log p$ and apply Theorem 10 with $\epsilon = \frac{1}{p \log p}$, $\gamma = \log \log p$ and $\phi = 0$. Then, the system has security $\log \log p + 1$.

5 Unconditional Security of Authentication Codes without Secrecy

This section studies authentication codes. We follow the notation in [Sti91] to some extent. An authentication code is a four-tuple $(\mathcal{S}, \mathcal{A}, \mathcal{K}, e)$, where $\mathcal{S}$ is a finite set of possible source states, $\mathcal{A}$ is a finite set of possible authentication tags and $\mathcal{K}$ is a finite set of possible keys. For each $k \in \mathcal{K}$, there is an authentication rule $e_{\mathcal{K}} : \mathcal{S} \rightarrow \mathcal{A}$ The message set is defined to be $\mathcal{M} = \mathcal{S} \times \mathcal{A}$. We consider only systems where each pair key / source state defines exactly one coded message.

There are two different types of attack by the opponent:

– *Impersonation*: The opponent sends a forged message (s, a). The probability of success of this attack is denoted by P_i.

- *Substitution*: The opponent replaces a valid message (s, a) with a forgery (s', a'). The probability of success of this attack is denoted by P_s.

5.1 Information Theoretic Security

We recall the results in the literature for the lower bounds on the opponent's chances of success.

The probability that the recipient will accept $(s, a) \in \mathcal{S} \times \mathcal{A}$ as authentic is

$$\text{payoff}(s, a) = \text{prob}_K (a = e_k(s)).$$

We define $P_i = \max\{\text{payoff}(s, a) : s \in \mathcal{S}, a \in \mathcal{A}\}$

Theorem 12. *([S85]) For any authentication code $(\mathcal{S}, \mathcal{A}, \mathcal{K}, e)$ without splitting $P_i \geq 2^{-H(K)+H(K|M)} = 2^{-H(A|S)}$.*

In the substitution case, the attacker knows a legitimate message $m = (s, a)$. The probability that the recipient accepts the forgery (s', a') is

$$\text{payoff}(s', a', m) = \frac{\sum_{k \in K : a = e_k(s), a' = e_k(s')} p(k)}{\sum_{k \in K : a = e_k(s)} p(k)} = p(a'|s', m).$$

As before, define $P_s = \max\{\text{payoff}(s', a', m) : s' \in \mathcal{S}, a' \in \mathcal{A}, m \in \mathcal{M}\}$.

From here we can easily show the following.

Corollary 2. *For an authentication code $(\mathcal{S}, \mathcal{A}, \mathcal{K}, e)$ without splitting $P_s \geq 2^{-H(A|S,M)}$.*

Theorem 13. *([B84]) For any authentication code $(\mathcal{S}, \mathcal{A}, \mathcal{K}, e)$ without splitting $P_s \geq 2^{-H(K|M)}$.*

Note that $H(K|M) \geq H(A|S, M)$ and so the first lower bound implies the second.

An authentication code is said to have perfect security if the previous bounds are attained, i.e., $P_i = 2^{-H(A|S)}$ and $P_s = 2^{-H(A|S,M)}$.

We generalise the notion of security in the following definition:

Definition 12. *An authentication code $(\mathcal{S}, \mathcal{A}, \mathcal{K}, e)$ has (δ, δ') security if*

1. $\log P_i \leq -H(A|S) + \delta.$
2. $\log P_s \leq -H(A|S, M) + \delta'.$

5.2 Instance Security against Impersonation

We define the security of an individual instance (s, a) of an authentication scheme.

Definition 13. *Let $(\mathcal{S}, \mathcal{A}, \mathcal{K}, e)$ be an authentication code without splitting and μ a distribution over $\mathcal{S} \times \mathcal{K}$.*

- *an instance (s, a) is γ secure against impersonation if $K(a|s, K(s|\mu), \mu) \geq \log(\#A) - \gamma$.*
- *an instance (a, s, m) is γ' secure against substitution if $K(a|s, m, K(s, m|\mu), \mu) \geq \log(\#A) - \gamma'$.*

The following theorem allows us to relate the deception probabilities to Kolmogorov based security of instances.

Theorem 14. *For any authentication code* $(\mathcal{S}, \mathcal{A}, \mathcal{K}, e)$ *without splitting, for any independent variables* S, K *over* $\mathcal{S}, \mathcal{K}$ *with computable distribution* μ *and any large enough polynomial time bound* t,

1. *for any instance* (a, s) *of the authentication code,*

$$2^{-\max_{a,s} K^t(a|s,K(s|\mu),\mu)} \leq P_i \leq 2^{-\min_{a,s} K^t(a|s,K(s|\mu),\mu)}.$$

2. *for any instance* (a, s, m) *of the authentication code,*

$$2^{-\max_{a,s,m} K^t(a|s,m,K(s,m|\mu),\mu)} \leq P_s \leq 2^{-\min_{a,s,m} K^t(a|s,m,K(s,m|\mu),\mu)}.$$

Proof. For the first statement,

$$\begin{aligned}
\max_{a,s} K^t(a|s, K(s|\mu), \mu) &\geq \sum_{a,s} p(a,s) K^t(a|s, K(s|\mu), \mu) \\
&\geq H(A|S) \\
&\geq \log(1/P_i) \\
&\geq \min_{a,s} K^t(a|s, K(s|\mu), \mu).
\end{aligned}$$

The first inequality is trivial; the second follows from Theorem 5. The third is Theorem 12. Finally, the last inequality follows by using the Shannon-Fano code, which encodes a source $\{(x, p(x))\}$ with codewords of length $\log 1/p(x)$. This encoding can be carried out in polynomial time if the distribution μ is given.

Similarly, for the second statement (using Theorem 2 instead of Theorem 12)

$$\begin{aligned}
\max_{a,s,m} K^t(a|s, m, K(s, m|\mu), \mu) &\geq \sum_{a,s,m} p(a,s,m) K^t(a|s, m, K(s, m|\mu), \mu) \\
&\geq H(A|S, M) \\
&\geq \log(1/P_s) \\
&\geq \min_{a,s,m} K^t(a|s, m, K(s, m|\mu), \mu).
\end{aligned}$$

Corollary 3. *For any authentication code* $(\mathcal{S}, \mathcal{A}, \mathcal{K}, e)$ *without splitting,*

1. *if all instances* (a, s) *are* γ*-secure against an impersonation attack;*
2. *if all instances* (a, s, m) *are* γ'*-secure against a substitution attack;*

then the authentication code is (γ, γ')*-secure in the information theoretic sense.*

6   Conclusion

By the close relation between information theory and Kolmogorov complexity, we have shown that there is also a very deep relation between Kolmogorov complexity and cryptography. Shannon's entropy can almost be replaced by Kolmogorov complexity in the most important definitions of perfect secrecy of a private key cipher system, with the advantage that this gives us a notion of security of individual instances, instead of having a statistical notion.

We have only studied information theoretic cryptosystems in this paper, and many problems remain to be studied. The practical implications of the security of instances remains to be explored. However, we expect that the most promising extension of this work is to study computational models of security, such as in public-key cryptosystems. We expect that time bounded Kolmogorov complexity, and notions such as instance complexity [OKSW94], will be the right technical tools to achieve this.

References

[Bla79]   Blakley, G.R.: Safeguarding cryptographic keys. National Computer Conference Proceedings 48, 313–317 (1979)

[B84]   Brickell, E.F.: A few results in message authentication. Congressus Numerantium 43, 141–154 (1984)

[Cha66]   Chaitin, G.J.: On the length of programs for computing finite binary sequences. Journal of the ACM 13(4), 145–149 (1966)

[Cha75]   Chaitin, G.J.: A theory of program size formally identical to Information theory. Journal of the ACM 22, 329–340 (1975)

[G88]   Gács, P.: Lecture Notes on Descriptional Complexity and Randomness (1988), http://www.cs.bu.edu/faculty/gacs/papers/ait-notes.pdf

[GV04]   Grunwald, P., Vitányi, P.: Shannon Information and Kolmogorov Complexity (2004), http://www.citebase.org/abstract?id=oai:arXiv.org:cs/0410002

[Har83]   Hartmanis, J.: Generalized kolmogorov complexity and the structure of feasible computations. In: Proceedings of the 24th IEEE Symposium on Foundations of Computing, pp. 439–445 (1983)

[Kol65]   Kolmogorov, A.N.: Three approaches to the quantitative definition of information. Problems Inform. Transmission 1(1), 1–7 (1965)

[LR05]   Lee, T., Romashchenko, A.E.: Resource bounded symmetry of information revisited. Theoretical Computer Science 345(2-3), 386–405 (2005)

[LV97]   Li, M., Vitányi, P.M.B.: An introduction to Kolmogorov complexity and its applications, 2nd edn. Springer, Heidelberg (1997)

[OKSW94]   Orponen, P., Ko, K.-I., Schöning, U., Watanabe, O.: Instance Complexity. Journal of the ACM 41(1), 96–121 (1994)

[S84]   Simmons, G.J.: Message authentication: a game on hypergraphs. Congressus Numerantium 45, 161–192 (1984)

[S85]   Simmons, G.J.: Authentication theory/coding theory. In: Blakely, G.R., Chaum, D. (eds.) CRYPTO 1984. LNCS, vol. 196, pp. 411–431. Springer, Heidelberg (1985)

[Sha79]   Shamir, A.: How to share a secret. Communications of the ACM 22(1), 612–613 (1979)

[Sh49]   Shannon, C.E.: A mathematical theory of communication. Bell System Technical Journal 27, 379–423, 623–656 (1948)

[Sol64]   Solomonoff, R.: A formal theory of inductive inference, part i. Information and Control 7(1), 1–22 (1964)

[Sti91]   Stinson, D.R.: Combinatorial characterization of authentication codes. In: Feigenbaum, J. (ed.) CRYPTO 1991. LNCS, vol. 576, pp. 62–73. Springer, Heidelberg (1992)

Author Index